Colonial Strangers

Colonial Strangers

WOMEN WRITING THE END OF THE BRITISH EMPIRE

PHYLLIS LASSNER

RUTGERS UNIVERSITY PRESS
New Brunswick, New Jersey, and London

Library of Congress Cataloging-in-Publication Data

Lassner, Phyllis.
   Colonial strangers : women writing the end of the British empire / Phyllis Lassner.
      p.   cm.
   Includes bibliographical references (p.   ) and index.
   ISBN 0-8135-3416-X (hardcover : alk. paper) — ISBN 0-8135-3417-8 (pbk. : alk.
paper)
   1. English fiction—20th century—History and criticism.   2. Imperialism in
literature.   3. Decolonization—Great Britain—Colonies—History—20th century.
4. Women and literature—Great Britain—History—20th century.   5. English
fiction—Women authors—History and criticism.   6. Huxley, Elspeth Joscelin
Grant, 1907—Criticism and interpretation.   7. Bottome, Phyllis, 1884–1963—
Criticism and interpretation.   8. Godden, Rumer, 1907—Criticism and i
nterpretation.   9. Manning, Olivia—Criticism and interpretation.
10. Decolonization in literature.   11. Colonies in literature.   12. Sex role in
literature.   I. Title.
   PR888.I54L37 2004
   820.9′358—dc22   2003019798

British Cataloging-in-Publication data record for this book is available
from the British Library.

Manufactured in the United States of America

CONTENTS

Acknowledgments

THIS BOOK GREW out of my earlier studies of British women writers of World War II and the collegiality with other women scholars so committed to bringing attention to their remarkably intrepid lives and writing. Among those who read and listened to my work in progress and shared their wisdom and learning, I thank Jane Marcus, Carol Troen, Kristin Bluemel, and Elizabeth Maslen. There are many conference organizers and audiences to thank for their responses to this work, including Frédéric Regard, whose conference on British biography and autobiography provided my work on Elspeth Huxley with thoughtful and critical feedback, as did audiences at the City College of New York and the Graduate Center. The Space Between Society must be singled out for the dedication of its members to the study of culture and literature from 1914 through 1945, which has been crucial for sustaining interest in neglected British women writers. I am also grateful to Marilyn Hoder-Salmon for her research on Phyllis Bottome, research that led to the discovery of five suitcases of her papers, and for the generous hospitality of Frederica Freer, in whose home I could read of Bottome's courage in her own words. I must add to this tribute Anne Summers, who recognized the significance of Bottome's papers and approved their purchase for the British Library.

With the unwavering support of Bob Gundlach, Northwestern University has generously contributed to my ability to write this book with a sabbatical, as university research grant, and a Hewlett grant to develop my course, Colonialism, Race, and Gender Relations. Students have challenged me with their questions and insights. I wish to express appreciation to the following for their help in gaining permissions to reprint previously published materials: the editors of the *Journal of Narrative Theory* and Graeme Harper, who published earlier versions of parts of this book; Kristine Krueger, at the Fairbanks Center for Motion Picture Study, for help in tracking down sources; Camilla Hornby and the Rumer Godden estate, for photos from Rumer Godden's autobiography; Heather Jones, for photos of Elspeth Huxley and her family; Caroline Raudnitz of Carlton International Media Ltd., for publication of movie stills from *Black Narcissus;* and Stephanie Freidman, at Janus Studios, for stills from *The River.* Leslie Mitchner's suggestions for the shape of this book were nothing short of inspirational, including the integration of film versions of several novels.

As always, there is Jacob Lassner, whose patience with colonial stories and postcolonial theories represents only the latest chapter in a saga of unfathomable support and companionship.

Colonial Strangers

Introduction

LETTING GO OF an empire is very hard to do. Although the British Empire was just about bankrupt by the end of World War II and had surrendered most of its colonies by the 1960s, it wasn't until 1998, and with as much regret as flourish, that Britain finally yielded Hong Kong, its last Crown Colony. This long duré and the momentous events that defined it produced a literature by British women writers that represents an indispensable if neglected bridge between the colonial and postcolonial eras and discourses.[1] In the decades following E. M. Forster's skeptical but symbolically hopeful colonial critique, *A Passage to India* (1924), British women produced a saga of imperial self-delusion that confronts their own critical positions. In novels and memoirs that mock, castigate, and grieve the ravages of colonialism, these women show how imperial self-deceit repressed the violence that would lead to the end of Empire. From the 1930s, as Britain's power was threatened by the rise of fascism, these women witnessed and recounted the failure of Britain to recognize the malignity inherent in all imperial ideologies, policies, and practices. From their divergent but overlapping positions as settlers, exiles, and anticolonial activists, these women confronted not only how imperialism was self-destructive, but how its ideology of racial supremacy could be transformed into a threat not to Britain's global power alone, but to humankind itself.

This literature remains captivating and challenging today when empire as an idea and as a practice still rules as the force many consider responsible for the fate of postcolonial nations and peoples. As I write this, we are hearing calls for the assumption of new imperial burdens. In other respects, empire makes itself felt as it has mutated into neocolonialism, globalization, and cultural imperialism.[2] But despite the devastating human costs resulting from the reign and defeat of the twentieth century's most malignant imperial power, the Third Reich, empire by any other name remains a haunting presence in a postcolonial world. The British women who wrote the end of Empire interrogate its hold on our critical and creative imaginations.

In its most approachable form, empire grips the imaginations of widely divergent audiences. From the 1980s through today, there is no end to the spate of TV miniseries and feature films based on colonial memoirs, such as Elspeth Huxley's *The Flame Trees of Thika,* on serious novels, like Ruth Prawer Jhabvalla's *Heat and Dust,* and on popular romance fiction, such as M. M. Kaye's *The Far Pavilions.* Most recently, the sixth remake of A. E. W. Mason's 1905 colonial epic, *The Four Feathers,* has played to full movie houses. Even postcolonial Bollywood can't let go of the Empire; witness the hugely successful 2002 film *Lagaan,* which narrates the defeat of the British in India as a cricket match, and in which impoverished and exploited Indian villagers are instructed by a rebelliously sympathetic young English woman. Whether this panoply of colonial and anticolonial intrigue should be seen as a sign of nostalgia for the Raj, as a critical sigh of relief for the official end of Empire, as a crisis of Western cultural confidence, or as representing ongoing tensions between East and West is still a subject of heated debates.[3]

The urgency of these questions is evident in the concerns of postcolonial studies, which have complicated our views of an oppressive imperial past with arguments for the agency and resistance of the colonized, and with complex views of colonial relations, including non-Western perspectives. These very efforts, however, endow that oppressive past with power over the present, especially as an oppressive colonialism is found to infect postcolonial polities and literature even today.[4] And yet, as Frederick Cooper and Ann Laura Stoler remind us, the "Manichaean world of high colonialism that we have etched so deeply in our historiographies was nothing of the sort" (1998, 8). In agreement with Cooper and Stoler, British women writers not only bear witness to colonialism's complex relations and consequences, but also narrate actions and arguments to expedite its end. In 1974, Olivia Manning published *The Rain Forest,* a searing satire of British functionaries clinging to their colonial protocols in a seedy boarding house. While they shuffle their irrelevant papers and their wives compete for imperial status at the bridge table, the natives blow them all up. Like Manning, other British women writers opposed those "progressive social scientists of the 1950s" who may have recognized "that colonial rule in Africa or Asia was morally unacceptable" but who were also more committed to modernization than to dispatching colonialism "to the past" (Cooper and Stoler 1998, 15). Writers like Manning, Phyllis Bottome, Rumer Godden, and Elspeth Huxley unsettle this imperial timeline by confronting the abusive marriage of modernity's new technological violence and imperialist oppression with the urgent need for all empires to end. And so they challenge the generalized view that "an imperial outlook had been an integral feature of British public life for generations" (Ward 2001, 4).

Individually and collectively, these writers unsettle the political and imaginative power that is still awarded to colonialism today. In writing careers that extend from the 1930s through the 1970s, headlong into the postcolonial experience, many British women writers challenge assumptions about boundaries between colonial and postcolonial writing. Including Phyllis Shand All-frey, Muriel Spark, and Ethel Mannin, these writers show how the inconsistent and contradictory policies of the British Empire foretell its end and after-maths. In Mandatory Palestine, for example, British promises to support both Arab nationalism and Zionism produced no resolution except an embarrassed British withdrawal. In their novels, memoirs, and reportage, we find racial and cultural entanglements growing out of the historical crises of the 1930s and 1940s, crises which blurred the boundaries of colonial identity and power and created new insights about anticolonial movements, world war, and postcolo-nial nationhood. We discover that the identities and politics of British sojourn-ers in Palestine, settlers in Kenya, and colonizers in India are intertwined with those of colonized and resisting peoples, but not only within British imperial politics. They are also entangled by their collective vulnerability to other imperial antagonists: the Axis of the Japanese Empire and the Third Reich. From Africa, India, and the Caribbean to the Middle East, these women writ-ers narrated the end of Empire as it was necessitated by the most horrific and global consequences of racially defined imperial self-justification.

Race, Modernity, and the End of Empire

While by definition modern literature is always expanding and revising its boundaries, this inclusiveness has been compounded by intense attention to race as a category of analysis. It is therefore surprising if not startling that the specifically racialized decade of the 1940s and its literary concerns have found no points of convergence with postcolonial studies.[5] Most significantly, despite the fact that World War II was launched by the Axis powers as an imperial con-quest based on racialist ideology and precipitated the end of all European empires, there has been little attempt to integrate this most cataclysmic event into the racially defined and ever expanding and complicated postcolonial narrative. If, as postcolonial critics argue, "modernity, in all its incompleteness and instability, was made through colonialism," where is that most globally destabilizing event of modernity, the Second World War? (Burton 1992, 1). No matter how we define history, there is an inextricable relationship between the "racial modernities" that reached their apogee in the Holocaust, the necessary and decisive war to end fascism, the end of Empire, and the indecisive victo-ries of anticolonial, antiracist narratives (Burton 1992, 3).

My argument that these British women writers are central to postcolonial debates is deeply rooted in this racial modernity. The nadir of that modernity, the Second World War, in all its totalizing constructions and destructions of difference, in its global displacements, is often said to be so ethically and expe-rientially exceptional that it destabilizes its own discursive position. And yet as we are reminded by British women's writing, because this war is the defining moment that leads to the end of Empire, it can no longer remain absent from the postcolonial narrative. As I learned when I began to read British women writers of World War II, there were many who defied the prevailing view that fascism could be appeased and, in effect, dismissed. These women were all too willing to risk the scorn of critics and colleagues alike for a purpose rarely permitted in literary writing. Defying social and political decorum, they challenged political leaders as well as other writers and literary critics to hear their pleas for the victims displaced by Nazism in the 1930s and 1940s. As I followed their writing beyond the war, I should not have been surprised that the tragedies resulting from twenty years of fascist persecution would remain imprinted on their literary imaginations. Just as they were convinced that the Holocaust was the horrifically logical consequence of racist supremacism, so they confront us today with the dangers of marginalizing that story from the history of colonialism.

It was the persistent political and literary courage of these writers that inspired me to engage postcolonial studies and to see each of their concerns in the light of the other.[6] What became so important about this mix of writers and their colonial complications was that they provide unsettling points of direction on the "compass for taking readings of the legends of women's maps" of Empire (Marcus 1989, 271). This study begins the work of reality-testing those legends. It explores the critical tension between what has already been concluded about colonizers and colonial relations and what we have yet to learn. The lessons are embedded in accounts of women witnessing the ending of the Empire into which they were born. Though they were expected to identify with this imperial space, these women refused to be fixed, marginalized, or victimized by their historic and geopolitical conditions. My plural—conditions—is a crucial part of my argument. The movements of these women writers across the borders of colonial identities should be seen as an invitation to construct a more flexible model of postcolonial judgments. Their inclusion in the postcolonial conversation extends both the center and the periphery of what we mean when we speak of empire and colonial and postcolonial consciousness. For what happens in their writing is that the center and periphery of the British Empire, its colonizers and colonized, move outwards and inwards toward each other. The narrative results negotiate the distance between these writers and the British Empire as they are surrounded equally by the lethal threat and memories of fascist persecution and extermination.

INCLUDING WORLD WAR II
AS THE END OF EMPIRE

Phyllis Bottome and Olivia Manning predicted the fate of Hitler's multicultural victims if the führer could not be stopped in Europe. For I think we can safely say, from our historical position today, that if Hitler's conquests had succeeded and he had therefore been able to institute his racialist policies beyond Europe, he would have globalized the Nazis' supreme command as the Master Race. And while this command included enslavement, its racial ideology was also designed to exterminate all those who the Nazis constituted as the degenerate races.[7] Extermination, of course, would ironically obliterate those very multicultural and racial differences Hitler's racial ideology designated. At this crisis moment in the history of European empires, Bottome and Manning demand that we notice how the ideologies of the Third Reich ride herd over any construction of race and racism that even today excludes antisemitism and ethnic hatreds. For what Hitler and his pseudoscientific muses brutally show us is that blackness is a sign not merely of color or biological difference, but of social disease and corruption. In this train of thought, blackness can therefore infect those who might not otherwise be identified or identify as black.

In dramatic contrast to racially pure white Aryan Germans, blackness, for Hitler, is the symptom, "written on the skin" for "all to see": blackness "captures [the] essence" of the impure African races (Gilman 1991, 101, 99). But for Hitler's muse, the racial scientist Houston Stewart Chamberlain, this included the Jews because they also originated from Africa. Writing in 1913, Chamberlain maintained that the Jews made the lethal mistake of inbreeding and becoming "'hybridized'" with black Africans during their ancient Alexandrian exile, and so they became "'a mongrel' (rather than a healthy 'mixed') race" (Gilman 1991, 174). Mixed, but forever fixed. And while Chamberlain and Hitler affix the Jews to blackness, Hitler's agenda is not concerned with their black African kin. Chamberlain's use of the word "hybridized" is a startling reminder of Homi Bhabha's theories of hybridity. But unlike Homi Bhabha's celebration of hybridity as a new and adaptive human strain, resistant to racial oppression, Chamberlain's meaning produces a lethal weapon—Hitler's death machine. As so many British women writers saw, the Nazi construction of race included not only antisemitism, but its most virulent form. What we learn from the inclusion of the Jew and antisemitism in the writing of British women is that to exclude the Second World War from postcolonial analysis erases categories of race and racism that illuminate colonialism's savagery on any designated Other. Moreover, to exclude the Third Reich from colonial and postcolonial discourses is to forget and ignore that Hitler's racialist policies and practices represent the quintessential endgame of colonial oppression.

The urgency of ending racist oppression drives writers such as Phyllis Bottome, Ethel Mannin, and Olivia Manning to construct a correspondence "between imaginative means and historical goals" (Van Alphen 1997, 28). While this correspondence is hardly new to fictional writing, when it involves the subject of antisemitism and the Holocaust, a distinctive and urgent problem emerges. Holocaust critic Ernst Van Alphen analyzes fears that literary figuration, as it strays from historical facts, causes "historical reality . . . to recede behind the rhetorical and narrative effects of our discourse" and, as a result, diffuses the particular, if unfathomable horrors of the Holocaust (1997, 32). I fully acknowledge this danger, but precisely because so many of the writers in my book inscribe World War II and some refer to the Holocaust as an argument for the end of Empire, I view their writing not as a test of Van Alphen's point about Holocaust representation, but in the light of it. Although their arguments are about the racist underpinnings of both the Holocaust and colonialism, these writers are not creating an equivalence. In fact, as they demonstrate in so many different facets and forms, colonialism is about brutal and murderous exploitation, but it is not about exterminating an entire people for the purpose of purifying the world of their poisonous presence, in short, through a purposefully conceived policy of lethal social engineering. Referring to Conrad's controversial anticolonial classic, Lawrence Langer pungently critiques the comparison: "When someone exclaims 'The Jews—they dead!'— between five and six million of them, to say nothing of the countless other victims of German barbarity—we enter a realm of annihilation undreamt of by Marlow, Kurtz, or indeed the ruthless colonial exploiters whose greed knits together the threads of Conrad's tale. Notwithstanding the suffering and deaths of which they were guilty, the main interest of these exploiters, as with American slaveholders, was in keeping their victims alive. The will to murder was not an intrinsic part of their scheme" (2002, 81). As all of us now know, Hitler's policies and the practices of his concentration and death camps could have completely destroyed the world's Jews and Gypsies.[8]

For many British women writers who witnessed the Hitlerian translation of imperial racism into mass extermination, no further evidence was needed to prove that all empires must end. As they embed their arguments in their novels, they create a "moral friction" between their imagined colonial landscapes and historical reality, and that friction becomes a necessary critical tool (Van Alphen 1997, 28). Not only does it help them clarify distinctions and continuities between the Third Reich and their own Empire, but in all their various plots and locations, that "moral friction" interrogates their relationship to imperialism as well as their own status as colonial strangers.

From the 1930s, when Elspeth Huxley is embedding her fears of fascism in Kenyan murder mysteries, across the 1942–43 desert battlefields of Olivia Manning's *Levant Trilogy*, and over the Caribbean landscape of Phyllis Bottome's novel *Under the Skin*, the map of Empire is being altered forever by the rise and fall of the Nazi Empire. As late as 1965, Muriel Spark situates the 1961 Eichmann trial as a test case in a plot interweaving questions of Empire and its determination of racially and historically determined identities. A primary reason my book is arranged geographically is to dramatize how this protracted siege of the Third Reich, with its terrifying new definitions of subjectivity, agency, victimization, and oppression, also affects the meanings that define colonialism in different parts of the British Empire. As Hitler conquered and occupied other imperial centers, as his armies threatened both the center and periphery of the British Empire, he changed the meanings of indigenous inhabitant, settler, and occupier, as well as those of colonizer and colonized. As chapters on the Middle East, the Caribbean, India, and Kenya will show, British women writers delineate how these changed meanings help us understand differences in colonial relations and identities as they were felt and enacted across the British Empire. In turn, as Frédéric Regard observes, such differences, in their conjunction of geography and discourse, create a context that stimulates a rich conception of the relationship between self and Other, a relationship that includes the critic (2003, 380).

There were many British women writers who did not fail to notice that the war to defeat fascism and Nazism would embed and embody another struggle: that at the same time their nation would be fighting for its own life, it would be stifling the lives of other nascent and would-be nations. Phyllis Bottome, Elspeth Huxley, Rumer Godden, and Olivia Manning recognized how the priorities of World War II created a definition of just war that also disguised and concealed the colonial injustices of those democratic nations fighting for their right to live. What catches the eye of these and other women writers is that racism and oppression are not just the obvious and sole provenance of Nazi evil run amok; they are the hidden agenda of any imperial plot, however benign in its articulated mission.

The moorings of Hitler's racist bridge from Europe to Africa were blown up on the sands of El Alamein, but what was not destroyed was the racism that underwrote the victorious Allied empires. And yet, even as many British women are impelled by the Holocaust and other fascist horrors to protest the racism of their own Empire, they articulate the definable difference between the ideologies and consequences of the Third Reich and imperial Britain. The Allies never conceived of genocide, but our writers remind us how British, French, and other imperial actors, using guns and other forms of colonial coercion, exploited the world's colonized people and guaranteed their suffering. As we will see in such novels as Olivia Manning's *School for Love* and Phyllis Bottome's *Under the Skin,* the British Empire planted the seeds of its own destruction when it was forced to recognize that the values cherished at home were just as significant to their colonial constituents. Woven through so much of women's writing in this book is the recognition that those principles of freedom and self-determination which Britain carried in its fight to survive and defeat Nazism had to be extended to their colonized subjects. And so even as they supported and endured the war against Nazi domination, these writers represented two other struggles—that of the colonized to become their own political agents and their own conflicts about the place of British subjects in colonial and postcolonial worlds.

Of course, it is no surprise that while World War II raged on, little attention was paid to unsettling questions about the meanings attributed to war aims by Allied propaganda. For while the fight for freedom was authentic, its rallying cry did not accord with attitudes toward Hitler's victims. Not only were most refugees denied entry to safe harbors, but plans to bomb either the rail lines that carried the victims or the camps themselves were rejected. By the same token, little notice was given to the ongoing struggles for freedom in the Allies' colonies. To have done so would have positioned the already besieged Allies not as valiant defenders but as oppressors. But many British women writers persisted with a political courage that demands our attention. Even when the war against the Axis powers was won, they mounted narrative and activist attacks on the last bastions of imperialism. They argued that if the last just war won the fight for democracy, it also rehearsed a serial battle to bring down the curtain on imperialism's grand masquerade as a democratizing mission.

THE DISPLACEMENT OF WOMEN WRITING THE END OF EMPIRE

In the shadow of a global imperial battle, British women writers constructed their own racial analyses and gendered verdicts of the end of Empire. And yet despite a deluge of theory and analysis of colonial and postcolonial experience, representation, and its gendered amendments, the white colonial woman writer remains invisible or marginalized.[9] Illustrating this marginalization are the cases of Doris Lessing and Nadine Gordimer. Despite or perhaps because of their prominence, they are often dismissed for false consciousness, that is, even as they represent the evils of apartheid, they are condemned either for the failure to represent the consciousness of the racialized colonized or for exploiting their consciousness for the care and feeding of white colonial creativity.[10] Damned if they do and damned if they don't, these women writers and others never fail to speak self-consciously from their social location or identity. Their novels and memoirs fully recognize the privileges accorded their status at the same time that their own racial, economic, and gendered positions may have denied them privilege.[11] In the case of Phyllis Shand Allfrey, despite years of working tirelessly on behalf of Dominica's independence and workers' rights, she was ousted because she was a white woman. And so just as the traditional canonization process had its criteria for ignoring the troublesome figures of women writers, so we now have postcanonical, postcolonial criteria setting boundaries and perhaps settling scores. The result of these latter criteria is to reduce the complex cultural and political identities and agendas of white women colonial writers to paradigms of complicity with imperial racial ideologies.

Now this dismissal carries a burden so heavy that we can say it has an effect of double destabilization. Many postcolonial critics argue for the necessity of destabilizing such oppositions as oppressor and victim. The category of victim denies women subjectivity, agency, and voice because it assumes their passivity, regardless of whether this passivity is perceived as part of women's nature or as enforced.[12] As a remedy, feminist critics have listened to and analyzed the voices of colonized women. In this restoration, colonized women defy the objectifying discourses of victimhood by narrating a wide variety of activity, decision making, and resistance. In the very act of recognizing the right of colonized women to represent themselves, however, postcolonial critics do not issue the same license to such colonial women as Elspeth Huxley and Rumer Godden, who might also have critical stories to tell. Instead, colonial women are treated with equal doses of righteous indignation, depicted either as victims of men who coerced them from the manicured greens of Tunbridge Wells to the heat and dust of the Veil of Kashmir, or as agents of the imperial project, loading their Liberty chintzes onto the bent over backs of their blacks.[13] Settler writers in particular, such as Elspeth Huxley, are seen as succumbing to the lure of adventure, profit, and power, and duped into believing they could be authentically British. Such criticism does not accept the possibility that colonial writers can have a political identity with integrity equal to that of the critic. To refer to "white, middle-class solipsism" is to dismiss with contempt the idea that white, middle-class British and colonial women could politicize their views beyond the perspectives of their London drawing rooms, Assam bungalows, or Land Rovers (Donaldson 1992, 9). To claim that "the plurality of [British women's] voices is increasingly a closed conversation within a sealed room" and a "monologue of dominant, imperial power" closes the book on the impassioned "discursive interruption[s]" these writers construct, not only in dominant colonial discourses but in their own thinking and imagining and in that of their critics.[14] Because such critics are committed to the belief that their own ideology is untainted by racism, sexism, culturalism, or ethnocentrism,[15] they cannot imagine how utterly prejudiced is their view of colonial writers as people who cannot escape the indelible inscription of British imperialism into their political consciousness.

This all-encompassing paradigm, which any postcolonial theorist would deplore for colonized women, stereotypes colonial women. It not only renders their range of individual and communal differences invisible, but denies them a variety of identities and narrative voices that might just provide a fruitfully tense interaction with those of colonized and postcolonial women. Imagine Rumer Godden and Kamala Markandaya discussing the sexual relationships they construct between English and Indian protagonists in their novels *Peacock Spring* and *Some Inner Fury*. What kinds of critical questions emerge for each of them in light of the way they define racial and national identities, and how might they see this as related to their differently ambivalent resolutions? How might their questions amend our own? To begin with, stereotyping British women writers prohibits such critical relationships and questions because it not only reinforces oppositions between colonizer and colonized, but makes each invisible to the other. Such stereotyping also falsely represents the historical, political, and "regional complexities of colonial women," as Claire Midgley points out; for example, white settlers "were both colonizer (in relation to indigenous inhabitants) and colonized (in the sense of being under British imperial governance)" (1998, 6). Without the presence of the late colonial woman and her narratives, there is a problem with conceptualizing colonial roles and values as well as national, colonial, and historical identities.

These categories of experience and expression are destabilized not only by racial, ethnic, and linguistic differences, but by gender relationships in colonial settings.[16] In order to be useful and responsible tools for analyzing women's late colonial writing, these categories must also be compounded by the fears, dislocations, losses, and aftershocks wrought by the historic moment in which this writing is produced. Stereotypical assumptions about the political and narrated identities of colonial women writers can be tested by viewing their writing through important questions feminist critics have raised about women's autobiography: "How does the narrator take up and put off contradictory discourses of identity? How does she understand herself as a subject of discursive practices? How does she come to any new knowledge about herself? What has been 'repressed' in the narrative which dis/identification erased? By locating autobiographical subjects in a historically embedded context and probing the conditions for gaining agency, critics have reframed the discussion of women's 'experience' as nonessentialized" (Smith and Watson 1998, 23). Because this quote applies to the late colonial woman writer, it is startling to discover her absence. Those analyses of identity which deconstruct the "universal" lead to the inclusion of women and such fluid and destabilized categories as "in-between" or "multicultural subjectivity" as well as the "migratory, diasporic," or "mestiza"; but in Smith and Watson's discussion, these apply only to the history of decolonization (1998, 29). To include the late colonial women provides a necessary argument that also serves as a prelude to the history of decolonization.

To introduce the colonial woman as a life writing subject with complicated identity politics of her own offers new strategies for the production of new knowledge. As we see how many late colonial women become critically constructed subjects of their own stories, we are rewarded with newly expanded meanings of "in-between." All the writers in this book are cases in point. The positions of second-generation settler writers such as Rumer Godden and Elspeth Huxley, and of Phyllis Shand Allfrey, whose family roots in the Caribbean date from the seventeenth century, question the terms "national identity" and "cultural identity" because these writers don't have just one of each. The sense of cultural identity they portray is, as Stuart Hall argues, "a matter of 'becoming' as well as of 'being.'. . . Far from being eternally fixed in some essentialized past, . . . [it is] subject to the continuous 'play' of history, culture and power" (1996, 112). Though they grew up in colonial homes, were British subjects, and lived in Britain as adults, all three settler writers identify with the spaces and historical crises that define their movements. There is no homeland that endows them with a stabilizing citizenship. Each one, moreover, abandoned the colonial culture in which she was raised to become a writer who questions the very ethos of colonial settlement. Because England was an unknown and alien place until they were adults, these writers can see English political and social culture from a critical distance. Alienation provides them with the recognition that British superiority is merely an arbitrary signifier that loses its grip under imaginative scrutiny. Another group of writers I discuss, Phyllis Bottome, Olivia Manning, Ethel Mannin, and Muriel Spark, may also be British citizens, but most of their writing, political, and emotional lives were spent in destabilizing circumstances, on the move, from Central Europe to the Middle and Far East. It was from these crisis-ridden places that they recognized the convergences and differences between the British Empire and its would-be conqueror.

For all of these writers, home is often makeshift and undomesticated, sometimes war torn, and in some instances a chosen state of exile. I would certainly agree with Judith Kegan Gardiner that these circumstances produced "a fruitful unsettledness that makes [these] women simultaneously inheritors of and antagonists to imperialism" (1989, 134–135). The lives and writing of these women traverse more borders and boundaries than colonial conquest erased and created. None of them, moreover, ever stopped testing the grounds of her life journey against the displacements of her colonized and war-torn neighbors. In fact, there may be no better subject to "unsettle rather than to consolidate the boundaries around identity" than the second-generation settler woman (Smith and Watson 1998, 28). She also serves as a conceptual and historical transition, shifting her identities among the "patriarchal discourses" of the romantic adventures of rugged individualism, the resisting agency of the colonized, and the emergencies of the historic moment (Martin 1998, 390).

It is this tense "unsettledness" that calls for a more flexible model of analyzing the polymorphous relationships among British women writers, their subjects, and their critics at the end of Empire. Many of these writers plotted fictional as well as autobiographical relationships in which the values, felt experiences, and insights of the colonizer and colonized not only intersect, but intertwine in clashes as well as in their attempts at mutual understanding and rapprochement.[17] In Phyllis Bottome's 1950 novel of Jamaica, *Under the Skin,* seething racial tensions in a school of mixed-race students and staff explode as a murder plot against a well-intentioned English headmistress.

Elspeth Huxley's 1959 childhood memoir, *Flame Trees of Thika,* depicts the inevitable failure of English settlers to dominate the Kikuyu social justice system. They and other writers use their imaginative renderings of historical, social, and political contexts to raise critical questions about categories of colonial identities, about their constructed subjects and their cross critical perspectives.[18] Their questions, moreover, relate directly to those Jeanne Perrault addresses about constructing "the categories into which 'I' and 'we' fit ourselves ... [for] those who are named by others have no way to exist in and for themselves" and "are vulnerable to being named from the outside and thus, paradoxically, created for others' purposes while being eliminated for their own" (1998, 192). Though Perrault is discussing racial politics on behalf of women of color, surely her "we" can be part of a decision and not an assumption about who is included in those "borderlines" she and other feminists would like to see as "mobile" and socially transforming (Perrault 1998, 192). British women writing the end of Empire must be included as they unsettle those borderlines from their unexpected perspective.

These women write to understand and critique the Empire, while sometimes struggling and then failing to find a place for themselves within it or outside. In all cases, they provide a critical response to the complaint that they are beset by nostalgia for an idyllic colonial Eden.[19] Among their many critical insights, these women question the relationship between direct and indirect imperial rule. Often overlapping, under direct rule, local governing councils and rulers cooperate with colonial governors; while, in indirect rule, control is exerted through local rulers who find it economically and/or politically expedient or necessary to cooperate. While some writers could be accused of attributing too much autonomy or responsibility to local rulers' compliance with colonial rule, as we shall see, they construct intricate connections that give equal weight to the historical and political interests of each group. In Phyllis Shand Allfrey's 1953 novel, *The Orchid House,* the heirs of an old English colonial family are forced to decelerate their progressive plans when faced with an alliance between Dominica's only independent newspaper and the Catholic Church, with its deeply conservative and colonizing power. The necessity of an eventual compromise, about which Allfrey is both resigned and rebellious, occurs in the historically crucial space between the Spanish Civil War and the coming of World War II. As her novel veers between identification with leftist causes and colonial loyalties, it carves yet another indeterminate facet of difference out of the critical mass of theories of colonial ambivalence and mimicry. As Homi Bhabha explains his theory, "in order to be effective, mimicry must continually produce its slippage, its excess, its difference. The authority of that mode of colonial discourse that I have called mimicry is therefore stricken by an indeterminacy: mimicry emerges as the representation of a difference that is itself a process of disavowal" (1998, 153).

Over time, as other critics have responded to Bhabha's theories of mimicry and hybridity, the metaphoric use of these terms has become intertwined in constantly shifting relationships between dominant and subject groups and individuals, institutions of power, and the production of cultural artifacts.[20] When Bhabha insists that colonizer and colonized are inextricably engaged, he bears witness to that complicated sense of the racialized, ravaged self that has led so many postcolonial theorists to disavow any relationship with the colonizer except adversarial.[21] According to Bhabha, however, colonized and colonizer are not locked in a fight to the death in their state of attraction-revulsion but are engaged in a process of giving life to a hybrid identity constructed out of circumstances inherited from the colonial condition. This construction, moreover, embeds the consequences of choices made by the colonial subject, including broad and varying degrees of adaptation and adoption. As in *The Orchid House,* the effect of this combination is that each, colonial subject and object, becomes part of the other, each is both self and Other, and each becomes something other than colonial subject or object.

This hybrid identity does not imply that each disappears into the other. Instead, once the colonial subject and object have met on each other's grounds, neither the vast and haunting continents of India or Africa, nor the vast and haunting English novel can disappear from either the character of colonized or colonizer in their imagined or prefabricated identities. The result is that instead of a divide between them, their intertwined history of cultural transformation is a haunting and therefore anxiety-ridden shaping force. I explore the resonances of these hauntings in reading *The Orchid House* through its multifaceted relationship to that other postcolonial novel of colonial Dominica, *Wide Sargasso Sea,* and its progenitor, *Jane Eyre.* We can also see this haunting in Bhabha's argument that the ambivalent mirroring of colonial relations renegotiates postcolonial national identities and narratives. Like Allfrey, he recognizes the irrevocable tensions in negotiating these identities and narratives. Allfrey's novel delineates the process by which this tension comes into being as she dramatizes the uncertain relations between colonial and anticolonial discourses by grafting an anticolonial critique onto the authority of her characters' colonial experience and locating their tense hold on each other in a definable moment at the end of Empire.

The tensions underlying and resulting from the ambivalent relationship between colonial and anticolonial discourses reproduce an endlessly frustrated narrative, not only in Allfrey's novel, but in others. Ethel Mannin's 1963 novel, *The Road to Beersheba,* becomes both defensive and offensive in its construction of a liberation narrative for the Palestinian people. Even in its more humane arguments and effects, Rumer Godden's 1950 novel of India, *The River,* is composed of desires for the British presence to have been benign, desires which cannot be met in the hybrid identities of the newly postcolonial state, no matter how fruitfully they are negotiated. One can also see this frustration in following the character of Barbara Vaughan in Muriel Spark's 1965 novel, *The Mandelbaum Gate,* as she stumbles through her religious pilgrimage and hybrid identities—British/Jewish/Protestant/Catholic. Her crossings over the tense postcolonial landscapes of Jordan and Israel defy the meanings of hybrid. Missing from theories of hybridity, even those that Susan Stanford Friedman shows are "'thick descriptions' of historically and geographically specific situations," is the critical perspective that details the ending of the British Empire (1998, 90). This protracted but transformative historical crisis exposes the failure and rejection of hybrid identities and the emergence and assertion of differences that may not be negotiable.

LATE COLONIAL ANXIETIES

Like Rumer Godden, many postcolonial theorists have argued that despite the power wielded by the British Empire, anxiety prevailed as the political psychology of its overseers. Even with all the trimmings of upward mobility and authority that the heights of Empire afforded, British colonial agents suffered dislocation in conflicted cultural climates that could never become a home away from home. Their Liberty decorated bungalows and gated tennis clubs could only camouflage the tensions created by colonialism's incompatible exclusionary and missionary policies. Goals and principles the British considered progressive were undermined on two fronts. The colonized but ancient and polysemous civilizations resisted transformation into unified but self-alienating national entities. British claims to superiority were subverted by their own logic; how could one claim to be superior to that which one did not understand?[22] The paucity of happy colonized faces reflecting the Raj's good intentions only served as a constant reminder of colonial insecurity and instability. Compounding this affront, as the British Empire ended, history denied the colonizers any laurels which might have made withdrawal less vainglorious. And so, as many memoirs, fictions, and reports attest, leaving the Empire behind was fraught with ambivalence about cultural and social identity, sense of purpose, and moral righteousness.[23]

The bridge between these historical anxieties and literary narratives of the end of Empire can be built by taking up "the interpretive problem" posed by Simon Gikandi: "How to read the grand narrative of imperialism when it has lost its authority and legitimation? Do we read it, within its dominant mythology, as the confident imposition of the European narrative (civilization) over historically belated local narratives (barbarism)? Or do we read the imperial story, within its contradictions, as a trajectory haunted by a sense of its doom . . . [?] Or do we read the imperial story as a dialectic in which the confrontation between the culture of colonialism and local resistances to its hegemony have generated interdependencies?" (1996, 32–33). As the official imperial relationship drew to a close, British women writers translated their experiences and responses into fictions of women's internalized colonial anxieties and contradictions. Such writers represent an "imperial femininity," according to Gikandi, recording "the female subject's ambivalent interpolation by the ideologies of empire" (1996, 146). They understood only too well the colonizing import of representing the Orientalized Other as a menacing if spellbinding mystery. Writers such as Manning, Godden, and Huxley satirize the fears and attractions both colonizer and colonized project onto each other and how this ambivalence constructs each as the objectified Other. At those moments when the colonial was becoming postcolonial, these writers delineate the process through which the female colonial agent is made to recognize her anachronistic and untenable position. She discovers her own Otherness at a site which has already rejected any possibility that the colonial project will not contaminate itself. In turn, those who are labeled the colonized resist the term's oppressive designation by becoming agents of their own distinct moral visions and political fates.[24]

This imaginative and complex representation effects a political and historical critique through another transformation, writing the denouement of the colonial novel. Instead of providing a model for political and aesthetic resolution, the muted, romantically wistful ambiguity of E. M. Forster's conclusion to *A Passage to India* is rejected.[25] Through a variety of tragic-comic colonial encounters, British women writers resist the narration of imperial history "as a romantic . . . compensation for its tragic acts and consequences"(Gikandi 1996, 103). Their fictions show how the lingering effects of colonialism can be understood by reflecting back on the deferred pace that characterized the protracted denouement of the Empire. In representing that lingering plot as a defining moment instead of an anticlimax, many of these women's novels show how the intensity of feeling on both sides of the colonial divide could produce a reverberating violence even as the world was engaged in its most violent war.

Where some writers use satire, others, such as Phyllis Bottome and Phyllis Shand Allfrey, use forms of melodrama to show how the disorder and instability represented by colonized sites and peoples become catalysts for resistance and insurrection against the Empire's civilizing and romanticizing impulses. It may very well be that for Rumer Godden such violence could also be translated into comedy precisely because the game of Empire was finally up. But as she shows, comedy also serves the trenchant purpose of analyzing colonial self-delusion as the cause of British agony at the end of Empire. To ignore the critical hybridity these women's narratives embed, to silence them, commits what Gayatri Spivak argues has been the result of silencing subaltern women: limiting historical knowledge (Gyan Prakash 2000, 131).

THE PLACE OF THE BRITISH WOMAN WRITER
IN THE POSTCOLONIAL CONVERSATION

To hear the critical hybridity of these women's voices from a postcolonial position also requires recognition of what Jane Marcus calls "the ethics of the woman writer's elsewhereness": "For elsewhere is not nowhere. It is a political place where the displaced are always seen and see themselves in relation to the 'placed.'. . . One is 'put in one's place' by the process of 'putting her in her place,' in that the gesture of placement reveals itself as authoritarian and academic, the naming and judging game played by the alternate rules of 'Who is most marginalized?' rather than 'Who is Central?'" (1989, 270).

The British women writers in this book refused to be put in their place by the historical and political pressures of their day. Their writing repudiates those categories that would elide either those pressures or the places within them that they construct for themselves. That these historical pressures ultimately wrenched colonizer and colonized apart haunts these writers and drives them to negotiate their own distanced positions. For as the British Empire dissolves, they are displaced into the postimperial periphery of the independent center of new nations. As they construct dialogues between resistance leaders or citizens of new nations and questing British subjects, I would like to see them as representative of a new kind of multicultural and postcolonial perspective, shaped not only by the embrace of hybridities, but by the tensions necessitated by the continuing evolution of their different political, cultural, and social realities.

CHAPTER 1

Strangers at the Gates

THE MIDDLE EAST

OLIVIA MANNING: THE GATES BESIEGED—WORLD WAR II

When there was no doubt about who would win the war, the Egyptian Government brought its treasures up from the cellar and unlocked the doors of the museum. . . . The hall glowed with [Tutankhamen's] gold as the British soldiers wandered round and we wandered round with them. The display was a gift for us. A farewell gift, I think.

—Olivia Manning, "Cairo: Back from the Blue"

Christmas 1941: a feast without food. In the Middle East, the dispossessed of Europe gave thanks for Pearl Harbour and waited for the war to turn round.

—Olivia Manning, "The Tragedy of the Struma"

Of all the exotic sites of imperial imagination, the Middle East is closest to the heart of Western civilization. As the birthplace of the West's foundational religious texts, the Middle East is where Western subjectivity, with its claims to enlightened righteousness and moral superiority, could be said to originate. But as the traumas of the crusades and imperial conquest show, the Middle East has inspired violation as much as it has reverence for the moral lessons of the Hebrew Bible and New Testament. In turn, those same sacred texts have been used to justify that violation. With its political and ideological conflicts reverberating from the ancient past to present, one would think that this historic epic would be of crucial interest to postcolonial studies, but this is not the case. Though books written by writers from all over the Middle East are now being translated from Arabic, Turkish, Persian, and Hebrew, its colonial and postcolonial literature by British writers, especially women, is mostly absent.[1]

This is not to say that this writing isn't read. Muriel Spark's prominence guarantees that her novel of Israel and Jordan, *The Mandelbaum Gate,* always receives honorable mention. Olivia Manning's *Levant Trilogy* has been in print ever since its Masterpiece Theater production introduced Kenneth Branagh and Emma Thompson as the exiled Guy and Harriet Pringle. But like an anti-Orientalist dream come true, such film and TV renditions, like Agatha Christie's *Death on the Nile,* are easily accused of offering more lessons in vintage couture than in history. The novels, on the other hand, entertain us with unsettling political dramas. Those by Agatha Christie, Olivia Manning, Muriel Spark, and Ethel Mannin portray the modern Middle East as a palimpsest of ancient narratives in conflict not only within each of their own textual outlines and with each other, but with the competing narratives of contemporary political history.[2]

Olivia Manning, whose writing life was propelled by world war and the end of Empire, set the tone for her career with her 1937 novel, *The Wind Changes,* which depicts the Irish rebellion against British rule and provides witness to the Empire's final blows. Manning's finest moments as a novelist are expressed as she dramatizes Britain's greatest threat, the Nazi siege on Europe and the Middle East. Manning began her journey across the European war fronts with her marriage to R. D. Smith in 1939, when she followed him to Bucharest, where he lectured and organized cultural events for the British Council. Instead of a romantic honeymoon, however, their trip began years of exile on the run from the Nazis. Fighting for its own life, the British Empire could offer little protection, and so Manning faced an onslaught that overwhelmed the security and confidence the Empire's civilizing missions once promised. She and her husband fled across the Balkan peninsula, through Athens, and on to Cairo and Jerusalem, where the British Empire held sway while the Allied forces were under siege in the nearby deserts. The scope and passion of her epic construction of this war are narrated from the perspective of a writer who is an outsider, not only to the indigenous cultures around her, but to the British mission from which she chose to remain aloof.

She cannot, however, be accused of detachment, for this perspective enabled her to develop empathy for those oppressed by any imperial force. Nowhere did this become clearer than in the Middle East, where refugees from Nazi-occupied Europe found themselves competing for safe ground with those who could barely remember when the land was not colonized. Though Manning also wrote short fiction and novels that have nothing to do with the war, there is no doubt that her strongest writing engages the emotional experiences of combatants and noncombatants alike, none of whom emerged unscarred from the necessary but bloody battles on and behind the lines.

Manning wrote short fiction, essays, and a draft of *The Balkan Trilogy* during the war, but the stresses of facing the threat of one Nazi invasion after another delayed the completion of her World War II novels: *Artist among the Living* was published in 1949, *School for Love* in 1951, *The Balkan Trilogy* between 1960 and 1965, and *The Levant Trilogy* between 1977 and 1980.[3] While all of her fiction is concerned with political anxiety, these particular

novels establish her "as historical witness" not only to Nazi conquest and decisive battles on two continents, but to the war's relationship to the end of
Empire (Mooney 1982, 41). Resonant with a complex range of responses and
wartime experience in Europe and in the Middle East, these novels represent
historical witness as multivocal and dialogic. Manning shows that in the struggle to survive racial supremacism no one is an innocent bystander, least of all
the writer as witness. As she told Kay Dick, "I write out of experience. I have
no fantasy. I don't think anything I've experienced has ever been wasted"
(Dick 1974, 31).

Great Expectations in Jerusalem

Palestine, as you know, is full of uncertainties. The first thing you have to do
here in Jerusalem is to find out in which particular century anyone else is living.
There are people who still think it's the Middle Ages and claim to have been
living in the same house for 1700 years. To us it is 1947, but the Jews are in 5707
and the Arabs have it that it's 1366. . . . As there are also three official languages
(English, Arabic and Hebrew) a large part of the population are more or less
continuously engaged in translating. But the strain of this is relieved by the
existence of three holidays a week; Friday for the Moslems, Saturday for the
Jews and Sunday for the others. The authorities hope that the Palestine problem
will be solved before anyone else accustomed to holidays on Monday or
Thursday wants to come here. Jerusalem the golden; or, as Josephus put it, a
golden bowl full of scorpions.

—Sir Henry Gurney, British Chief Secretary in Palestine, 1947

In the wartime novels of Olivia Manning and in Muriel Spark's 1965
novel, *The Mandelbaum Gate,* Jerusalem is the place that captivates the imaginations of the ancients, the romantics, and the moderns. It is a place that also
unsettles the boundaries between ancient and modern, East and West, history
and mythology, fragmentation and unification. Jerusalem in these fictions is
both a city of the mind and of realpolitik, a city that resists not only political
control, but authorial and critical control as well. The Jerusalem of Manning's
1951 novel, *School for Love,* may be an icon representing universal love and
peace as the holiest site for three monotheistic religions, but, as she reminds us,
its very sanctity has also inspired world-class and profane battles for political
sovereignty. In 1943, the time of the novel, despite Britain's military successes
across the Middle East and North Africa, Jerusalem represents a precarious
sanctuary as the capital of British Mandatory Palestine.[4] Reverberating with
past and present conflict, the crowded space of 1943 Jerusalem may be home
to colonized Arabs and an ancient homeland for Jews fleeing Hitler's death
camps, but it also encapsulates the imperial battle between European titans for
control of the entire Middle East. Despite the enormity of this battle and the
vast space it occupies across the Middle East, because it is shunted offstage, its

significance could easily be read as receding into atmospherics—transforming contested space into mood. And so it might seem that a world-shattering crisis becomes merely a gloomy backdrop for the novel's focus, a sad tale of an English orphaned boy—a warning that his odyssey into adulthood with its awakening of social consciousness may run aground on the alien rocky hills of colonial space. *School for Love* casts its love as an accomplice to both global and localized racial violence.

Even as the plot never ventures beyond Jerusalem's gates, however, this portentousness marks Manning's assessment of the fate of individual and collective consciousness in the post–World War II literary imagination. Instead of suggesting the bumpy road toward a developing individual psychology, the boy's episodic encounters with conflicting social codes reflect a narrative confrontation with the politics and history of colonial conquest and its waning days. The novel stages the fate of individual consciousness and of colonialism through Felix, an orphan stranded in the Middle East since his parents' death in Iraq.[5] Because Felix is not really wanted by anyone else, he is shunted from one temporary caretaker and one besieged site to another. Confronting enigmatic and conflicting political realities, with no resources or power to be responsible for himself, Felix could easily represent Palestine itself. He, too, becomes the target of projected hopes for a triumphant and restorative postwar future while he embodies the failed promises of triumphalist imperial power.[6]

The novel exploits the great expectations of that European tradition, the bildungsroman. Manning shows that unlike Dickens's Pip, when an English boy's odyssey into disillusionment lands on colonial soil, comeuppance exposes more than the colonial origins of wealth and privilege. In 1943 Palestine, Felix's fate is caught up in the recognition that the British Empire is being bankrupted by a war to save not its privilege, but its bare bones.[7] Despite military and diplomatic strategies to maintain control over global influence and resources, the only sustainable future for Manning's British colonials is imprinted on a one-way ticket back to a dissolving imperial power. Reading *School for Love* through the lens of Dickens's *Great Expectations* exposes the consequences of colonial power on novelistic romance and the fate of social and individual mobility. In turn, these imagined consequences highlight Manning's revelations about the corrupting circumstances of imperial power and their relationship to its racist and antisemitic discourses.

As a prelude setting the course of Felix's odyssey and return to England, the death of his parents marks the fragility and lost battle of imperial privilege: his mother succumbs to typhoid and his father is shot by Iraqis in "a German-inspired rising" (Manning 1982b, 55). Flown from Baghdad, where he and his mother had been waiting out the war, Felix is sent to Jerusalem, which, along with the Egyptian cities of Alexandria and Cairo, is the remaining center of

British influence in the Middle East. As though questioning the progressive, civilizing mission of the Empire, the novel's Jerusalem becomes the site that tests the Western cultural ideology of an individual's journey of discovery. Belonging nowhere, the figure of the English boy wandering around Jerusalem calls attention to the British colonial presence as an inauthentic and degenerating vestige. The novel pits Felix's uncertain individual will against that destabilized colonial presence.[8] Through the perspective of the boy's developing political consciousness, Manning dramatizes the tightening hold of the British on a shrinking space. That this space should ultimately be defined by racial and antisemitic exploitation marks it as imprisoning for Britain's Others. This desperate but mercenary hold is personified ironically by Miss Bohun, an English spinster whose power, based on the promise of beneficence, mocks the missionary project. A distant relation of Felix, she takes him in for her own advantage. As leader of the evangelical Ever-Ready Group of Wise Virgins, Miss Bohun embodies and genders the dangers of colonial self-delusion in the guise of a withholding lady bountiful and false prophet. Proselytizing apocalypse, she awaits Armageddon while presiding over an old Arab house, and, as though she were dispensing spiritual favors, she extorts inflated rents from refugees for its tiny, sparse rooms. With this satiric portrait, Manning positions Miss Bohun as a female agent of colonial ideology whose traditional role of making an English home in alien space has come to a perverse end.

Twenty years later, when Manning writes *The Balkan Trilogy* and *The Levant Trilogy*, she creates Harriet Pringle as an exile who has no opportunity to make a home, traditional or otherwise. For Harriet, this is a condition that robs her of any power and yet also liberates her from the destructive implications of that power. Unlike those modernist texts that engaged apocalyptic images to express "the standpoint of a distanced intellectual mourning the loss of traditional life," Manning's text mocks such responses as a luxury few can afford at a time defined not only by exile but by extermination.[9] Miss Bohun's apocalyptic fervor is linked to the most destructive moment in modernity to highlight the contribution of individual self-deception to the process that led to complicity with atrocity.

Like Dickens's Miss Havisham, Miss Bohun constructs her self-enclosed world around a plot to exact retribution, exploiting what little British privilege and prestige is left to a woman alone in this eroding colonial power base. Imagine the dark cold of Miss Havisham's gothic character and house as the consequence of colonial exploitation. In Manning's vision, and in that of Phyllis Bottome and Phyllis Shand Allfrey, the ambiguous darkness of the gothic and of modern individual psychology is exposed as an ineluctable historical force. Felix's first impression of Miss Bohun is the "face of some sort of large insect," and her "hostile" house is seen "as though he had entered an enemy country" (Manning 1982b, 10, 27, 14). The relationship between Miss

Havisham's claustrophobic space and the gated Jerusalem lies in power that denies the subjectivity of others by luring those others with self-serving promises for a self-determining future. Those very promises, however, turn out to be prisons. Like Miss Havisham's house and the colonial project itself, no romantic glow will emanate from Miss Bohun's unheated rooms, and the only wisdom she can impart is the exploitation of others' needs.

The first stop in Felix's voyage of political disillusionment is a recognition of colonial power and its connection to the war that has victimized him but has also distinguished him from other kinds of victims. He discovers that Miss Bohun has expropriated the Arab house from the Leszno family, Jews on the run from the Nazis, who have rented it from a local Imam.[10] In its multilayed history of contested occupation, the house cannot make any of its tenants feel at home. Having convinced the Lesznos that she has their well-being at heart, Miss Bohun offers security in return for their slave labor and, adding insult to injury, banishes them once again to the servants' quarters. While the narration of this exploitation mocks the spinster's justifications, it also suggests a more insidious connection. The gothic atmosphere of the house resonates with the conflict between those in dire need of a stable, nurturing home and its manifestation as a punitive concentration camp. In the novel's retrospective evocations of Jewish persecution, this resonance should also be understood in terms that extend to that of the uncanny, which Ernst Van Alphen attributes to houses haunted by their relationship to the Holocaust. Such houses are experienced as tomblike or "as a dead body," haunted by "a problematic experience in the past that . . . is then projected in the present onto something alien, outside the self "(Van Alphen 1997, 197). As though manifesting the threat that would historically affect the Jews in the present time of the novel, Miss Bohun's house produces anxiety in all its boarders: "repressing . . . a problematic experience"; this experience, however, does not occur "in the past," as Van Alphen describes it (1997, 196). Instead, it invades from far away, from a horrific European present that Manning confronts several years afterwards in this novel (Van Alphen 1997, 196). To exploit Van Alphen's discussion of the uncanny further, if the haunted house "only serves to *situate* the uncanny experience" and there is always a person "who has agency over it, albeit unconscious," Miss Bohun is "the original agent of repression," confining her Jewish tenants in spaces and conditions that portend an apocalyptic event outside her political imagination but with which her callousness complies (Van Alphen 1997, 198, italics in original).

Resonating with imperialist rhetoric and missionary earnestness, Miss Bohun's self-righteousness translates into a form of racism that is particularly resonant in 1943: antisemitic complaints about Jews deserving their fate because they're too poor and "subservient," the fate they deserve for having been too rich and "pushing" (Manning 1982b, 44). Blaming the Lesznos for their stateless fate and victimization, and congratulating herself for her altruism, the Englishwoman assumes a mantle of moral and political authority, the seams of which connect British imperialism and fascism a bit too uncomfortably. As in Manning's World War II epic, *The Balkan Trilogy,* this novel takes the risk of deploying conventional stereotypes in order to characterize the Jew as victimized by antisemitic rhetoric. On the one hand, testimony by other characters and by the narrator's asides corroborates Frau Leszno's complaints of being abused by Miss Bohun's self-serving machinations. The problem, in that this is a post-Holocaust text, lies in the narrator's assessment of the Jewish woman's "voice," which is described as "pitched on a note of self-pity and self-righteousness and accusation that roused in a listener neither remorse nor compassion, but rather a murderous irritation of the nerves" (Manning 1982b, 72). The risk here is that the reader can all too easily share the response of this designated "listener" who, more dangerous than merely unsympathetic, blames the Jew for her fate (72).

What rescues Manning's suspicious depiction of Frau Leszno's crude, repulsive wail is that this listener turns out to be none other than Miss Bohun herself, whose own "voice, breaking in, was in comparison reasonable and dignified" (Manning 1982b, 72). Unsullied by a feminized sentimentality, Miss Bohun's pragmatic rationalism resembles the rationale of British imperialism. This is the rhetoric that claims benevolent patriarchal trusteeship over a site and people viewed as otherwise incapable of evolving out of their primitive emotions and conditions. In *Artist among the Missing,* Manning dramatizes how this same imperialist rationality is tautological and self-canceling. While Geoffrey Lynd complains that "pity" for the persecuted Jews is an emotion that has become "too much for [him]," yet another assault on his depressive state, he also registers a hallmark of British colonial politics (Manning 1975, 42). His plaint is mirrored by a friend who accuses someone else's concern for the Jews as the opposite but equally debilitating malady—"hysterical" (42). Between the lines of this bipolar discourse, an imperial politics is articulated that is so even tempered, so shorn of the residual scars of protracted assaults on being and identity, that it is truly transcendent. The assaults reflect a vision that has levitated to a self-protected space, way above and beyond the material histories of Other's abject persecution. In *School for Love,* defending oneself against the charge of antisemitism represents politically balanced rational judgment and so, for colonial actors, affirms the mental and political health of an otherwise dying Empire. As stated in *Artist among the Missing,* "There are good Jews and bad Jews, honest Jews and dishonest Jews, clever Jews and stupid Jews—but suffering is not peculiar to their race" (42). From the perspective of imperialist rationalism, these Others delegitimize their own claims on sympathy because they cannot escape the sustained and irrational history of their suffering. The erasure of humane concern here exhibits the danger hidden in political rationalism. Not only does

it cancel the Empire's claims for benevolence, but the material realities and legitimacy of Jewish suffering as well.

In this gothically domesticated colonial site, we can imagine the offstage
colonial adventures and onstage violent end of Dickens's Magwitch as being
translated into the theater of world war and a tragic-comedy of the end of
Empire. Just as the characters and fates of Magwitch and Miss Havisham are
intertwined, we can see them both encased in Miss Bohun and her house, as
the perversion of great expectations. But unlike Miss Havisham's privations of
selfhood, which are afforded by a sheltered private space, the drama within
Miss Bohun's frigid house is invaded by a contested political sphere.[11] The
deprivation of private space in Manning's novel means the loss of public protection against imperial designs and interests. The threat is intensified by the
battles between empires. In the case of Jerusalem and its Middle Eastern contestants, public and private protection can only be guaranteed by statehood, by
the sovereign right to defend one's own interests.[12] At the very beginning of
the novel, as Felix is being driven to Miss Bohun's, he sees a divided landscape—the Arabs in the hills and the Jews in the valleys—but like the attitudes
reflected in the policies of the Mandate, Felix is "ignorant of the problems of
Palestine" and assumes that the topographical "arrangement" is something that
could be "agreed on by both parties" (Manning 1975, 8). On the very next
page we discover how easy it is for the colonial presence to ignore these problems: it is winter, and "snow-capped Jerusalem" looks "like nothing so much
as a wintry English village street" (9). This image, representing the imaginative
consciousness through which the British naturalize and neutralize their imperial dominance, serves an analytical role throughout Manning's Middle East
novels; in *Artist among the Missing,* Jerusalem is "not merely another Middle
Eastern city," but "as severe, clean, and permanent as a Cotswold village" (22).
In *School for Love,* the narrator's conflation of the image into imperial chastity
is ingratiated into Felix's consciousness, revealing a tensely divided and colonized city, but one that is transformed into a quaint English village—frozen in
the timeless image of nostalgia.

Quite like a Victorian postcard, reminiscent, in fact, of a scene from Dickens's novel, the vision imprints and establishes the grounds for Manning's critique of the colonizing British political imagination. The image shows how the
British make themselves comfortable in a foreign, harsh landscape by contain-
ing it within their own insularity. In 1943, however, the conflated image has
squeezed out a conflicting reality: while defending the English village from the
Nazi barbarian, the British Empire foments violence in the villages it has conquered and promised to protect. In Manning's political imagination, writing
this novel in 1950, two years after Arab nations fused their rage against the
United Nation's partition of Palestine and invaded Israel, it was the British
presence that exacerbated the tensions that led to the Arab-Israel War of 1948.[13]

In both *Artist among the Missing* and *School for Love,* the decline and nec-essary retreat of the British Empire becomes the logical consequence of extending the discourse of imperial rationalism into the realm of a balanced, evenhanded diplomacy. The casting of this balance, however—"the good Jews and the bad Jews"—subjects the Jews to categories of judgment that not only place the British in an unambiguous, morally superior position, but deny the Jews their own complex, sometimes irreconcilable and often overlapping cul-tural, social, and political differences. Acknowledging these complicated dif-ferences and their historical contexts defies the idea that moral oppositions like "good" and "bad" are equivalent to balance or evenhandedness. Fitting the Jews so neatly into these moral dichotomies only results in squeezing out their various struggles over time and place to maintain their foundational identity while confronting the necessity of change and complying with laws that pre-scribed their social, economic, and political roles. The collapse of their differ-ences into a Manichaean vision makes it all too easy to see both "good" and "bad" as extremes, conditions that mark them as not human and so ready-made for Nazi persecution and their destabilized status as exiles in Jerusalem.

Manning relates the dangers of eliding cultural differences to the even-handed politics of British imperialism in the Middle East. In order to justify and sustain its own cultural supremacy and political domination, the British treat the opposed nationalist aspirations of the Jews and Arabs as differently but equally childlike. In contrast to the British sense of their own enlightened and pragmatic politics, the Jews and Arabs are viewed as obsessed with their primitively passionate and irrational ties to an ancestral homeland. As a cor-rective to these politics, *School for Love* depicts an anxiety in the condition of the Jewish exiles that distinguishes them from the condition of the colonized and yet enfolds them into it. In the historicized and politicized topography of this novel, both the Jews and Arabs of Palestine are positioned as subjugated Others, but with differences. And it is for reasons of these historically marked differences that this fictional representation of Jerusalem cannot be appropri-ated by the postcolonial concept of hybridity, intended as a reconciliation of opposed differences. The implications of these opposed differences—the Arabs' status as an indigenous people under British Mandate and the stateless Jews seeking to establish a polity of their own—become clear through Felix's odyssey. His road to disenchantment leads not to Miss Havisham's singular sadism or his personal ethical crisis but to a vision of a political and experien-tial hell for Others, a hell which he, as a white Christian British subject, will be spared.

Like the British soldiers who in April 1945 will accidentally come upon Bergen-Belsen, Felix wanders into a scene where one of Miss Bohun's ser-vants is catching and setting rats on fire: "The smoke that arose filled the air with an acrid stench of burning fur" (Manning 1982b, 78). Unlike Dickens's

Miss Havisham, whose rage for vengeance engulfs her own body in flames, Miss Bohun's pernicious designs safely guard her. If Miss Havisham can be said to represent the self-consuming narcissism of economic exploitation, Miss Bohun suggests the outwardly rippling effects of political manipulation. Prizing her own advantage in a world where local conflicts reverberate and complicate the boundaries of a world war, Miss Bohun and her designs collude with imperial plots on all sides. In the rhetoric of spiritual redemption, transformation, and transcendence, she coerces her Others to accept her economic manipulation of them as protection against the vicissitudes of attempting some kind of self-determination. Unlike the effects of Miss Havisham's plotting on individual destiny and consciousness, the fate of millions is implicated in Miss Bohun's strategies.

The connection between the image of burning rats and the novel's setting in 1943 Palestine constructs a searing connection between the Holocaust and imperialism.[14] That 1943 is an escalating moment in the Holocaust draws our attention to the policies of the British Home and Colonial Offices. Even as they claimed the moral high ground against the barbaric Nazis, these offices plotted their own mission of racial purity, obstructing any efforts to rescue European Jews like the Lesznos from the burning that awaited them. In a 1970 article for the *Observer,* Manning describes one of the most heinous examples of that obstruction, the tragic story of the *Struma,* a 112-year-old decrepit ship overflowing with 760 Jews escaping from Nazi-occupied Rumania and heading for Haifa via Istanbul. Not permitted to disembark at either port, suffering from starvation and dysentery, the passengers languished while Turkish and British officials refused to intervene. After the ship was sent floating in the Black Sea with no workable engine, an explosion finished off all but one passenger. At one level, Manning expresses understanding of Britain's bind, trying "to maintain a balance of power between two peoples [Arabs and Jews], each of which believed that anyone not with them was against them" (1970, 13). But then, from the vantage point of thirty years later, she concludes, "The Mandate is ended, but officialdom goes on, impedient, intractable; cold as the sea" (17).[15] Manning's images of the burning rats remind us all too well that for the Nazis, Jews were filthy poisonous vermin that, for the health of the German Empire, had to be exterminated. Her coda shows us the poison of all imperial politics.

Manning is constructing a lacerating critique in that image of the burning rats. Her novel suggests that the British presence not only is complicit in allowing the Holocaust to continue, but at the same time, as Miss Bohun's gestures and political stance reveal, is provoking a political conflagration in the appropriated garden of Palestine. On the one hand, Miss Bohun typifies a romantic gesture that defined the British presence in the Middle East from its inception in 1798 until its final administrative departure in 1971. Signifying goodwill toward other people's customs, in practice, Britain's policies reflected another form of laissez-faire imperialism. In order to support this thesis, Manning takes a risk similar to that in her portrait of the Jewish Mrs. Leszno. The fact that the servant burning the rats is an Arab easily leads to the conclusion that the novel is not only marking Arabs as culturally primitive, but, worse, implicating them in the Holocaust. Instead, Manning positions Miss Bohun's tolerance of the practice as the culprit. The scene exposes a pragmatic morality that reflects the political hierarchy and double message embedded in indirect imperial trusteeship. As servants to the Mandate, the Arabs have no subjectivity and therefore no license to create and implement their own policies; in their voiceless narrative presence, silently tending a colonized garden, they represent pawns to be deployed as showpieces who demonstrate the higher morality of the British. In turn, this higher morality justifies "thinking the worst of everybody while trying to do the best for them," in short, using the language of responsibility to control the fate of the inadequate Other (Manning 1982b, 42).

In Manning's construction, the logic of the British Mandate works by aestheticizing its politics through its trusteeship of the indigenous garden which, while its authenticity is preserved by the native, is being transformed into a colonial enclosure. Representing both a project of modernization and an appreciation of the primitive, the politics of the colonized garden can be seen to employ a metaphorical conflation that helps the Empire ignore its own contradictions. In such fashion, the politics of the colonized garden dictate that its subjugated Other must assume responsibility for its own local customs and practices. And so, when Felix runs to tell Miss Bohun about the burning rats, he catches her at prayer, which, combined with irritated tolerance—"It's the way the Arabs do it"—articulates another justification of the British presence as a moral model (Manning 1982b, 79). Because the novel's publication in 1951 provides a critical perspective on its 1943 setting, the novel's metanarrative includes the commentary that this very model of liberal indirect rule will ignite a political violence. Standing for the British Empire, Miss Bohun will persuade herself she has no responsibility. Condensed and imprinted into Miss Bohun's character, British self-justification is dramatized as a self-deluded rhetoric of an irresistibly reasonable, pragmatic, but transcendent morality. As Miss Bohun instructs Felix, "I think the Arabs appreciate our spirit"(94).

Felix is unlike other child characters in this study. Rumer Godden's child characters ask guileless but critical questions that mock the deluded good intentions of their colonial elders. The child Elspeth Huxley develops her own consciousness of both forming an African identity and denying others theirs. Felix represents the vicissitudes encountered in the development of a questioning consciousness, including the pressures that may thwart it. As an exile, Felix's British identity falls prey to the rhetorical props that promise stability, including those discourses through which colonial agents internalize loyalty, not only to the Empire but to its paradoxically romantic and pragmatic point of view. Felix occupies the colonial space that has been destabilized by the tensions between its romanticism and pragmatism, by external threats to its authority, and by the silent seething of its mutually antagonistic colonized. Coupled with his own experience of the violence and losses of war, Felix's only access to stability is through the cultural codes and language of his compatriot, Miss Bohun. The revelation that these coded systems of meaning are themselves unstable and instruments of distortion is plotted as Felix's various encounters with refugees. In their own tenuous positions in Jerusalem, these stateless people become firmly destabilizing forces against colonial dependence. Their languages of experience and expression mark their social and political positions as incapacitated and delegitimized, not only by the conquests and persecutions of the Third Reich, but by their status as unassimilable aliens in both the center and outposts of the British Empire.

Embodying exile and diaspora, they have been deprived of their native languages but have also been endowed with a language of critical heteroglossia. As readers stumble across their awkward English, their "joke accent[s]"and laughter become the precise instruments to expose Miss Bohun's religious turpitude (Manning 1982b, 47). In addition to the Lesznos, we share this point with Felix as he makes friends with his fellow lodger, Mr. Jewel, and is invited to join him and his friend, Frau Wagner, for one of the denuded dinners offered by Miss Bohun's kitchen. Responding with mocking laughter, Frau Wagner highlights the impossibility, at this historic juncture, of taking the religious and moral rhetoric of imperialism seriously. In a stinging indictment of the debauched religious eschatology that justifies the ingathering of colonizing agents, Nikky Leszno wryly comments, "And for this our house was stolen from us" (112). All together, the voices of these refugees form a jury standing in judgment on Miss Bohun as an agent of the British Empire and its withdrawal from moral and political responsibility. Their most potent influence, however, emerges as their laughter becomes the instrument by which Felix begins to see through Miss Bohun's imperial power.

Caught up in efforts to assure their own survival, the refugees are ultimately powerless to translate their critique into an effective riposte against the administration that tolerates their desperate presence. But between their stateless position and that of Miss Bohun stands a British subject who, because she is both an insider and outsider to colonial and British identity, provides the novel's guide through its colonial critique. Jane Ellis, raised in India and Egypt and a pregnant widow of a British air gunner, guides Felix into "venturing into reality" (Manning 1982b, 136). With a comparative design, the novel dramatizes reality as a process of critically reading the competing discourses of political and cultural identity as they are expressed within and outside Miss

Bohun's walls. As with Dickens's Estella and Pip, Jane Ellis becomes the elusive object of Felix's infatuation, drawing him into experiences beyond the emotional scope of both his former status and his ability to understand. Unlike Estella, however, and unlike Miss Bohun, Jane Ellis can be a reliable guide because she is "not stiff, narrow, proud, prudish and contemptuous of 'the natives' " (132). She is more like Dickens's Biddy in this sense, all the more attractive because her lack of self-absorption allows her to empathize with the needs of a young boy while providing a reality test of them. With her, Felix learns to deconstruct "the romantic . . . story-book world which his mother always somehow produced around her," a vision which loses its benign associations when connected to Miss Bohun's insularity and to the imperial project (136). It is only when Jane Ellis takes him along one evening to the Innsbruck Café, into the melee of Jerusalem's underground cultural life, that reality is exposed as two kinds of deceptions. And although there was a Café Vienna in Jerusalem at the time, Manning's use of the Austrian name suggests the birthplace of both Hitler's aggressions and the Freudian discovery that self-deception perpetrates such urges.

The most obvious deception is figured as Miss Bohun's home hospitality, where the censorious, self-serving, and manipulative discourse of imperious largesse is exposed every time she turns off the lights or heat and, more by will than necessity, serves her ersatz meals. That the truth of such parsimony is more metaphorical and critical than substantiated by the historical record can be gleaned from the fact that by the end of 1942, despite rationing, "foodstuffs were plentiful and varied [and] could always be supplemented from the flourishing black market" (Sherman 1997, 162). A more subtle lie and one that encapsulates romantic denial is figured as the Innsbruck Café. At first glance, the Innsbruck Café appears to be playing the critical card against the apparently irreconcilable tensions that form the political claims of the city's Arabs and Jews, for the café is a place where they and other refugees share a community based on their talk of art and sex rather than on political tension and cultural difference. The scene, however, also plays against a literary convention, where, in the murky light of a surreal night town setting, political, social, and sexual taboos are supposed to be broken and exposed as the folly and frailty of repressive cultures. As the cafe's name suggests, Freudian talk joins with nostalgia for gemutlichkeit, but the value of both is undermined by the identification of Austria as the birthplace of the dictator who drove those Jewish refugees to Palestine. What actually takes place in this den of multicultural conviviality is the repression of political reality by the romantic lie of talking the talk of " 'Kafka, Palinurus, Sartre' " (Manning, 1982b, 131).

What is ironically concealed by all the literary allusions and conviviality between Arabs and Jews are the political realities of the colonial discourses and policies that exacerbate their conflicts. Just how impotent these colonized

men have become is made dramatically clear as their sexual repartee expresses
the stereotyped images that disenfranchised them in the first place—"ignorant
Arabs" driven "wild by the swing of [Jewish women's] breasts and buttocks"
(Manning 1982b, 132). Along with the complicity of the men's internalized
prejudice, the narrator's arch voice exposes the political distance between the
liberal sounds of the men's sexual talk and their domination of women. In fact,
what enables these Arab and Jewish men to be friends is their agreement about
curtailing the social and sexual freedom of Moslem and Jewish women. For
the passion with which this shared value is felt overrides the fact that these
men never speak about "Palestine's private war that was marking time now
until the World War ended" (132). Though their patriarchal attitudes construct
a comfortably shared space in 1943, by 1947, when Britain withdraws, Palestine more closely resembles a combination of texts by the writers they
invoke—Kafka's *The Trial* and Sartre's *No Exit*. Like the fantasied atmosphere
of these texts' unreality, the café represents the dangerously manipulative rhetoric of political denial.

Just how dangerous this rhetoric will turn out to be is dramatized as the
women's position in the reality of that fabled place, Jerusalem. In a colonized,
contested, and destabilized world, the women living in exile expose the stakes
of local and global wars through their tenuous claims on domestic space and
the possibility of regeneration. Because Miss Bohun's house is owned by a
local Imam and can never belong to any of the women, it suggestively dis-
mantles the theology of homeland as a sacred place, especially if sacredness
implies universality. The fact that all the women—Miss Bohun, Frau Leszno,
Frau Wagner, and Jane Ellis—are constantly threatened with eviction highlights their transient status in this novel's colonized space and the maleness of
a sacralized homeland.[16] Because the women are tied to the most meager
material necessity, they cannot afford to mystify the idea of homeland, regardless of how they identify with a place of ethnic, cultural, or nationalist origins.
With her depictions and references to women of so many different histories
and identities, Manning is working against an opposition between British
women's privileged position as British citizens and other women's victimization by inferior cultures. But rather than universalizing the gendered conditions of women's citizenship, she questions universalized interpretations of
homeland. When the idea of homeland takes on a transcendent meaning, radically separate from the political and cultural conditions of a contemporary
lived experience, it assumes a romantic aura and becomes a foundational
myth, not of universal proportion, but solely of male power.

We can hear how this romantic myth is both deflected and expressed in
the gendered cadences of the men's talk in the Innsbruck Café. For in denying women an equally shared space, they put the lie to their multicultural conviviality. In the rhetoric of a man's world, they express what Ian Baruma calls

a "romantic nativism, celebrating the national soul" (2002, 13).[17] This home-land is constituted as a place belonging to a homogeneous male people whose identification with it grants them a mythically pure status. As it excludes women, this male homogeneity duplicates the oppositions of self and Other, of us versus them. In colonial history, these oppositions are translated into indigenous and settler identities, both of which incorporate the domestic management of and by women. In *School for Love,* the showdown over Jerusalem takes place in a very local homeland, over domestic proprietorship, and occurs when Miss Bohun reneges on subletting her house of displaced aggression to Jane Ellis. Recalling and acting as an agent of the men's displaced sexual expression, Miss Bohun equates Jane's pregnancy with sexual "deprav-ity" and "corruption" of Felix (Manning 1982b, 159). This condemnation of the younger woman not only assumes that the evangelical spinster is morally superior, but that, on the basis of being a pure Ever-Ready Wise Virgin, she is the rightful claimant to her colonial site.

Miss Bohun's service on behalf of men's sexual displacement also recalls the role of the femme fatale, a time-honored convention in Orientalist plots. As a sexually corrupt woman, Jane Ellis is cast in the role of Other, unquali-fied to occupy the mythically constituted, immaculately conceived colonial state or nativist homeland. At the same time, however, Miss Bohun condemns Jane on the same grounds that the religious and moral rhetoric of imperial-ism uses to construct the colonized male as a savage Other. With a mocking twist, however, the pregnant Jane Ellis not only calls attention to Miss Bohun's colonial repression, but represents the fecundity that undercuts its continuity. Jane Ellis embodies an anticolonial critique with her pregnant body, for it mocks Miss Bohun's moral condemnation as both sterile and inhumane. Not only is the spinster's hold on the house nonregenerative as it rejects the mother-to-be and her baby, but, as Jane accuses her, Miss Bohun has translated the belief in a Christian "Second Coming" into inhumane practices (Manning 1982b,160). In her statement that "true religion should give practical results," Jane draws attention to the duplicity of Britain's prag-matically romantic imperialism (160). While claiming to honor the compet-ing religious devotion of Arabs and Jews to the Holy Land, the only "practical result" of the British Mandate is the protection of its own interests. Despite the multicultural mix of its colony, British rule recognizes only its own cul-ture as legitimate. As each of those peoples waits for their own version of a Second Coming, that is, the restoration of their national homeland, the mythical and political power of messianic promise has all but disappeared to satisfy the omnivorous appetite of the British Empire. Like Miss Bohun, who represents the self-righteousness of imperial gluttony for expansion, the Empire needs to satisfy its own yearning for self-justification as its end draws near.[18] The trust granted the British Empire by the League of Nations has set the stage for a battle between colonial intransigence and resistance. But the product created by colonial exploitation is a combustible throwaway.

Just as Miss Havisham raises Estella only to consign her to an abusive, sterile marriage, Miss Bohun has taken in a pregnant Mrs. Ellis only to ensure her miscarriage. By metaphorical extension, Mrs. Ellis's miscarriage represents the aborted outcome of the British imperial presence in Palestine. As witness and colonial bystander, Felix is transformed by seeing the colonizing custodianship of Miss Bohun erupt into the violent gesture that sends Mrs. Ellis tumbling down the stairs. He becomes the disillusioned byproduct of an imploding British imperialism. Like Pip, he must be exiled from the place in which romantic dreams of love and adventure are both born and dashed. At the end of the novel, as Mrs. Ellis and Felix are being evacuated back to England, instead of focusing on the characters' woefully romantic sadness that shapes the conclusions of *Great Expectations* and *Passage to India,* Manning focuses on the nation itself. In an exhausted post–World War II era, Britain must embark on a new political odyssey No longer the center of imperial power, in the wake of its costly victory, Britain has become a periphery in the postcolonial world.

Olivia Manning's "Unreal City"

Though unlike any other place I had known, it was suffocatingly familiar. While other countries have an ethos never quite caught by the artist, Egypt is exactly like an old-fashioned color supplement: *The Land of the Pharaohs . . . The Finding of Moses.*

—Olivia Manning, "Cairo: Back from the Blue"

Manning's epic fiction of this war is unlike that of almost all those British women writers who recounted World War II from their besieged home fronts, from behind the lines. Her *Levant Trilogy,* in particular, crisscrosses the cityscapes that provided precarious refuge for civilians and soldiers and then reaches imaginatively into the terrain of the battlefront. If her position behind the battle lines made her a bystander, her writing conveys the emotional and moral risks of evaluating the felt experience that pursues the fighting men even when they can leave the battlefield. As she writes in 1944,

We could recognize at once men who had just returned from the desert. Meeting them at parties, we felt their nervous consciousness of their surroundings. . . . We felt acutely in some of them the strain of energy becoming exhausted. Their hands trembled when they smoked. . . . We knew they were on the fringe of the same panic we had been skirting when we arrived. Danger had an advantage over them. The news that one of them had been killed often came as no more than confirmation of a suspicion felt on his departure.

> It seemed a matter for Kafka, the life they lived out there, dug into sand
> . . . where even a man might pick up a tin of bully beef or a glove and be
> blown in an instant to fragments . . . and the life we lived in the unreal
> city, feeling always in the air the vibrations of desert victory or defeat like
> the vibrations of cannon. (1944, 78).

Like Morse code, the "vibrations" across the desert front communicate the immediacy of war's unimaginable putrescence to the eavesdropping bystander. But they also foretell the ongoing crises of a postcolonial Middle East, crises that victory at El Alamein couldn't resolve and that involve us yet today. We can hear Manning's anxiously prescient voice in her 1949 novel of wartime Egypt and Palestine, *Artist among the Missing*. With its multicultural tableau, this novel relates indigenous Middle East political tensions to the World War II battles for the Middle East and to the global reaches of imperial racism.[19] As the Third Reich challenges the British Empire in the western desert, the global war between them expands not only territorially. In this fiction, global war includes the fates of those, like the Jews, who have no way of escaping this war on themselves or those, like the Arabs, who have no say about this war being waged on their soil. On the Jaffa road in Jerusalem, "among the dark and light faces, the peoples of all countries of the Levant and the priests of half a dozen denominations, went the British troops swaggering in their nervousness of alien surroundings and in the long-ingrained consciousness of British superiority," a mind-set that Manning judges elsewhere as "gross" (1975, 65; 1944, 75). The ironies of this panoramic swathe encapsulate Manning's critique of the British presence in the waning days of their Middle Eastern rule. Instead of a universalizing solution to cultural supremacism, in this novel and others, the wedding of multiculturalism to an imperial presence creates not only cultural barriers, but racial tensions that the war against fascism both challenges and supports.

Artist among the Missing locates the Empire's most nervous center in the character of Geoffrey Lynd, who as "a staff officer, must represent for [those serving under him] all the evils of British imperialism" (Manning 1975, 46). The artist of the title, Geoffrey suffers from a kind of shell-shocked depression. As it forms the novel's defining consciousness and perspective, this malady of mind becomes bound up with the body politic to implicate the artistic imagination. Four years after the Allies' victory, this novel assesses the conflict between the necessity of defeating the fascist Axis and the necessity of sustaining British imperialism. Throughout her fiction of World War II, Manning elaborates and analyzes this conflict as both incitement and entrapment for the creative and critical imagination, as both opposition and interrelationship between the political and the artistic. These novels evaluate the political bind as follows. The fascist mandate calls for eradicating freedom by exterminating those it racializes as poisonous Others. The humanistic freedom for which the British are fighting includes the colonial right to elevate the lives of those it racializes as inferior Others, even as it exploits them. As a novelist/witness, Manning must decide whether her own representations of these Others exploit them as well, and, even more dangerously, represent them in ways that risk replicating the racial and ethnic stereotypes that put these Others in harm's way. Despite the hindsight and shifting geopolitics that accrued with the passage of thirty years between the publication of *Artist among the Missing* and *The Levant Trilogy,* Manning's political imagination continued to translate the political-artistic bind into a vision of imperial entropy. This vision intensifies as she replays the British defeat of German forces in the western desert in the light of increasing knowledge of the Holocaust. But instead of declaring a moral victory for the British, she shows them mired in the politics and moral ambivalence generated by their own waning power. In her own role as artist, Manning ultimately decides that British ambivalence becomes the prison house of Others.

The depression that drives Manning's vision in 1949 and that overwhelms Geoffrey Lynd also serves as a critique reflecting Britain's sense of its "unsustainable" Empire in the Middle East—what has been called "imperial fatigue" (Yapp 1999, 10). This is a very different mind-set from the shell shock of World War I, as depicted by Phyllis Shand Allfrey's *The Orchid House,* where the soldier's debilitation forces him into critical retreat and reflects his decaying colonial society. In Manning's novel, the very distortion and negativity symptomatic of depression provide an acutely critical view of the ideological double bind fostered by citizenship in the British Empire. The bind consists of defeating Hitler's murderous empire while serving and defending both Britain's democratic values and its colonial exploitation. For Manning, the depressive narrative voice retains its power to analyze the war and imperialism even in their aftermath, in the late 1970s. The depression that besets Harriet Pringle paradoxically galvanizes the critical consciousness of *The Balkan Trilogy* and *The Levant Trilogy.* Harriet's response to the war provides a realist method through which we can understand history as a process that is dramatized as political effects on the psychological depiction of character. Harriet's depression not only serves to register the war's immediate emotional and life-threatening urgencies, but figures Manning's deep concerns about victory.[20] Victory over fascism has, from the start, been "politically compromised" by eroding "this barren ground that was now the field of victory" (Manning 1975, 8; 1982a, 281).

The Levant Trilogy, which followed *The Balkan Trilogy,* is set primarily in Egypt and continues to plot the trajectory of Harriet and Guy Pringle's exile along the eastern and southern escape routes from the Nazi-occupied Mediterranean. In *The Levant Trilogy,* the centrality of Harriet's depressed perspective, which begins in Bucharest, when war and a sense of her own power-lessness overtake her, now alternates with that of a young British soldier, Simon Boulderstone. In the thick of the prolonged battle at El Alamein, Simon becomes disoriented and depressed himself, as the streams of the tanks and infantry he follows lose their way in the dust that arises from their own tracks and from the debris and smoke of the fallen.[21] As a signal carrier, Simon represents an instrument of Allied efforts to give their war aims coherence. The queries and responses he carries back and forth between temporary head-quarters and the fighting front are designed specifically to synthesize and then create the information necessary to coordinate the next battle moves. For Manning, the question arises whether any meaning at all can be created out of the rhetorical and consequential distance between the promises of a war for freedom, its exploited subjects, and its maimed and dead. But as the questions Simon carries to the front turn out to be no longer relevant to the besieged division commander, the meanings of the means of war evaporate like water in the desert. Manning's trilogy disassembles the professed meanings of war by showing how they become as lost as the subjectivity of the soldiers, Hitler's potential victims, and the exploited North Africans. All of these are made invisible by the battles that envelop them. Meanings apart from official war aims do emerge, however, in the alternating narratives that connect the plight of Hitler's designated victims and the colonized landscape. Just as the desert landscape seems to disappear under the weight and breadth of the war's tanks and infantry, it mounts its own resistance in the form of its rising, blinding sands. In effect, this is a storm against a war that in this desert land promises only to reconfigure the boundaries and alternate the names of imperial vic-tors, like the ebb and flow of ancient empires.

Although much of postcolonial theory depends on the assumption that developing an empire means creating peripheries, the embattled colonized landscape in *The Levant Trilogy* is figured differently. The desert outpost becomes its own resisting center and thus instrumental in the decentering of imperial power. In Manning's vision, El Alamein is a center of action that, even as it becomes the site of British victory, destabilizes the imperial presence. The disorienting winds and sands of El Alamein defy all imperial claims and incor-porate them into their own symbolic battle against occupation. Although the historic outcome of the battle will not be tampered with in this realist fiction, the novel embeds the fear that represents a different outcome—what would have happened if the Allies had lost at El Alamein and in the western desert? Like the rest of Europe and beyond, they would have become the colonized Other of the Third Reich. It is this fear that drives the Allies across the desert and produces the anxiety that accompanies its victory and defines Manning's narrative voice. As she projects the historical knowledge and perspective of the 1970s back onto her wartime fiction, she introduces a critical gloss on the fears of the Allied armies, including their embattled isolation in the desert and among the colonized and refugees.

This gloss takes the form of another Other, one whose presence has been made invisible by the world war that overtakes the desert as part of its strategic sphere to restore freedom. Positioned like searchlights in the desert, the Egyptians emerge within and between the brutal slaughter of the battle lines to expose and put the lie to intertwined imperial myths: how the isolated courage of the Allied armies came to the rescue of the empty, harsh lands neglected by natives too ignorant to know how to cultivate and govern them. After a prolonged history of coextensive imperial incursion and occupation of the Middle East, and now squeezed between the Allies and Axis, the Egyptians, at least in Manning's representation, claim subjectivity for their land and for themselves.[22] Iqal, Harriet's translator-assistant at the American Embassy, is one of the voices in an Egyptian chorus Manning deploys as critical commentary, questioning the legitimacy of the occupier's fear: "What do you British do with my country, Mrs. Pringle? You come here to rule yet when the enemy is at the gate, you run away" (Manning 1982a, 73). Asked how he feels "about a German occupation," he shows how the continuous history of imperial occupation has eroded away differences between the current combatants (74). For the disdained Other in his relentlessly occupied land, this erosion is exposed by a dangerous slippage between the rhetoric of the combatants: "What do these Germans promise us?—they promise freedom and national sovereignty. What are those things? And what are these Germans? They are invaders like all the invaders that have come here for one thousand four hundred year. They come, they go, the English no worse than others. But to govern ourselves!—that we have forgotten, so how do we do it? And why should we believe these Germans, eh? For myself, I am brushing up my German to be on the safe side, but all the time I am asking myself, 'Better the devil we know'" (74).

Though, like the soldiers, the natives have been rendered invisible by their embattled landscape, the voices representing their body politic are not lost. On a train to Alexandria, Harriet hears "the gleeful yells of the porters" joining Iqal's to create a defiant political chorus: "Even when poor, diseased and hungry, they maintained their gaiety, speeding the old conquerors off without malice. No doubt they would welcome the new in the same way" (94).[23] Harriet can easily be considered as patronizing of the Egyptians as the British ambassador of the time, Lord Killearn, who assessed them as "'essentially a docile and friendly people, but they are like children in many respects'" (quoted in Louis 1985, 226). Though Harriet's mockery is directed at the conquering contestants, its sarcasm requires and exploits the assumption that the Egyptians deserve their fate because they lack the resolve of their more mature saviors: they will accommodate any conqueror. The novel, however, questions this very assumption by celebrating Harriet's consistent sympathy for the

Egyptians and criticism of the British Empire. If the natives are given very little presence or voice in the trilogy, their subjectivity is asserted in the
responses of both Pringles to the vexed relationship between their own status
as colonial exiles and that of the colonized. And in turn, the perennially colonized Egyptians represent a critical bridge between the Allies and Axis armies.
The Egyptians are caught between the combatants, not only in this world war,
but between this war and others the West has brought to North Africa, including their imperial conquests and cultural takeovers. If the victory against the
Afrika Korps is decisive for the Allies, it registers differently through the lens
of the local Egyptians. Guy Pringle realizes that "lecturing on English literature, teaching the English language, he had been peddling the idea of empire
to a country that only wanted one thing; to be rid of the British for good and
all. And, to add to the absurdity of the situation, he himself had no belief in
empire" (Manning 1982a, 513–514).

Manning provides a critical guide to the problems of representing indigenous peoples, not only by imaginative writers, but by theorists of colonialism
and postcolonialism. Rod Edmond points out that "even when ironized,"
when "the language, categories and the anxieties" of a theory are used for the
purposes of critique, they replicate the terms of their "own concepts, becoming in the process self-fulfilling" (2000, 55). Let us see what happens if we
apply this observation to postcolonial theory. I think we would have to conclude that in its criticism of colonial and anticolonial writers, the very language it targets would have to seep into its own words. The language of
postcolonial theory would then turn out to objectify, exoticize, and exploit
the very natives whose subjectivity it seeks to rescue. I maintain that this
method also objectifies, indeed ossifies, the white colonial woman writer. And
while for some theorists this might seem like poetic justice, it reduces the
terms of analysis to the same one dimensionality in which they draw the
white woman writer. Unlike those writers who may undermine their own
colonial critique by creating self-canceling ironies (Conrad and Forster have
been so accused), Manning's irony, like that of Rumer Godden in particular,
always targets the British. This is a self-conscious strategy that includes themselves as imaginative writers responsible for any political ironies they commit.
Where Godden uses the voice of an English child or that of her narrator,
Manning represents her critical ironies in several voices and positions: in the
colonized, in the critical distance between the Pringles' and Simon's reflections, and in their positions and hers as agents of Empire. Even as characters
like Harriet and Guy Pringle and Geoffrey Lynd are presented sympathetically
as voices of conscience, their complicity with imperialism is not excused or
considered irrelevant as though they were innocent bystanders.

In fact, part of Harriet's complexity lies in the way her depression is
presented sympathetically. Rather than serving as an inward-turning or

self-absorbed and abject form of consciousness, Harriet's depression is presented as registering the anxieties of others. Hers is a self-effacing perspective
that allows her to observe others with a combination of empathy and emotional detachment. This strategy may derive from devaluing her own feelings,
but is acutely attuned to the articulated and nonverbal responses of others
(Manning herself developed such powers of observation while gathering
information for MI5 [the British FBI] when she lived in the Balkans, according to Ruth Inglis). Most of Harriet's criticism is registered as unexpressed
thoughts, as though her analyses must remain secret and therefore uncontaminated by the self-absorption of her comrades. When she does rouse herself to
comment, it is in the interest of political critique, as in her assertive correction
of Simon's "fresh and innocent" belief in "the British Empire [as] the greatest
force for good the world had ever known" (Manning 1982a, 24).[24] In rebuttal,
she tells Simon that the British "expected gratitude from the Egyptians and
were pained to find themselves barely tolerated" (24).[25] Part of her insight is
gained from and supported by her own gendered position, which runs parallel to the cultural and political history of the Egyptians. While her political
observations are fiercely independent, she could be describing her own
dependent, pacified position in relation to her husband and to the colonial
administration. As we shall see, unlike the character of the mulatto in Allfrey's
The Orchid House, Harriet's dependent character is not subject to institution-
alized racism, but the only privilege her female whiteness affords her is drawing attention to the paucity of options for her activism.

     The little critical work on *The Levant Trilogy* is divided, applauding Man-
ning's complex treatment of both Simon's desert war and the Pringles' marriage. No attention is given to Harriet's implication in and understanding of
the relationship between the meanings of colonial racism, the war, and those
Others caught in the middle. As Elizabeth Maslen and Margaret Stetz point
out, for far too long critics have assumed that female protagonists and women
novelists are driven by interpersonal relationships and "individual 'erotic experience,'" rather than by the critical social and political issues of their day (Stetz
2001, 95). Nowhere is this more apparent than in one affirmation of Manning's
"uniqueness," especially in her "reflections on historical events [and] contemporary violence" (Inglis 1969, 26). At the same time, however, we are told that
the subject of the *Balkan Trilogy* is the Pringles' marriage and that "the disintegrating wartime Balkans" serves only as "the backdrop"(Inglis 1969, 25). As
though in response, Manning asks, How is the marriage plot affected by a war
story? If we add the ingredient of colonialism into the theoretical mix, as Manning's plotting demands, we see how the subjugated position of the colonized
sheds light on the subjectivity and agency of a modern married heroine. As
postcolonial theory now recognizes, to designate the colonized as powerless is
to pursue the endgame of the imperial project. Rather than reducing the col-

onized to position of victim, we are beginning to grant agency not only to their resistance, but to the maneuvers that one could too easily call complicit with colonial power. That is, by recusing ourselves from judging the accommodation strategies of the colonized, it has become possible to see their political maneuvers as satisfying the fundamental need to survive and to maintain an indigenous cultural and social order. In this light, the relationship between colonized and colonizer is far more intimate than a simple opposition of power and powerlessness would attest. If we apply this perspective to Manning's portrait of Harriet, we can see how, within her depressed state, Harriet constitutes a robust critical selfhood while her relationship with her husband enacts her assent to the primacy of his charismatic powers.

The trilogy links the depressed Englishwoman's lack of options and the survival strategies of her elated Egyptian porters through their historical contexts; they include clashing empires, the fate of a colonized people and land, and the emotional and political costs of imperialism. As the horrors of war and the oppressions of colonialism are gradually imputed to Harriet's consciousness, her response provides a feminist gloss on the porters' "gleeful yells" of farewell to the colonizers. With equal spontaneity, she tries to say farewell to her subjugating marriage. Like the colonizers, who create a world bounded by their own myopically expansive vision, Guy's nearsightedness signifies a self-justifying narcissism. As we shall see, this myopia also marks the romantic visions of colonial characters in the writing of Elspeth Huxley, Rumer Godden, and Phyllis Bottome. Just as the colonizer exploits the colonized without noticing how this only wears them out, so Guy's dependence on Harriet's presence exposes his indifference to her needs. Nowhere is this more powerfully represented than in his blindness to the emotional depletion inscribed on her wasting body. Embodying the nearly invisible status of the colonized, but endowed with the consciousness of resistance, Harriet tries to save herself by accepting a ride with two women journalists on their way to Damascus. But, like the porters who wait patiently for the next wave of interchangeable conquerors, Harriet returns to Guy. Even with a renewed sense of her individuated separateness from him, she takes her place in his shadow once again.

Though they might both be objectified by colonizing interests, as this narrative turn interprets history, the Englishwoman and the Egyptian porters are granted very different subjectivities. The Egyptians have discovered that history can be read as supplying a model for flexible strategies of survival. In a 1967 essay about her stay in Cairo, Manning notes the Egyptians' response to the ebb and flow of German and British offensive and retreat: "They had been ruled by outsiders for 2000 years and were still ready to believe that a new master could mean a good time for all. And now the old master was on the run. Speeding us away, they shouted their derisive amusement, letting us know we were done for. They could have behaved a great deal worse" (1967, 53).

Unlike Harriet, whose developing political consciousness belies the tor-
por of most of her behavior, the Egyptians are given a consistently resistant
political strategy concealed by their good cheer. Guy Pringle's reflection about
his Egyptian students, quoted earlier, reveals that the language of the colonized
constitutes a self-assertive power that relentlessly resists the language of
Empire. Because Guy's lessons and any communication between the British
and Egyptians must be conducted in English, they represent a one-way siege,
easily leading to the conclusion that the Egyptians are silenced. Moreover,
because their service to the British and their characters are presented as one
and the same, Manning can be accused of denying the Egyptians the integrity
of a complex experience. But unlike the English lessons that promise civilization but efface the student's culture, the language of the native retains its
integrity precisely because it is never uttered. The rhetorical effect is that the
native's language and the experience it represents remain beyond the pale of
colonial appropriation. Though the Egyptians are only shown serving and
speaking the language of their colonizers, their usage mocks the very message
carried by Guy's lessons. Iqal and the porters refuse to see the warring colonial empires as representing moral oppositions or the moral and political
imperatives of the Allies as representing a higher civilization than the childlike
Egyptians could ever cultivate. Instead, the Third Reich and the British
Empire are perceived by the Egyptians as interrelated agents of chaos pitted
against Egypt's own internal struggle to remain intact.

Manning's strategy, like that of other British women writers, is problematic for many postcolonial readers. The white woman writer transcribing the
native voice is easily interpreted as a censor. Instead, the novel represents the
Egyptians as launching a critique of its author's self-conscious anticolonial
questions. In its own counteroffensive, the combination of Egyptian voices
and narrative strategy ironizes colonial discourse. Rather than following a
design "which is typical of imperial writing," according to Nigel Rigby, Manning's self-mocking narrative not only avoids, but speaks out against "the possession of [the natives'] thoughts" (2000, 228). As their choral echoing calls
attention to their voices as fictional contrivance, the Egyptian porters implicate Manning's artistry in her political imagination. Expressing Manning's
own political critique, her own "gleeful yells," the Egyptian porters assert a
reality that remains out of reach to both the English characters and their
author. The Pringles' understanding of the natives' resistance is shown to
develop not through direct confrontation, but only through their anxious
sense of their own irrelevance. Manning's representation of the Egyptian characters enables them to withstand not only imperial subjugation and exploitation, but any critique that would deny them a voice and presence in the
narrative of a British writer. In the discourses and practices of both, the sub-

jectivity of the native may go underground, but it remains sufficiently intact to emerge with revitalized self-determination.

At the end of *The Levant Trilogy,* with the Allies' victory, the spoils belong to the colonized, who regain their nation after the British are forced to retreat from both Palestine and Egypt. Manning's coda tells us, "Two more years were to pass before the war ended. Then, at last, peace, precarious peace, came down upon the world and the survivors could go home. Like the stray figures left on the stage at the end of a great tragedy, they had now to tidy up the ruins of war and in their hearts bury the noble dead" (1982a, 571). As "stray figures," the British are not only decentered, but bit players or stage hands. Their agency is confined to discovering some coherence in the interstices between the end of the heroism that defeated fascism, the end of Empire, and the beginning of mourning both.

MURIEL SPARK AND ETHEL MANNIN: THE GATES BREACHED AND THE STRUGGLE FOR POSTCOLONIAL IDENTITY

Disguised and Exposed Strangers: Muriel Spark's The Mandelbaum Gate

The man said something in Arabic. Freddy had thought he was a Jew. You couldn't tell the difference sometimes. Some of them had extremely dark skins, almost jetters. Why couldn't people be moderate?

—Muriel Spark, The Mandelbaum Gate

It should have really been a much better show in our colonial effort.

—Muriel Spark, interview with Martin McQuillan

Long after Britain yielded its mandate over Palestine, after it left India and most of its Empire was being dismantled elsewhere, its struggle to remain a global power continued. If its last imperial gasp was drawn at the defeated incursion into the Suez Canal crisis of 1956, Britain was still insinuating itself by more diplomatic methods so as to protect its economic and political interests. By 1965, when Muriel Spark published *The Mandelbaum Gate,* her novel of the Middle East, Britain's performance as a power in the region could be satirized as make-believe. In the same work, however, she surveys the potential damage of the enfeebled British presence to nations engaged in their struggles for self-determination in a postcolonial age. It may very well have been this concern about Britain's postimperial anxieties that drove her to say of this novel, "I felt I had done my *Passage to India*" (McQuillan 2002, 215).

Though greatly admired for her narrative innovations, Muriel Spark's place in the canons of modernism or postmodernism remains unsettled. In part, this may be due to the identity politics surrounding her conversion to Catholicism in 1954, after which, as she has attested, she also converted from writing poetry to novels. Though she wrote her first novel only in response to a request from a Macmillan editor and, as she told Frank Kermode, she thought novels were "an inferior way of writing," her religious conversion made her think differently (Spark 1977, 132): "The Catholic belief is a norm from which one can depart. It's not a fluctuating thing. . . . Nobody can deny I speak with my own voice as a writer now, whereas before my conversion I couldn't do it because I was never sure what I was, the ideas teemed, but I could never sort them out, I was talking and writing with other people's voices all the time. But not any longer" (Spark 1961, 60). Critics continue to wrestle with the problem of how to read Spark's conversion into or out of her novelistic voice, especially since many of her plots play with a determinism that, as Bryan Cheyette suggests, has led critics to exercise their own determinism; many critics interpret her fiction as though it keeps replaying an "ongoing conversion, transforming the author anew and distancing her from her previous self"(Cheyette 2000, 7). In its constancy, this critical determinism performs its own kind of ritual, as though the repeated practice will in itself reconcile an unsettling paradox or contradiction in Spark's plotting, where Catholic conversion is often a bit too close for comfort to Calvinist determinism.[26] For postmodern and feminist critics, the combination of Catholic conversion, Calvinist plotting, and Spark's "great" belief "in providence," may also add up to a cultural conservatism at odds with current literary critical-ideological missions (Spark 1961, 63). Spark's conversion inflects her novels in myriad guises, but, as we shall see, these guises not only inform its structure, but emerge as the actual subject of *The Mandelbaum Gate*.

Compounding the intricacies of Spark's religious valences are the spare structures of many of her novels, even those which gesture toward a more open realism. Influenced by the conciseness and precision of neoclassical poetry, the French *nouveau roman,* and British postmodernism, the unadorned prose style and logic-defying connections of her novels work in counterpoint with her baroque plotting, often making it unclear where her ideological sympathies lie. In fact, as Patricia Waugh has noted, "Spark embraces neither a complacent liberalism nor an anarchic postmodernism. Her stories, [Spark] says, are neither 'true' nor simply 'lies'; they are neither mimetic representation nor simply the play of signification; they neither assume a fixed human moral order nor abjure morality altogether" (1989, 217). This ideological indeterminacy is further complicated and even undercut by Spark's sly humor, which targets not only the social conventions and politics represented by her narrators and characters, but her own self-conscious plotting and stylistics. And if these features aren't daunting and distancing enough, Spark disavows any ideological relationship with her characters or narrative voice: "I have to decide what the author of the narrative is like. It's not me, it's a character. In some of the contemporary novels I'm not too keen on, the narrator is always the author, whether it's first or third person narration. That gets monotonous.

Every theme demands a different sort of commentator, a different intellectual attitude" (Spark 1961, 62).

While her fans have taken great delight in parsing Spark's idiosyncratic narrative voices and intensely compressed plots, and in discovering paradoxical plays of meanings between their lines, they have been less enthralled with that one novel, written early in her novelistic career, which doesn't fit the patterning she established before and after.[27] *The Mandelbaum Gate* is her longest novel, and therefore the least poetic. Especially as she "did it in the form of short stories . . . each . . . with a different point of view," it is also her most discursive and "baggy," but it wrestles with an identity politics that defies paradox (McQuillan 2002, 215). In fact, as I will argue, the novel's delightful satire of British colonial ineptitude and the muddle of Middle East politics is plagued by an underlying essentialism about which there is no playfulness.

Placing her own identity issues on the line, Spark engages religious conversion as the disturbing principle of the plot and of her female protagonist, Barbara Vaughan. Barbara's conversion to Roman Catholicism motivates her religious pilgrimage to Jerusalem, a place whose history unsettles any notion of either Catholicism's universalism or ritualized harmony. Like the plotting of the novel itself, which consists of intricate patterns of dualities, doubling, and self-reflexive connections, Catholicism and conversion turn out to be messy, ambiguous, open-ended processes that, as the combination wrestles with its own designs, can also be self-parodic. If these complications have unsettled her critics, they have also led to the novel becoming a problem for Spark. While she expressed great affection for it when it was first published and won a prize, she has since admitted that its two-year-long creation "exhausted" her (McQuillan 2002, 215). She also declared, "I don't like that book awfully much . . . it's out of proportion. . . . I got bored, because it's too long, so I decided never again to write a long book, keep them short" (quoted in Whittaker 1982, 79). The length of *The Mandelbaum Gate* not only spotlights a change in Spark's preferred formal structures, but, much more radically, raises questions and problematic responses to the meanings Spark attributes to conversion. Critics mark her indelibly as a "wholly Catholic writer in the British tradition" of Graham Greene (Cheyette 2002, 100), and they see her conversion as an ongoing determining split which keeps replicating "a rather too facile act of redemption," rather than the more fruitful "fluid" and "sustained dialogue" which offers an opportunity to play with "a range of possible national or religious identities" but which also allows her "to deny the efficacy of all forms of classification" (Cheyette 2000, 7, 11).

Such fluidity and ambiguity are both supported and questioned by the connections Spark makes between her writing novels and her being converted. While she maintains that Catholicism has given her the "security" to find her "style" by "not caring too much," her conversion also gave order to her thinking (Spark 1961, 62, 63). As we shall see, however, *The Mandelbaum Gate* questions the viability of conversion itself. Set in the same year as her essay "My Conversion," in a narrative voice Spark would insist is pure invention, the novel's combination of intensely serious and satiric styles works in tandem to provide a critical gloss on the statements Spark makes in the voice she claims as her own. In turn, the questions confronting the viability of conversion unfold as constituting, perhaps even necessitating, her most realistic writing. This includes enough historical contingency to open up her narrative strategies to unsettling external pressures.

The novel's setting in Israel and Jordan questions both the harmony of any religious faith and the stability of conversion in the light of political history, including Israeli-Arab tensions and their connection to British imperialism, racism, antisemitism, and the Holocaust. Spark has often spun her spare tales around particular historical events, for example, Miss Jean Brodie's infatuation with Il Duce and Italian fascism in *The Prime of Miss Brodie* (1961) and World War II in *The Girls of Slender Dreams* (1963). Unlike these novels, in *The Mandelbaum Gate* history appears and functions as more than a single event or a backdrop. Instead, it plays as a primary character, with all the particularity of the moment and yet in flux. Spark imagines history here as tensely open-ended, calling attention to itself as a force that is distinguished from and indeed competes with the determining power of the author. That this powerful historical force produces no violence in this novel also sets it apart from her others. Despite its setting amidst real political conflicts, no bombs are arranged to go off and no character is sent off to die in a war. Instead, the novel enacts a kind of narrative conversion, in which the violence of history is played as a comedy of manners until it confronts that ultimate atrocity, the Holocaust. As it appears in *The Mandelbaum Gate,* history also challenges the absoluteness of the truths in which Spark believes. She tells Frank Kermode that while she doesn't "pretend that what [she is] writing is more than an imaginative extension of the truth," she writes "fiction because [she is] interested in truth—absolute truth": Distinct from "metaphorical truth and moral truth, and what they call anagogical, . . . there is absolute truth, in which I believe things which are difficult to believe, but I believe them because they are absolute" (Spark 1977, 133). If this sounds tautological, Kermode interprets Spark's "absolute truth" as "revealed religion" and a function of what "happens in the author's mind as he writes" (Spark 1977, 134). In Spark's earlier novels, whatever the historical event against which the plot is set, character is often fixed and wound into motion only to be revealed as predetermined by Spark's tightly grasped and compelling plotting—designs that can be seen as functions of her "absolute" beliefs.

In *The Mandelbaum Gate,* the historical moment cannot be reined in by belief or any hermeneutic; it insists on its absolute reality even as it eludes our grasp. Even as the novel confronts claims made on behalf of any historical truth, the protracted history of the Holocaust remains a crisis for which there seems to be no preparation, no hermeneutic, and no protection from its horrors. This includes not only the characters and the narrative design, but readers as well. And this is the case despite the novel's many concerted efforts to both discover and evade the impact of historical and fictional plotting: the separate and combined attempts by its British diplomats and spies, the workings of the Eichmann trial, Barbara Vaughan's open inquiry, and a narrative that juggles and weighs each of these efforts against the other. Asserting a narrative integrity and resistance of its own, the relationship between conversion, cultural and racial identity, and the Holocaust in this novel also dodges any propulsion of narrative suspense that would conventionally hold readers' attention or that would assuage them by appealing to their own imaginative and critical gifts. Set in 1961, following Spark's two-month stay in Jerusalem, the novel's historical tension between past and present develops as an irresistible force that moves even beyond the ending. So taken was Spark with this dynamism that it not only inspired her to transcribe events in her visit into the novel, but set the tone, direction, and style of several following novels.[28] In all its turbulence, history here ensures not only that characters are destabilized, but, paradoxically, despite the novel's commitment to spying, disguise, and subterfuge, that the indelible historical moment overwhelms the characters' ability either to effect change or to change themselves. The conflicts between ancient and modern history embrace the entire narrative structure, including the author, narrator, characters, plot, conceits, and structure.[29]

Despite its particularity, as it informs the 1961 Middle East setting, with its Arab, Israeli, and English characters, history is an all encompassing determinant, remaining obdurately material but also indeterminate. Calling attention to division or two sides, the title, *The Mandelbaum Gate,* marks the political tensions between Israel and Jordan, tensions that were founded on and would ultimately lead to explosion once again. A security checkpoint between the two nations, the Mandelbaum Gate stands for the contested foundation of the State of Israel as well as the detente that defined Israel and Jordan's relationship until the 1967 war, when the Israelis defeated the Jordanians and occupied the West Bank. A real peace accord between Israel and Jordan was only signed in the 1990s.[30] That Spark should choose the rigid but unsteady border as her title in 1965 invites a political and historical reading of the novel. Unlike Spark's other novels, where Catholic faith vies with Calvinist determinism in an otherwise secularized, even faithless Europe, *The Mandelbaum Gate* is set in the terrain that gave rise to Christianity but which is defined by the religious fervor of its political conflicts between Muslims, Christian Arabs, and Jews. Barbara Vaughan's inherited Jewish and Protestant identity signifies and confronts these conflicts as she embarks on her religious pilgrimage. As she encounters the political implications of her multifaceted sense of self, the novel ponders the unkempt relationship between religious and historical identities. This history, moreover, not only is about local and personal tensions, but implicates imperialism even after the end of Empire. The brief saga shared by Barbara and a foreign service officer, Freddy Hamilton, highlights the historic role of the British Empire as well as Britain's self-conception nearly twenty years after it left its colonized contestants to their own devices. In the 1961 setting, as well as during the two years of the novel's composition, the British are positioned as an anomalous presence; their insistence on moderation only denies the passions motivating the Israelis, Palestinians, and Jordanians. As Barbara enters their midst and shakes up Freddy, she exposes the turbulence that remains in the wake of Empire and its relationship to the Holocaust.

If political moderation represents rationality and other civilized virtues, Spark exposes its underlying and self-canceling passions as well as its violent implications. Freddy, who prides himself on representing British diplomatic decorum, is suddenly overcome by amnesia, a disease which is diagnosed as afflicting "white men in the tropics" and which allows him to forget his brief political and erotic adventure (Spark 1965, 141); and this is shown to be an imperial defense mechanism against the "pathogenic environments" endemic to "colonial outposts" (Edmond 2000, 45). Akin to the lassitude of British neocolonial diplomacy, Freddy's amnesia conveniently denies the unsettling primacy of emotional agency and intimacy, both of which he considers irrational and uncivilized. It is only during those few feverish but forgotten days that he acts with any political and sexual decisiveness. And true to his defensive amnesia, this determination is threatening both to his "subdued" if stiff upper lip and to the politics of diplomacy that avoids direct involvement and which he has served so well (Spark 1965, 3). Such diplomacy recalls Britain's futile evenhandedness in Arab–Jewish relations as well as its lethal rejection of Jewish refugees during its mandate. The state of amnesia resonates with Britain's denial of responsibility for the tragic consequences of both histories. Until Freddy meets Barbara Vaughan, his partner in political intrigue, and Suzi Ramdez, his partner in sexual ecstasy, his innocuously "agreeable" style finds its correlative in thank-you notes whose classically constricted poetic forms express "scarcely a word," avoiding "murderous attachments, the sort of emotion that . . . led to international incidents" (Spark 1965, 7, 3). *The Mandelbaum Gate* deploys Freddy's minor consular position to show how postimperial Britain in 1961 Jerusalem needs to feel it is important enough to incite such political feelings and powerfully wise enough to abate them. That Freddy should lose the memory of his most intensely felt experiences attests to the self-deluded machinations of a postimperial power.

Spark's satiric analysis of Britain's postimperial mind-set takes the form of a plot precipitated by Barbara Vaughan's commitment to computing her multiple identities evenhandedly, just like the postcolonial British presence in divided Jerusalem. The British also pin their hopes for conciliation on being fair to all sides of the Arab-Israel conflict. But like Barbara's "beautiful and dangerous gift of faith," these politics represent a reassuring if self-deceptive illusion (Spark 1965, 20).[31] As the novel shows, in the Eichmann trial and elsewhere, historical documentation betrays the construction of such an accommodating fusion as an unwieldy fiction. A multicultural identity only highlights the tensions caused by neglecting the interests and dangerous tensions of cultural and political difference. In the novel's postcolonial setting, where multicultural identity, as befitting a celebration of hybridity, might be considered a solution to intractable differences, it functions as a self-reflexive joke or hoax. Consider, for example, the case of Suzi's father, Joe Ramdez, whose name, like his fictional identity as an Armenian Arab and like his nickname, "the Agent," only calls attention to his double-dealing character and political playacting (Spark 1965, 69). In an evenhanded gesture of her own, Spark portrays Joe and his various agencies as being as harmless as postcolonial British diplomacy. His elaborate network of information-gathering and controls turns out to be as irrelevant as the spying of an English expatriot, Mrs. Gardnor, hunting down water pipelines that no one cares about. Gently mocking the state of postcolonial Middle East politics, their plotting turns out to be no more serious than the cloak-and-dagger popular fiction of postwar–cold war foreign intrigue.

Reminiscent of Manning's trope of anticolonial resistance, Spark's satire begins with the tense landscape of the Middle East strategically avoiding a takeover. In Spark's novel, the Middle Eastern land has been domesticated into an English garden. Its vibrancy, however, depends on the inscrutable presence of an Arab boy who tends it but who remains beyond the reach of English desire. Graceful but deformed, associated therefore with both sexual temptation and the wages of sin, the boy triggers Freddy's sexual memory of another boy gardener. In Spark's carefully plotted doublings, Freddy's homoerotic desires are then translated into lust not only for the Arab woman, Suzi Ramdez, but for her brother Abdul, a doubling that mocks the legacy of evenhanded British diplomacy. Following his own strategies of colonial usurpation, self-justification, and denial, the mild-mannered consul translates and therefore tames the garden's sexual and political suggestiveness into a tale of moral edification. And so he associates the garden with an old tale about English spinsters who went around the Empire, scattering their English wildflower seeds, "doing something to unite East and West" (Spark 1965, 59). Political and sexual desire, redolent in this colonial myth, are thus sublimated and sublated into good intentions that conceal but also justify desire for the Other's land. The piety of this imperial strategy, however, is also betrayed by colonial cognitive science, a rationale that silences the Other in his colonized garden: "It's the Arab mentality. They think in symbols. Everything stands for something else. And when they speak in symbols it sounds like lies" (Spark 1965, 59, 75). The analysis here, spoken by an Englishwoman, could easily be applied to Freddy's own self-censored forms of self-expression. While the colonized Others' pent-up desires for self-determination are always perceived in colonial terms as threatening violence, Freddy's circumspection, like the silent withdrawal of British diplomacy, shows that perception to be nothing more than a projection. As history and the fictions of Manning and Spark attest, such withdrawal is tantamount to the abrogation of the responsibility the Empire once so proudly felt it should assume.[32]

The effect of silencing self and the Other also backfires when the Other learns to mimic the imperial discourse of disguised motives. The information networks of Joe Ramdez function not only in competition with the British, but as a way of communicating to the former imperial power that the British are being manipulated out of their own decorous silence for the purpose of strengthening Arab self-determination. In their inscrutability, the Arabs embody a strategy of double messages that keep their own political needs untranslatable in their disguise of gracious but always confusing helpfulness. As Joe Ramdez advises his daughter and principal agent, Suzi, "[Freddy] will communicate more if you make him feel an intruder in our land; that's always the way of the British" (Spark 1965, 253). In contrast to the Arabs, the cool distance on which the British count to protect their neo-imperial presence and interests is erased by the transparency of their discourses of disguise. But Spark's own evenhandedness mocks this information highway because British interests contain secrets "already available in publications which had not reached them, or which lay forgotten in their files" (Spark 1965, 253). Instead of fomenting political unrest, the mutually canceling espionage plots of the British and their former imperial wards create an interdependent relationship that nourishes a sense of competing but ineffectual cultural hegemony.

Spark's satire as her critical tool places her in a literary tradition she chose for herself—"a marvelous tradition of socially-conscious art" (Spark 1971, 23). In her 1971 invocation speech at the American Academy of Arts and Letters, she calls for mockery as being far more effective in holding the moral attention of the audience than representations of "depicted suffering," which can produce a "cult of the victim," which "is the cult of pathos, not tragedy" (Spark 1971, 23, 26). The problem is that "sympathies and indignation" could lead audiences to "feel that their moral responsibilities are sufficiently fulfilled by the emotions they have been induced to feel" and so to feel "absolved" (Spark 1971, 23, 24). "Crude invective," on the other hand, is likely to end in violent action (Spark 1971, 25). Years after her depiction of the Eichmann trial in *The Mandelbaum Gate*, Spark uses the example of World War II to demonstrate how tyrants such as Hitler and Mussolini "wouldn't have had a chance" had they faced a "massed" response of "ridicule" and "helpless laughter" at their "goose-stepping troops"—they would have been denounced as "absurd" (Spark 1971, 24, 26). In *The Mandelbaum Gate,* Spark's satire is not targeted against tyrants, but saved for those British individuals and institutions already marked as absurd by the historical moments that have passed them by and for those Arabs, like Joe Ramdez, whose machinations serve to mock the ineffectual designs of the British while sustaining a strategic independence. And so it is with a fair amount of affection that she gently mocks these characters whose happy endings are assured by a plot that will not allow them to serve as either victims or villains. Though Barbara Vaughan is another target of satiric opportunity for Spark, there is a powerful element of serious interrogation invested in her character that we don't see in either Freddy's or Joe's portraits.

As though it were a guide to reading the novel and all its identity issues, the second chapter, "Barbara Vaughan's Identity," has received much critical attention. Combined with Barbara's own growing self-awareness, the narrator and Barbara's Israeli guide take us through a labyrinth of genealogical, psychological, religious, social, and legal issues, all to establish the instability of her cultural-religious identity. Since the novel is about a woman who is half-Jewish, half-Protestant, and a convert to Catholicism on a pilgrimage to the Holy Land, it invites us to read it as another imaginative rendering, if not test, of Spark's own identity and conversion.[33] Early on, the novel was called "The Gentile Jewesses," but then Spark used the title for a short story that explains the difficulties of being even marginally Jewish in 1920s Edinburgh. Despite the fact that the narrator's great-grandmother was Christian and her father Jewish, though "she would have been amazed at any suggestion that this attitude was a weak one or a wrong one, . . . she had not liked the Jewish part of her origins to be known, because it was bad for business" (Spark 1985, 272).[34] Spark herself uses the phrase "exile in heart and mind" to describe her persistent moves away from monocultural, homogeneous environments "which cannot accommodate" her (1970, 151–152). Religious identity in *The Mandelbaum Gate* questions how individual identity can matter in a setting where there is no such thing as personal identity without political and historical identity. Like the influence of postimperial Britain, Barbara's religious pilgrimage to ancient sites in Israel and Jordan is predicated on negotiating three faith traditions: Judaism, Islam, and Christianity. The way becomes thorny for her, however, because the bases of these beliefs question each other and because Barbara's conversion to Catholicism is caught between political tensions. If the presence of Catholicism is predicated on the ritual of pilgrimage, both Judaism and Islam lay ancestral claims to the land itself. Neither fabulistic nor futuristic, this novel gives its narrative power to those voices that insist on facing history as a force competing with faith.

Like the peoples of the Middle East among whom she travels, Barbara seeks self-determination, and yet she also dodges it. Even though every risk she takes enacts choice, it also restricts her movements and self-expression. The fact that her "self-image was at variance with the image she presented to the world" affords her the privilege of relishing a delightful emotional privacy, but it also means that she is always at risk of being misunderstood (Spark 1965, 40). Unlike Suzi Ramdez, who exploits her inherited identity in a tradition-ally gendered society to exercise her freedom, Barbara's "inexplicable identity" forces her into hiding, into covering her body and her purpose, when she crosses from Israel to Jordan (42). As if she weren't "displaced" enough, the plotting of her pilgrimage splits her identity even more, until its secret and contested movements and dual motives come to resemble the fractured polit-ical worlds across which she travels. The novel's bridge between Barbara and the political divide is her escapade with Freddy. Though Barbara negotiates her multiple identities self-consciously, her cultural and sexual disguises as well as her political subterfuges resemble Freddy's less conscious sexual dualities. Her sense of conversion, that it is "insignificant" to be "a Gentile and a Jewess, both and neither," to be "a wolf in spinster's clothing," aligns religious conver-sion with sexual politics and performances, with the transformation of Freddy's dormant homosexual desire into lust for Suzi, and with his politics of fair play (50).

While Barbara's masquerades lead to the recognition of her own sexual and cultural Otherness, Freddy's espionage exposes the equitable politics of British neocolonialism as impotent even as it constructs the Other as a sexual object. As their alliance parallels the machinations of political contestation and diplomacy, these English characters become identified with the history, pres-ent, and future of Palestine, Israel, and Jordan, with their conditions as the for-merly colonized, and with the self-proclaimed reluctant colonizers. But even as the novel deploys satire and sexual roundelay for the great pleasure for its readers, these romps are haunted by the horrifically inequitable politics of another imperial conquest. Implicated in the tumultuous present and unde-termined future of the postcolonial Middle East is the unatoned past of Nazi Germany, an empire which exercised its own sense of fair play by rendering all the objects of its domination impotent. This included not only the claims of faith and any homeland except that it claimed for itself, but the power of its Others to resist. As the novel shifts to the terrain of Barbara's pilgrimage, it makes all of these claims problematic.

Instead of resolving her competing and even incompatible identities, as Barbara is driven around northern Israel over an increasingly rocky terrain, categories of identity keep crisscrossing each other. At every turn, like the Hydra's heads, unexpected signs of irreconcilable differences crop up once again, until the cheerfully hybrid identity of the British convert is forced to confront questions that defy her quest. The catalyst for this confrontation is an Israeli guide who goads her with questions that traverse Jewish legal and political history. Barbara responds by trying to find a "definition" for an "essential" sense of herself (Spark 1965, 27), "the human soul, the individual. Not 'Jew, Gentile' as one might say 'autumn, winter.' Something unique and unrepeatable" but also "unspoken, uncategorized and unlocated" (38). As Bryan Cheyette argues, Barbara's response represents a "welcome intellectual skepticism" (2000, 66). Having affirmed its own method of inquiry, however, the novel also insists on a form of contingency that, paradoxically, challenges "intellectual skepticism" even as it also embarks on its own pilgrimage to define an "essential" sense of self. Although historical contingency also unsettles categorical imperatives, in the case of this novel, it creates an indelible marker of identity and selfhood. Even if, as Cheyette argues, Barbara places herself "outside of both a dominant nationalism and an orthodox conversionism," the historical record shows her and us the fragility of this choice and another kind of determinism (66).

What makes Barbara feel "displaced," that "her personal identity [was] beginning to escape like smoke from among her bones," is the inescapable modern Jewish history brought to light by the relentless questioning of her Israeli guide. This is also a history that Barbara's religious pilgrimage can, on the grounds of its universalistic solidity and narrative boundaries around the life and lessons of Jesus, assiduously avoid. For her the Eichmann trial is "political and temporary" (Spark 1965, 208). As the guide's questions begin to wear her down and she feels "deprived of fresh air and civil rights," the image of smoke escaping from her bones assumes historic connotations that destabilize the mythic, transcendent meaning of her pilgrimage (26). Her own choice of language shows that her identity may be conditioned by factors where choice is not only a fiction but no longer relevant. The image of smoke escaping from human bones can, of course, be taken as a purely imagined trope or as a mockery of Barbara's self-dramatization, but this brief reference reminds us of Spark's penchant for making language both transparent and opaque, literalizing the suggestiveness of her metaphors. Because this image literalizes a historic fact that is so insistent in this novel and from which there is no transcendent escape, it insists on a historicized interpretation. No longer safely confined to the loss of individual identity, the juxtaposition of this image with the deprivation "of fresh air and civil rights" points to a more collective destiny, one that can't be kept at bay by a religious commitment to alter one's relation to history. Instead, Barbara's quest is linked to a collective history that the novel imposes on her consciousness and ours.

The metaphoric allusions may be a function of Barbara's singular consciousness, but her guide is positioned to confront not only her but the reader as well with their materiality. Not letting any of us off the hook, he presses his inquiry with an aside "to some invisible witness": "I ask her a question, she makes a big thing of it that I am Gestapo" (Spark 1965, 26).[35] Unlike the narrator's affectionate mockery of British and Arab characters, the Israeli's joke establishes him as a determining agent. Whereas Joe Ramdez negotiates his political position by maneuvering lightly around the innocuous constraints of the present, and Freddy forgets the present to safeguard the never-never land of earthly delights, the Israeli guide has confronted himself and Barbara with a threatening past. Instead of providing a comfortably comic distance from catastrophe, the paradoxically peaceful tension of Spark's political comedy of manners erupts in a violence that cannot be escaped by fiction, by myth, or by comedy. If the guide's self-mockery is also affectionately rendered, it positions Barbara's responses to his questions as another maneuver to deny the past's intrusion on the present. Typical of Spark's gallows humor, the juxtaposition of the two quotes on one page—the image of smoke and the Gestapo-like questions—produces a deadly seriousness. Here they connect, all too tellingly, with the role of the Eichmann trial, the historical event which not only disrupts all of the novel's many plot trajectories but questions the novel's comic mode and voice.

If Barbara thinks her identity can be negotiated through cheery memories of "Golders Green Jewishness" and her father's "rural Anglicanism," Spark undercuts any romantic nostalgia by forging links between Barbara's personal history and the history of the Holocaust (Spark 1965, 27). That her father died after being thrown by his horse into a ditch is immediately countermanded by her guide recounting that his father also died in a ditch, "Shot by the S. S." (25). In their exchange about religious identity, Barbara's chosen identity is situated in opposition to the guide's insistence on the impermeability of Jewish legal identity. She may claim a combined identity—"the peculiar independence of the Gentile-Jew"—but she remains tied to Jewish law, where, because her mother was Jewish, she is wholly Jewish (27, 28). Her insistence that her identity can be fluid and unresolved because it is both "essential" and "displaced" is not only questioned by the laws of Jewish identity, but declared a fiction by the identity laws which instituted Eichmann's power in the Third Reich—the Nuremberg laws.

Preparing the way for the Holocaust, the 1934 Nuremberg laws of Nazi Germany erased the Gentile half, denied the possibility of choosing one's identity, and destroyed the viability of Jewish laws of identity. The Nuremberg laws marked anyone with even one Jewish grandparent as Jewish enough to be "deprived of fresh air and civil rights." In their indelible presence at the Eichmann trial, the Nuremberg laws cast a long shadow over the novel. From this potent center of the novel, no plot turn is exempt, including the comedy of Freddy's amnesia. As it stands for British diplomacy in the Middle East, this repression of its responsibility must extend to closing the gates of Palestine to

Jewish refugees from Hitler. The Nuremberg laws also shadow Barbara's identity questions as well as her romance plot. On the one hand, the novel treats the "outcast status" of Barbara and her lover, Harry, as well as their ignorance about his forged Catholic identity, as the stuff of romantic comedy (Spark 1965, 44). But the affectionate irony with which Harry's forged identity and the legal logic of Catholic canon law are treated only spotlights the ominous linkage of Barbara's constructed identity to the Nuremberg laws. More urgent than a romantic romp or stroll down the lanes of religious memorials, Barbara's pilgrimage challenges whether her bones can escape the smoking memory of the death camps and whether a constructed religious history of a universal faith can supersede a history that cannot be identified with or universalized. Ultimately, the novel asks whether any fiction of modernity can escape that memory.

Setting the novel in Jerusalem and featuring the Eichmann trial marks a well-documented event with certain outcome, but as Spark uses the trial, its historic implications mutate into the unforeseen. On the one hand, Spark shows how the trial was deliberately plotted to imprint the brutal history of the Holocaust on world consciousness—"an implanted image in the public mind" (Spark 1965, 210). In pitting Catholic, Jewish, and the Nuremberg laws of identity against the Eichmann trial, Spark's novel challenges its own verdict about the stability of a converted identity. It also sets up a conflict between sacred stories and the profanities of history. With the presence of the Eichmann trial, the novel confronts the relationship of the great powers of God and a universal church to a history of Jewish identity. Both religious belief and identity are superseded by a relationship to a historical particularity—the great powers of human tyrants. Demonstrating the significance of the Eichmann trial, Shoshana Felman argues that it not only holds Eichmann captive to a predetermined guilt, but effects "a conscious closure to the trauma of the war; to separate ourselves from the atrocities and to restrict, to draw and demarcate a boundary around a suffering that seemed both unending and unbearable. Law is a discipline of limits and of consciousness. We needed limits to be able both to close the case and to enclose it in the past. Law distances the Holocaust. Art brings it closer. We needed art—the language of infinity—to mourn the losses and to face up to what in traumatic memory is not closed and cannot be closed" (2001, 202).

Spark's novel enfolds the Eichmann trial into her art as a historical event that Barbara and readers must "face up to," approximating what Felman calls "this space of *slippage between law and art*" (2001, 202, italics in original). In pitting Catholic, Jewish, and the Nuremberg laws of identity against the Eichmann trial, Spark's novel tries to keep its balance in that space "between law and art" and, in so doing, challenges its own verdict about the instability of identity. Felman sees the Eichmann trial not just as being about history but as being a "living, powerful *event*" in itself (2001, 210, italics in original). The word "living" is particularly important here because what made this trial "monumental" and "revolutionary" was its "unique representation of the victims' previously unheard, unknown, and unnarrated narrative" (Felman 2001, 213, 210). "In the Nazi scheme, this narrative was meant to be erased as part of the erasure of the Jewish people. The articulation of this narrative as a living, active, historical, and legal force is therefore in itself an unprecedented act of historic (and not just of legal) justice" (Felman 2001, 213). Unlike other Nazi war crime trials, which focused on the perpetrators and where Holocaust survivors provided corroborating testimony, the Eichmann trial confronted the watching world with the collective voice of survivors who spoke for the six million Jewish dead. The trial's chief prosecutor and Israel's attorney general, Gideon Hausner, recalls asking himself "what the victims would have wished me to say on their behalf, had they had the power to brief me as their spokesman, now that the roles were reversed and the persecuted had become the prosecutors" (quoted in Felman 2002, 214). What he did say to the world's witness was this: "When I stand before you, judges of Israel, in this court, to accuse Adolph Eichmann, I do not stand alone. Here with me at this moment stand six million prosecutors. But alas, they cannot rise to level the finger of accusation in the direction of the glass dock and cry out *J'accuse* against the man who sits there. For their ashes are piled in the hills of Auschwitz and the fields of Treblinka. . . . Their blood cries to Heaven, but their voice cannot be heard. Thus it falls to me to be their mouthpiece and to deliver the heinous accusation in their name" (quoted in Felman 2002, 214).

In *The Mandelbaum Gate*, the Eichmann trial affirms the survival of the Jews and Jewish identity in opposition to the history of the Holocaust and the prevalence of antisemitism and anti-Zionism.[36] The very meticulous legal and performative efforts to achieve this affirmation, however, also represent a fear that haunts the Jews—that the threat of persecution will not end with Eichmann's guilty verdict and execution. It is this overlay of an unendurable and indelible history that translates the trial into the anxious plea that the Holocaust can never be allowed to recur. It is also this history that is implicated in the insistence, indeed, urgency of the Israeli guide's questions. With this focus, the novel makes history both very palpable and elusive, rendering it as a force that must be contended with even as it evades confrontation. The characters' confrontation with ancient and modern history becomes a challenge to the religious, political, and narrative systems of belief that typically represent Spark's novelistic conflicts.

History in *The Mandelbaum Gate* resists any search for order as its "crazed unreality" interferes with all strands of the narrative. On the one hand, the novel definitively and intricately connects Barbara's pilgrimage with the past as both religious mystery and political history. Her pilgrimage traces the life, miracles, death, and resurrection of Jesus as sequential markers for the staging of her commitment to Catholic faith and fate. But always threatening to detour this pilgrimage is the crossroad to and from the Holocaust, where the universal embrace of Catholicism cannot elide her historic identity, especially as she is made to be a witness by attending the Eichmann trial. That Spark is questioning the nexus of Catholic faith and identity is confirmed by having "the plot set in motion on Mount Tabor, the site of the New Testament's paradigmatic Transfiguration" (Glavin 2000, 296). As Glavin argues, the New Testament meaning of transfiguration forecloses transformation because it "is evanescent, momentary, elusive, and illusionary. It may mark a difference epistemologically, but it doesn't, can't, make a difference ontologically. Just the reverse: this sort of transfiguration is always about the poignant gulf between what we may from time to time chance to see and what we, all the rest of the time, do and are" (2000, 296). In a novel writ large with many forms of disguise, hidden in the margins of Barbara's transfigured identity and disguises is the historic fact that for Jews caught by Hitler's transformation of the Jewish self—conversion—didn't work, either as effective disguise or as salvation. If we take this context seriously, it then becomes impossible to apply whatever meanings Spark's conversion has for her to this novel. It may very well be, as Cheyette claims, that Spark's "narrative voice locates her 'Gentile Jewish' identity as a creatively disruptive force," but in this novel, a hybrid identity, like conversion, only "destabilizes" our thinking about postcolonial theories, not about "modern society," as Gauri Viswanathan claims (Cheyette 2002, 104; Viswanathan 1998, xvii).[37] In historical context, the already multiple identities of Barbara are further complicated by her visit to Israel, where her pilgrimage to the ancient source of Catholic faith is taking place at a pivotal moment and with testimony to the shattering of faith in modern history: the Eichmann trial.

As though testing the idea of a flexible identity or the postcolonial concept of hybridity against historical consequences, this is the moment when the Jews of Israel are demonstrating that the destructive history of which Eichmann was a perpetrator did not allow European Jews either the optimism hybridity connotes, a fluid identity, or indeterminacy. It refuted the idea that conversion is an act of will, a gift of grace, or both. It rejected the idea that conversion creates transcendence as a willed belief that can overcome history. Where God is immanent in Catholicism, God became a problem for Jews in the Holocaust. In the conflict between the power of the Nazis and God's power, the Eichmann trial asks, Who was the master of the Jews' fate? The actions of the Nazis override the claims of hybridity to erase indelible, absolute racial categories and to respect and tolerate fluid racial and ethnic boundaries. But now, sixteen years after the liberation of the death camps, the Israeli setting of the trial defies the value of such a modern sense of fluidity by demonstrating that no history or plot can decenter their ancient and essential identity. Inscribed in the legal arguments about Eichmann's guilt, the trial is announcing the moral and political necessity of recognizing the historically stateless and vulnerable Jews as a people whose identification with their ancestral homeland reaffirms the coherence and centeredness of their identity. The vulnerability of the Jews' status also challenges the idea of multiculturalism, which in its theory and practice lies outside the Holocaust and outside Jewish survival. While the dispersal of the Jews endowed them with the ability to live in exile almost anywhere, their distinct religious and historical identities always placed them beyond complete assimilation or acculturation in their local habitats. Even as they adapt to local customs in appearance and behavior, they both choose to stand apart and are labeled as alien. In short, they remain bounded by a paradoxical sense of difference that obtains across all cultures in which they live. What is unbounded in this novel is the historical memory of their belonging to themselves alone and their displacement from other worlds. It is this historical memory that has been etched into their identity.

That Barbara should attend the Eichmann trial only after it "had entered a boring phase" distances her from the "impassioned" testimony of the survivors, which is now concluded (Spark 1965, 210). But this next phase, in which Eichmann is testifying and she is a witness, offers her and us a new meaning of both "boring" and "identity." "Boring" now refers to the language of a bureaucratic death machine—language that underwrites, contains, and denies the terror that victimized so many and therefore hovers over the trial and the survivors, like a ghostly threat, as though it could still erase the reality of the survivors and their testimony. Because Barbara does not have the survivors' words as buffers between her and Eichmann's testimony, their absence highlights her presence as embodying the identity that victimized the Jews. Taken by surprise "by the certainty, immediately irresistible, that this dull phase was in reality the desperate heart of the trial," she realizes that boredom signifies the horror of the "massacre" (210). What is boring is the mechanistic ritual of Eichmann repeating his defensive litany—he was only "in a position . . . to obey orders" (211). It was this meaning of "boring" in Eichmann's performance that led Hannah Arendt to conclude that evil could be banal.[38] What is horrific is that this repetitious testimony echoes the relentless workings of the death camp machinery.

In its attempts to establish its veracity through repetition, Eichmann's testimony, portions of which are reprinted in the novel, uses a language of bureaucratic detachment. Deploying the passive voice forecloses individual and collective responsibility by ascribing functions to "the system" or by eliding the subject from sentences altogether: "Listed there. All the matters" (Spark 1965, 213). In this way, Eichmann's language disguises its material consequences by avoiding references to human subjects. In direct opposition to the chief prosecutor's brief, as though Eichmann is defending himself by rhetorically replicating "the system's" death machinery, his testimony allows no space in which the victims and survivors can appear, and therefore suffocates them once again. Of course, this language of entrapment resembles the concern of so many of Spark's fictions "with freedom," where characters are in danger of "being trapped within someone else's order," whether it is "the 'plot' of God's creation, ideology or fate" or "within language itself," the latter reflecting the postmodern sense of "an arbitrary system of signification which appears to offer no means of escape" (Waugh 1989, 121). The difference in *The Mandelbaum Gate* is that the history of the Holocaust cuts through any postmodern indeterminacy. The Nazi "order" of entrapment is no metafiction, and, for all its playfulness, this novel is deadly serious about the material consequences of a language grounded in a specific historical moment. The resonance of this moment and its consequences haunts Freddy's classically timeless, depersonalized, and otherwise silly thank-you poems, written as though language had only form and no consequential meaning. As though it must enact its own judgment, the novel's only representation of Eichmann is through the language of his testimony; in denying him a presence, it refuses to grant him any more agency.

While the transcribed samples of the trial are mechanistic and boring in their enumerated detail, they perform a drama that opposes Eichmann's banal defense. As Spark negotiates the "space of slippage between law and art," these bits and pieces of documentation are made to perform as a historical event, but not as though it is extant, reified, transparent, or as though it can stand by itself. Instead, this representation engages in an argument with Barbara's construction of personal identity. Positioning Barbara as a witness to the trial confronts her with ineluctable documentation that her identity, rather than being fluid or "displaced," has been historically mandated by the laws which Eichmann followed and which implicate her in his "pre-written destiny" and rage for order (Spark 1965, 212). Juxtaposed with the trial's silenced witnesses, Barbara's "deaf and dumb" masquerade and rescue mock the idea of identity as a choice (196). Like self-proclaimed Jewish identity, or the ambiguous identities of half or quarter or assimilated Jews who were silenced, erased, and exterminated, Barbara's Jewish identity would have enfolded her into the very system that Eichmann implemented so religiously. This system, which enacts the well-oiled mechanistic order of the Nazis, reflects back on Spark's own desire for "a sense of proportion," which she felt at the time of her conversion was concomitant with "a sense of order" (63). But as her literary experimentation shows, over time she became more committed to a self-reflexive questioning of the more inflected meanings of "order" through her changing formal structures. In *The Mandelbaum Gate,* because "order," as associated with Eichmann and the Nazi order, leads to "proportion" being replaced by a monstrous misproportion, her usual playfulness is abandoned for an intensely serious meditation.[39]

With its presence at the heart of the novel, the Eichmann trial connects Barbara's religious, cultural, and historic identity with another historical strand. The history that the trial represents, that of World War II, concerns not only the fate of Europe and its identity as comprising either independent nations or satellites of the Third Reich, but that of the embattled Middle East. Until the Germans were defeated at El Alamein, Britain's own identity as an empire, its access to vital resources, and its sense of responsibility to the trusteeship of the Middle East were threatened by the empire of the Third Reich. During the North African campaign, Jerusalem was the capital of the British Middle East, and its fate represented the future of the British Empire. Once the war was over, Britain had to face two intricately related realities: that its attempts to administer two competing populations had failed and that the Holocaust had created a new impetus for the creation of a Jewish state in Palestine. After the United Nations declared the State of Israel, the British were left in a newly vulnerable postcolonial position. They needed to sustain diplomatic relations with those Arab nations which now controlled its trade routes and oil and also with Israel, whose purpose it had both supported and subverted. In turn, as Palestine was transformed into two contesting nations and a destabilized population of Palestinian refugees, its own multiple identity became grounds for an ongoing state of crisis. As a British subject whose pilgrimage dramatizes her nation's impossible imperial dream of Arab-Jewish reconciliation, Barbara is implicated in the history of the end of Empire. As her pilgrimage threads its way around the ongoing political and religious conflicts of Israel, Jordan, and Palestine, their histories cast a shadow over any resolution the novel suggests about multiculturally happy families and endings. The denouement that suggests that Barbara will manage her mixed religious identity with the grace of her conversion is overwhelmed by confronting any reading of the novel with the unavoidable knowledge that this happy fate is only possible outside the historical tragedy of the Holocaust and the vicissitudes of the Middle East that shape her story.

At every turn of plot, what underlies Spark's concerns with narrative and religious identities are her unsettling insights about historical irresolution and her disorienting representation of sexual desire. Scattered throughout the novel, like the English spinsters' wildflower seeds, these insights and disturbances destabilize the novel's topography and the way the novel ties up its end with good cheer.[40] Freddy's amnesia and constricted self-expression do not indicate solace in innocuous and evenhanded diplomacy, but rather a return to repressed sexuality and deflected rage, the combination of which defines his mother's lethal relationship with her companion, Bennie. Like his classical poems, which deflect the political rage around him, his letters ignore the women's mutual hostility and deny their lesbian undercurrent, leaving the way open for Bennie's murder of Mrs. Hamilton and Freddy's abrogation of responsibility. The hostility in which these women's relationship is conceived extends, moreover, to the lesbian suggestiveness of the relationship between Barbara and Ricky, the headmistress of the school where Barbara taught. Ricky's bond with Barbara, like that of Mrs. Hamilton with Bennie, is also represented as threateningly obsessive. Marrying Ricky off to Joe Ramdez resettles, indeed, disposes of her as a disturbing character and lesbian desire as a disturbing force. Such a resolution, however, is equally disquieting, for it also effects a narrative amnesia about Freddy's homoerotic desires. Where, early in the novel, Freddy's desire for the Arab boy is presented as a pastoral colonial comedy, by the time Barbara and readers have been through the Eichmann trial and Mrs. Hamilton's murder, we, at least, should be asking critical questions about the relationship the novel has established between transgressive sexualities, cultural identities, and the role of historical violence in their fictionalized destinies. At the end, despite its gift-wrapped playfulness, the novelistic desire to experiment with homoerotic desire and fluid identities vies with its urge to expunge the former and to reassure itself of a cultural choice and fictional stability that the novel undercuts with its own historical incisiveness.

The rhetorical effect of such approach/avoidance is to create a contrast with the novel's treatment of Freddy's homoerotic desire as benign and with the evenhandedness of the British relationship to Arab-Israeli tensions. The novel's 1961 setting in Israel and Jordan, in which the ongoing history of the region is imprinted, gives the lie to claims for a happy ending. Even as Barbara Vaughan and so many other characters leave Israel and Jordan, marry, and settle down, what is left behind and haunts their stability is the staying power of the tense irresolution that their adopted, adapted, and fluid identities cannot escape. Cheyette has argued convincingly that Spark's own multifaceted identities have "enabled her to become an essentially diasporic writer with a fluid sense of self," encouraging a reading of her fictional identity crises and conversions as rejecting a single, unified view of "the world" (2000, 10, 11). I see Spark as ambivalent, if not critical of such fluidity. She is always questioning "the quest for order, as in her own conversion," because it resembles "a form of crazed unreality as it expunges an all too human 'confusion and ferment' from the world" (Cheyette 2000, 12). Even as Spark proffers her own evenhanded, indeed, "fluid" diplomacy in her representation of contesting subjects and desires, it is through the irresolution faced by her characters that we also find a deeply complex and nuanced analysis of the political world she creates in *The Mandelbaum Gate*. But however she conceives her own multiplicity, her novel attests to the historical conditions that create a "crazed" order of reality, not unreality.

Like Manning's *School for Love, Artist among the Missing,* and *The Levant Trilogy,* Spark's novel embeds a time which represents the political and cultural confusion that arises out of inhuman conditions and that creates not diaspora, but exile, and not exile as a chosen condition, as when Spark refers to herself as "an exile in heart and mind . . . moving from exile into exile" (Spark 1970, 151–152). The historical exile around which *The Mandelbaum Gate* agitates leads into incarceration and murder. The allusions to the Holocaust in these novels speak to the consequences that issue from a single, unified view of the world. In this case it is Nazi Germany, whose world view shackled Others to its crazed order of reality. The Jerusalem of these novels, though separated by the twenty years between a world war and threat of a regional one, is represented as a map of the clash between ongoing human and political confusion. With their final irresolution, these novels suggest that this clash continues, not just into those twenty years between the events they depict and embed and their narration, but beyond. More volatile than fluid, the changing nature of this clash shows the erratic multiplicity not of individual identities, but of cultural and historical forces that are connected to both the aftermath of the Holocaust and a long history of other conquests, occupations, contested sites, and resistance. Paramount in both Manning's and Spark's novels is a resistance to the homogenizing effect of the British Empire and its grand narratives. However powerfully that Empire may have exerted its dominant culture and politics, it was competing with other imperial and local determinants. As we see the Pringles, Felix, Jane Ellis, and Barbara Vaughan return to England, albeit in different times and under different conditions, they testify not just to the end of the British Empire, but to a history that must take its own course without the Empire's presence.

A History Stranger Than Fiction

History has seen great empires and whole civilizations pass away. In our time we've seen the passing of the British Empire. It used to be said that it was the empire on which the sun never set—though the Indian nationalists used to say that was because God couldn't trust the British in the dark! . . . And Hitler's Third Reich, which was to last a thousand years. So why shouldn't young people . . . live to see the passing of Israel—the liberation of Palestine? In the end injustice destroys itself—all evil does. History demonstrates the fact.

—Ethel Mannin, *The Road to Beersheba*

While Manning and Spark depict the British Empire as an incendiary presence, inflaming the desires and tensions that define the partition of Palestine, Ethel Mannin imagines a British persona that empathizes and identifies with a unified Palestinian cause. Mannin's own career as a writer of about 100 books is shaped by her social and political activism. From her early novels about women's and men's economic oppression, she explored the intersection and impact of political and social systems on people around the globe, from the United States to Burma, people who were caught by local and colonial power and who invariably demonstrate a heroic resistance both at the level of individual desire and collectively. This is not to say that she was never critical even of those systems where she found hope. In 1936, Mannin visited the Soviet Union, hoping to see the ideal socialist state in operation, but, as she recorded her response in her book *South to Samarkand* (1936), the socialism she saw was embroiled in an obfuscating bureaucracy.

Mannin's novel, *The Road to Beersheba,* published in 1963, takes us back in time to the Arab-Israeli war of 1948 and represents the experience of Palestinian refugees as "the story of the *other* exodus," from the town of Lydda and its surrounding villages to Ramallah, on the Arab side (note, italics in original). Basing her narrative on reports she received from refugees, Mannin creates a family headed by Christian Arab Butros Mansour and his English wife, Marian. Their son, Anton, becomes the focus of the novel's demonstration that the yearnings and frustration of the Palestinians cannot be satisfied, assuaged, or deterred either by a hybrid identity or by the best intentions of the British. After the death of his father, Anton returns to London with his mother, and, though nurtured by his English grandfather's sympathetic politics, the boy renounces a future designated by Britain's homogenizing values of pragmatic and gradual progress and becomes a resistance fighter. Crossing with his comrades over the Demarcation Line into Israel, he is killed by gunfire from an Israeli kibbutz.

Mannin introduces her novel with a foreword that provides a "necessary" historical context or "explanation" (1963, 11). For a comprehensive picture and for historical accuracy, she relies on well-known demographic statistics and public policies from both the British government and the United Nations as well as memoirs and public statements by such figures as U.S. president Harry Truman and Israeli foreign minister Golda Meier. Mannin's unabashed sympathy for "the Palestinian diaspora" provides a critically humanized shape to this historical tapestry at the same time that it raises significant questions about the use of history to construct fiction (1963, 13). The historical foreword prepares us, indeed, teaches us how to read the novel, but by the conclusion we learn the reverse. The fiction has taught us how to read Mannin's history. Mannin's guide is very different from that of Spark's chapter, "Barbara Vaughan's Identity." Spark's narrative guide lures the reader into accepting the dialogue, the Israeli guide's questions and Barbara Vaughan's tensely hybridized responses, as providing the key to the chapter title's conundrum. But as we've seen, this is not the whole story; the introduction of another essential historical perspective challenges the relationship between identifying and identity. Mannin's narrative guide insists straightforwardly that we identify with a people whose urgent historical perspective challenges how we read and understand claims to the historical identity of a people and a colonized land.

Mannin's novel is impelled by the rescue of a narrative that she feels has been silenced by global institutional power. Since the United Nation's

partition plan in 1947 which led to the creation of the Jewish state the following year, the voice of the Palestinians is heard only "as the forgotten people" whose "Arab nationalist aspirations" were relegated to displacement and
dispossession (Mannin 1963, 217, 13). A significant intervention in the literary
history of Middle Eastern late colonialism, *The Road to Beersheba* foregrounds
the Palestinian people as subjects who not only are victimized by modern history, but claim subjectivity through an ancient identity and modern political
activism. Unlike Manning's Arab servants or Spark's sexualized Arab boy, Mannin's Mansour family is rescued from subjugation by giving voice to the noble
wisdom of Butros, to the romantic and political growing pains of his son,
Anton, and to the passion of his friends' political resistance. Mannin also
humanizes her Palestinian subjects by representing Butros and Marian Mansour as equitable partners in marital love and companionship and in the
respect each gives to the other's difference. Situating their story in the literary
history of British domestic fiction, Mannin politicizes the Western conventions of family romance and subjects them to a multilevel critique. Where
British domestic fiction typically ends with marriage and the restoration of
traditional social and cultural codes, *The Road to Beersheba* begins with a marriage that, despite the tragic death of Butros, represents the more perfect union
of identifying with a collective Otherness. Tested by the loss of social and economic status and political stability, the complex and successful bicultural relationship of Marian and Butros highlights the one-dimensional insularity of
the romance bounded by the inviolate gates and greens of an English manor.
Just as history interferes with the workings of romance in Manning's novels
and the idea of fluid identity in Spark's, the very concept of domestic romance
is undermined by the events that blast the walls of home and individual
choice. Even as Mannin's novel mourns the loss of intimate love and political
self-determination, it confronts the necessity of political passion. It is this passion that gives agency to Mannin's colonized subjects and shapes her novel.

The Road to Beersheba keeps pace with the revision of domestic fiction
sparked by women writers during and after World War II.[41] In the postwar era,
a common fictional theme was concerned with women's domestic roles as the
nation rebuilt its sense of cohesion and security. In a critique of this national
rally, Mannin's novel shows how domestic and national stability are terms that
retain their coherence only when national identity is not under fire. Though
British women's postwar fiction, from the self-consciously intellectual to popular, represents women's unequal married lives with "ambiguity," it is often
critical of the middle-class status of most female protagonists (Baker 1989, 22).
A middle-class desire for economic and social security was imagined as providing only limited choices and alternative fates. Taking the Englishwoman
out of that setting and into colonized territory offered Mannin the imaginative opportunity to create a domestically and politically active married

woman. Unlike the stereotypical British colonial woman who romanticizes and recreates English parlor manners and morals in her colonial bungalow and ventures out only to the gated British club, Marian Mansour grafts an unexpected "moral and physical stamina" onto her role as "mistress" of an Arab household (Mannin 1963, 25, 22). Instead of "long[ing] for England's green and pleasant land," about which her husband teases her, Marian develops a "long[ing] for Lydda, and their estate, Darat el Kheir" (100). If the idea of England is derogated as a myth of cultivated and domesticated national origins and continuity, the idea of Palestine is valorized as a documented history that is robbed of its continuity by a historic epic of exile. Marian's identification with Palestine begins with her love for Butros's noble solidity, which resembles the "integrity" and "distinctive personality" of her father, Robert Melby (53). Like her growing devotion to the Palestinian cause, this love is "so intensely willed that" it becomes a driving political force (53).

And yet despite the assertion of her willed desires and the differences Mannin establishes between Marian's equitable position and the oppressive dependencies of the Arab women in her household, the Englishwoman is not made to be free. It is only after Butros's death and Marian's return to England, where she now has to find work and a new direction, that we are told that her identification with Palestine cannot be viewed independently of her relationship to "Butros in whose benign shadow she had lived" (Mannin 1963, 120). Mannin's construction of Marian resides in another shadow as well. "She was a small thin dark-haired woman with . . . surprisingly blue eyes, which Anton had inherited; she could have passed for an Arab, and frequently did; there was nothing distinctively English, or even European, about her" (26). This makeover of the English rose questions not only the Western racialized model of human evolution, but the inherent superiority of a European species. Marian's ability to pass suggests not so much a willed personal resistance to racial or cultural categories of identity as it does a genetic, embodied mockery of their political implications. Marian's ambiguous profile does not escape a racialized condition of the subjugated colonized, but rather the subjugating position of the colonizer. It is as though the depth and integrity of her emotional and political identification with the Palestinians have found their objective correlative in her hybrid physiognomy. No longer an outsider by dint of political or cultural hierarchies, the Englishwoman's identity has been biologically naturalized as not merely affiliated with but belonging to her adopted homeland.

The novel's racialization of Marian as a hybrid of East and West, dark and light, also gives her a fluidity that history denies Barbara Vaughan. Where modern racial theory and its translation into political practice reifies Barbara's Jewish identity and mocks her decision to convert, both sides of Marian's chosen dual identity are legitimized. While Arab identity has been politically and culturally racialized as part of an amalgam of Oriental inscrutability, exoticism, and danger—"dark shifty greasy . . . traders"—Mannin rescues Arab culture and validates Marian's Arab identity by showing the coherent and rational order of Arab family, economic, and community arrangements (Mannin 1963, 190). On the other hand, the novel's English sections show the safety awarded to English identity by its unflappable cultural caché and political self-confidence. And even as the novel depicts Britain's evaporating role in Middle Eastern politics, Mannin's construction of English characters sympathetic to the Palestinian cause restores the political integrity of British right-mindedness. In another graft, the resemblances between the integrity of Butros Mansour and Robert Melby demolish the cultural hegemony of West over East. Finally, it is Mannin's own sympathy for the Palestinian cause that creates a safety net for Marian's political self-determination. As the Palestinians suffer and endure their exile, the legitimacy of their cause is confirmed by the commitment to it of Marian and her father.

That Mannin should choose to validate Marian's political commitment through physical embodiment also raises critical questions about her fictional and historical method. Can the Englishwoman only be made an authentic member of her Palestinian community and family if her face can pass as an Arab's? And conversely, do her blue eyes provide her with another kind of safety net, one that leaves her fellow Palestinians behind in exile while she can escape back to her English identity, comfort, and stability? Unlike Spark, who creates the blue-eyed Arab Suzy in order to mock racialism, Mannin addresses these questions by positioning Marian and her father as representing another hybrid form—that of British colonial politics. Mannin's foreword foregrounds British colonial politics as a betrayal of Arab nationalism. As their reward for "fighting with the Allies in World War I against the Turks," the Arabs were awarded British and French Mandates instead of the independence they envisaged (Mannin 1963, 11). Her sarcasm expresses her sense of British betrayal in reneging on their agreements to support Arab nationalism even during the war. This injustice was compounded, according to Mannin, when "by the outbreak of World War II the Jewish population had increased from 50,000 to 600,000 and the operation of the Mandate gave the Jews an increasing economic hold on the country. Zionist industries were government-protected, Arab villages were demolished to make place for Zionist settlements, and the Jews had their own hospitals, schools, political institutions, and preferential treatment from their British sponsors" (12).[42]

Situated as opposed to this betrayal is the brand of British politics that, ironically, could rescue its imperialism from infamy. Working against both political pragmatism and ideologies that justified imperial supremacism, the novel's sympathies for Palestinian self-determination are based on combining faith in historical inevitability with the rationalism of freethinking doubt.

Anton's tutor, Gerald Johns, teaches him, "In the end injustice destroys itself—all evil does. History demonstrates the fact" (Mannin 1963, 128). Johns invokes "history" as progressive, with "the passing of the British Empire" following on the heels of the end of "Hitler's Third Reich," to be followed by "the passing of Israel," culminating in "the liberation of Palestine" (127–128). Creating a chorus of anticolonial critique, Johns's voice is joined with a narrative critique that also positions the Palestinian story in history as opposed to the religious myths that supported oppression.

The symmetry here achieves an irony beyond its inherent structure. On the one hand, imperialism is made more oppressive in the collectively even-handed voice and target of this condemnation than it might seem if different empires were examined separately. Mannin's references to World War II do not include particularities of the Third Reich. The combined effect deletes the distinctively British intellectual and political traditions that lead Robert Melby and his daughter to sympathize with Palestinian nationalism. For even as the novel's historical and imaginative narratives impugn the exploitative good intentions of British imperialism and Christian sentimentality, it is the combination of British organization and Christian charity that allows Melby to help run a school for blind Arab boys. Mannin would like to create a separate category for Melby's vocational devotion, but it remains tied to the very institutions she repudiates. Unlike the embedded politics of Manning and Spark, which identify an interrelationship between the self-interests of the colonizer and the different communities of the colonized, Mannin's narrative valorizes Arab political ethics, shifting its earlier emphasis on interdependence with the best of the British.

Mannin's history of Palestine is unlike those constructed through the narratives of Spark and Manning. Instead of finding legitimacy in the claims to Palestine of both Jews and Arabs, Mannin's history is created out of an opposition which pits a legitimate Palestinian identity struggling to retain its homeland and build "an independent democratic Arab state" against Zionist "pressure and tactics" and "Israeli terrorism" (Mannin 1963, 12, 13).[43] This opposition finds its ontological confirmation in Mannin's declaration that Palestine is the rightful ancient homeland of the Arabs, whose presence she traces to "the ancient Philistia of the Philistines, a predominantly Arab country" (11). In this interpretation, Palestinian history is naturalized, so that the people are one with the land, not in a racist replay of the black primitive, but as the regeneration of a high-achieving ancient civilization. In contrast, the Jewish presence in Palestine is a modern contrivance and the result not of ancient history, identification, or identity, but of modern Zionist ideology and invention. While Spark and Manning show the interrelationship between contested claims to Palestine's ancient and sacred sites, Mannin's history and fiction recognize no contest, especially as her combination erases Jewish

identification with ancient Israel. Interestingly, her erasure of Jewish identification with ancient Israel takes the form of appropriating the terms of Jewish
historical consciousness to protest the plight of "the Palestinian Refugees."
Her dedication shows that the novel is her response to their request, "Why
don't you write *our* story—the story of the *other* exodus—*our* exodus?" (italics
in original). If Jewish identification with ancient Israel is based in part on the
biblical epic of their exodus from enslavement in Egypt to self-determination
and nationhood, Mannin's foreword establishes the Palestinian exodus as the
authentic story, in opposition. The Palestinian exodus is from self-determination to oppression, and Mannin's writing of their history removes the kind of
doubt that accrues with viewing the narratives of biblical stories as constructed myths.

For Mannin, it is not only the ancient history of Palestine that belongs
solely to the Arabs, but its modern history as well. Unlike Spark and Manning,
who examine the history of tensions in Mandatory Palestine as related to the
crisis of Jewish statelessness during and after the Holocaust, Mannin interprets
the implications of "the Nazi persecution of the Jews in Germany" not as
leading to the murder of 6 million, but to being "a powerful ally of Zionism"
(Mannin 1963, 12). This conjuncture marks an elision of documented history
that stands in stark contrast to the sympathetic confirmation offered not only
by Manning and Spark, but by Phyllis Bottome. If we compare the publication
of Mannin's novel in 1963, two years after the Eichmann trial, to Spark's 1965
confrontation with the trial's reverberations, the effect is even more startling.
The rhetorical effect of Mannin's argument shows that the Jews exploited
their own suffering, not even as justification, but as propaganda for the ideology that would provide a state of their own. Fulfilling this antihistorical interpretation, the novel's Jewish dramatis personae are presented as having no
historic consciousness of collective suffering, either of their own or of those
who are displaced or who die as a result of the formation of the State of Israel.

Mannin's language demonstrates this moral failure in propelling her story
of the Palestinian's "exodus" with an Israeli violence that is sealed by her
indictment that the Israelis would "shoot down thousands of unarmed people" who, in a gesture of Gandhiesque nonviolence, might empty out of the
refugee camps (Mannin 1963, 19, 244). At the beginning of the novel, as the
Mansour family is preparing to leave their home, a married daughter is raped
by a laughing Israeli soldier who, when graciously offered a glass of water, des-
ecrates his own tradition by dashing it. Building the momentum of Israeli savagery, this scene is followed by one in which a young Israeli woman soldier
with "a strong Germanic accent . . . butt[s] [Butros] in the back with a sten-
gun" and spits on him, an act which, when combined with the German
accent, resounds with Nazi associations (22, 23).[44] Marian later interprets this
event as a cause of her husband's death.

That this depiction has purposes beyond historicizing the Palestinian cause is made evident in the portrait of an English Jewish young woman with whom Anton briefly becomes involved while in London. In contrast to the novel's Palestinians, who in exile and suffering maintain their cultural pride and authenticity, Rosa's family are secure "Londoners," and she conceals her identity from Anton by disguising herself as Spanish, Rosa Rosado (Mannin 1963, 163). What is not disguised is Mannin's contempt for Rosa, who, though "common," is at least honest enough to recognize that Anton is "the inter-lekchal type" while carrying out her assigned role as the sexually voracious Jewish woman—"I intend to have a good time with [Anton], and no one's going to stop me!" (171, 160, 165). All too "common" indeed, such stereotyping raises difficult questions about Mannin's project to restore legitimacy to the Palestinian cause. If Mannin's purpose is to rescue the Arabs from their Orientalizing stereotypes, she has succeeded by giving them a complex face and voice and by showing the immersion and integration of a empathetic Englishness into Arab social and political culture. And while the domestic counterpart to this political empathy may cast a romantically uncritical glow over its development, it also raises significant questions both for Mannin's politics and for postcolonial theory. In the first place, her vision of a romantically domestic bonding of Arabs and Britons does not accord with the evolution of her politics from socialist forms of collaboration to her more anarchic contempt for national levels of organization, whether they involved colonial or independent peoples.

It is true, however, that the domestic and political relationships established by Marion and Butros undermine the colonizing politics that rely on racial hierarchies and an irrevocable supremacist separateness. But what happens when this critique supports another kind of supremacism? What happens to this cultural harmony when it not only excludes the Jew but, as with the Israeli woman soldier and her "Germanic accent" and with Rosa, reconstitutes the Jew as a monstrous Other? For in stark opposition to the noble British Melbys, Rosa Rosenberg is the novel's only bad Briton. If the Melbys signify an ideally humane and selfless British colonialism, Jewish Rosa embodies the self-serving betrayal that in her critical foreword Mannin attributes to the realpolitik of British policy for Palestine.

The opposition suggested by this construction has significant implications for Mannin's historical fiction. However one might interpret the history of Palestine's partition and the fate of its peoples, does the legitimization of the Palestinian cause require demonizing and therefore delegitimizing that of the Jews? In Mannin's depiction of nameless, faceless, and—except for the noise and violence committed by their weapons and bodies—voiceless Israelis, this would seem to be the case. And when Zionism isn't represented either as callow propaganda or as a siege on innocent victims, its proponents falsify their

own political vision and identity, as we see with Rosa's Zionist friend Alice
Meyer, who only "fancied herself cultural" (Mannin 1963, 163). By contrast,
the authentic identity and nationalistic strivings painted for Jews in this novel
must be contained in Diaspora, as in the case of Rosa's parents, who "had no
use for the great ingathering; you belonged where you were born and bred;
nationality was one thing, religion another. So far as they were concerned they
were Londoners, of the Jewish faith" (Mannin 1963, 163). This belonging,
however, excludes any meaningful relationship between the Arab boy and
Jewish woman. If he is sent to enact a resistance against the Israeli oppressor
responsible for his exiled condition, she is meant to enact another necessity.
Constituted as culturally inauthentic as well as a temptress, Rosa is made to
deserve her fate as happy in her exile. For her and for her compatriots in Israel,
the "Zionist dream" can't even achieve the status of a mythic longing (163).
With no historical context of its own, Zionism is a corruption of authentic cultural tradition. There is no place in Mannin's rendering of Palestine's history for
the historical context of an ancient Israel, the documentation for which Muriel
Spark depicts in the work of the archaeologist character, Saul Ephraim, on the
Dead Sea Scrolls. With the erasure of their historical identification with ancient
Israel, modern Israelis are given only a denaturalized response to the topography they are accused of having usurped. Unlike the Arabs, with their reverence
for the ancient towns and villages of Palestine, Israelis are seen as having "mod-
ernized the little market town of Beersheba out of all recognition" (255). Having misappropriated the garden, the Jews of this novel must not only remain in
exile, but sacrifice their foundational narratives.

Not coincidentally for an anticolonial novel, Conrad's *Heart of Darkness* is
invoked to conjure up "phrases spoken in nightmares'" (Mannin 1963, 192).
While this suggests the nightmarish exile of the Palestinian people after partition, Mannin has inadvertently alerted us to another meaning. Just as scholars
still debate the ambiguity of Conrad's critique of colonialism, whether he is
indicting the barbarity of European politics or victimizing the natives once
again by reinscribing their savagery, Mannin's novel is poised on a critical
brink. By granting the Palestinians no responsibility for the war of 1948, the
only subjectivity and agency they are granted is that of victim. By showing the
Israelis' role in the war to be solely one of colonial conquest and oppression
and their nature as essentially savage, the only subjectivity and agency they are
granted is that of villain. In the construction of this historical fiction, she may
have exposed her own heart of darkness.

Mannin's novel, like *The Mandelbaum Gate* and Manning's Middle East
novels, challenges the boundaries of Empire as it emanates out of complicated
political historical contexts and representation of the peoples of the Middle
East. But, by contrast, Spark and Manning create political comedies to dramatize the tensions that arise from identities which precede and follow colonial

domination and with which they challenge their readers. Mannin's novel creates its own foundational and polemical myth to legitimize Arab nationalist claims to Palestine and delegitimize those of the Jews. Instead of challenging her audience, she relies on another stereotype: the romantic appeal of the desert Arab. An iconic figure since the days of Lawrence of Arabia, this image presents its own ironies. Like the blue-eyed Marian, T. E. Lawrence was, after all, an Englishman mimicking an Arab. And if this mimicry distances us from Arab subjectivity, it also calls attention to how Mannin represents Arab identity and subjectivity, for the noble Butros Mansour, who is made to represent the Arab cause, is a Christian. There are no Muslims to be found in the novel.

Mannin's romantically racialized depiction of the Palestinian people coincides with her depiction of the end of the British Mandate, where remorseful Britons sympathize with the Palestinian cause. In stark contrast, Manning and Spark implicate even the best intentions of the British as exacerbating the tensions of Palestine and Israel. Situating these writers in an all too relentless debate exposes the problematic status of the language of colonialism and its postcolonial critique as it continues today. If the policies and practices of the British Empire in the Middle East have been canonized as easy targets for vilification, the relentlessly contesting voices of Manning's and Spark's Middle East can be seen as transgressive. Unlike Mannin, with her efforts to create a gothic tale of villainy and innocence, Manning and Spark represent their contesting characters as confronting their responsibility for their resistance and liberatory narratives. As Manning and Spark remind us, however, writers must address questions about their responsibility to the subjects they create as objects of their historical and critical imaginations, but so must we as readers.

CHAPTER 2

Strangers in a Walled Garden

RUMER GODDEN'S ANGLO-INDIA

I want to stay here the rest of my life. Live here, flying to England only now and then. I want to see these springs as long as I live and have the harsh discipline of the winters to keep me hard and alive.

—Rumer Godden, *A Time to Dance, No Time to Weep*

Our house was English streaked with Indian, or Indian streaked with English. It might have been an uneasy hybrid but we were completely and happily at home.

—Jon Godden and Rumer Godden, *Two under the Indian Sun*

THE NOSTALGIC YEARNING which impels these statements could easily mark Rumer Godden (1907–2000) as an all too willing victim of her memsahib memories, expressing her imperial whiteness through novelistic visions of an idyllic colonial childhood. Her position at the end of Empire, looking backwards at an Anglo-Indian childhood from her inevitable expulsion, constructs a different narrative, however.[1] In Rumer Godden's fictions of India, which depict the decade just before independence and immediately after, the word "streaked" is neither neutral nor aesthetic. Instead, it suggests the violence that tarnished any dream that the British could be "happily at home" in India. In her representations of India, there is no reconciliation between "happily at home" and "an uneasy hybrid." Not only does that "uneasy hybrid" invade her fictional colonial homes, but it dissembles the foundational idea of a politically or culturally viable British India. Whether India is invaded by well-meaning nuns or diplomats, whether it inspires British women to seek adventures of self-determination or their children to recognize cultural oppression through their own constraints, it is the stuff of romance fiction. To be "completely and happily at home" in Anglo-India is an act of political denial that Godden's Indian novels expose. If Godden's 1966 references anticipate Homi Bhabha's happy hybridity, they also challenge the term through the unsettling positions of Rumer's female protagonists, who more often than not find Anglo-India an oppressively walled garden.

Rumer Godden's early life was shaped by the nurturing promises of an Anglo-Indian walled garden. She was born in Sussex, England, but from the age of six months until 1945, when she moved to England with her two daughters, India was her home and Anglo-Indian the identity bestowed by the Empire. Her novels of India dramatize the fictionality of this identity as well as the felt truths of living in a place mapped by Empire as Anglo-India. Despite her provocative position as a critical insider, unlike those critical tourists, E. M. Forster and Paul Scott, no place has been found for her in the postcolonial canon. Writing both during the colonial era and after, as an insider to the settler's experience and an outsider to indigenous India, Godden offers us the quandary of what it meant to discover that her own genealogy and experience as Anglo-Indian were the objects of critical attention, that her identity would be judged as resting on false and oppressive claims. Such criticism also assesses her wide readership and popularity as signs of her work colluding with Raj nostalgia. Though, like many critics, she would question the authenticity and integrity of the white British writer's relationship to her colonized subject, she has not been invited into their conversation. Unlike Kipling, whose ambivalent relationship to his Indian subjects excites the interest of critics, Godden has been unduly neglected.

Godden's story begins with that of her father, Arthur Leigh Godden, who brought his family to India. A shipping agent, Godden was one of many Englishmen whose career ambitions were welcomed by British India's bustling commercial networks. While sharing in the wealth of privilege and comfort offered by a confident colonial elite, Arthur Godden and many like him were not adorned with aristocratic pedigree or pretensions. Unlike the minor British gentry who reconstituted their exclusive worlds of country estates in an illusory African wilderness, the businessmen and professionals who came to India built their share of the Empire by developing a mercantile economy.[2] The adventure of running a British business in India was supported by a well-ordered home life, managed in tiers of authority by an English wife and her regiment of Indian servants and tradespeople. As Godden writes in her novel, *The River,* "young men . . . came out raw and young to learn the trade and ended up as magnates. Later on, they married, and too often, Father said, their wives ended up as magnums" (1946a, 19–20). Unlike Elspeth Huxley's mother, Nellie Grant, Katherine Godden sought neither adventurous dislocation nor a new beginning, but adapted to an intensely domestic life, presiding over four daughters and Narayanganj, a large "monstrous house" on the river Lakya in East Bengal (Godden and Godden 1966, 21).[3]

Though their plush lifestyle, supported by cooks, nanny, gardeners, housemaids, and seamstresses, was actually far more luxurious than that of

1. The Godden House at Narayanganj. Courtesy Camilla Hornby.

Kenyan aristocrats, and seemed no different from most of their own expatri-
ate community, it also reflected many ironies of colonial relations that Rumer
and her sister, Jon Godden, never lose sight of in their writing. The Goddens
may be associated with the ruling class, like Huxley and her family, but their
economic and social lives reflect a far more fluid middle-class experience
than aristocratic allegiance would allow. Narayanganj turns out to be a
"facade"; instead of representing an imperial takeover of India, it was rented
by Arthur Godden's company from their "imposing Muslim butler," Azad Ali
(Godden and Godden 1966, 29; Chisholm 1998, 10). Moreover, as Rumer
Godden's biographer observes, because they lived far away from the city-
centered "ritual snobbery and competitiveness of Anglo-Indian life," the
Goddens could relish the pleasures of having made "their own small world"
(Chisholm 1998, 6).

Unlike the timeless Orient of which so many white colonial writers are
accused of evoking, "the timelessness of India" for the Goddens is always subject to disruption and even resistance on both sides of the walled garden.[4]
Together and individually, Rumer and Jon Godden point to the disparities of
thinking in time that warns of the inability of "We Westerners" and "Orientals
to feel they occupy the same place at the same time. As the pandit storyteller
in their coauthored *Shiva's Pigeons* reminds us, "life evolves in cycles, a process
of gradual change, unceasing transformations, while behind them is the force

that never changes, 'prakriti'—nature—the implacable 'law,' a recurring continuity. India is changing, not for the sake of change but because she must—
there is no place for stagnation in continuity—but underlying the surge of
human movement is the changeless rhythm in which it is held" (Godden and
Godden 1972, 9). Unlike Forster and Kipling, whose India, according to
Michael Gorra, is "eternal" and outside "the sense of historical development
and change," Rumer and Jon Godden plot "the Raj's illusion of permanence"
that intensified Indian desire for self-determination and "made it impossible to
perceive" (Gorra 1997, 29). Rumer Godden's fictions of India represent a conflict, changing constantly in itself, between India's sense of its own ecological
balance and its adversary, the wrenching "transformations" wrought by the
British colonial presence in its final phase.

Rumer and Jon Godden were themselves subject to the abrupt changes
integral to the colonial mission. At only five and six years old, but typical of
Anglo-India, Rumer and Jon were sent back to England to preserve those
most outward expressions of their English essence—their accents and manners. In 1914, after a year in the compulsively ordered home of their "ascetic"
aunts, Rumer and Jon atypically returned to India, where the Goddens' social
order was so lax that they were contaminated with their Eurasian governess
Nana's "chi-chi" accent (Godden and Godden 1966, 5, 69). Because their
walled estate was insulated, not only from the hyper-Anglo manners of British
India, but from the repressions of England itself, it also encouraged their imaginative gifts. Their lives and identities were therefore shaped differently than
those British children, called "outposts of Empire," who were shielded and
entrenched so that they could "shoulder their share of the burden of Raj"
(Macmillan 1988, 125). As they grew into adolescence, the Godden children
could very well have been isolated from Indian life, especially on a river estate,
but their lives were more deeply and yet more ambivalently entwined with
India. The throbbing life of the bazaar, which abutted their house, became an
enticing and familiar playground. But Narayanganj was also set off from the
Indian community, not only by its gates, but by the parapet from which the
Godden children flew their Indian kites and from which they could entangle
and cut loose the kites of village children. Tied to "those invisible children . . .
in the kinship of enmity, . . . the kites could have been taken as a symbol of our
lives" (Godden and Godden 1966, 47).

This sharply ambivalent divide, however, did not create an anxious sense
of an unknowable India or even a sinister Otherness. The monkey man, for
example, who figures so threateningly in Rumer Godden's Indian novels, is,
in the sisters' memoir, only a harmless clown directing his monkey's sexual
hijinks. Symbolized by their garden, which was more like a carnival than a
retreat, the lives of Rumer and Jon and their younger sisters, Nancy and
Rose, were both segregated from and exposed to the local popular culture.

They were not, moreover, oblivious to either "the poverty and suffering" of their Indian neighbors or to the problematic status of their governess (Godden and Godden 1966, viii). Her "heartless isolation in the nursery" was only compounded by her Eurasian identity, which, as Rumer Godden was to explore in both her 1937 novel, *The Lady and the Unicorn,* and the 1975 *The Peacock Spring,* made her "one of those luckless hybrids despised then even more by Indians than Europeans" (Godden and Godden 1966, 34, 32). But as the family traveled throughout India and cultural and political awareness caught up with the protected clarity of their childhood, Rumer and Jon Godden also realized that India's social and economic order was far more complex than any picture of a deep chasm between rich and poor could depict. In addition to their own complicated relations with Indian servants of many castes and classes, they discover those "millions of people in the middle way" often ignored by "dismayed authors" who see "little beyond the big, often squalid cities," the distasteful if unavoidable itinerary of Western tourists (Godden and Godden 1966, viii). Despite the multivalent social picture the Goddens draw, they can be criticized for emphasizing "the picturesque and the melodramatic" in their writing, and thus segregating their story of India from the imperial history that offers "a more meaningful context for understanding . . . the relations of political and economic power," according to David Spurr (1993, 48). But instead of a mythic vision of an unchanging, homogenized immersion in an invented, expropriated cultural landscape, Rumer Godden uses the river on which her family lived to express a time-bound, historically situated Anglo-India. In their teeming commercial, human, and animal traffic, the "big rivers . . . gave a sense of proportion" to the feeling of belonging it nurtured in the Godden children (Godden and Godden 1966, 26).

In all of Godden's Indian fictions, any sense of India's timelessness is overwhelmed by her affinity with "the Indian concept of truth [which] is that it changes and flows so fast that you can only hope to catch a few drops in your hands" (Godden 1986, 20).[5] Even her most elegiac novel, *The River* (1946a), advertised by the dust-cover blurb as a story of "the human heart," decenters its timeless, universalized themes with the violent costs of colonial blindness as exposed by the cataclysms of World War II. As Michael Gorra reminds us about Paul Scott's characters, Godden's characters "know that they are living within history," and this is a historical crisis in which the British will confront not only the end of Empire, but the translation of their cultural and political superiority into the language of waste and irrelevance (1997, 29). In many of Godden's novels of this period, it is the crisis of World War II that disrupts the timeless meanings attributed to "death, birth, cruelty, kindness, retribution, and the shadow of love" (Godden 1946a, jacket).

MISSION IMPOSSIBLE: *BLACK NARCISSUS*

Is it just the thin mountain air . . . or has the exotic world awakened passions in the sisters they can no longer deny?

—MGM Home Entertainment, video cover blurb

Godden's 1939 novel, *Black Narcissus,* and its 1947 film version bracket the world war that led to the end of Anglo-India and disrupted its meanings. The dates form a significant frame of reference for their subject. Godden finished the novel in August 1938, only a year before the British nation was forced to enter World War II, and she realized that, like so many, she "would have to break . . . the Peace Pledge" she had signed (Godden 1987, 130). The novel offers both a reprieve from the terrors to come and a confrontation with the war's necessary consequences. The movie version, produced in 1946 and released in May 1947, could afford to ignore the war, especially now that it was over. But at the very moment India is becoming independent, partitioned, and engaged in its own civil war, its colonial subject must confront itself more directly. The story is built entirely around the tense anticipation that the school and clinic founded by a group of five nuns in an abandoned harem in northern India are doomed to fail. While the novel is quite stunning, its evo-cation of a doomed colonial enterprise is dramatically glossed and interro-gated in the film version. The differences between the two versions highlight the ideological frameworks that had both justified the British colonial pres-ence in India and made its withdrawal a foregone conclusion. The film also illuminates issues about the late colonial representation of colonial and indige-nous characters and their relations. Set on a remote cliff somewhere north of Darjeeling, overlooking the Himalayas, featuring a group of Anglican nuns, the story offers a drama of good works thwarted by mysterious atmospheric forces and intense psychological need. The interplay of personal and unearthly dynamics is a far cry from the geopolitical conflicts raging thousands of feet below and halfway around the globe.

The novel, which was a best seller, was inspired by Godden's visit years earlier, when she was eighteen, to an isolated mountain village near Chera-punji, where she discovered a cross-shaped headstone marked with "Sister" and dates indicating she "was only twenty-three" when she died (Godden 1987, 129). Later, "as the evil of Nazidom spread over the world," and Godden despaired over her children's fate and that of the world's Jews, she felt that she was rescued by writing *Black Narcissus* (Godden 1987, 130). The emotional truth Godden invested in the novel was dashed for her by Michael Powell, who directed the film version and told her that he "saw the book as a fairy tale" (Godden 1989a, 51). While the screenplay, written by Emeric Press-burger, adopts so many of the novel's elements to almost exacting detail,

2. Deborah Kerr as Sister Clodagh, Jean Simmons as Kanchi, and David Farrar as Mr. Dean in *Black Narcissus*. Courtesy Carlton International Media Ltd.

including dialogue, facial expressions, and plot movements, Godden saw it as "counterfeit" (Godden 1989a, 52). She derided the casting of Sabu, "a thick-set, snub-nosed South Indian coolie boy as a young Rajput prince," as "deliberately blind," while fully appreciating the talents of the major actors, including Deborah Kerr, David Ferrar, and Flora Robson (Godden 1989a, 52, 105). Interestingly, though she found the English-speaking and singing Indian peasants a travesty of her standards of authenticity, she had no complaints about Jean Simmons, the English actress, playing a Nepalese peasant girl. Her most lacerating criticism targeted the sets and costumes: "the snows were white muslin blown up on bamboo poles; the remote Himalayan valley was a garden in Surrey; the palace looked a ramshackle imitation of the Pavilion in Brighton" (Godden 1989a, 52).[6] Although the movie became "a classic," appearing regularly on TV and in film retrospectives, it almost kept her from ever allowing another of her novels to be adapted to film (Godden 1989a, 53). Changing her mind, she did go on to enjoy such successful film adaptations and TV miniseries as *Greengage Summer, The River,* and *Peacock Spring,* but she remained wary of the translation, not only because of visual authenticity as an isolated issue, but because the visual was key to expressing her attitudes to her subject accurately.

Connections between this artistic concern and its political context are invoked in her short story, "Children of Aloysius," which dramatizes her persistent theme of an inauthentic and damaging neocolonial presence. Its plot mocks the desire of a film director to find an authentic "elderly Eurasian woman" to portray a nursemaid in an Anglo-Indian family (Godden 1989a, 61). Echoing an attitude that Godden would critique relentlessly throughout her career, the story's filmmaker declares, "I want the truth and simplicity of these people" (62). The truth developed by the story is that despite the promise of "five thousand rupees," a car to transport her to and from work, and a boxed lunch, the very authentic, very poor old Eurasian woman they find refuses to abandon her own creative responsibility (67). Mocking the film director's artistic and political integrity, the Eurasian actress refuses to hold anyone hostage to her exacting standards. She insists, instead, on being far more comprehensively involved in her own cross-cultural project—supervising the handmade lace handkerchiefs her "Ladies" buy for charity (69). Perhaps because Godden was also recalling her very rewarding experience working with Jean Renoir on the film version of *The River,* she also rescues her fictional filmmaker. At the end of the story, he acknowledges that the constructed reality of his "celluloid world" can "spoil" everything it touches (70). Perhaps, too, Godden was thinking about her own attitude toward artistic representation "as an interpreter between the Western and Indian worlds" (Godden 1989a, 105). Feeling so strongly that "in cinema the authenticity is truth," she would have to confront the meaning of this claim for the fictional representations on which the film versions were based (Godden 1989a, 105).

In the film version of *Black Narcissus,* the painted sets, fancy costumes, and heightened melodrama that Godden felt travestied her novel can also be seen working as an epilogue or political gloss on the novel, which was conceived in a time of different historical and political significance. With its shadowy corridors and hotly colored murals, the film's rendition of Mopu, the abandoned harem, reeks with the murky sexual atmospherics that were so conventional and taken for granted by a 1947 Western audience, but which today seem to fit so easily into the Orientalist catalogue. With what today we might consider an equal lack of subtlety, the machine-driven howling winds and fluorescent bursts of spring that characterize the cliff convey a pungent and incisive anticolonial message. Intemperate at all times, the mountain weather both reflects the colonial ruler's anxiety and expresses the danger brought by the English mission. The heightened sounds and colors of the film's mountain clime convey not only the external threats to the nuns' mission but their fragile belief in it and themselves. Working analogically as well as etiologically, the weather and the local political climate soon have the nuns veering between spiritual and sensual ecstasy and depression. As their defenses succumb to the irrepressible temptations of being surrounded, indeed, engulfed by the harem's profane sublime, the nuns' story becomes a self-fulfilling prophesy. Just as the previous mission of monastic brothers was dislodged suddenly and mysteriously, so the nuns find they must retreat from their debased Shangri-La to the more moderate climes below.

This psychodrama, with its conflict between the hypertension inspired by an atavistic exoticism and the repressive defenses of English civilization, is interwoven with a late colonial narrative.[7] Desirous of bringing Western education and medicine to the hill people, the nuns are caught off guard by the customs their students bring to school, including a sensuality that defies the discipline their own tightly wrapped bodies represent. That their presence is anachronistic even before they settle in is verified by the equally disturbing figure of Mr. Dean, an Englishman who serves as the overseer of the general (as a Maharajah prince is called in Nepal), who in turn owns the palace. An agent not of the British, but of the Indian ruler, Mr. Dean is situated astride a political and cultural divide.[8] His advice may be pragmatically English, but his sandals, shorts, and floppy hat signify a languid style and hint of yielding to the seductions of the native. Though it might appear that this cultural crevice is bridged by the general's Western tastes, it is also undermined by the resistance of the valley natives and the narrative presentiment of the Empire's ending. Dean's voice, which varies from gentle to caustic mockery of the nuns' projects, expresses the contradictory historical mission that ultimately deconstructed the logic of British India. At one moment supportive of native customs and traditions, at another he calls them "primitive," and while he is reputed to consort with local women, he anticipates danger not only in local resistance, but in Britain's place between two worlds; the Empire has trapped itself by colonizing the "back of beyond."

The expressionistic design of the film merges the individual and imperial psychologies that constitute the disintegration of the nuns' House of St. Faith at Mopu. As David Boxwell observes so acutely, the film is both deeply affecting and analytical because of its "optical effects" which represent "an India losing its reality to its possessors, who are in the process of reconstructing a dreamscape to replace that reality" (1999, 5, 9). Through close examination of the cinematography, including "glass shots, superimposition of one image over another, and matte work" which imposes human actors on "striking Olympian aerial views of India," Boxwell shows how the film renders "what was real and historical now unreal and mythical" so that Britons could begin to accept Indian independence (1999, 5, 6, 9).[9] Boxwell ultimately finds the film conservative and pessimistic as it leaves the Indians in the hands of a native ruler who, despite his humanitarian support of local health and education, does nothing to relieve the poverty and prejudices of a caste-bound society.

As we will see, however, in Godden's later writing, she will not endorse a one-sided critique of oppressive power; as in Elspeth Huxley's novel, *The*

Walled City, she locates political and economic oppression in the mutually supportive system established by both local native rulers and British imperialism. With independence on the horizon at the end of both novel and film, like the nuns who are leaving, the general, too, will be forced to retreat from his power base. A parting shot shows us the failed collaborative performance of an anomalous missionary presence and an anachronistic local throne of power. As rain clouds are superimposed over a painted one-dimensional image of the Mopu palace, it suggests a final curtain falling on a canceled performance. As the camera pans from Sister Clodagh's saddened view of the palace to the wistful look on Mr. Dean's face, we are certainly being invited to recognize a lost romantic opportunity, but this also connects with Godden's political theme. Dean is being left behind with a denuded colonial romance. He faces the prospect of being agent to no power, of losing his mediating agency once both the British and the Maharajah are out of the picture. As his drinking increases over the course of the story, so we see his agency and that of the Empire's indirect rule dissipate.

Just as Dean's increasingly irrelevant position suppresses any romantic narrative of British hegemony in India, so Sister Clodagh's impossible mission expresses denial of connections between her repressed memory of a failed Irish love affair and the romance of the harem. Though she fails to recognize the dangers that were faced by the absent women of Mopu, every flashback to Sister Clodagh's failed romance comments on them. Her romantic drifting becomes our critical attention. Though critics have dwelled on the film's theme of sexual repression, none of the women's romances is about sex. The man Clodagh loves rejects her for the riches of the American dream and the opportunity to escape yet another stultifying colonial position, this one being an inherited burden which includes a suitably insulating Anglo-Irish marriage and an impoverished estate. With only a little money of her own, Clodagh has only enough agency to retreat from one anachronistic narrative into another.

Like her, the Maharajah's women occupy a tenuous position in a patriarchal ruling structure; they have been dispersed from a romantic story that kept them dependent and vulnerable. Signifying the dangers of a sequestered but dependent life, the screened windows of the harem could not protect them from their protectors. As the camera pans across them, what we see is the empty space that epitomizes their lack of subjectivity. The screens also comment on the nuns' enclosed life, a vocation they have chosen, but which is no protection from the consequences of the colonial romance in which they play a supporting role. As she will continue to do throughout her career, Godden here exposes the double bind in which women's choices for self-determination are already scripted as a problematic fiction within the realpolitik of colonial relations. The absent women who are never seen or heard in either the novel or film haunt the nuns' story with the illusion that any of them could

matter. The story of the general's mother, who was exiled for some unidenti-
fied transgression, is recounted third-hand. We are never given the women's
version of their story. In dramatic contrast, the film only presents us with the
harem's living room, the bareness of which spotlights not only its faded
frescoes, but the women's dispossession. The frescoes, which depict women
frolicking in their water gardens, are also disintegrating decorative objects,
reflecting on the women's dissolution.

As though reconfirming and forecasting the continuing displacement of
women in colonial spaces, the empty room and its faint memories of women's
ebullience also reflect on the doomed fate of the only human occupant in the
scene. Kanchi, the Nepalese girl who for Godden is "like a basket of fruit piled
high, luscious and ready to eat," dances in preparation for seducing the young
rajah, who is studying with the nuns (Godden 1942, 101). With its psychedelic
contrast between the fresco's dissolving sensuality, the missing women, and its
screened windows, the brilliantly lit room telegraphs Kanchi's abandonment,
not only by the young rajah, as we would expect, but by the beneficent nuns.
Kanchi's solo performance in this scene, which does not appear in the novel,
serves our critical attention well, for it points to a relationship between Godden's concern for her own artistic integrity and the film's representation. Jean
Simmons's painted brown face highlights not only the film's stylistic artifice, but
the critical question of how to read the fact of a white English actress performing as a Nepalese peasant. Having criticized so much of the film, Godden felt
that Simmons, "at sixteen, perfectly fulfilled [her] description of Kanchi" (Godden 1989a, 52). Is this just another Orientalist instance which illuminates Godden's hypocritical concerns for authenticity? I will argue that the painted face
works expressionistically, to signify the layers of political and representational
power that colonize women in both the film and the novel. Precisely because
Godden can be held directly responsible for her own creative production, we
can accept her novel's critique of women's colonized roles as authentic. In a film
that is preparing its audience to abandon the romance of imperial power, it is
not only the character of the Nepalese peasant woman that is being discarded as
an acceptable representative of her own subjectivity. In disposing of Kanchi, the
film also stresses the idea that colonial power cannot protect indigenous women.
Even if Godden is oblivious to the problem of her own Janus-faced critique, she
creates a guide for our more complex response. Her approval of casting the
white English actress may be seen as a colonizing gesture, but the novel, *Black
Narcissus,* like her other Indian fictions, exposes the colonial presence as a dangerous illusion. At the level of its plotting, her narrative shows how imperial
contact cannot ever be benign, whether that contact is imagined or real, because
it irrevocably alters the subjectivity, the self-definition of the subject. The casting of Jean Simmons only magnifies the impossibility of the colonizing gesture
understanding or improving the lot of the native girl.

3. Jean Simmons as Kanchi in *Black Narcissus.* Courtesy Carlton International Media Ltd.

The film's scene of Kanchi's solo represents the dire consequences of imagining the character and fate of the colonized woman. Totally absent from the scene, the nuns are symbolically present as having screened out from their consciousness any recognition of their mission's colonizing impetus. As Kanchi's dance is shown to define her wayward character and as she throws away her dust rag, we know that she, too, will be thrown away, not only by the rajah and the nuns, but by both the film's and novel's narratives. When she disappears from both, never to be seen or heard from again, all that is left of her is the incomplete and self-serving tale the young rajah tells Sister Clodagh. Local power has once again colluded with the imperium's good intentions. Working together, they eliminate a responsibility that could not be confined but remains a confining obstacle to an unencumbered rule. As a peasant girl, with no economic resources and no social supports, Kanchi's fate reflects that of Sister Clodagh. Once again a young woman is ejected from the world that cast her into an anachronistic narrative, in Kanchi's case, as Mr. Dean reminds us, into the tale of the beggar girl and the king. Having Jean Simmons play Kanchi calls attention to the character's vulnerability. The painted exoticism of the English actress and the emblazoned set testify to the impossibility of allowing a Nepalese peasant ward of British missionaries to play her own glamorous role.

The critical context of this casting is also pressured by the wider canvas of the space between the production of the novel in 1938 and the film in 1946.

In that space a war has been fought against the mastery of a race that obliterates difference by exterminating it. Jean Simmons's painted face and body are uneasy reminders of that horror. Her whiteness has been erased, but in the artificiality of her brown painted body what we have is not the resurrection of the racialized Other, but the sign of its erasure. Whiteness here is the power that is moving the brown figure. At this moment of the film's production, Britain is reeling from the victory that cost it its ability to hold onto imperial power and mastery. Britain expresses its destabilized position by hiding behind but controlling the expression of racial self-determination. Both Kanchi and Sister Clodagh are ejected from their romances because like the story that allowed the harem a life of its own, their lives have become an anomaly in the tale of economic and political power that supersedes them.

Romance stories in Godden's writing are invariably overwhelmed by the repressive mechanisms that govern colonial institutions. In turn, the repressive atmosphere instituted by the nuns mocks the notion that they will be offering the natives a transfusion of moral and physical well-being. The nuns' school and clinic are but a prescription for the end of their mission in India. On the one hand, the malaise that strikes them could be seen as another Orientalist tale succumbing to the inherently diseased East, especially as it climaxes in the story of Sister Ruth's sexual hysteria. But Godden's story embeds a different politics. The fact that there is no role that can contain Sister Ruth—as nun, lover, or apostate—aligns her and the other nuns with the stultified, transgressive, and exiled condition of the women of the harem. The tale of sexual repression, as the film advertises itself to audiences, is simply the mass appeal plot, another popular romance, like the tale of the beggar girl and the king, and one that camouflages a narrative of political oppression. The mysterious deadliness of the palace, expressed in gothic images that combine the stories of the nuns and the Indian women, represents a different kind of assault as well as a form of resistance. Instead of being victimized by their own defensive repression, all the women in *Black Narcissus* are subject to the joint political venture of the imperial mission and the general. As the beat of the village drums vies with the bells of St. Faith, as opaque white draperies blow shadows across empty passageways, the mystery enshrouding the palace can be seen as blindness to how the complicity of the Maharajah with Britain overpowers the women's story. But as its painted film image remains intact, defying any resemblance to realism, the veiled palace also keeps itself unknowable to its foreign intruders—film characters and viewers—and therefore untouchable. Godden's exposure of the duplicity of imperial good intentions and the complicity of local power remains an uncomfortable truth at the center of her writing.[10] As she wrote years later, "What lies behind them [stories by herself and Jon] is, I think, compassion—or lack of compassion—a 'sharing' even in cruelty, horror and grief because, if an author is trying to achieve what we early learned to call 'truthful writing,' this 'sharing,' whether we shrink from it or not, is the source of all creative inspiration, however small" (1989b, 159).

DOMESTIC AND GLOBAL WARS:
BREAKFAST WITH THE NIKOLIDES

Rumer Godden's novel *Breakfast with the Nikolides,* which was written in 1941 while World War II was raging, depicts the timorous nature of the relationship between colonial relations and the historical disturbance bracketed by the novel and film *Black Narcissus.* Though the East Bengal river setting and shoreline house of the later novel are based on the Godden's beloved childhood home, the particular historic moment infects any sense of the idyllic. But instead of disturbing her creative momentum, the global emergency drove her to write *Breakfast with the Nikolides,* about which she said, "Of all my novels [it] comes nearest to our 'truthful writing' and nearest to the India I love so deeply" (Godden 1987, 161).

Breakfast with the Nikolides is a very disturbing novel for a feminist critic. While its plot is driven by an abusive marriage, the character of Louise, the beaten and raped wife, challenges any impulse to view her as a victim, either of her violent husband or of the social prescriptions and bonds of British colonialism. Indeed, the novel's indictment of her imperious maternal control and imperialist racism would seem to defy any effort to defend or rescue her character. While such a conundrum presents challenges to literary analysis, the novel offers it as a heuristic through which to interrogate the crisis of a historic moment. Plunging Louise Pool into the emergency of war was inspired by Godden's need to protect her own two daughters from the Nazi siege on Europe in 1939. Like Louise, Godden escaped with her girls to India. But whatever sympathy this close call might generate for her fictional character is complicated by Louise's distrustful withholding and emotional cruelty toward her twelve-year-old daughter, Emily. Godden's biographer, Anne Chisholm, speculates that this relationship may reflect the tensions Godden felt with her daughter Paula, as well as her anger toward her irresponsible husband. Biographical evidence notwithstanding, the novel's own entanglement of an abusive family with the threatened state of the Empire transports a subject of interpersonal relations onto a global stage of compelling importance to the study of imperialism and postcolonialism.

Louise Pool is abused both by her husband's violence and by the violence of war. Having fled her husband, Charles, when he raped her eight years earlier, she is forced upon the outbreak of war to leave Paris, where she and her daughters had been living. Such a clear vision of the impact of history on character is immediately eclipsed, however, by our first view of Louise. Wearing a veil, she is also obscured by "rumors" circulating in the Indian community of Charles Pool's "hidden past," not to mention any questions we might have about her choice of his home as a safe haven (Godden 1985, 13).[11] Repudiating definitive answers, the novel only heightens the sense of mystery that permeates each of these characters and their marriage as well. As Godden's India novels cumulatively show, however, rather than representing a mysterious subcontinent, Louise suggests the willed ignorance that enforces late colonial denial about its own damaging effects. Although narrative ambiguity is often preferable to a more obvious tendentiousness, Godden's inscrutable portrayal of Louise becomes problematic, especially if we compare it to her portrayal of Charles. Where Charles is authoritative and charismatic and, despite his often blinkered vision, is deeply committed to India's well-being, Louise is hysterical and often repugnant, qualities demonstrated by her emotional abuse of her daughter Emily and her disgust with India. The problem is not with the instability and untrustworthiness of her character, the combination of which is a tried and true convention of modern literature. What is ultimately so distressing about her profile is that it creates a double narrative barricade: against sympathy for the victimized woman and against criticism of her violent husband. On the one hand, an exchange between Charles and Louise at the time of her return confirms that he raped her and smashed up their house eight years earlier. And yet despite this evidence of his violent instability, the novel precludes a quick verdict by presenting Louise's continuing flares of desire for Charles and her decision to remain with him. This representation would seem not only to undercut the validity of her original flight, but the value of any further resistance. At the end, when we witness the couple's cheery arm-in-arm promenade, we are led to ask if the novel is fostering belief in the colonial marriage as a model of ameliorating the violent means and end of political colonization.

The image of an Anglo-Indian happily ever after is unsettled, however, by the novel's depictions of relations between the British and their Indian subjects. That Godden is deploying the relationship between individual and colonial violation as a critical tool is evident in the aggression with which Charles prods East Bengal into agricultural progress. The Government Research Farm he builds is "impressive" not only for its "model crops" but for leading the local Indians out of their traditional fatalism toward belief in modernization, in their ability to effect change (Godden 1985, 5). The magnitude of his success is confirmed by his popularity, but when we are also told that "he was pushing the whole of India before him," we recognize the arrogance that impels the work of imperialism (Godden 1985, 5).[12] The aggressive clarity and absolute certainty of Charles's vision are all too consistent with Britain's modernizing mission, and just as self-righteous and coercive. What solves the mystery of the Pools' marriage and Louise's character, and destroys any sense of an inscrutable Orient, is the contextual plot where imperial certainty is destabilized by the historic moment of the Second World War. Like the Indian peasants and students who are overwhelmed by Charles's takeover, Louise has lost the ground on which she had staked her self-discovery. Paris, the place where she gives birth to Binny, the child born of rape, inspires hope for a new life in an aura of enlightenment. When radical change occurs, however, Paris becomes another site of violation. The city of light succumbs to the dark ambiguities of imperial conquest and the power relations of collaboration when it surrenders to the Nazis. In 1940 there is no safety for Louise except as an imperial ward, and so she chooses the devil she knows—her husband and his colonial fortress. Like Harriet Pringle's struggle in Manning's *Levant Trilogy,* Louise's emotional travail can thus be seen as a critical perspective on imperial dependency. Just as the war has clarified the position of these women, so it connects English domestic politics to those of the Empire. In 1940, with their imperial masters threatened by the global assault of the Japanese and Nazi empires, the colonized Indians have no recourse to self-determination. Instead, they are promised protection by the British Empire, a double bind, as it turns out, which includes conscripting them to protect imperial interests by asking them to sacrifice their own lives.

Godden articulates this double bind in the story "Possession," published in her collection, *Mooltiki,* where the alien world war calls for the sacrifice of the only son of a peasant family:

> "War. What is this war?" No one in the village knew what the war was, though the schoolmaster and the post-office clerk from Pasanaghar read the newspapers. To the villagers, Narayan and the young men from the villages round who had been recruited were, simply, gone. . . .
>
> "But what *is* war?"
>
> "War is like locusts. . . . Like a plague of locusts devouring . . ."
>
> "But—locusts leave nothing." (Godden 1957, 7–8)

The void left by this insurmountable loss is filled with Godden's anger at the self-righteous British offer of compensation. After years of compounded tragedy, a colonial agent finally appears in the village, only to rail at Narayan's parents for not having applied for their son's military pension: "'These people are helpless. Helpless! What fate sends them, they accept'" (Godden 1957, 21). Turning British bigotry against itself, the ending shows the self-determination of the Indian couple. Having prudently invested the pension in their land, they cultivate it with a vigor derived from their own act of repossession and regeneration, the combination of which reclaims their son as Indian from his status as British subaltern.

The contempt shown by the British in this scene finds resistance in the Indians' pragmatic orthodoxy. In Patrick Hogan's terms, as we will see with Elspeth Huxley's representation of the Kikuyu, empirical reasons often produce a "modernizing tendency" in indigenous peoples, where they can distinguish themselves from "Europeanization" while making advances on "traditional ideas and practices" (Hogan 2000, 11). Engaging Gayatri Spivak's discussion of "third-world women," we can see how these meanings and implications of "tradition" and "modernization" are shaken by the modernity Godden depicts in her 1941 story and 1942 novel, where World War II intervenes in the representation of Indian colonial relations (Spivak 1988, 306). According to Spivak, because an Indian woman is caught "between patriarchy and imperialism, subject constitution and object-formation," she "disappears, not into a pristine nothingness, but into the violent shuttling which is the displaced figuration of the 'third-world woman' caught between tradition and modernization" (1988, 306). Godden's engagement with the particular historical crisis of World War II in her story "Possession" and 1942 novel challenges any stable meanings of "tradition and modernization" and provides a different objective correlative for the trope of "violent shuttling." Their very dissimilar histories and wartime displacements are woven into a narrative relationship between Indian and British women.

In the context of Godden's life and writing at this late and violent date in the waning history and narratives of British imperial India, the definition of "tradition" can also apply to the British Empire, to meld with its modernizing mission and then to be dislodged. Over its 200-year-long presence, the British Empire had paradoxically formed a tradition of its own in its state of deeply entrenched colonial continuity. Using her own experience, Godden shows us how this tradition is embedded in the continuity of the colonial lives of British women. In order to protect her children from the war, Godden lived for a while in an isolated bungalow on a tea estate in Chinglam. Here she relied upon *The Indian Cook and Housekeeper,* by Flora Annie Steel, published in 1888, to take her "back fifty years into a former quiet graciousness" (Godden 1946b, 42–43). This is not just an escape from the violence of war but an emotional defense that provides order in the face of cultural isolation. Such a defense is facilitated by the retrieval of a myth that denies the colonial violation that made such "graciousness" possible.

We see this traditionalism highlighted and also questioned in all of Godden's Indian novels. Even as recently as in her 1991 *Coromandel Sea Change,* both British and Indian women characters must leap with great agility, persistence, and strength to resist the stealthy demands of gender roles whose isolating codes and expectations have not disappeared in the modern independent state. It is thus not at all jarring that in its 1941 setting *Breakfast with the Nikolides* should depict the English wife as being powerless and ultimately complicit with a marital role that recalls the violating confinement to which wives are so often subjected in nineteenth-century gothic novels. With World War II occupying Godden's narrative space and presaging the end of Empire, neither tradition nor modernization can be figured as stable oppositional categories or, in the language of war, as barricades against one another. As these categories continue to mutate, even in Godden's postcolonial imagination, the modern postcolonial India is often threatened by the ghostly return from the past of an unfulfilled colonial adventure or an unresolved traditional English domestic fiction like the gothic. Godden shows that the very idea of narrative resolution in the late colonial novel is threatened when the British imperial tradition must face its own "violent shuttling" in the form of another modernizing but dystopian project—the industrialized warfare being waged by the empires of the Japanese and the Third Reich. In the battle of these imperial titans, the figures of Indian and British women in *Breakfast with the Nikolides* can "illuminate" not only the disordering of modern and gothic literary traditions, but their relation to the violence that inheres in "the vexed historical continuity between colonial and nationalism and other global movements such as diaspora and transnationalism" (Ray 2000, 2–3). At the moment of World War II, modernist and gothic experiments are shown to be inadequate to the task of representing a global violence that overwhelms how postcolonial has configured colonialism.

We must also consider how these displacements do not arise from or originate in the postcolonial, but rather at that moment when the nationalism undergirding colonialism is being threatened. However one assigns responsibility for the violence generated by diasporic modernity in Godden's novel, its invasion of the domestic sphere spares neither the colonial agent nor subject. Godden's representation of a "vexed historical continuity" as a feature of the embattled late colonial moment offers a significant historical intervention in the relationship between colonialism and postcolonialism. Sangeeta Ray argues that despite partition being "the apocalyptic event for the subcontinent," few studies connect it with Indian nationalism (2000, 126). Godden's novels remind us that Indian nationalism was supported by that other "apocalyptic event," World War II. It was the war's assault on Britain's own nationalism and colonialism that gave rise to the postcolonial moment, for the catastrophic economic and human costs of this war made it all too clear to the British that they had to relinquish their jewel in the crown.

What drives this war are the designs for conquest by the Axis empires and the defense of the British Empire and nation of Britain and its allies. In both cases, the idea of empire is interdependent with the nationalisms not only of the combatants, but of India, with its own struggle for self-determination against the British Empire.[13] The setting of Godden's novel is that very moment when India is desperately needed by the British and is resisting its colonized role as a bulwark against the Japanese Empire in the eastern sphere of a global war.[14] The two and a half million Indian men and women who had joined the British armed forces and who represented so many ethnic Indian groups fighting in Burma and elsewhere in southeast Asia cohere as a colonized people and also as a nation fighting an eastern empire.[15]

Breakfast with the Nikolides depicts the polymorphous and interdependent colonial relationships, within British India, that are entrapped and liberated by world war. For Godden, colonizing conditions extend across cultural, gendered, geopolitical, and domestic spheres. For example, like the Indians and like her daughter Emily, Louise is positioned as a dependent child, needing and deeply attached to the promise of protection. The form of protection Charles embodies is in turn similar to imperial power, the result of conquest and occupation. Devoid of nurture, this protection is intensely patriarchal and militaristic, intriguing in its "commanding" presence and threatening in its violent control (Godden 1987, 9). Confined to and silenced by her subjugated position, Louise has every reason to wear a veil when she returns to Charles; like a curtain, it signifies the purdah of the colonial wife. If Louise is driven to yield to Charles's dominion, her irresistible attraction to his power is no longer mysterious in cause or effect. With no resources or shelter of her own, lacking a lexical frame of reference to explain her relationship with Charles, her only form of expression is hysteria. At its most feverish pitch, her hysteria translates her rage at Charles into sexual desire, the fulfillment of which imprisons her once again in his arms and inspires an escalation of her fears. But her hysteria is not confined to her marriage. As Godden connects its power politics to imperialist ideology, it is also symptomatic of her fear and rage at Indian contamination. It is far safer to deflect her raging anxiety at subjugated Indians than at her "commanding" husband. We see this most melodramatically in an act that recalls E. M. Forster's critical deployment of a woman's hysteria. Louise is like Adela Quested in that she has come halfway around the globe to be married to an Englishman whose colonial power conflates rage, fear, and sexual desire. And just as Dr. Aziz is accused of rape, so Louise accuses the Indian student, Anil, of molesting Emily.

The sense of power and control Louise gains from victimizing Anil derives from a combination of political and psychological conditions. In turn, the novel predicts that these conditions will produce an explosion marking the beginning of the end of India as a safe haven and outlet for British power. If Anil's helpless condition mirrors the British wife's belief about her own powerlessness, the novel notes marked differences. Despite the fact that Anil's family is Brahmin and wealthy and Louise has no resources of her own, she is situated within a power structure that will use her fears to justify its subjugation of the Indian. And so she is given license by her own political culture to identify with her abusive husband by articulating his power: "If I were a man I should horsewhip you. That is what they would do to you in England. Flog you so that you should never forget. Don't try and defend yourself" (Godden 1985, 224). In its reach from domestic to political violation, the relationship between the abused British wife and colonized Indian also reflects that between direct and indirect colonial rule, where the British manipulated the interests of local power elites and trained Indians to administer the laws and regulations they imposed. In this way, we can also see Louise as serving her own interests and as having been trained all too well in the language of British power. But if the British wife is the lawfully marked target and tool of her husband's unfulfilled aggression, the effects of her rage expose them both as symptomatic of the self-destructiveness of the colonial system. For the very core of that system is damaged when Louise finds a doubly safe scapegoat— her daughter. Combining the vulnerability and dependency of the Indian, Godden's portraits of Emily and Louise show how the colonial project is embattled from within at the very moment it is fighting for its life in a global war.

My layout here of a psychodynamic that in our day has become quite conventional serves as a model of imperialist psychology, where, as we have seen with *Black Narcissus,* individual desire collaborates with collective power.[16] Like his coercion of the Indian peasants, Charles's violation of Louise is legitimized and protected by the power of his authoritative colonial position. And at this historic moment, when Britain's imperial subjects are being conscripted to protect the Empire from its own vulnerability, neither Louise nor the Indians have access to psychological or physical mechanisms of self-defense. In this association of domestic and colonial oppression, the novel embeds the most extreme consequences of the idea of colonial conquest in the historic moment of the Nazi conquest of Europe and the Japanese conquest of Asia.

In its intricate weave of colonial, wartime, and domestic violence, the novel depicts not only an English abusive marriage, but that of an Indian couple, Narayan and Shila Das. Read together, these marriages inscribe the fractured whole of Anglo-India. As it depicts tradition clashing with modernity, the novel casts East Bengal as a microcosm of the British conquest and its intensely imposing presence. Each side, the British marriage and the Indian one, figures as a broken but illuminating mirror of the other's domestic space and its spillover into colonial politics and relations. Rather than a symmetrical parallel structure, the marriages of the Dases and the Pools reflect the jagged but intersecting lines of their respectively abusive power bases. Unequal though these power bases may be in British India, they work together in Godden's fictional construction to show the relationship between colonial and gender relations, in short, how modern colonial domination supports men's traditional domination over women in both cultures. Though the ideological sources and traditional practices of this domination are obviously different in each culture, the colonial power of the British imposes a modernizing model that provides new impetus for old Indian habits. And yet the direction of this confrontation with modernity is not linear.[17] Instead, Godden shows how the colonial relationship ruptures what appear to be not only intractable gender relations, but the imperatives of modernity.[18]

Educated in Western medicine to be a veterinary surgeon, Narayan Das is the overachieving student of the Empire's modernizing mission, committed to the lessons of his masters, "who bothered to take up a gutter-boy and give him life" (Godden 1985, 42). That this "life" promises upward mobility at the cost of cultural ambivalence and alienation forms the emotional and imperial plot that develops his character. In this latter-day setting of the imperial sun, Narayan is not so much Other or hybrid as "in-between" colonial and post-colonial. The pragmatic promises of British imperialism drive him to apply the lessons of Western progressivism to his professional ambitions. The more ephemeral prospect of social mobility and acceptance leads him to translate his lessons into homework. Fulfilling "the British . . . passion for alteration," he becomes an agent of the Empire, taking its lessons home by uncritically accepting its modernizing mission as a critique of his Indian heritage (Godden 1985, 42). This critique marks the mimic man whose smiling acquiescence is actually a scar from having internalized colonial violation. That this scar will not heal is revealed in actions that we can label cultural rape. This violation includes prohibiting the traditional behavior and customs of his wife and imposing on her the designs of a Western secular and companionate marriage.[19]

Unlike the sense of mystery that pervades the depiction of the Pools' marriage, Narayan's emotional and cultural assaults on Shila are made very apparent, but not as a sign of the Other's transparency. Instead, Godden is contrasting the unselfconsciously enacted imperial psychodynamic of the Pools' marriage with the deeply reflective and articulated anguish of the objects of cultural imperialism. The contrast between the two marriages therefore reflects critically on accusations of Orientalism in colonial fiction. Reversing the charges of Orientalism, the Pools' colonizing English marriage could be described as timeless in its persistent patterns of desire and violation, while the Dases enact India's confrontation with the historical contingencies of modernity and resistance. This confrontation includes not only the political and military pressures of World War II, but the war's conjunction with the tensions between a lingering colonial and emerging postcolonial identity. It is the combination of these uncertainties and displacements that shapes the characters and marriage of Narayan and Shila. Instead of Indian culture being portrayed as the mysterious Other, the idea of mystery or the unknowable becomes an extended metaphor for the self-deluded and irrational violence that colonial relations incorporate.

We see how this dual violation infiltrates the domestic politics of India in the Dases' marriage. Though Shila tries to please Narayan, her fearful efforts reflect the anxiety of losing herself in a role that makes her a misfit in both the world of the British and her own. She can emerge from purdah to host Narayan's Brahmin friend, but her husband's dismissal of her interests renders her invisible, as do the exclusionary social codes of the British.[20] Like Kanchi in *Black Narcissus,* despite class and regionally defined cultural differences, Shila is thus consigned to a modern or even modernist purdah, a disjunctive status of nonbelonging. In turn, Narayan's constant disdain and rejection of her, as they mirror British attitudes toward Indians, point to the double bind of his taking "life" from colonial paternalism. Their marriage, which resides on the margins of Anglo-India, reflects the social and emotional costs of becoming an imperial mimic man and of being his Indian wife. The unequal power of Indian husband and wife may originate within their culture's prescribed gender roles, but it is legitimized by imperial modernity.

The struggles for cultural and domestic power between the Pools and between the Dases are illuminated by their relationship to another asymmetrical relationship, one that defaces any idyllic picture of the colonial domestic landscape: the war between Louise and her daughter Emily. That the emotional cruelty of an Indian husband should reflect an abusive and abused English mother and child complicates the relationship between the structures of colonial and gender roles in the novel's domestic politics. The powerless status of the Indian wife is reinforced by India's relationship to the British colonial structure. Dependent on British favor, Narayan resembles Louise in being an imperial ward and in abusing the only power he has, in the domestic sphere. His uncontested status as a husband in Indian culture enables him to strip Shila of the authority she would ordinarily wield over her household and to reduce her position to his own in relation to the colonial structure. They are thus intertwined in a union dominated by the power of his shame as an unmanned, colonized Indian. Transcribing his status as Other, he reinforces the subordinate position of his wife, who then becomes doubly colonized as his Other. In this recasting of colonial power and powerlessness, Narayan mirrors Louise's power over Emily by prescribing his wife's role as that of a dependent child. He has thus internalized and fulfilled the promises of imperial power by projecting his own violated condition onto his dependent wife. Like Emily, Shila has neither the confidence that would accompany an education of her own nor a supportive peer community, much less one with any of its own authority. In Shila's case, there is simply no Indian community to which, as an apprentice to English-style domesticity, she can belong.

In her analysis of imperial modernity, Godden also considers how its conflict with Indian tradition leads to cross gendering the colonized Indian male. A significant cost of Narayan's mimicry is his own traditional male gendering, which is destabilized, as shown in contrast to Charles's hypostatic, hypermasculine aggression. Charles is portrayed as embodying the spasmodic violence that erupts from a repressed and repressive colonialist belief in imperial self-containment. Narayan represents the loss of belief in a selfhood that can remain beyond the reach of colonization. When he rejects Louise's order to kill her children's dog, suspected of rabies, we are led to cheer his insubordination, for what is at stake is his professional and cultural integrity. But the fear of rabies, as it extends to Louise's hysterical fear of congenital Indian contamination, must be assuaged by undermining the very knowledge the modernizing mission of colonialism has granted the Indian.[21] Just as colonial power both endows Narayan with authority and robs him of confidence, so his only form of retaliation is to derail his wife's self-assurance, a narrative move that situates him as a mirror image of her helpless femininity. Even as Narayan mirrors Charles's aggression and imposes Western modernity on his wife, he is not only excluded from the colonial social order but denied the masculinist identity instantiated in colonial domination. Caught between his thwarted efforts to become a man in British terms and the feminizing effects of his own dependency and subservience, his position mimics that of Louise and Shila. As he discovers that he cannot restore his manhood by remaking his wife, he becomes a mimic man mimicking women. Furthermore, elevating his wife to a Western model of equality will not substantiate his upwardly mobile status. Instead, the semblance is a mockery of his hopes and distorts both their positions in the two cultures which shape their identities.

In another facet of the novel's mirroring effects, the gendered interweave of colonial and domestic relations is complicated by Narayan's relationship with Indian social culture. Whatever the differences between attaining mobility among the British and attaining it in his own Indian spheres, their combination shows that his position blocks the construction of hybridity as a site of social and cultural negotiation. In Godden's cross-colonial critique, no matter how fluid and fluent his social and professional skills, Narayan bears indelible marks that render him immobile, in perpetual stasis. However far his British training has carried him beyond his birthplace in the alleyways of Calcutta, the illusory nature of that progress is reflected in his status among Indians, where "the tradition and the heritage of Brahma" make him feel "the only caste-marks [he] shall ever know" (Godden 1985, 42–43). In both cultural systems these are the marks of racial inferiority: his "crossed blood . . . that makes [him] dark and thick and slightly squat," the hair that "grows close to [his] head like a Negro's" (41). In an ironic contrast, Godden constructs Charles as also dark and hairy, but his "brilliant" blue eyes and tall, "commanding" presence mark him as the romanticized manly conqueror (9). Fulfilling another modernizing mission of the British, Charles embodies the shift away from nineteenth-century masculinist ideals. Ronald Hyam explains this shift "from the ideals of oral strenuousness, a Christian manliness, to a culture of the emphatically physical . . . from serious earnestness to robust virility, from integrity to hardness" (1976, 72). Unlike Narayan, whose racialized body signals his subjugated position, the source of Charles's darkness is the Indian sun, the relentless power of which, as it never set on the British Empire, reflects his assigned role as master of all he surveys.[22] In contrast to those analyses that hold colonialism either totally responsible for the racial and social inequities of indigenous cultures, or at least exacerbating them, Godden offers an equal opportunity for mutual cultural manipulation. Narayan is the pawn of both. Embedded in his racial shame is the declaration by each culture of its inherent superiority, an identity position untouched by the fluidity of modernity or the crosscurrents of colonialism.

The novel, however, effects a crosscurrent of its own by considering the implications of social class and racial identity within Indian culture. Having failed to convert Shila into accepting Anglo-Indian culture, Narayan is forced to confront a racial and social barrier that divides Indians from each other and that he has internalized. Feeling that his "dark" presence would "contaminate" the Brahmin home of his friend Anil, Narayan attempts to transform Anil into his own colonized image (Godden 1985, 44). The metamorphosis begins with being "in love with Anil," a desire for homoerotic union that will overcome Narayan's shame by erasing their caste differences, colonial rejection, and Shila's presence: "You are myself. You are all that I want to be" (Godden 1985, 40, 49–50).[23] Their union, however, is impossible, but not because the novel condemns it as transgressive in any sexual sense. Instead, this erotics of sameness reflects a vision of colonial relations that erases the possibility of resistance because it assumes Indian complicity with the promises of colonial privilege.[24] Independently of each other, but forming a joint colonizing venture, both Narayan and Anil's father pressure the young man to achieve first-class honors at the College of the Government Farm, a colonial reward for accepting cultural domination. In an act of passive resistance, however, Anil writes poetry and sits by the river instead of studying; he creates his own culture instead of losing himself in the British cultivation of Anglo-India. His death from being infected by the Pools' rabid dog only confirms how the vision of a hybrid Anglo-India is poisonous to India, while the celebration of his poetry affirms India's voice.

India's voice is also expressed in the figure of Shila Das, who, from an Indian woman's perspective, complicates not only the nationalist and colonial bind but the author's relationship to it. Shila is caught between her husband's expression of colonial identification and allegiance and, like many in her nation, her own resistance to it. Like Anil, a paragon of nonviolent resistance, she becomes more intensely herself. In contrast to her husband's frenetic work to emulate the British, she settles into a stillness constructed out of her culture's ancient ecology and reconstructed by Godden: "On the tumbledown pillar in the garden Shila would sit while minutes and whole half-hours slid away. 'Where is the knitting they taught you at school? Where are the books I like you to read?' They lay forgotten, and the small red ants that inhabited the pillar came out and ran across them. The sun lay hot there, and in the evening there was a breeze warm from the river, and Shila like one of the ants or a little lizard could never have enough of warmth and sun . . . and all the time the river ran below and she watched the water running, running past" (Godden 1985, 75–76). Any suspicion that this passage represents a stereotype of the indolent Other must be discounted in light of Shila's victory against Anglophilia at the end of the novel. Though Narayan has prohibited Shila from observing her traditional ceremonies, she wages her own insurrection, aided by the surreptitious and subversive rituals of their maidservant, Tarala. Like the river's flow, their unrelenting conspiracy withstands his assaulting ambitions until it becomes clear that this is where Godden situates Indian integrity. This integration of nature and culture, like that in the passage above, does not eschew modernity or reinscribe the primitive or exotic or the feminine as a view of Indian culture.[25] Instead, this depiction subscribes to a view of Indian tradition as defined by a historian of India, Ainslie Embree: "Not a fixed residue handed down from the past; it is, rather, an enduring structure with adaptive mechanisms that permit it to be both historically determined and a continuously renewed creative force" (1989, 4).[26]

What the novel's depictions of Shila's and Tarala's traditional rituals assert is the guardianship of Indian culture against the self-deceiving cultivation of Englishness. While some might argue that this portrait represents a purifying isolationism, Godden's narrative vision is far more integrative. The novel closes with more than one alternative to British cultural hegemony and masculinist domination. In one instance, Emily meets with Narayan to learn why and how her dog died, but his expert scientific testimony must vie with Emily's discovery of a more profound wisdom. As the girl watches Shila sculpt a goddess, a two-way connection is forged that contributes Indian creative expression to the lessons of cultural diversity Emily is gleaning from her life in India. Though Emily attempts to speak to her in the local Indian vernacular, Shila replies in her own inflected English, not "clipped like . . . Narayan's," in mimicry of the British, but shaped by the rhythms of her own language, giving "her words a musical lilt" (Godden 1985, 272). Her sculpture, too, though traditional in form and purpose, integrates a declaration of Shila's independence from Narayan's pressures to assimilate. The intricate patterns generated by her quiet, fluid movements are expressions of both her self-containment and its woman-centered cultural heritage. Emily asks, "How do you know the pattern?" Shila replies, "I know it. My mother knew it and her mother. Even my mother's mother's mother" (272).

Within the unsettling moment that combines pressures to accommodate cultural identity to colonial modernization and those pressures on the British Empire to end, "the figure of the woman" does not "disappear" into or become "displaced by the violent shuttling" between "tradition and modernization" (Spivak 1988, 306). It isn't even overwhelmed by war. Instead, Godden's figures of a British woman and girl and of an Indian woman show how that unsettling moment liberates traditional roles in both communities. To explain how this productive disturbance works, I would like to return to my own trope of the fractured but illuminating mirror. The destabilized positions of Louise and Emily Pool and Shila Das are narrated separately in order to highlight how each reflects the similarities and differences in the respective social and cultural spheres that fracture women's sense of wholeness. But as the separate narratives shape the novel, their simultaneous connection and discordance also represent a coherent modernist whole. Though Louise and Shila never meet, their stories, combined with Emily's encounter with Shila, support each other's claims and arguments, forming, in narrative effect, a community.

The cohesiveness and coherence of this colonial community is made possible by the conjunction of war and resistance that ironically forms its support. As though echoing the violence that invades from without and within, the students of the Government Farm College rise up in protest at their belief that Anil has been imprisoned by the British and, in so doing, mock the commanding presence of Charles. Perhaps it isn't a coincidence that in August 1942, at about the same time this novel was being published, protests broke out across India in the wake of the British detaining Nehru, Gandhi, and other leaders of the All-India Congress for ratifying Gandhi's Quit India Resolution. Like the Empire itself at this moment, Charles "looked at them with tired naked eyes" and with a final paternalistic reprimand—"Hush!"—he yields British paramountcy to Indian rule, to Narayan (Godden 1985, 283, 284). In this prelude to the end of Empire, the "sahib" knows he "has got to act like a sahib," as Orwell wrote in "Shooting an Elephant," but for Godden this now means that the "mask" he wears has grown thin and transparent, and to keep his English difference he must enact his power by showing that the choice to relinquish it is his (1953b, 152). This is more than a recolonizing gesture, where the colonial banner is passed on to the ruling elites created by colonial occupation. Narayan's hybridity—the marriage of modernization and Shila's tradition—represents a self-made decolonized man. After recognizing that "all this force and striving, this breaking away and smashing down of obstacles, has been wrong," Narayan dreams of going "back to the only mother I have, to India herself. . . ." (Godden 1985, 283, 284, 44). If women have traditionally been cast as icons of nationhood while being subordinate to it, the Indian woman in this novel liberates India's mimic man from his Anglophiliac coercive lessons and mandates a new kind of Indian masculinity. At the end of the novel, like the river which resists the altered course Charles imposes on it, the integrity of Shila's beliefs emerges triumphant over the pressures of British colonial progress. On the one hand, this resistance is integrated into a negotiation with Narayan's wish for a companionate marriage. But, as well, his own

Anglophone mimicry will be distilled into Shila's commitment to Indian traditions they can share. In this sense Shila solves the problem Kumkum Sangari
and Sudesh Vaid locate in constructing "an inspirational model of the past"
that cannot "deal with our present problems" (1990, 18). What Shila constructs
is "an inspirational model" *from* "the past" that reforms the confused and
oppressive present in which Narayan has participated. It is in this sense that
Godden herself is inspired by a particularly Indian identification of the nation
with a "manifold . . . great Goddess":

> Some of us say she is one of her own eager young professional women,
> burgeoning with new ideas. . . . Others insist she is that ageless mother,
> calm and untroubled, whose customs . . . have not altered for thousands of
> years. Or she is a golden princess who has awakened after centuries of
> sleep. A princess? She is a beggar woman, her children starving in filth and
> rags, her hand outstretched to the world for alms. Which "she" is she? The
> answer is "all" . . . and, though she has the mysterious goddess power of
> reconciling her contradictions so that they do not clash but, rather, give
> her a peculiar richness, an added or double meaning, they often make her
> seem utterly baffling. (Godden 1972, 8)

Among Godden's many accomplishments in this novel is her ability to imagine, from her position as Anglo-Indian colonial woman, an Indian woman
who, as she resists the dubious temptations of anglicized meanings and interpretation, is an agent of Indian independence.

The negotiation extends the categories of colonial and postcolonial identities enwrapped in theories of mimicry. As Parama Roy insists, "Setting the
powerfully suggestive notion of colonial mimicry to work in new—that is,
non-European—contexts (while also situating it within familiar ones) shows
us the ways in which indigenous models of identity formation. . . . are often
traversed by it, but in ways that might be functional to the interests of Indian
nationalisms" (1998, 174). The question of Rumer Godden is particularly tantalizing here because she dares to negotiate the distance between indigenous
and colonizer from constantly shifting critical positions. As her child characters develop their own independence by scaling the walls of their Anglo-
Indian gardens, Godden offers them and us a vision of working against
"colonial mimicry." Adding her writing to the mix of categories Roy and others keep expanding, we can see Godden "as a salutary warning against the
reduction and thoughtless commingling of categories" precisely because there
is no sign of her complicated identity among any of the extant critical categories—"gender, ethnicity, sexuality, religion, class, and competing nationalisms" (Roy 1998, 174). Indeed, we must consider how her identity as an
Anglo-Indian woman writer negotiates among those competing nationalisms.

The Endangered Garden: *The River*

Nothing can mollify the sky,
the river knows
only its weight and solitude.

—Rumer Godden, "Bengal River"

It was between the writing of *Black Narcissus* and its film release, and four years after the publication of *Breakfast with the Nikolides,* that Rumer Godden wrote her most personal evocation of Anglo-India, the novel *The River,* published in 1946. Deeply autobiographical, the novel is set in a big house and walled garden exactly like Narayanganj, on a busy and crowded river, adjacent to both the Indian village and the jute works managed by the English father. The central consciousness in a family much like Godden's own, and with her own first name, is that of Harriet, an awkwardly shy second sister, whose lyrically universalized coming-of-age story and passions are directed toward the wounded visiting war veteran, Captain John, and expressed in her precociously gifted writing. As Godden herself and her critics read the novel, the detailed particularities of the narrative are all in the service of "the timelessness of a spell," a myth to which Harriet's writing contributes (Godden 1989a, 105):

The river runs the round world spins.
Dawn and lamplight. Midnight. Noon.
Sun follows day. Night stars and moon.
The day ends. The end begins.
(Godden 1989a, 126)

Universalizing and naturalizing human experience, this precocious poem certainly encourages critics to thematize the novel as "the passage from innocence to experience" (Rosenthal 1996, 28) or "the reality of evil that no paradise . . . can keep away, in India or anywhere else" (Chisholm, 1998, 199). Godden's biographer concurs: "There is not a political thought or word in *The River*"(Chisholm 1998, 198).

Like *Black Narcissus, The River* was adapted into a critically acclaimed and widely popular film, and both novel and film should be read within their respective historical and cultural contexts as well as in relation to each other. To begin with the critics' comments above, it is certainly true that neither the novel nor the film ever directly addresses the Second World War, the independence of India, or the effect of both on Godden's family. If, however, we consider the political and narrative relationship between the time frame of the novel's composition and the film's, as we did with *Black Narcissus,* we see once again how they work as intertextual commentaries on the time bound theme that critics read as timeless. The mythic structure of both the novel and the film version of *The River* enfolds a critical relationship between the narratives the British constructed to justify making India their home and those Indian narratives that made leaving inevitable. The narrative and contextual relationship between the novel and film begins with the political import of their times of production. The novel was published a year before Indian independence, and the film, though it represents that immediate postwar time, was made in 1950, after partition and at a time when India was creating public institutions that would borrow models from the British while distancing itself. Within the tensions of this defining period, Godden portrays the experience of an Anglo-Indian family discovering that India's timelessness is not theirs (Chisholm 1998, 198).

It was on one of the visits she would make to India, after returning to England permanently, that Godden knew "*The River* was one of these rare books that are given to you" (Godden 1989a, 39). Her feeling that it captured an emotionally accurate representation of her childhood experience is matched by the lyrical intensity of the novel's language. The subject of this lyricism is the novel's questioning of an ongoing British presence in India; the lyrical language represents the development of Harriet's social and political consciousness. The opportunity to translate the novel into film presented itself three years later, when the renowned French director, Jean Renoir, committed himself to filming it. The fact that there is little plot or action in the novel made this an interesting challenge for Renoir. He described his project as dramatizing the "very touching relationships between [the characters]" (Chisholm 1998, 200). Most significantly, he intended to film it not on some studio sound stage, but on location in India. The cost of this would have been prohibitive had it not been for Kenneth McEldowney, whose fortune supported the project and whose marketing imagination inspired him to be the film's producer. Most of the cost of filming in India was covered by the Ward of Princes, mainly Prince Fatehsingh of Limbi. Before it could begin, however, Godden went to Los Angeles to write the script with Renoir, a collaboration that produced her respect for his artistic integrity. She saw that her vision would be sustained rather than sacrificed if some "characters disappeared" and "new ones came in. We changed, unchanged, but not the idea, the flavor" (Godden 1989a, 105). Renoir agreed "passionately" with Godden that in this film there would be no Bengali peasants "singing or talking in English as they did in *Black Narcissus*" (Godden 1989a, 105). There are also no English actors playing Indians.

The integrity of the British woman writer is expressed in the film as Harriet's struggle and as a Western narrative tradition of love and loss, the combination of which gives coherence and meaning to Godden's Anglo-Indian representation of regeneration and forgiveness. Integrating the Anglo-Indian

4. Rumer Godden with cast of *Black Narcissus.* Courtesy Janus Films.

story with its Bengali setting necessitated a great deal of effort spent on translating local environments into filmed images and narration, as we can see in an opening close-up of an Indian woman painting a traditional pattern on her floor with rice water while the voice of an unseen, adult Harriet explains its Hindu meaning. Like our first glimpse of Harriet's father speaking Bengali to his workers, this prelude offers an integrative proposition, that even though the Empire is over, there is a place for the British in their respectful relations with Indians and their benign business enterprises. Not only is the family depicted as essentially happy and harmonious in itself and with their Indian servants, but the English tunes and dances with which they celebrate Diwali, the Hindu festival of lights, are designed to show the Britons' celebration of Indian culture. This narrative line, however, does not stand unquestioned, either as fiction or life writing or as a timeless myth.

An incident during the filming could, indeed should, be seen as its politically time-bound context. During the direction of one of the Diwali festival scenes, "hundreds, perhaps a thousand or more" students from the University of Calcutta converged on the scene, chanting in Hindi and Bengali, " 'Hai. Hai. Foreigner film.' 'Hai. Hai. Foreigners out,' " setting fire to the set, and beating some of the crew (Godden 1989a, 130). Godden attributed the protest to "sensational tales" about " 'filming Hindu women [who] were forced to appear naked!' " and Renoir assuaged the students by showing them the film rushes, by discussing the film's respect for India, and then by involving some of the students in its production. The event, however, cannot remain incidental to the film's story (130). The student "invaders" resist the film's primary elegiac narrative by inserting a violently clashing postcolonial moment (130). As a result, the story of a congenial British presence is no longer timeless or universal.

Disruptions to the film's claims for postcolonial harmony are reinforced by its multivalent narratives, and so the relationship between characters and actors is integral to its structure. One of two significant changes from the novel, about Godden's desire to represent "the essential link between truths [of] East and West," reflects our questions about the location of representational agency in colonial and neocolonial fiction (Godden 1989a, 122). The novel links its Western protagonists to the East through Harriet's lyrical description of the Indian landscape. The film dramatizes this linkage through Harriet's voice accompanying a panorama of the river's life. But then the film introduces the Eurasian Melanie, the convent-educated Eurasian daughter of an American neighbor and his Indian wife, now deceased. None of the three appears in the novel. Melanie's combined identity may embody the linkage between East and West, but she also challenges it. From the moment she exchanges her convent uniform and braids for a sari and traditionally folded hair, the film questions the idea of linkage. Though she and her American father are shown to have a very loving and trusting relationship, the film depicts Melanie as painfully drawn to a relationship with the wounded American veteran, Captain John, but then ultimately retreating from a Western identity. While this transformation is dramatized through the development of her character, its political implications are announced in its relationship to Godden's Eurasian characters in other novels. Where Godden allows Melanie to choose her Indian identity, elsewhere she presents the status of the Eurasian woman as deeply problematic.

In her later novel, *The Peacock Spring,* Alix Lamont's desperate desire to rise above her impoverished and denigrated status in Indian society creates a disabling and ambivalent relationship with her Indian mother and a tortured sense of herself. As Godden writes in her preface to this novel, "in those days [the 1930s] Eurasians were ostracized by both Indians and Westerners" (Godden 1975, n.p.). Historically, "those days" extend from the nineteenth century when Eurasians petitioned the British government to be called Anglo-Indian in order to designate a place in English society with shared cultural values. By the 1930s, they were considered a degenerate result of debased colonial desire and more Other than those who were identified as Indian only. In this sense, Melanie's choice seems more like a romantic retreat into another mythic colonial garden, one where the American father can offer his Eurasian daughter the fulfillment of her Indian desire by protecting her from any attempt at integration. This retreat does not allow us to think of Melanie's character as representing any kind of happy, fluid, self-actualizing hybridity or expression of essentialist identity or authentic experience. Instead, as Bill Ashcroft, Gareth Griffiths, and Helen Tiffin argue, "the inauthentic and marginal is in fact the 'real'" (1989, 41). In this way, we can see Melanie as positioned in between, registering a cultural dissonance created by Godden's expression of her own identity: "I suppose, in a way, I am a divided person, having two roots: Sussex, England . . . and India. . . . [W]hen I am in one I am homesick for the other" (Godden 1975, preface, n.p.). Godden's desire to achieve artistic and autobiographical authenticity is thus expressed as a tension between the enforced racialized condition of the Eurasian woman and her own ability to choose division.

In its film version, *The River*'s attempt to link East and West draws attention to the racial and political implications of its casting. Instead of an English actress, as in the case of Jean Simmons in *Black Narcissus,* the prominent Indian dancer Radha Sri Ram plays Melanie. Consistent with his passion for veracious detail, it was Renoir who insisted on hiring Radha, whose talents extended beyond her exquisite performance of the classical dance of the Bharata Natyam tradition. Exercising her own integrity, she refused to have her smile transformed by "'television teeth'" or her skin color changed: "'If you want me, you must have me as I am,' she said" (Godden 1989a, 127–128). The choice was not only providential for its artistic effect, but critical for its political import. Capitalizing on Radha's talents required a center-stage performance, which would include a narrative sequence of her own in addition to her role as Melanie. Like dialogic voices, Radha's performance and Melanie's story assert an Indian presence, the power of which contests the primacy of the Anglo-Indian story. The latter, which is doubly layered, consists of Harriet's narration of her family's story and, within that, the story around which Radha's dance is performed. Invented by Harriet and read to Captain John to capture his attention, the story's only connection to Indian narrative is its mime of Indian marriage ceremonies. Its integrity lies in its parallel exposition of a young English girl's sexual yearning through the conventions of Western romance. But despite all the effort to convey the innocence of the *jeune fille,* Harriet's role is also constituted as a neocolonial writer, usurping and exploiting indigenous traditions to fulfill her own desires. Writing vicariously, Harriet makes sure that the desires of her Indian heroine are providentially fulfilled. Her story represents a young Indian woman falling in love with a young Indian man, but her desires are thwarted when her father insists on an arranged marriage. With as much sorrow as ceremony, the young woman marries the man her father chooses, only to learn, at the lifting of the veils, that he is indeed her loved one. Despite this happy ending, the young woman's story remains linked to an English plot, especially as it is indebted to Harriet's interpretation of the Indian father's desires and her own.

5. Radha Sri Ram performing Indian dance in *The River*. Courtesy Janus Films.

Linked and indebted, but not fused. Radha's performance frees the Indian tale from Harriet's wish-fulfillment fantasy and offers it a critical commentary. Portraying the young woman, Radha performs a dance that cannot, by its very Indian nature, be Harriet's invention, a translation of her plot, or the creation of the Anglo-Indian novelist and French filmmaker. Instead, Radha's dance is a text belonging to itself and moving within its own contextual sphere, from its own thousand-year tradition and in its combined language of Indian symbolic and nonrepresentational movement. Even if the camera's framing attempts to contain her, the meanings of her movements lie beyond it. Her physical movements cannot be equated with emotions known to a Western audience. Compared to the languid movement and lambent prose of the Anglo-Indian family story, the dance and pageantry of Radha's performance represent a vital expression of Indian separateness and autonomy. Even if the gaze belongs to the Western filmmaker, the confident energy and self-contained relationship between dance and dancer represent a mockery of Harriet's all-knowing voice-over narrative. The combination of Radha's embodied authenticity, her character's refusal to integrate into Anglo-India, and the interpellated Indian tale she enacts is integrated into the film structurally but remains distinct in its form, content, and interpretive possibilities. If the film, like the novel, seems to focus on the Anglo-Indian family, Melanie's character and Radha's performance function as a powerfully reinforced rejoinder and resistance narrative, enfolding the Anglo-Indian plot into itself and marking it as Other. Together, they posi-

6. Radha Sri Ram performing Indian dance in *The River.* Courtesy Janus Films.

tion the Anglo–Indian novelist and the French film director as indebted to an independent Indian nation. As Melanie's story and Radha's performance cohere with the students' own Quit India demonstration, it becomes impossible to view the lyrical style of the Anglo–Indian narrative as nostalgic. Instead, it suggests the flagging energies of the postcolonial British presence.

This enervation is reflected in a tableau the film version preserves from Godden's novel. Bogey, Harriet's young brother, is killed by a cobra that nests

7. Patricia Walters as Harriet, Godden's nephew Richard Foster as Bogey, and Indian Sikh snake charmer in *The River*. Courtesy Janus Films.

in a peepul tree in their walled garden. That the British presence has always been on shaky ground is symbolized by this enormous tree which cannot be contained. It not only straddles the garden wall and the outside village lane, but its roots thrust upward from the soil and then double back into it, defying the carefully cultivated symmetry of the rest of the garden. An indigenous life form, the tree keeps reclaiming its primacy over its native and colonized habitat. It also harbors the snake that tempts the British into thinking that they are safely ensconced within their garden walls, but that kills Bogey. No reader can be faulted for seeing this tragic incident as a canonized evocation of the colonial paradise spoiled by an indigenous presence. The colonial myth is shattered, ironically, by the child's sweetness and innocence, the very nature of which typecasts him as a sacrificial lamb to the colonial myth, the unwitting agent of a persistent colonial self-delusion. If the cobra belongs, Bogey is the reminder that the British delude themselves that they do, too. Though looked after by a Sikh servant, Bogey is pretty much left to his own devices and his otherwise harmless fascination with the garden's creatures is called into question by his own role as tempter—offering the cobra milk and the music of his own reed pipe, and then turning temptation into abuse by poking the snake with a stick. When Bogey dies from the cobra's bite, the novel and film elegize the loss of life by associating it with Harriet's loss of innocence. She is guilty of knowing about Bogey's hobby and failing to report it to her parents. As the narrative's lesson of responsibility extends to firing the negligent servant, it reasserts the colonial message that native peoples have no more sense of responsibility than children.

This colonial message has been taken by postcolonial critics as almost timeless in itself, as extending from the economic invasion of the East India Company through neocolonial incursions by the rest of the world exploiting India's resources and talents. But this same episode about Bogey also questions the message about native irresponsibility. In one sense, Bogey's actions are modeled on the long-established tradition of the British exploiting India for their own needs. By implication, the film suggests that this narcissistic sense of responsibility is no less cruel than that of a child whose enclosed world gives him no reason to question his domination of it. In addition to Bogey's story, Harriet's narrative of the Anglo-Indian garden puts the lie to any Edenic colonial fantasy. Another change from the novel to the film shows that when it is time bound, the issue of responsibility questions Britain's neocolonial presence after Indian independence. This change refers to the character of the wounded Captain John, who is English in the novel, but an American in the film. Drawing on the immediate memories of World War II, the invasion of Anglo-India by a one-legged American who has also lost his sense of purpose questions the "moral friction" between that war and the logic of the British staying on. Reversing the narrative image of the native cobra, Captain John represents the temptation to see the colonial garden as restorative and redemptive as well as a confrontation with its damaging effects. As Melanie, Valerie, and Harriet vie for his attention, his role echoes "the legend of Paris and the apple" (Godden 1989a, 122). But because his war melancholy intrudes on any romantic idyll, the figure of the American veteran confronts the colonial myth with the insurmountable costs of all empires as an evil waste. All this desire for the grieving soldier merely highlights how there is no colonial space where Westerners can belong. Melanie's infatuation reflects the Eurasian woman's identification with Captain John's longing for a stable sense of self; they have both been caught between a complex of wars against imperial domination and a struggle to locate both autonomy and relatedness between their own colonial antecedents and an uncertain future. One of the three women infatuated with Captain John is Valerie, the spoiled daughter of a colonial entrepreneur who reflects the thwarted desires of a neocolonial presence.

If the neocolonial presence remains fraught with self-perpetuating disappointment, the film assures us that its desires can be contained by postcolonial self-consciousness and artistic representation. At the very end, we hear Harriet recognizing her desire for Captain John as a passage into postcolonial consciousness. As her voice turns back to the unrelenting and yet unpredictable flow of the river, we are reminded that she is speaking from the perspective of a distance established by time and political tide. Just as Rumer Godden had to leave India at the moment it betrayed her own desires for finding a sense of purpose within her childhood memories, so Harriet's voice registers a post-colonial reconciliation with the exile of the Anglo-Indian. The resonance of timelessness in her coming-of-age story will be revised as she reconstructs her colonial identity. She does so by writing it as a confrontation with Anglo-India in the form of a personal fiction.

STRANGERS IN ANOTHER'S GARDEN: *KINGFISHERS CATCH FIRE*

In India a woman alone does not go and live alone—not, at any rate, far from her own kind, not unless she is a saint or a great sinner.
> —Rumer Godden, A Time to Dance, No Time to Weep

Tensions between postcolonial reconciliation and the exile of the Anglo-Indian form the plot of Godden's 1953 novel, *Kingfishers Catch Fire.* Though they share much in common, unlike *Breakfast with the Nikolides, Kingfishers Catch Fire* is a pleasure trip for the feminist critic. Not only is it a comedy, but its postcolonial production affords its heroine an adventure of self-discovery that is prohibited for Louise Pool in 1940. Combined with its self-appointed mandate to speak for the subaltern, this adventure continues the struggle of both the English woman and her Indian neighbors to break free of British cultural domination. *Kingfishers* is based on an incident that actually drove Godden to leave India after an ill-fated struggle to live there with her two children. The incident, in which a servant poisoned her, is fictionalized as an analysis of the self-deluded thinking that even after a two-hundred-year rule, the British could enlist the respect and support of those they had colonized.[27] Whether Godden herself is guilty of this delusion is a question the novel embeds autobiographically, but ultimately cannot answer. As her biographer tells us, this is because the incident "remained disturbingly open" to the point where "Rumer came to dislike the book and to wish she had never written it" (Chisholm 1998, 177). Like this disturbance, the novel dramatizes a painful ambivalence, what we can even call an "in-between" genre, as it attempts to balance its satire of a woman's British neocolonial settlement with its abrasive consequences.

Unlike *Breakfast with the Nikolides,* this is a novel about a woman's resolve to achieve independence. And yet it is fraught with lack of resolution. In contrast to Louise, because Sophie has been liberated from a difficult marriage by her husband's death and the end of war, she can imagine a new life for herself and her children, and she attempts to build one on the margins of both British and Indian societies. Using archly critical voices which in dissonant harmony mock and deflate her characters' best intentions, Godden unmasks the vastly complex social and cultural infrastructures that seemed for so long to make coherent sense of Britain's imperial presence in India. By the end of her post-colonial plotting, it is clear that these bases of knowledge produce not wistful understanding or nostalgia, but the chaotic and destructive expression of fierce mutual desire that can neither be explained nor understood as romantic.

The novel evokes an anachronistic British presence in a time that isn't identified, but as it follows Godden's own story, would be set moments before or after Indian independence. This netherworld becomes the imaginative site for a portrait of a young colonial widow who decides to embark on her own Indian adventure of self-discovery and independence. The narcissism of her decision, however, forecloses the narrative possibility that she will be able to recognize the civil war waging around her. Insulating herself within the tale of adventure she spins, Sophie rebels not only against any historical contingency, but against her dependent state of impoverished English widowhood. Assuming a fresh start, she plunges headlong through the "helter-skelter" of India (Godden 1994, 226). Her only other option is to return to England, to "forsake her life and end in Finstead" with Toby, her Mr. Knightly look-alike, and the stability of his tightly starched "teatime" (30, 226). Based on Godden's own experience, Sophie decides instead to take her two daughters to live in a decrepit cottage in the foothills of the Himalayas, where she will attempt to integrate them into the far more unpredictable and therefore romantically ineffable, if risky, climate. That this was a daring decision is confirmed by her autobiographical statement: "In India, a woman, any woman, Western or Indian, does not live alone unless she has a label: school inspector, missionary, or, if Indian, holy woman or guru, and, 'If you do this,' said the Provost Marshall, 'you will be out of my jurisdiction.' . . . The missionaries were more blunt. 'You have lost your mind'" (Godden 1989, 186–187).

Sophie believes she can prove her self-sufficiency by integrating Western habits into what she construes as the natural ecology of Kashmiri culture. With more zeal than knowledge of the local economy or arts, her first maneuver is to learn the crafts by which Kashmir's various peoples subsist off the land's scant bounty. While this reverses the nuns' project in *Black Narcissus,* the lesson is the same. The nuns' Western medicine, which shows their disdain for indigenous practices, turns out to be symptomatic of their poisonous project. Sophie, by contrast, exchanges "castor oil" for "anemones" and "blood-cleansing tea" in order to enhance the unspoiled simple life of the Kashmiris while recreating her own in their image (Godden 1994, 113). But instead of beneficence, Sophie's expropriation of Kashmiri culture becomes a destabilizing translation. She has positioned herself in "the liminal stage" of an unsettling comedy in which individuals "have neither their old selves and old positions in society nor their new ones" (Little 1983, 3). Certainly Sophie's quest to

8. The Dove House, the model for Dhilkusha, Sophie's mountain bungalow in *King-fishers Catch Fire*. Courtesy Camilla Hornby.

superimpose British pragmatism and its modernizing mission onto her own mystifying and retrograde vision of Kashmir places her "betwixt and between . . . socially and psychologically" (Little 1983, 4, 3). The humor in *Kingfishers Catch Fire* derives from the correspondence between liminality and the "patterns of quest comedy," that is, between the always tentative status of being displaced and the linear progression of a search that is resolved as a productive reordering of experience (Little 1983, 4). In Godden's rendering, however, the very instability of liminality reflects and leads to the violent consequences of Anglo-Indian relations that imaginative fiction cannot ward off.[28]

Violence breaks out as Sophie reaps the consequences of ignoring how her presence subtends the fragile rapprochement between the different ethnic and religious communities that comprise Kashmiri society. In her exploitation of their economic interdependence, Sophie believes she is creating a harmonious social order, but the distortions she produces only mirror her own vexed role. This vexed role is implicated in the social politics of romance plotting as well as of colonial agendas at the end of Empire. In turn, this microcosmic debunking of the resolute missionary spirit of British colonialism is shaped as a comedy of misguided manners. As Sophie restores her rented cottage, Dhilkusha, to pristine simplicity, it ironically and critically assumes an imperious outlook.[29] Her employment of local labor and her use of local resources

are all in the service of self-interest while she congratulates herself for bringing progress to those below her lofty vista. Even when a desperate servant
concocts a poisoned love potion, impairing Sophie's already blurred vision,
and her enclave disintegrates into violent resistance, she allows herself to be
seduced by her own understanding of "those people" (Godden 1994, prologue). Sophie's Indian odyssey progresses toward a sense of responsibility for
her intervention in the fate of the Kashmiris, but a multivocal narrative stands
in the way of her moral self-satisfaction or ours. The novel's many voices, dissolving the primacy of Western rationality and modernization, also clarify why
neither Sophie nor her postcolonial compatriots are willing to relinquish their
fantasied relation to India: the subcontinent's "beauty in people and things" is
a kind of love potion in itself, an elixir whose life-enhancing qualities make
the Britons believe they can be even better colonizers now that the Empire is
over (prologue).[30]

The comedy that exposes this fantasy as a poisonous self-delusion derives
much of its effect from what Mikhail Bakhtin has theorized as a discourse of
tension, which is made up of dialogic voices competing with one another
from different perspectives. In turn, this tension is translated into comedy
through the technique of parody, which can "expose to destroy" the expressed
point of view of another through implied mockery (Bakhtin 1981, 364). In
terms of Godden's comedy of cultural tension, parody dramatizes the ongoing
power struggles between a woman whose search for independence recreates a
colonizing project and those who resist her exploitation. Judy Little's analysis
of women's comic writing exposes a subversive element in dialogic discourse
by showing how the language of power can be deployed to mock that of colonial self-delusion: "When these writers humor the sentence, they make it
unsay, or partly unsay, what it seems to say. In so doing, these women expose
the ambivalent structures of language and its implied worldview. Power is
revealed as a linguistic posture . . . while gender categories unravel in the linguistic stripping" (1991, 31). In *Kingfishers Catch Fire,* the gender categories
established by literary romance conventions and by colonial relations unravel
as they form a tense and mocking dialogic discourse in narrative relation to
each other. Instead of being resolved as comedy, however, this narrative relationship explodes from pressures—as the power of Sophie's fantasy is invested
in the now anachronistic imperial project, as the novel invests power in the
woman escaping from her own colonized subjectivity, and as the novel asserts
the power of the resistant recolonized subject.

Dialogic tension sets the tone of the novel at the very start. In the prologue, an exchange between Sophie and Toby establishes the playful yet defen-
sively expressed ambivalences that mark Godden's relationship to her heroine.
It is within this tension that the prologue deploys and mocks the conventions
of romance writing. And while romance as a vision has been integral to so

many colonial novels but is now condemned as "nostalgia for the Raj," romance in *Kingfishers Catch Fire* is a critical device. Godden deploys conventions of popular romance to show how they support ambivalence about the end of Empire in serious colonial discourses.[31] Resonating with the fairy-tale incantation, "Once upon a time," the prologue's opening words are "Long Afterwards," a rhetorical move which debunks the fantasied sense of a timeless elsewhere by establishing a time-bound relationship between past and present. Instead of guaranteeing that Sophie and Toby are entwined in domestic harmony forever after, the prologue questions its own narrative desire to do so. Holding the ground on any idyllic future, this opening also establishes the narrator's resistance to romantic fantasies about Britain's relations with India (Godden 1994, prologue). Godden's objection to such fantasies is twofold. The first element concerns the structural expectation in fairy tales of imminent domestic or supernatural danger where female characters are constituted as unprepared to defend themselves against the terror of oppressive control or unfathomable monstrousness. Compounding the woman's vulnerability is the narrative defense against both fears that sacrifices her to a ritually expected "happily ever after." For Godden, the ultimate danger in fairy-tale or romance plotting is the Manichaean duality that plots innocence and evil as distinct, unrelated, and inhuman forces, devoid of human responsibility. Such evocations of a timeless English decorum or mysterious Orient condemn the English woman to unchanging gender roles and show the Indian subcontinent and its people as inherently threatening. Equally dangerous is the implication that neither the Englishwoman nor the Indians will learn to resist the ways of knowing that are thrust upon them. In self-conscious and critical opposition to the antihistorical safety net of romance, the prologue's "Long Afterwards" marks the beginning of a narrative set in a place bound by historical rupture. As the rest of the narrative takes a long look backwards at the interlocking behaviors and events that lead up to the prologue's English setting, it plays out the prolonged but particular time of ending Britain's presence and complicated relationship with India.

The consequences of this revision can be imagined as threatening the life of romance as a literary convention, especially as readers' expectations of "happily ever after" are mocked and therefore resisted by the dialogue which follows "Long Afterwards." In their sidestepping repartee, which contests each other's interpretations of narrative time, Sophie and Toby, her implacable if patronizing knight errant, defy the idea that narrative resolution means domestic harmony. Indeed, their contest draws attention to the gendered politics of romance: " 'Not so long,' said Toby, 'it's only two years.' . . . 'Ages afterwards,' said Sophie," echoing and therefore invoking the narrator's support (Godden 1994, prologue). Toby, whose exacting sense of time marks him as prototypically and imperially commanding, pragmatic, and grounded in realist conventions of male authority, is mocked as a romantic in disguise by Sophie's recognition. This mockery begins with the prologue, continues with Sophie's resistance, and persists to the end, to his "always rescuing [her]" (8). To accept Toby's romantic paternalism would mean recapitulating colonial ideologies of race and gender at the very moment the novel is connecting Sophie's struggle for independence with India's. Like the native, it is assumed that the woman cannot evolve into rational maturity. The novel's critical connection between imperial racism and sexism is thus reinforced by Sophie's fear of Toby's offer. To embrace him would mean abandoning her vision of Kashmir's delights to his "savagely" protective denunciation of its people as "rabble, ugly and menacing"(prologue, 225). In its offer of sanctuary, Toby's green and gentle England is only a gentler and kinder form of protection than Charles Pool's India. For as *Kingfishers* interpolates English scenes, it is clear that the distance between imperial homeland and colony is not so great, as both would tame the wayward Englishwoman. Toby's English sanctuary denies the efficacy of Sophie's resistance to Anglo-India's vision of her as a charming but undisciplined child.

Unlike the predetermined resolution of romance, Sophie's odyssey of self-determination not only remains suspended throughout the novel, but is represented as a risk. As we shall see, however, no matter how the ambiguity which drives the prologue's domestic scene is interpreted, it is even further destabilized by the novel's conclusion, where Sophie may be on the run from Toby. In a tense dialogic relationship of their own, prologue and conclusion produce a multivalent critical awareness that involves interlocking relationships between colonial and domestic politics. Sophie's longing for Kashmir in the prologue and the chaos her presence later instigates become directly implicated in the colonizing domestic order Toby offers her.[32] At the end of the novel, convinced that she has recognized her "mistakes" and learned to "respect" the Kashmiris' "own truth," Sophie takes off with her children to romp through yet another adventure, this time in Lebanon (Godden 1994, 229).[33] In this sense Sophie fulfills the poetic prophesy depicted in Gerard Manley Hopkins's poem, "As Kingfishers Catch Fire," which inspired Godden's title. On the one hand, because the domesticated prologue presents her as acquiescent to Toby, her adventure-seeking conclusion is self-mocking. At the same time, however, though it nearly immolates Sophie, her passion for self-discovery is regenerating. For Sophie's escape at the end does leave Toby behind and asleep, suggesting that the story he embodies is an idea as moribund as Britain's two-hundred-year conviction that it was rescuing India from itself. Rather than accepting the prologue as Godden's conclusion, we need to attend to her interrogation of its romantically timeless sense of a woman's fated domestication. Another way of viewing the relationship between the prologue and the conclusion is as a fluid metaphor. Situated at the edge of

India's independence, Sophie's neocolonial adventure story can be seen as a travelogue that questions the English supremacism Toby claims.

Godden's trope of narrative time is particularly resonant here. For just as the Raj continued to cling to the anachronistic social codes and cultural attitudes celebrated by Queen Victoria's jubilee, so Godden's modern setting paradoxically evokes the manners and morals of an earlier age. Sophie's temptation to find stability and safety in Toby's embrace recalls the nineteenth-century "ideology of the lady," which, according to Gail Finney, not only implies "the passivity and desire for male approval associated with ladylikeness," but is "antithetical to the creation of humor" (1994, 2). But as Godden's reversal of "Once upon a time" suggests, modernity in the form of a woman's struggle against stability and safety will also "necessitate [the] aggressiveness, satire, and ridicule, not niceness," that defines comedy (Finney 1994, 2). Sophie's aggressive quest for self-determination becomes the target of satire, not because the novel assesses her escape from a prescribed dependency as ridiculous, but because she thinks she is shedding the "ideology of the lady" without noticing that it is attached to her economic and political position high above the Kashmiri villagers. The assumption of individuation and autonomy on which Sophie's self-determination is based still makes her the memsahib, obscuring those Others on whom her quest depends for support and who are exploited without regard to their own subjectivity.

Despite their differences, in the figuration of Sophie's blindness and Toby's open but vise-like arms, the novel assumes that they share the self-enclosed social and cognitive spheres of colonial authority. Neither of them, therefore, has any critical perspective on their roles as controlling the fates of others. In contrast to this imperial narcissism, Godden represents wisdom, as she does so often in her fiction, in a child.[34] Of Sophie's two children, Moo, a small boy, and eight-year-old Teresa, it is the girl who is set in dialogic tension with her mother. Teresa begins her own quest to understand and shape her fate by raising insouciant questions and commenting archly on her mother's plans:

> "We shan't be poor whites," she [Sophie] announced to Teresa. "We shall be peasants."
>
> The thought that they were not peasants did come into Sophie's mind, but she pushed it down.
>
> "How shall we be peasants?" asked Teresa fearfully. (Godden 1994, 31)

While there is always humor, as Judy Little reminds us, in "the inversion of the usual authority so that clowns mock kings" or children mock their elders and betters, the use of mockery also shows deep understanding of the rhetorical structures of authority (1983, 2). We can see this in the fact that mockery is only funny if it captures the precise diction and tone of the powerful. Teresa's question achieves its comic effect for this reason: inverting Sophie's definitive declaration into a question exposes the absurdity of their being either "poor whites" or "peasants." Unlike the peasants of Kashmir, the Anglo-Indian mother and child have the option to return to genteel if confining comfort. Teresa's question points to the impossibility of their becoming peasants—that the very effort would be farcical, parodying their misunderstanding of what it means to be a peasant, not to mention the power invested in their political ability to choose roles.

That such a choice is supported by their neocolonial position is also linked by Teresa's question to another source of Sophie's power. It is as though Sophie's self-centered search for a new kind of woman's authority has blinded her to the power invested in her by her maternal role, one which the child must resist to locate her own sense of self. With the narrator's guidance, which affirms and supports the child's naive wisdom throughout the novel, the reader is invited to share the rebellious satire that is the effect of Teresa's anxious question. For Teresa's question exposes the exploitative relationship between her mother's quest for self-determination and the colonial condition of Otherness. As it forms a narrative pattern, Teresa's questions and answers work as an epistemological strategy that deromanticizes the exotic mysteries of Otherness. Though her position as dependent child would prevent her from seeing this, Teresa's unequal and unreasonable power relationship with her mother parallels that of colonial relations and identifies Sophie's arbitrary self-righteousness as the reconstruction of a colonizing project. What assuages the reader's anxieties, if not Teresa's, are the hints that self-determination for the English woman, her children, and the Others among whom they live is inconceivable so long as to "Sophie [India's] strangeness was romance," a perspective that for the Kashmiris "was part of her terrifying cleverness" (Godden 1994, 91, 107).[35]

While the narrator's support of Teresa's suspicious questions serves to guide our responses to the childlike mother and precocious child, the plot leaves the child to fend for herself. The radical isolation to which Teresa is subjected is not merely the function of alienation between mother and child, however, but of the political psychology of colonial relations, as we see with Emily and Louise Pool in *Breakfast with the Nikolides.* Just as Sophie cannot tolerate the child's interrogating challenge because it asserts an authority that reverses the roles of mother and child, so she clings to her maternal imperative in relation to the Kashmiris. She constructs them as children who can't possibly know what is best for themselves, as when she offers her servants a day off each week for rest and their own affairs: "They were still more astounded. 'You pay us,' said Nabir. 'You should try and get all the work you can from us.' Anything else made them uneasy, but Sophie was firm" (Godden 1994, 108). This maternalism is exposed as part of Sophie's self-delusion in aligning her with those she accuses of colonial manipulation—the missionaries, who, for "all their love and zeal . . . wanted to bend" the people they worked for (229).[36]

The comic irony of Sophie's anticolonial critique boomerangs when instead of victimizing or colonizing either Teresa or the Kashmiris, Sophie's maternal discourse turns out to be a blessing. It spotlights her as the enemy while protecting the Other. Recalling Sophie's resistance to the danger Toby represents, the Kashmiris may be embraced by her discourse, but they remain sufficiently unknowable so as to wage a clandestine rebellion. In turn, Sophie's all too obvious condescension makes it easy for the Kashmiris to know her and to mock her desire to improve their lot. The form of the Kashmiris' rebellion is to refuse to assimilate to her ignorant view of them and her ideology of selfless and mutual help. Just as Teresa's question undermines the governing power of Sophie's self-righteous rhetoric, so the Kashmiris find "something corrupting in Sophie's new ideas": " 'But—if everyone helps themselves, who will need all this help?" ' they ask of her (Godden 1994, 111).

The interpretive effect of this question aligns Teresa with the Kashmiris and creates "two texts within one: the parody itself and the parodied or target text: both present within the new text in a dialogical relationship" (Paravisini and Yorio 1987, 182). While the "target text" here is Sophie's willful naivete, the novel assumes the risk that the instrument of parody may deflate itself. If Teresa's naivete is developmentally appropriate, if it prompts us to find her and her questions cute, the narrative is taking a big risk. The danger lies in that the questions attributed to the Kashmiris, like those mocking responses Olivia Manning gives the Egyptians, might also target them as cute, as precocious natives, thus branding them as backward. Godden's depiction of the Kashmiris, however, includes an acute sense of difference and blossoming anger that resists the colonizer. This representation also parodies Sophie's assumption that she can know them and hence enfold them into her English domestic order, just as Toby would embrace her.

Parallel to this parodic relationship, Teresa, like the Kashmiris, will struggle to extricate herself from the strings attached to maternal self-sacrifice. Rather than affirm the conservative self-replication of maternal ideology and follow her mother's lessons, she destabilizes both by showing the absurdity of a woman searching for her own autonomy while exploiting another's (Finney 1994, 11). Teresa chafes against Sophie's maternal pedagogy by noting through a series of mocking questions that her mother's choice of primer, "*The Wise Teacher*," is too "full of ideas"; teaching "arithmetic in a new way, by clapping and hopping"; it drives the student-daughter to ask, " 'Can't we learn it the old way by writing it in sums?'" (Godden 1994, 79). By twitting the tenor of Sophie's authoritative voice, Teresa's old-fashioned preference exposes Sophie's progressivism as an oppressive form of control. In its reflection of colonial relations, Sophie's pedagogy is a regressive anachronism. Supported

by the intervention of the ending of Empire, Teresa's nostalgia creates a critical space in which her own subjectivity can thrive. In contrast to Teresa's
method, the servants learn to mimic Sophie's methods as a way of earning her
approval and absorbing her power. Despite their differences, however, as child
and servants appropriate maternal colonial power, they also use "the one voice
to subvert the other, [and] such parodic dialogizing functions as an emancipa-
tory strategy" (Finney 1994, 8).

This alignment and opposition of Teresa and the servants creates a different kind of risk for the novel's critique of Sophie's colonial reconstruction. It
does this by addressing two questions, posed by Gayatri Spivak, that drive so
much postcolonial theory: "Can the subaltern speak," or what kind of agency
is possible in situations of extreme social inequality? (1988).[37] The novel anticipates and addresses these questions by ridiculing the Englishwoman's assumption that she and the villagers can get to know and understand each other.
Read in the political context of its 1953 publication, the success of this satire
is based on the trust that the colonial discourse supporting Sophie's assumption is already thoroughly discredited. Sophie is an appropriate satiric target of
affectionate teasing because there is no harm done now that the Empire is
over. In turn, however, this trust suggests a critical perspective on Spivak's
question which not only assumes but demands integrity and authenticity for
the speaking colonized subject. For nowhere in this question is there to be
found its own Other: integrity and authenticity for the speaking colonial Englishwoman. Without this mutual respect, there is no postcolonial relationship,
only a one-dimensional construction that, as it essentializes the colonizer, mirrors that which is so disturbing when the subject is the colonized.

The novel shapes our response by building a conflicted relationship
between Sophie and her Kashmiri servants. Sophie's Victorian cri de coeur,
"Servant troubles!" conflates all those who work for her into a homogenized
mass, totally ignoring Kashmir's indigenous, multicultural tensions (Godden
1994, 75). Such tensions are all too apparent as they reflect Kashmir's rule by
a Hindu rajah and administration over a largely Muslim population, a polity
that is complicated by the internalized vision and presence of a neocolonial
power (9). Nabir Dar, Dhilkusha's longtime Muslim caretaker, and Sultan
Sheikh, Sophie's Hindu servant, are not merely dusky and infantilized com-
petitors for the white woman's affirmation, but scions of two village families
whose acrimonious rivalry formed the "etiquette" of the political structure of
the village long before a British presence (127). Despite its ubiquitous power,
however, for Sophie, the stakes of this rivalry are so paltry, "some of it was
almost funny" (72). Like Sophie, Godden herself was ultimately to discover
that "it was difficult to believe the lengths to which these people would go for
pitifully little; that this was because they had pitifully little, [she] had not yet
understood" (Godden 1987, 198). Sophie's idea of what is "funny" evaporates

when the local political balance is upset by her blindness to her own position as irritant in the well-being of the village. Blaming Nabir for the cycle of petty crimes her arrogance has set into motion is the catalyst that explodes the political and social balance of the village. In effect, her behavior stands for the debilitating consequences of colonial ambivalence about its indirect rule. She has failed to trust the local ethical and political ecology which she had claimed to understand and even assimilate.

When Nabir disappears, his rival Sultan is left with no mediating agent between his ambitions and Sophie's, and his vulnerability drives him to appropriate Sophie's illusory power and knowledge. That is, with the desperate logic of a recolonized subject, he catalyzes the dubious science and artistry of Sophie's herbal workshop—her "alchemy"—and concocts a love potion (Godden 1994, 121). The result, however, is a deadly mockery of the expropriating power of English knowledge and imperial trading practices, for Sultan can only reconstruct her English recipe with an ingredient he can afford: ground glass instead of the required pearls. In its mimicry, this love-hate potion also targets colonial maternalism for believing it could authenticate the integrity of the colonized. And so the novel indicts Sophie's attempt to impose British empirical rationality and the imperial order of its economic exploitation on the complicated commerce of village healing practices. The horrific and comic affect generated by this alternative medicine coalesces as the critical symbolic scene that guides us through the novel's anticolonial conclusion.

Sultan's love potion incites mood swings and erotic longing in Sophie, raising the ghost of "one of the central and most potent fears of the British community"—rape or revenge (Chisholm 1998, 180). According to Godden's sister Nancy, "what happened to Rumer was nothing exceptional, especially in Kashmir—'It happened all the time'" (Chisholm 1998, 181). The novel's incident may very well represent that fear as well as recall the persistently narrated but distorted memory of the Sepoy rapes of 1857.[38] It also inscribes what is left out of those narrations—both mutual attraction and revulsion. The only sexual intimacy that results from Sultan's potion demonstrates how the power of Sophie's colonial maternalism feminizes the postcolonial manservant. Both Nabir, who is constructed along the lines of the stereotypical manly Muslim, and Sultan, as the effeminate Hindu, are rendered ineffectually passive-aggressive agents by Sophie's rule.[39] And yet it is from within this frame of colonizing reference that these men assert their most effective threat and speak for themselves in a subversive discourse of their own. As the shock of their insurrection opens Sophie's eyes, she is forced to see that her power has turned them into a parodic reflection of herself and that she has "turned into some sort of monster," in effect, as though she and the colonial idea had poisoned themselves (Godden 1994, 208). If Sophie has committed that most insidious act of colonialism, appropriating and recasting the Other into the sameness of her solipsistic image, Rumer Godden makes sure that we recognize her heroine's occupation of a different, critical space. At the end of the novel, the indigenous beauty of Kashmir answers the question of "Who speaks for the subaltern?" by violating the greatest fear of Sophie, the neocolonizer. As Kashmir pronounces its irrevocable separateness and wholeness from Sophie's peripheral vision of it, the only authentic healing the postcolonial Englishwoman can represent is to leave.[40]

CHAPTER 3

Red Strangers

ELSPETH HUXLEY'S AFRICA

There was the Empire, and there were we at the heart and center of the world. No one questioned our position. Everyone else was a barbarian, more or less.

—Elspeth Huxley, *Love among the Daughters*

AMONG ALL THE women writers I study in this book, Elspeth Huxley has not been neglected or ignored. In fact, she has won the unequivocal, if not visceral, attention of critics. Huxley, who died in 1997, retains the power, even today, to ignite a raging bonfire of criticism of her African identity and writing. Her African critics, most notably Chinua Achebe, find her guilty for "consider[ing] herself an African, like so many other white settlers in the fertile, comfortable highlands the British had taken away from the Gikuyu in Kenya" (Achebe 2001, 57). Achebe's totalizing indictment reflects back on his own identity experience and creates more of an affinity with Huxley than he would seem to desire. For like the white woman settler writer, he, too, received a British-based education and left the Africa he loved to become a writer who complicated what an African identity means. And so Huxley, too, over fifty years, wrote about Africa as she imagined it before colonization, as she experienced it as a child settler, and as she tried to understand it after independence. After she left, she never lived in Africa again but, like Achebe, sustained a passionate love and concern for the land and peoples who shaped her multivalent identity. If this passion underwrites a form of nostalgia, it is not, as Michael Gorra argues about Paul Scott, "for imperial rule," but is "a persistent search for what he just as persistently does not find, for an idea, a belief, that will give a purpose . . . he knows cannot be found and which he would have to discount even if it could" (1997, 24–25). Whatever knowledge Huxley acquired, however, is seen as ill-gotten gains, as when she is accused of using her "sound grasp of the Gikuyu language" and customs to justify colonization (Githae-Mugo 1978, 122). The identity politics with which this lifelong journey becomes entwined earns her the opprobrium of being "called the spokesman for the white settler community" (Achebe 2001, 57).[1]

Though Huxley left Kenya at the age of eighteen, she forged a career out
of Africa, writing fiction, biography, travel books, and analyses of the continent's changing landscape, all of which, for Achebe and others critics, adds up
to "the colonization of one people's story for another" (Achebe 2001, 43).
Though she was only six when Kenya became her home, the story of how the
colony shaped her identity is taken as a misappropriated foundational lesson. That the child would find the Highland forest with its duikers and
chameleons a place of enchantment is read as an affront to its indigenous people. Based on this premise, her critics conclude that her attention to the forest's beautiful complexity only shows how she could easily "explain . . . her
black characters" without "seriously bother[ing] to penetrate" their thinking
because she already believed in "the inferiority of the black man" (Githae-
Mugo 1978, 18). To write Huxley off in this way, as a colonial racist, is to foreclose an open inquiry into the British colonial experience in Africa, without
which we cannot fully understand its effects on the indigenous Africans. To
claim, as does Micere Githae-Mugo, that the only "portrayal of fellow-
Kenyans" that has "depth . . . is likely only to come from a native son" leads us
back to a question that has not been put to rest: who is authorized to represent people unlike themselves? (1978, 132).

To erase the colonial voice in order to hear that of the colonized not only
repeats the conflict between them, but places the voice of the colonized
beyond scrutiny. Most dangerously, to vilify the colonial writer's representation of her experience is to erase that Other with whom she shares her narrative and historical space and therefore to deny part of the critic's own
subjectivity. On the other hand, to open Huxley's books once again allows us
to begin a new knowledge quest—to understand what a white colonial
woman writer may have discovered about her own multifaceted identity and
colonial politics, what Penelope Ingram calls "the precarious positionality of
the settler" (1999, 81). By 1959, after forty years of writing, Huxley's colonial
identity had become infused with a "complicated psychology," to use Carolyn
Steedman's term, a shifting mind-set that confronts us with questions about
the political boundaries that govern our own criteria of what we value in
women's life writing (1998, 247).

In a pamphlet Huxley published in 1954, during the Mau Mau uprisings,
she clings to the belief that despite its "complicated" mix of races, Kenya can
overcome its "inter-racial bickering" and find a way to create a new kind of
nation out of "different customs, mentalities, standards of living and faiths"
(1954a, 3). Her vision would include a place for European settlers, "the middle way between the white supremacy of South Africa and the black
supremacy of the Gold Coast," a way that had been paved by those like her

own parents who came to Kenya in 1911 (Huxley 1954a, 36). Arriving two years later, Huxley was part of that British settler movement she herself mocks as "White Mischief," the "notorious . . . gin-soaked . . . Happy Valley" crowd of "raffish" gentry who, in the 1920s reigned over the White Highlands (1964, 112). These are the people who have also been castigated for imagining Africa as their Edenic playground, transforming it into their "ideal of domestic order and tranquillity which suppresses the underlying desire" for colonization (Spurr 1993, 31). The settlers were the snakes in this garden, tempting the Kikuyu and Masai peoples to exchange their freedom to serve and imbibe the ways of an alien people who considered themselves a superior civilization.[2] The success of Huxley's 1959 childhood memoir, *Flame Trees of Thika,* is explained by postcolonial critics as nostalgia for that order, for its imperial grandeur and rugged individualism at a time of national decline.[3] This was also the year the White Highlands were declared closed to white settlers. The huge success of the book's 1981 TV version is attributed to a romantic erasure of every trace of colonial oppression while Britain struggles with the return of its repressed colonized to the metropolitan center.

To read Huxley's writings according to her own mandate reveals a sustained critique of the romantic dreams through which British colonial settlement could justify its incursions. The variety of her representations in novels as well as memoirs and reportage lends complexity as well as inconsistency and irony to her lifelong engagement with Africa. An example of this critical reading of colonial folly in Africa is Huxley's biography of Lord Delamere, a founding father of British Kenya. Her preface, which contextualizes Delamere's story within colonialist ideologies and politics of his day, asserts a critical distance that critics most often elide. After presenting a summary of "European standards," which viewed Africa with great certainty as "wholly primitive," Huxley wryly notes, "The intricate social mechanism[s] underlying tribalism, that enabled these groups to maintain a relatively stable life amid a hostile environment, were equally unknown" (1967, v). Rather than arguing for British colonialism in Africa or having Africa all figured out, Huxley writes in many different forms and in various historical contexts to explore the effects of British ignorance on the Kenyans and on themselves. Throughout her writing, this would include her changing relations to the land and its people as a colonial and postcolonial woman.

A prime example of this inquiry is her 1939 novel, *Red Strangers,* in which she ethnographically investigates the condition of the Kikuyu people before, during, and after colonial settlement. That the attitudes of Huxley and her mother would change radically over time is announced in the dedication to her mother, who "suggested this book and helped to bring it into being." Nellie Grant's interest and admiration of the Kikuyu's intelligence and "enterprise" not only opposed those settlers who thought the Kikuyu "deceitful,

crafty," and quarrelsome, but led her to challenge her daughter by proclaim-
ing, "You've done *White Man's Country.* What about *Black Man's Country*
next?" (Huxley 1987, 182). A foreword confesses to Huxley's lack of anthropological expertise and to her hopes for imaginative construction, but also to
reliance on interviews with Kikuyu who could offer their memories of the
first encounters with white men. Though she doesn't mention the help she
received from the British Kenyan administration, she announces her purpose
as dramatizing Kikuyu beliefs and experience to a European audience because
"that rapidly dwindling number" of "old Kikuyu men who remember life as
it was lived before British rule, cannot present their point of view to us . . . in
terms which we can understand" (1939, viii). It was also because the "young
educated man," with his European education, like his teachers, cannot "interpret the feelings and outlook of the generation to whom the processes of
European though were always alien" (1939, viii).

Her research, which informed her later writing, also became her critical
guide. It was conducted through the Grants' foreman, Njombo, other Kikuyu
elders living at Njoro, and among the people of Chief Murigo, who helped
smooth the way, so successfully, in fact, that "it seemed that no secrets were
withheld" (Huxley 1973, 120). Huxley and her mother were invited to witness several sacred ceremonies, including female circumcision, "a sign of trust"
attested to by the fact that "the Government, as well as the Missions, disapproved of the custom" (121). As though anticipating postcolonial criticism, she
"disclaim[s] any intention of speaking for the Kikuyu people or of putting
forward their point of view. . . . I am well aware that no person of one race and
culture can truly interpret events from the angle of individuals belonging to a
totally different race and culture" (Huxley 1939, viii).[4] Despite and/or because
of these disclaimers, Huxley stands accused not only of usurping the role of
"the African writer who considers himself the authentic spokesman of his
people," but for the reason that she finds the African "unqualified" (Githae-
Mugo 1978, 40).

In its misreading of Huxley and her relationship to other African writers,
this accusation questions its own plea to authenticity. On the one hand, Huxley never positions herself as anything other than an "outsider looking in," but
her portrayal of Kikuyu society resembles Chinua Achebe's depiction of the
changing Ibo society in *Things Fall Apart* (Githae-Mugo 1978, 47).[5] Unlike
Achebe's novel, however, which remains a hallmark of African fiction, Huxley's African writing maintains its status as the colonial woman's problem.
Though they would disagree about reasons, Huxley and her critics may share
an ambivalence about how to represent the evolution of a culture from its
own narratives of the precolonial through anticolonial struggle and the shape
of its independent state.[6] We can see how this ambivalence operates in
Achebe's novel, which also bridges African and Western narrative conventions,

where he has to confront the influences of his father, a Christian minister, his Western education, and his own anticolonial mission. Moreover, like Huxley, Achebe charts the complicated interrelationships between an indigenous culture confronting the viability of its traditions and beliefs and their consequences at the crisis point of colonial encounter.[7] Working with such traditional English novelistic concerns as ideologies and the representation of individual character development, fate, and chance, Huxley's fictions also subject these features to Kikuyu beliefs and practices. By the end of her career, both the Kikuyu and the British have been viewed through the lens of each other. In this way, despite the bulk of narrative attention to the Kikuyu, Huxley constructs a balance in perspective that, unlike Achebe's *Things Fall Apart,* is critically unsettling. Nowhere is this role of unsettling outsider made more palpably precarious and multivalent than in her African mystery novels, which I discuss later in this chapter and which serve as my own metaphorical critical guide.

I maintain that Huxley wrote murder mysteries about Africa precisely because she didn't have it all figured out, not during or after colonial settlement.[8] Never satisfied with answers, she relentlessly raised questions that address Simon Gikandi's concern about whether the white colonial woman writer can represent African peoples "as autonomous entities rather than mere projections of European fantasies" (1996, 150). The fact that Africa and its peoples might never be understood by a white colonial writer shapes the travels and writing she pursued almost to her death. What remained the most inscrutable mystery for Huxley was the short-lived epic of white settlement. To narrate the settlers' stories as a series of murder thrillers would demonstrate the risks that motivated much of their Kenyan odyssey. But despite the conventional solutions with which her detective novels are resolved, understanding of the settlers' failures remained a mystery over the many years in which she explored the genre.[9] In every one of her murder mysteries, every villain turns out to be a settler. In a microcosmic sense, this all-white melodrama represents the radical separateness with which settlers forged their African identities. No matter how physically close their black African workers lived, they remained worlds apart. True, one could easily argue that Huxley's thrillers, like so many colonial adventure stories, depict black Africans as background, an undramatized, an undifferentiated mass, denied their own historical processes and either the subjectivity or agency to be a victim, resister, or even a villain. But given her depiction of all the settlers as murder suspects who, over five novels, constitute a disordered community, I think we can say that as they kill each other off, so goes their fantasy of domination and belonging.

Huxley may very well be asking whether the settler enterprise, even as it changed over time, can survive the distemper that is symptomatic of its essential uprootedness and isolation from the imperial center. Related to this is the question of whether the settlers can sustain their desire for adventure and independence, not to mention their defiance of conventional English constraints. Why does the rugged individualism with which they identify themselves devolve into obsessive jealousies, deranged self-delusions, and megalomania?[10] If this is nostalgia, then the next question must be, For what? Huxley continued to ponder these questions as murder mysteries from 1937, with the publication of *Murder at Government House,* through 1965, with *The Merry Hippo.*[11] At the same time, she addressed these concerns from entirely different perspectives in other genres—her 1959 memoir and other novels that experiment with narrative perspective and chronology. As reading these works will show, Huxley has a great deal to offer our postcolonial concerns: an astute understanding of "the complicated psychology" of settler identities and experiences and of colonial relations.

A COLONIAL CHILDHOOD

In our circle of cool shade, as if under a rustling green parasol, we inhabited a different world from the sun-soaked Kikuyu ridges. . . . It was as if we sat in a small, darkened auditorium gazing out at a stage which took in most of the world.

—Elspeth Huxley, The Flame Trees of Thika

The Africa and its peoples encountered by the first agents of the West has vanished and will never come again.

—Elspeth Huxley, *Nine Faces of Kenya*

The Flame Trees of Thika is a fictionalized account of the first two years, 1913–1915, of the Huxley family's residence in Kenya, where they came to build a farm.[12] From the vantage point of 1959, with Kenyan independence still four years away, the spirit of adventure and fortitude which propels Huxley's story is supported by two colonial icons: the quest tradition of Rudyard Kipling and Rider Haggard and the belief in an innocent and benighted mission. Huxley's parents were members of that tribe of minor aristocrats and gentry spurred on by the British colonial office to abandon their dim expectations for the challenge of building a model community of an ecologically sound ruling class.[13] As Dane Kennedy assesses this effort, however, this benign self-image masked more urgent and problematic desires and effects: "The gentlemanly stratum of Kenya encouraged the promotion of a rural, hierarchical society, reminiscent of a half-imagined Britain more congenial to their atavistic longings, sustained by the appeal of 'acting as a sort of feudal lord' in relations with the indigenous population" (1997, 191–192). In its construction of a child's consciousness, Huxley's tale pleads innocent to this charge. At one level she relies on the convention of childhood innocence, but then she uses the myth of an unencumbered and unspoiled curiosity to question whether the child could remain uncontaminated by adult perfidies while learning to recognize them. The result is a narrator in the enviable position of feeling able to represent, mediate, and assess the settler experience. The overlay of Huxley's retrospective wisdom onto a child's narrative endows each perspective with a plea for authenticity and integrity disallowed by critics of British imperialism. Interrogating her plea, we must then gauge the meanings of authenticity and integrity in light of her own attempts at self-scrutiny.[14] Whether Huxley is writing self-consciously to her critics is open to interpretation, but by 1959 she had already established herself as a highly visible debater on behalf of the set-tler presence for many years. Witness her twelve-year-long heated correspon-dence with the Oxford political scientist Margery Perham, who argued that the settlers' desire for dominance needed stringent guidance from Whitehall.[15]

Huxley's memoirs guarantee the complicated multiplicity of the colonial woman's character by creating a weave of narrative voices. The perspective of Elspeth, the six- to eight-year-old child in *Flame Trees,* is narrated by an adult who in turn is the construction of Elspeth Huxley some forty years later.[16] From these interwoven vantages, the adult writer, performing as a child, con-structs childhood as a fictional site for exploring the formation of a collective imagination and history and questioning the future of the white settlement of Kenya. On the other hand, all the critical attention to Huxley's memoirs has either focused on her adult consciousness of the settler experience or con-flated the child's and the adult's consciousness and knowledge. And while it could be argued that the creation of a child's encounter disingenuously dis-places the more compromised conscience of the adult writer, the child's pre-sumed innocence doesn't equal a lack of critical questioning. In fact, Huxley's greatest achievement in the memoir may very well be the hybrid critical con-sciousness that emerges from the cross-fertilization of an adult author and her fictional child narrator. By dramatizing herself, the subject, as the object of her exploration, Huxley studies the complex interrelationships and conflicts of historical, social, and cultural matrixes that form colonial experiences and identities. The resulting narrative unsettles any "boundaries around identity" (Smith and Watson 1998, 34). Combining the cultural work of the bil-dungsroman and kunstleroman in the colonial setting, Huxley records the for-mation of colonial identity as the child Elspeth becomes a writer in *The Mottled Lizard,* her second volume of memoirs. Reading her memoirs and other explorations of Africa, we discover that Huxley recounts the emergence of a writing self that is formed by colonial history and that demands a role in shaping it as she searches and fictionalizes the colonial experience for its often antithetical meanings. Even as her writing faces the impossibility of this shap-ing role, she also confronts her readers with the many facets and relationships between her colonial identity and selves—child, adult, African, English, writer.

Unlike those colonial women writers whose identities were formed by wanting to escape their colonial "provincial backwater," such as Phyllis Shand

Allfrey and Jean Rhys in Dominica or Doris Lessing, whose family lived on a poor Rhodesian farm, Elspeth Huxley was encouraged to experience Kenya as exile to Eden (Gardiner 1989, 134). In many ways, not being the Empire's jewel in the crown was indicative of its pleasures; its highland climate was healthier than that of India and if its British settlers didn't prosper economically as well as their Anglo-Indian compatriots, they felt liberated from the social codes which constrained the Raj. Huxley was not "expected to grow up [like those] ladylike participants in white English culture" (Gardiner 1989, 134). Without ayah or nanny, with both parents working their farm, the child roamed quite free, casually home schooled, at first with a governess, but then by her mother with farm catalogues as textbooks. As the adult writer presents her, the child explores and learns about the land and people which have become her new home and neighbors. But instead of being an unselfconscious consumer of the bountiful landscape, she is represented as learning to question the categories of self and Other constructed by her parents and their community. And it is through this questioning that Huxley constructs childhood as a critical position from which to explore the checkered history of British settlement in Kenya.

Paradoxically, this critical position assures Huxley a "secure point of origin" denied to those colonial women writers whose home "demeans women and makes it impossible for them to identify with the mothers they yearn for" (Gardiner 1989, 141). Huxley's mother, Nellie Grant (called Tilly in the memoirs), was a model not only for laboring outside the home, but for exercising independent judgment about their social lives and changing her political beliefs as she confronted historical crises that necessitated change. However this history continued to reshape the race, class, and ethnic divisions besetting this colonial nation, the foundations of colonial ideology are also questioned by the writing that complicated Huxley's colonial identity and narrative self.

In the two years of this first volume of Huxley's three, *The Flame Trees of Thika,* the child is deeply attached to her parents and also in the process of wrestling for her own position in which to ground a constantly shifting sense of individuation. Like so many colonial women characters in my study, she combines that enlightenment concept of individual primacy with the adult's search for meaning and the childhood insouciance presented by the narrator. Neither static nor unstable, this position metamorphoses into the fictional character of the child Elspeth, who defies her colonial imprinting. Instead of incorporating the social and emotional pressures and codes which define her parents' values and language, she questions them. In this way, the fictional Elspeth can be seen as formed out of the "heteroglossia" that, according to Bakhtin, comprises a group's "social dialects" which "intersect with each other in many different ways" (1981, 292). As enacted in the narrative combination of the child Elspeth, her narrator, and her author, these social dialects "may be juxtaposed to one another, mutually supplement one another, contradict one another and be interrelated dialogically" (Bakhtin 1981, 292). For example, the narrator's knowledgeable voice constantly intertwines with the child's process of discovery and learning. This has led some critics to scoff at this as sloppy slippage, but Huxley's narrative strategies simply ask for more precise attention to her designs and distinctions.[17]

One of the most contested passages in *The Flame Trees of Thika* recounts the child's memory of her first encounter with Africa. In addition to its relationships between the child Elspeth, the narrator, Huxley, the author, and the Africa that is constructed among them, the passage should be read in relation to Huxley's critics: ". . . dry, peppery yet rich and deep, with an undertone of native body smeared with fat and red ochre and giving out a ripe, partly rancid odor which nauseated some Europeans when they first encountered it but which I, for one, grew to enjoy. This was the smell of the Kikuyu, who were mainly vegetarian. The smell of tribes . . . [who] were meat-eaters and sometimes cannibals, was quite different: much stronger and more musky, almost acrid, and, to me, much less pleasant. No doubt we smelt just as strong and odd to Africans, but of course we were fewer in numbers, and more spread out" (Huxley 1959, 4). The position of this passage at the very beginning of the memoir serves the purpose of critics who take it as a key to Huxley's lifelong and offensive perception of Africa. Githae-Mugo avers that Huxley's depiction of Africa and its peoples focuses on "their peripheral manifestations rather than with the inner man," and that "defining black people by their "'peculiar' smell" results in "depersonalizing and stereotyping" (1978, 15). This passage also inspires Achebe's sarcastic jibe, "So profound was her expertise about the natives . . . that she could tell their smells apart" (2001, 57).

That Huxley knew there was a problem in articulating her relationship to Africa is not considered by either Githae-Mugo or Achebe. What enables them to ignore her awareness is their omission of the first two and last sentences of the passage above: "One cannot describe a smell because there are no words to do so in the English language, apart from those that place it in a very general category, like sweet or pungent. So I cannot characterize this, nor compare it with any other, but it was the smell of travel in those days, in fact the smell of Africa" (Huxley 1959, 4). Huxley's relationship with Africa begins with one that she negotiates among her different narrative voices and moments. The voice of the present tense generalizes a problem that has become conventional wisdom since the heyday of poststructuralism: the failure of language to effect a transparent correspondence between itself and experience and itself and the objects of its perception. Because the colonial encounter is never fixed in Huxley's African writing, knowledge remains unstable. Huxley's emphasis on the limitations of her own language provides a cultural and narrative critique of this problem. Moving from the position of

Huxley the author in 1959 back through two world wars to arrive at the child Elspeth's first encounter with Africa, she finds herself stalled at a critical juncture. All the intervening years of global and local conflicts and colonial negotiation have led to a crisis of representation. No English language of definition or analysis has evolved to provide a precise lexicon through which the integrity of the African subject can be articulated by the settler: "In reality, it was like living in one world while another co-existed, but the two scarcely ever meshed" (Huxley 1959, 152). The English settler cannot know the alien black African peoples through her own language.

What she can do, however, is construct her remembrance as an analysis of a relationship between her childhood sensory experience and a thwarted adventure of discovery. The result is a representation not of the objects of her adventure or their presence as a mysterious Other, but of how they might possibly have to remain unknown. Therefore, "the smell of Africa" is only apprehended as "the smell of travel in those days," not one that is grounded in any specificity or is definitive and stable. Instead, that sensory experience signifies the disorientation of settlers whose stay is always threatened by their failure to understand the land they call theirs but which never ceases to defy their ownership. Though Huxley was expected to make Kenya her home, the reference to "travel" suggests a displaced process of transition that may never reach solid ground, may never be negotiated successfully or be completed. This is "travel" that, as the history of white settlement dictates, never achieves permanence and, as described by Simon Gikandi, is "no longer motivated by the desire to map unknown territory, to bring unknown spaces under the control of a rational grid; on the contrary, travel seeks to defy cartographical notions such as borders and boundaries and to show how culture can be organized and represented outside the taxonomies we have inherited from modernity" (1996, 184). Both in her parents' African experience and in the way she builds her own adult life, Huxley is always on the move within and to and from Africa. In the modernity created by the crisis of World War I, Tilly decides Thika has become too suburban, and so they set off on another dream of discovering the primordial, a trek to build another farm at Njoro. In ironic contrast to this dream of domesticating unspoilt nature, Elspeth herself is sent off to England to be civilized. Armed with this education, the experience of which has destabilized both her African and British identities, she then spends years traversing Africa searching for ways to understand its peoples, their relationships to their lands, and hers to them. The "smell" of Africa is never identified except as that of "travel." The narrator's consciousness of how the years of education, travel, and writing filter this experience only highlights the distance between the realities of the Kikuyu as they might define them and her ultimate inability to narrate them. Like those other sojourners, Rumer Godden's Sophie, in *Kingfishers Catch Fire,* Muriel Spark's Barbara Vaughan, and Phyllis Bottome's Lucy, Huxley cannot become a mediator of knowledge about the Other. As a permanent outsider, she can only witness her own felt experience and narrate her speculations about the Other in a language that is equally in flux and indeterminate.

That this epistemological distance is a two-way street is made dramatically clear in the last sentence of the paragraph, omitted by her critics: "No doubt we smelt just as strong and odd to Africans, but of course we were fewer in numbers, and more spread out" (Huxley 1959, 4). In its attempts to negotiate the chasm between what colonizer and colonized can know about each other and to grant subjectivity to the Africans, the sentence expresses both bemusement and anxiety. On the one hand, it recognizes that settler knowledge of the Africans is an imaginary and comforting construction. Its final qualification, however, is disquieting, as it exposes the settlers as so isolated from each other and from African peoples that their assumptions of knowledge have no available support.[18] The very ground on which the settler project is to be built is destabilized by the inadequacies of their language to identify with any accuracy the daunting obstacles they will face. That Huxley wants her readers to follow this travel advisory is clear from the first page, when she sets the stage for her family's settler adventure: "We were going to Thika, a name on a map where two rivers joined. . . . If you went on long enough you would come to mountains and forests no one had mapped and tribes whose languages no one could understand. We were not going as far as that, only two days' journey . . . to a bit of El Dorado my father had been fortunate enough to buy in the bar of the Norfolk hotel from a man wearing an Old Etonian tie. (1). The gently mocking voice of the narrator exposes the attempt of the English to negotiate a settlement between the Africa they claim and that of the Africans as absurd from the start.

With no access to the knowledge that would incorporate the natives' system of mapping, the English settlers rely on a foundational myth of colonial conquest—"El Dorado." The fact that after four hundred years colonial exploration could not translate the mythic gold mine into reality becomes a welcome rhetorical opportunity for Huxley. In this passage, she creates another distance, one that offers her narrator's voice as a critical gloss on her family's adventure. The mythic knowledge which guides their settlement cannot span the epistemological or political distance between the colonized land and peoples and the colonizer. Fixed outside its actual history, the mythic knowledge of Western imperialism bears no connection to the experiences of either the settlers or the natives. The unchanging status of myth paradoxically produces unsettling results not only because the story of "El Dorado" can't serve as a map or guide, but because there are no lessons to be learned from it. Failing as a foundational myth, it offers no models of sanctioned or transgressive behavior. We see this forecast in the narrator's use of "fortunate," a wry comment on Robin Grant's abiding trust in providence as an old boy's entitlement. Ritual-

9. Hayley Mills as Tilly in TV adaptation of *Flame Trees of Thika*. Courtesy Fremantle Media.

ized as a heroic quest, this entitlement is ennobled by the association we can't ignore of Robin's name with his legendary medieval namesake. As it plays out, however, the entitlement materializes neither as grail nor gold, but as a self-mocking, mythic imperial talisman—"an old Etonian tie." In its class-bound allegiances, the settlers' trust reflects and reinforces the self-enclosed and code-pendent relationship between the "gentlemanly" great illusions of the British settler and the "gentlemanly" great game of the land agents (Kennedy 1997, 92).[19] Huxley's gentle humor could easily be read as complying with the nostalgia of which her memoirs have been accused. From the vantage point of 1959, in the aftermath of World War II's catastrophic losses, the Mau Mau uprisings, and the beginning of the end of colonial Kenya, the naivete of her father's colonial adventure could be seen as his sentimental if liberal trust in humanity, an outlook that would extend to his relations with his native laborers.[20]

Certainly this nostalgic trust along with all the other criticisms of Huxley's memoirs is dramatically apparent in the 1981 TV miniseries based on *Flame Trees*. Although the plot lines remain quite faithful, the series has no critical voice intervening in its representation of colonial settlement, which resembles a makeup session for a Ralph Lauren safari. This airbrushed romance is fortified by the promise on the video box that "the creator of *Upstairs, Downstairs* has lavishly brought to life that magical but vanished world which long ago captured a little girl's heart." Indeed, the central consciousness, if that term

10. Nellie, Jos, and Elspeth at new house, Kitimuru, in 1922. Courtesy Heather James.

is even applicable to this rendition, is that of a girl of eleven, whose charm, clearly inherited from her parents, is unrelieved by any of the challenges or pitfalls Huxley records in her memoirs. Over four tapes and about eight hours of viewing, the sense of a timeless Edwardian Eden prevails. Poses rather than action feature Hayley Mills as Tilly, adorned in immaculate white lace, gazing with Robin over a landscape whose horizon is transformed into their boundless entitlement by a gesture of noblesse. As they lift their manicured hands to shield their eyes from the savage sun, what is revealed as dangerous are the consequences of their own willful blindness and inertia. Their exploitation of native labor and imposition of a British economy will never allow them to learn the self-sustaining ecology of the Africans. Such tableaux of denial are in complete contrast to Huxley's memoirs, where photos show her mother to be a New Woman of her time, defying conventional categories by dressing in jodhpurs, man's hat, shirt, and tie, with her hard work visible in sturdy, mud-covered boots. In the miniseries, whatever dangers the Grants encounter are identified by the ever wise but always wry and beautifully coifed Tilly and confronted and defeated by the stalwart if occasionally stuffy Robin.

    With its relentless pursuit of charming triumph over quaint adversity and with its Madison Avenue Edwardiana, the TV series disguises the specific cultural boundaries of settler experiences. In all its gentility and geniality, this family-hour series aggressively disavows the political clash of cultures between the English and the black Africans as well as their material and symbolic exchanges. Whether the producers were aware of the postcolonial critiques of the memoirs is unknown, but the seamless concordance between their fantasied celebration of Huxley and the critics' accusation of her engaging in fantasy is ironic. Though their goals are different, both filmmakers and critics stereotype Huxley's subjects and writing by interpreting them as a colonial project camouflaging itself in romantic garb. In so doing, both the critical and dramatic interpretations of Huxley disguise the historical and narrative complexities of her writing. Both versions have magically made Huxley's own world vanish.

Throughout her memoirs, despite her persistent efforts to distinguish her family from other settlers, despite her parents' equation "of freedom and space" with an unpopulated Africa, Huxley insists that nostalgia is part of the romantic and therefore dangerous unreality of mythic thinking (Huxley 1981b, 12). She fully recognizes that their imagined Edenic "garden" validates the settlers' "craving for the wilder places of the earth" as "genuine" and allows them to exploit their "bright jewels" (Huxley 1959, 6, 7). But even though Tilly repudiates this mythic thinking, the narrator expresses doubt. However intrepid, this pioneer woman could not have survived fifty years of struggling against a resistant land without the "guilty secret" of her own romantic myth (Huxley 1959, 7).[21] Whether she's importing English chickens or planting in English-style rows, Tilly's farm represents her hopeful hybridity, grafting an English garden onto the African landscape. But as Huxley presents her mother's efforts, it is clear that the native soil, climate, and wildlife will resist, producing disasters we call natural, but that metaphorically insist on Africa's own indigenous nature and ecology. This is a critique that struggles to distinguish the narrator's perspective from Tilly's, but cannot help implicating itself. While all of Huxley's writing searches for the benefits of white settlement, her parents' romantic goals become an extension of her own wishful thinking. Their vague goal of "building up the country" is repeated so often in Huxley's writing, but she cannot prod "an absurd, romantic and outdated dream" into reality, as she later acknowledges (Huxley 1987, 84).

The well-intended missions of the Grants are undercut by Huxley's narrative heteroglossia of different colonial voices, goals, frustrations, and disappointments as well as her characters' articulated contradictions and inconsistencies. In some cases, these differences between and within characters occur simultaneously, and so create an internally critical narrative weave. For example, the self-dramatizing character of the Grants' friend, femme fatale Lettice Palmer, clearly designed as a critical foil for Tilly, shows how a colonial critique of the colonized cannot conceal its debt to the romance of imperial superiority. Hence, Lettice projects her own inability to "resist" temptations onto her vision of Kenya, which she characterizes as "sloth," as "doing no more than is necessary to exist" (Huxley 1959, 62). The critical foil, however, comes undone when Tilly's respect for African customs is articulated as only a more energetic form of Lettice's colonial arrogance: "It's true the natives have done nothing yet with the country, but we shall" (63). Tilly's disapproval of the genteel sensitivities, pampered indolence, and fanciful ideas of her friend is thus mocked by her own inability to recognize self-indulgent futility and the conventionally Christian mission of her own dogged pursuits.

Readers could easily question whether such satire is inadvertent, unintended, and therefore a mockery of Huxley's ability to confront her own roseate vision. The answer, I believe, is far more self-consciously self-critical than her critics would allow. Huxley's colonial critique invites other networks of characters to comment on her representation of her parents' benign settlement. The most visible is the juxtaposition of Hereward Palmer, Lettice's husband, to Robin Grant and the Boer, Mr. Roos, especially in their relationships with their black laborers. Palmer's pride in his military training and bearing, which verges on caricature, extends to his plan "to create a healthy spirit of inter-squad rivalry" for his black workers (Huxley 1959, 59, 104). Tripped up by Kikuyu social norms and his ignorance of them, Palmer's posturing and defensive anger are exposed as "ludicrous" as he sputters, "'Not one [Kikuyu] has an inkling of the meaning of discipline! . . . I suppose I must just go on trying to knock it into them'" (104). Palmer's temper tantrums are effective only as they expose the dark side of a Colonel Blimp. Their contrast with Mr. Roos's Boerish, un-Etonian diction spotlights the brutal implications of the white supremacist mission, whether it is exposed by the verbal threats of an officer gentleman or by the Boer's beatings of his "stuck-up nigger[s]" (45). If the uncouth Roos represents a brutish masculinity, neither British officer nor gentleman, Palmer's masculinity is called into question by his spotless and starched military poses, suggesting an ornamental delicacy redolent of the feminine. But when orders aren't followed, the gentleman settler morphs into the savagery that feminized good manners cannot tame.

In contrast to Roos and Palmer, Huxley establishes Robin and Tilly as benevolent and respectful employers of their black labor. The Grants "spoke to their foreman, Sammy, as they would speak to a fellow European. In return, Sammy gave them his complete loyalty" (Huxley 1959, 44). The "feudal relationship" Huxley imputes to "African society," however, turns out to reflect the Grants' own relation to Africa (Huxley 1959, 44).[22] When Roos brings charges against Sammy, Robin defends his foreman because he needs his labor, not because he feels a reciprocal loyalty. It turns out that Robin's defense of his black worker is a sign of the "British feudal spirit that prompted them to protect their own men against, as it were, rival barons" (46). In this fantasy of medieval jousting, Huxley exposes the reality that black workers are the pawns in the project of creating a modern, industrialized system of cheap labor. They are also signs of settler "prestige," a term that, as Kennedy points out, recurs throughout settler writing to denote white security and "status maintenance" and is expressed primarily as "an aloof and inscrutable manner, unexpressive of doubts and undemonstrative of affections" (1997, 153, 154).

Huxley's memoir does not remain indifferent to this subjugation of black Africans. Along side the representation of Roos's, Palmer's, and her parents' more subtle exploitations, the narrator's voice, the child Elspeth's conscious-ness, and various black African voices intervene. In dialogue with the narrator, these Other Africans respond and resist their enforced labor and their repre-sentation by the narrative structure. Their presence denounces any naturaliz-ing view of the settlers' encounter with their new land or that its "savage country" is a sign of the black Africans' character (Huxley 1959, 117). More-over, instead of representing the benefits of British hybridizing and civilizing influences, the work of black Africans on white settlements illustrates their coercion as they struggle to maintain the integrity of their own cultural prac-tices. Entering this fray, Huxley stages the relationship between white settlers and their black laborers as an enforced end to the settlers' adventure of ruggedly isolated individualism. Neither white European settler culture nor black African culture can be defined except in relation to each other. Most importantly, this relation belies any sense or possibility of hybridity in that each remains radically separate.

The central episode in which the two cultures clash and are redefined involves the interrelationship between colonial domination and an inter-necine African rivalry: that between two of the Grants' black African workers, the Masai Sammy and Kikuyu Njombo, and that between the exercise of jus-tice by the British and by the Kikuyu. Despite their mutual enmity and his role in Njombo's near demise, it is the Masai who presents the story of the Kikuyu Njombo to Elspeth with judicial detachment. Sammy's narrative of Njombo's murder of another black African is only partial, however, as it erases his own guilt. He has put a curse on Njombo, who then begins to wither away toward certain death. Not only does this story originate within the system of Kikuyu justice, but its intricate plot of intertwined revenge and violence results in redefining colonial relations. Despite British appeals and threats to the Kikuyu chief elder, despite investigation by the district commissioner's office, British law becomes irrelevant as an instrument of truth and justice. As this Kikuyu story roams over a hundred pages of *Flame Trees,* it not only frus-trates the expected progress of British narrative detection and empiricist pol-itics, but dispenses with the rhetoric of self-justifying colonial intervention. As yet unaware that their judicial logic and order will be resisted, the settlers are given a scene in which they have a chance to express a range of colonial goals, all of which are undermined by the narrative shadow of Kikuyu resistance. Tilly's problematic defense of the stalwart British presence is a case in point:

"We may have a sticky passage ourselves, but when we've knocked a bit of civ-ilization into them, all this dirt and disease and superstition will go and they'll live like decent people for the first time in their history" (Huxley 1959, 117–118).

As though plotting an insurrectionist movement, a narrative fifth column, within its own structure, the entire memoir is infiltrated by the narrative of Kikuyu traditions of decency. And rather than allowing us to see this dual structure as an arrangement of coexistence or the construction of a hybrid form, the Kikuyu story surrounds and threatens the self-justifying rhetoric of the colonial mission. That this threat does not abate over time is evident in *The Mottled Lizard,* Huxley's second memoir, where a Kikuyu is accused of killing a forest-dwelling Dorobo. Here Tilly's critical sensitivities are tested by the Kikuyu as she questions them in order to construct a detective story that is coherent and satisfactory to both English and Kikuyu judicial logic. Whether this is another romantic myth, whether Tilly can effect a cultural détente by "being a European" but trying to think like a Kikuyu is a crucial question for Huxley's African writing (Huxley 1981b, 321). This question is also played out in her 1937 novel, *Murder at Government House,* where an anthropologist tells the chief detective, "In many ways . . . the functions of a detective in our soci-ety resemble those of a witchdoctor among native tribes. The witchdoctor's job, like the detective's, is to hunt down the enemies of society and prevent them from doing further harm" (Huxley 1989a, 78).

All of Huxley's writing about the Kikuyu dramatizes their system of jus-tice as integrating values and procedures that parallel the British system and ideology while opposing them. In addition to the operative features of prece-dent, forensic investigation, and evidential corroboration, Kikuyu civil and criminal justice is about individual and collective responsibility. Huxley con-tinually, throughout her writing, dramatizes the complexity of Kikuyu com-munity relations as a legal system that weaves traditional beliefs and justice through the social and economic practices of courtship, marriage, and family life. Through this kaleidoscopic perspective, the Kikuyu people emerge indi-vidually and collectively, and not as the undifferentiated mass colonial writers have been accused of representing. The life of the community that Huxley represents forms a cycle whereby the structure of rituals gives coherence and meaning to the vicissitudes of climate, disease, and warfare and enhances the meanings of work and human relationships. As she concludes in her third vol-ume, *Out in the Midday Sun,* "In Europe, we believe that the individual, if of sound mind, is responsible for his actions and that, if he breaks the law, he must be punished. Under tribal law the community and not the individual was held responsible for the misdemeanors of any of its members: and recompense to the victim's family, not punishment of the offender, was the usual aim" (1987, 143–144). In her ethnographic novel, *Red Strangers,* these Kikuyu relationships and meanings become a critique of British colonial justice; according to a Kikuyu leader, the British system defies and betrays its own judicial logic. After manipulating Kikuyu witnesses to implicate themselves in a murder they did not commit, it becomes clear that British colonial justice is designed to render the African powerless. The language of the British interrogation and that of an interpreter who is inept in both English and in Kikuyu create enough confusion to entrap the Kikuyu defendants. A Kikuyu leader provides the dissenting critique: "Now I understand how these strangers have become so exceedingly rich; when they sit in judgment they award nothing to the injured person, but everything to themselves" (Huxley 1939, 202).

Flame Trees recalls the self-inquiring narrator of *Red Strangers*. Every defensive effort by the Grants and the Palmers only calls attention to the self-deception embedded in their supremacist beliefs. As the competition between the Africans' story and that of the settlers gains momentum, Robin's paternalism loses the expressive logic of its professed benevolence. Instead, as it articulates the desperation of a losing battle, the "dreamy and benign" language of colonialism is shown to be a lethal weapon (Huxley 1959, 141). Huxley's critical narrator reveals how, in appealing to Sammy, Robin "could show two absolutely different sides of his nature, and yet both were the same": "You are behaving not like a man who can read, but like a savage," Robin accuses Sammy (142). The literacy and language of British culture, designed to demonstrate how black Africans need "a bit of civilization . . . knocked into them," backfires, like a badly designed defense, to expose its underlying brutal hypocrisy. That Huxley wants readers to know that the Africans get this double message loud and clear is made evident in Sammy's impassive resistance to it: "'I do not understand what you are saying,' Sammy stubbornly replied" (12).[23]

Huxley's representation of the Kikuyu encounter with Europeans romanticizes neither. In the first encounters, the stranger "with his warriors" is seen by the Kikuyu to possess powers that may be causing the drought that occurs at this time (Huxley 1939, 154). But then as always, Huxley's narrator assures us of the Kikuyu's "skepticism," a mark of Kikuyu empiricism that contests the British, in effect, casting doubt on British intellectual and cultural superiority (154). Coupled with irony, this doubt challenges both British belief in rugged individualism and privileged status in the pantheon of the righteous: "It was hard to believe that any individual could possess so powerful a magic as to influence rain, which was sent or withheld according to the will of God" (154). The empirical constitution of Kikuyu culture also enables its people to persevere toward disarming a destructive force that rivals British guns—the pestilence they carry within them: smallpox. Although the Kikuyu begin by imputing this disaster to "divine wrath," they soon yield to the powers of observation: "it was the continued presence in the country of a stranger of

unclean habits and evil intentions towards the Kikuyu people" (155). Through
trial and error, the Kikuyu then develop a preventative treatment that we can
only call a vaccine. With the consent of those few who recover, the medicine
man mixes a combination of "withered pustules," herbal remedies, and blood
to rub into cuts in the arms of "those who had not yet been attacked" (157).[24]

If scientific history confirms that it was the white settlers who carried
deadly infectious diseases, their scientific myths prevail nonetheless. Not, however, among the Kikuyu. The empirical evidence on which scientific history is
based can't debunk European myths about an inherently diseased Africa and
its indigenous black Africans. Nowhere is this more graphically displayed than
in the names imperial medicine actually awarded to the diseases of their conquered lands: "Congo Red Fever. Rift Valley Fever. Mozambique Ulcer.
Guinea Worm Infection. Congo Floor Maggot. West African Relapsing Fever.
Bullinus Africanus" (Boxwell 2002, 10).[25] As David Boxwell shows, such diseases were formulated by imperial scientists such as Sir Patrick Manson, co-
founder of the London School of Tropical Medicine in 1899, representing an
etiology that "speak[s] tomes about the persistent tendency to pathologize the
Other" (2002, 3). Names of diseases, like "Creeping Eruption," are infused
with the creepy feeling that they cross over from tropical climates to the
natives who then embody and threaten to contaminate the Europeans with
their oozing and elephantine turgescences (Boxwell 2002, 3). Although this
threat has been explored widely by historians and critics, their studies generally leave the Europeans in sufficient denial about their own diseased bodies to
focus only on their victims. In contrast, Huxley's writing shows that European
settlement in Africa is a misadventure, and its imminent bitter end represents
the wages of their "sin." The Grants' perseverance, adaptation, and good
humor can thus be seen as representing a defense against external signs of
foreboding about the European mission. For if Africa is diseased and deadly
contagious, as Huxley demonstrates in *The African Poison Mystery,* the colonial
project may suffer from its own incurable congenital disorder.

As Huxley weaves a Kikuyu plot into the colonial memoir, the combination clarifies how this disorder derives from the settlers who don't understand
the Africans' message of resistance. What the Grants begin to recognize, however, is that if they are to make an African life for themselves, they must question the logic of their own resistance to the wisdom of Kikuyu cultural
organization. The tension between their resistance and recognition is expressed in that time-honored language of Kipling's homage to the British
Empire, the Great Game: "Robin grumbled . . . and here we are playing their
game, instead of bundling the whole lot of them in to the D.C. and letting him
knock some sense into their heads" (Huxley 1959, 152). Representing British
physical, cultural, and political presence is this language of the "game," which
associates British colonialism with advancing and celebrating the superiority

of British culture with good sportsmanship, a significant component of which is good humor. Its goodness, however, derives from a brand of self-deprecation that actually registers self-appreciation while targeting any Other as the butt of the joke. British good humor trivializes Kikuyu cultural practices by reducing the possibility of serious political relationships to a running joke. But Robin's grudging reference to "their game" reveals that the joke may have run its course. He exposes the humor embedded in the British game not as an effective offensive maneuver, but as a feeble defense against the romantic myths of British cultural hegemony it supports. Huxley debunks such myths again by replaying the game metaphor in *Red Strangers*. Describing "the game giuthi," she comments that the game "involves such complicated feats of mental arithmetic that few Europeans can play it" (1939, 181). As these Kikuyu narratives refuse to accept defeat according to the rules of the British game, British sportsmanship and humor reveal their nostalgia for the boy's adventure story, the ending of which signifies a victorious passage into manhood and a well-earned colonial victory.

The genteel snigger which identifies upper-class British social culture and which defines so much of the dialogue of Huxley's British settler community is ultimately mocked by Africa's refusal to get the joke. As the Kikuyu narrative insinuates itself persistently, the ironic vision inscribed in British humor is forced to yield to the seriousness of Kikuyu cultural identity. When Njombo recovers from his mysterious ailment after a visit by Sammy, his Masai rival, the Grants recite a mantra of Western empirical disbelief, but that skepticism also constitutes a reluctant new vision of colonial relations: "We have no proof it was Sammy. . . . In fact proof itself seems to be an exotic, like those poor little oak trees we planted" (Huxley 1959, 153). The metaphorical association between the sanctity of empirical evidence and the fragility of its product testing offers narrative recognition that the British, not the black Africans, are the "exotic" Others. Like the inhabitants of Phyllis Shand Allfrey's *Orchid House,* the white settlers are hothouse transplants who are doomed to wither in the resistant soil of Africa. Indeed, as Huxley's critics have complained, in its representation of an all-encompassing environment, her memoir depicts a "cruel world" where human agency is given little credit (Sander 1976, 35). Her plotting of natural and manmade crises is seen as creating "a squalor" out of "the human world," despite the recognition that Huxley's representation of Kenya's landscape accurately and poetically reflects its beauty (Githae-Mugo 1978, 47). This depiction is questioned, however, by Huxley's assignment of responsibility. As her representation of Kikuyu justice shows, rather than mystifying human or natural violence, she interprets the responsibility for tragedy as needing to be shared among different opposing agents, including different African peoples, the British and their European antagonists, and British gender relationships.

Though Huxley wrote two later volumes of her African memoirs, the end of *The Flame Trees of Thika* portends the end of the great British game in Africa when World War I breaks out. This war, which transported the British men from their farms into battle, is viewed by them as a validation of both adventures. Sent off to defend the Empire, the retired officers, Robin and Hereward, embody the ideology that made war and colonial service the training camp for each other. As the men disappear into battle, the failure of their training is announced through the women's experience. Fought offstage, the Great War is experienced by the women as a memorial service for the great colonial game. After two years of demonstrating that she is a more successful adventurer than many of the white men, Tilly is forced back into a traditional feminine role when war breaks out. Though this takes place at the end of *Flame Trees,* Tilly's retreat reverberates back throughout the memoir, raising critical questions about the construction of her gallant character. Despite the memoir's critique of colonial romanticism, has Tilly's character been a function of Huxley's own romantic myth? *The Mottled Lizard* both mystifies Tilly's character and questions her own critical intelligence: "She sometimes brought a sixth sense to bear upon events and characters, and had a way of leaping over logic and appearances into the hidden heart of an affair" (Huxley 1981b, 316). Has Tilly's resourcefulness and critical good humor, both of which distinguish her from the men's romantic escapades and dreams, been a cosmetic touch-up for a more recalcitrant feminine stereotype and female dependency?

When the men go off to war, Tilly and Elspeth, along with other English-women, cannot stay behind because of the threat of German attack. Even within this historical context, however, and even with their eventual return (which drives the plot of *The Mottled Lizard*), the narrative ending of *Flame Trees* suggests a foreboding that haunts the restoration of their colonial settlement. As the women are packing up, Lettice assesses her response to Africa, and while this could easily be taken as a sign of her chronic fragility, it also provides a critical gloss on the whole settler experience: "It is a cruel country that will take the heart out of your breast and grind it into powder, powdered stone. And no one will mind, that is the worst of it. No one will mind" (Huxley 1959, 264). Once again, the indifferent heart of Africa's darkness besieges the white colonizer. But whatever mysterious powers are imputed to Africa find their catalyst in the mythic pantheons of the Great War and of colonial romance.

What is ground "into powder" at the end of *Flame Trees* is the heart of war, a bullet that strikes the heart of colonial romance. Lettice's inamorato, Ian Crawfurd, who represents an illicit escape, not only for her but perhaps for readers, from Hereward Palmer's straitlaced devotion, is killed in battle at the very beginning of the war. His disappearance into the offstage mists of war suggests the evaporation of an eroticized colonial dream of conquering and possessing the object that teases desire by remaining beyond its reach. Rather than continue her membership in the society of stalwart but deluded settlers, Lettice, too, drifts out of their narrative never to be seen or heard from again, in any of Huxley's three additional volumes of fictionalized memoirs. Fractured by the war, the foundations of colonial settlement cannot be repaired, despite succeeding narrative attempts. The violence that invades Huxley's Kenya with the Great War marks the beginning of the end of a myth whose center cannot hold the promises of both stability and trespass. That the colonial adventure should join forces with a European war foretells its destructive end. In addition, Huxley's retrospective narrative argues that it was violence on which the colonial adventure was founded. But if the British cannot recognize this irredeemable flaw in their colonial foundation, Huxley makes sure we know that the Kikuyu can. And so in her 1939 novel, *Red Strangers,* the Kikuyu assess the object of European warfare, "killing their enemy," as having "brought no advantage at all" (Huxley 1939, 270). The appearance of European warfare in Huxley's writing is only the external sign of the African-born violence that will finally bring an end to British colonization. In 1959, when *Flame Trees* was published, the Mau Mau uprising had evolved into negotiations for Kenya's independence. Despite Huxley's continued efforts to elegize and question her family's colonizing presence, she writes its demise into the ending of this memoir. She thus sets the innocence of childhood exploration against the questionable guardianship of the settlement project.

Lettice, the romantic heroine, plays a pivotal role in this questioning. It is she, in fact, in opposition to Tilly's censure, who encourages Elspeth "to be a private detective," to "sit quite still and pretend not to be looking," so that "all the little facts will come and peck round your feet, situations will venture forth from thickets and intentions will creep out and sun themselves on a stone; and if you are very patient, you will see and understand a great deal more than a man with a gun" (Huxley 1959, 264). What looks like stage directions for a coquettish performance are actually translated by Huxley into the hermeneutic that drives all her writing about Africa—the search for meaning in the British colonial mission in Africa—that in the end may have no meaning.

COLONIAL MURDER MYSTERIES

Nowhere does this detection and failure of meaning become more starkly related to the psychological isolation of settler experience than in one of Huxley's early works, the 1939 *African Poison Murders*. This mystery thriller telegraphs the doubts raised by *Flame Trees*. The date of the novel is especially significant in relation to African history, for while the coming disorientation of World War II is played as background, as a subplot, it also highlights the dangers of the settler community isolating itself not only from their black neighbors, but from the geopolitical concerns that marked the continuum from the

Great War. As an implied commentary on colonial relations, the novel forges a connection to the world the settlers have come to escape. The novel's original title, *Death of an Aryan,* refers to the first murder victim, a German farmer and Bundist leader whose death is a kind of poetic justice for his heinous politics.[26] But in a plot move that would seem to distract from either the coming Second World War or ongoing colonial tensions, the murder turns out to be psychologically motivated and the murderer is a deranged and apolitical Englishwoman. Despite the narrative move to isolate and individualize motivation for the crime, it charts a connection between the noncontagious mental disease of the murderer and the isolationist antisocial disturbance of her victim. The premeditated crime that brings them together and the investigation that follows confirm the fact that both the Nazi and the sexually repressed spinster are outsiders in the White Highlands. Though the Nazi is condemned for his suspicious politics, the spinster is marginalized for her lack of social status. By the late 1930s, the sexually free-wheeling society of "the once notorious Happy Valley" has sublimated the aftershocks of the First World War, economic depression, and sexual violence into a rigidly gendered social hierarchy, where the only role for the impoverished single woman, a governess whose lessons are barely relevant, occupies a rung only slightly above black enforced labor (Huxley 1964, 112). In her tattered hand-me-down dresses, denied even the uniform of the self-sufficient settler woman, the spinster is also stripped of her racial identity as the embodiment of white European pride. Not even an Other, she is no woman, a nonperson.

Connecting the spinster's individual but complicated psychology with that of the settler community, the solution to the murder mystery shows her to have internalized her unbelonging as a self so isolated as to produce madness. And while she can be explained away as deviant in the community, the novel suggests that she is merely representative of its self-willed and unsettling isolation. The fact that she works for the German links them as undesirables who represent not only doubly lethal agents but, in their marginalization, a radical projection and even scapegoating of the community's destructiveness. Thus condemnation of the German as cruel to his native workers is contextually associated with the brutalities being committed by the German nation at this very time. By contrast, the British community can indulge in a self-deceiving self-pity for the scant rewards of being so indulgent of their laborers and Others. Ironically, the condemnation of the German connects him to the spinster, for, as it implicates his Nazi racism, it deracinates her. If the Nazi is recognized as an external threat to the Empire, the mental dementia of the Englishwoman is a shock to its system. She is an internal threat, registering, in her social and economic isolation, the Empire's lack of racial and gendered self-confidence at this historical juncture. After all, this is the very moment when Britain is forced to defend itself against Nazi racial conquest, and so

Huxley's murder thriller reminds us of the racialist and sexist underpinnings of her own Empire. The political and psychological alienation of the German and the spinster are thus connected to the way the community lives on the anxious edge of its own legitimacy and ecology.

As the investigation veers between the Nazi threat and the more mysterious instability of the settler community, the novel warns that as World War II approaches, the colonial project is threatened by its own disordered logic. As a slightly dotty scientist tells the chief inspector, "Being faced with an insoluble problem, that's what sends [lab rats] crazy. Well, I guess there are insoluble problems here too, but you don't go crazy trying to figure them out, you just leave them over till next week" (Huxley 1988, 27). Where "next week" in 1914 could lead from Huxley's first to her second volume of memoirs, "next week" in 1939 turns out to be too late for the settlers, portending the end of their story. The coming threat of the Second World War signals the end of the settlers' self-righteous withdrawal from both the well-being of their African neighbors and laborers and the outside world they fled. The erasure of the needs of black Africans and the exploitation of their labor is a telling sign of colonial isolationism. The thoughts of the natives remain a mystery in this novel only to the settler community. In her articulation of a "barrier" that isolates the thinking of settlers from the needs of "Natives," Huxley is inviting her readers to recognize the survival strategy of the latter (33). That this would include a disengagement from the self-destructive community the settlers have built for themselves suggests a "blank" space which represents safety and the agency with which the natives think for themselves alone (33).

Through the genre of a murder melodrama, Huxley exposes the very relationship many settlers chose to ignore: the connection between their colonial relations with native Africans and their relations in the global context. That "investigations in Africa often . . . run into a blind alley," that Africa itself is experienced by Europeans with "an indefinable feeling of menace, of unexplained queer happenings" reflects a horror originating not in the imagined object of fear but in the colonizing self (Huxley 1988, 32, 40). As the "menace" materializes, it turns out to have less to do with Africa or Africans than with those settlers from whom such fears emanate. Huxley invites us to see the horrors of darkest Africa manifesting themselves as the weapon deployed by settler derangement: the murderous English spinster who has expropriated a poison used by African natives for "the legitimate purpose of hunting" (85). In its delegitimized form, the poison "paralyze[s] the nerves that control the muscles of the [human] heart," an action that reflects the poisonous nature of the colonizing imperative (85). The discovery that the murderer is both one of their own and one who reflects their self-defeating strategies to create self-protective boundaries is presented in the novel as a reality test of the colonial adventure. When it is discovered that both their fears and construction of darkest Africa lie within the white settlements, it "furnished proof that" the "nightmare" was of their own making, "and quelled, in doing so, a little of the brilliance of the sun" (104). It may very well be that in order to dramatize this self-made "nightmare" and its relation to the horrors promised by the Nazi Empire, this detective mystery had to exclude the satire and comic elements that shape Huxley's earlier *Murder at Government House* (1937) and *Murder on Safari* (1938).

The menacing mystery of Africa as embodied in the murder of a Nazi Bundist by a maniacal English spinster signals the beginning of Huxley's investigation into the geopolitics in which colonialism was implicated. This is the relationship between the instability of the colonial project and the fascist racialist ideology the British Empire would oppose: "Things that had long been hidden, festering in the dark, were bursting out, like pus from a rotten sore too long bandaged up. Once the boil had burst there was no retreat. The evil had to come out; but who would be corrupted by its poison none could say" (Huxley 1988, 120). The sensationalist language here, typical of detective melodrama, coincides with the novel's climax, where the detective falls into a deadly trap. But the metaphors of disease and entrapment also expose colonial terror, for they call attention to the trapped thinking that prevents the settlers from recognizing their own project as corrosive. As the settlers' local mystery is solved, what remains is the global denial of the murderous instincts of any colonial occupation. Throughout the range of Huxley's work, we find that every romantic gesture of reconciliation and resolution is undermined by her situating it in a context relating the racism of colonialism to the violence of war.

THE WALLED CITY:
WORLD WAR II AND THE END OF EMPIRE

Huxley's novel *The Walled City* was first published in 1948. But by setting it in 1942 and moving backwards to the 1920s, Huxley demonstrates that just as colonialism was threatened and also thrived in the wake of one world war, it was shaken to its roots by the fascist blitzkrieg. These intertwined events transform the colonial narrative from a timeless parable of dark forces and victimization into a historical critique of what we mean by the ending of Empire, the postcolonial, and the construction of a different modern moment. The connection between World War II and the end of Empire that Huxley had presaged in *The African Poison Murders* echoes at the very beginning of *The Walled City* from the deeply insulated walls of London's St. James Club: "It was not pleasant to sit by and watch an empire to which your life had been devoted coming to pieces in front of your eyes" (Huxley 1948b, v). The expression of such imperial devotion is so easily mocked, not only as the self-deceived bombast of a Colonel Blimp (imagine Hereward Palmer thirty years older), but as the delusion of the colonial novelist who thinks she can interrogate the imperial project while clinging to it. The placement of this statement, like so many of Huxley's, on the narrative's first page, suggests a more self-conscious confrontation.

As this presence of World War II haunts the novel's flashbacks to the 1920s, it serves as a critical checkpoint for the self-deceit of colonial characters and as a guide for our reading the postcolonial. The novel's intricate moves between 1942 and 1919 and then throughout the 1920s present an empire deluded about its staying power while besieged from inside and out. Composed in 1947, from the perspective of Allied victory, this novel, like Olivia Manning's *Levant Trilogy,* looks back at the 1942 German invasion of Africa as prefiguring the end of the Empire. And just as Huxley interjects fascist aggression as a gloss on the character and fate of Empire, so she introduces several voices, including two opposing colonial administrators, two very different colonial women, and the character that has earned hostile criticism for the novel, a colonized native rebel. It is in concert that these dissonant voices question the viability of a white colonial woman writing from a position that has been called complicit with imperialism or, even more demeaning, its dupe.

Instead of this political cartoon, however, Huxley offers an equal opportunity for self-deceived, self-serving, and "incompatible" power (Huxley 1948b, 16). On the one hand, colonial officers of the British Empire are shown to serve their "distant masters," an interweave of London's Colonial Office and the ideology that binds them all to their mission—"white supremacy" (15). Whether the novel is guilty of adhering to this ideology is tested in several different narrative strands. In part 1, set in 1929, we are presented with the perspective that supports racialist ideology through absolute belief in the Empire's "meticulous honesty," the trust in which is expressed as contrasting its "integrity" with the "ancient" and therefore intractable corruption of the local native culture (15). Articulating this judgment is Freddy Begg, a colonial officer who plans to realize his ambitions and responsibilities through a new policy that will show "respect" for "native laws and custom" (16). The definition of "native" here is instructive, for it creates a slippage between the Moslem Emir who holds the seat of local power and those Africans in his domain who are of different ethnicities and cultures and are denied power. Begg's policy, which elides the will of these African Others, recognizes that of the Emir while making the latter an agent of British colonialism. Authorizing the local power to collect taxes is nothing short of a boon for the colonial administration while reinforcing the allegiance of the Emir, for the policy makes "it appear as if these innovations had their source in [his] authority" (16). This layering of colonial and local authority is seen as hybrid by Robert J. C. Young in so far as it works "through the exploitation by the colonized themselves," manipulating their ambivalences and "contradictions" that are exposed by the confusing codes of colonial governance (1995, 161–162).

Huxley's approach to a colonial balance of power is revealed in her subtle narrative use of indirect free discourse, a rhetorical strategy that can melt the boundaries among the characters and narrator. That Freddy's policy manipulates the local power of the ruling Emir is assessed by the narrator but attributed indirectly to Freddy as being "skillfully masked" (Huxley 1948b, 16). Whether Freddy approves of such a stratagem and therefore inadvertently exposes his own pragmatic politics and that of the Empire as hypocrisy is complicated further by the pragmatism of the Emir, who recognizes the usefulness of such "subterfuge" for wielding his own power (16). As the narrative weaves this relationship into the competing self-interests of local and distant masters, what emerges is a discourse that extends to the reader. The unarticulated but manipulative interplay between the Emir and the British is made public; it becomes an open secret that we share with Huxley as an exposé of the mutually self-deceived colonial relationship that leads to its defeat. In this way, readers are asked to join Huxley in her investigation of the ethical parameters of the final struggles to maintain the Empire. As the novel dramatizes both a clash and complicity between the indigenous ruling polity and imperial domination, it questions the very foundational assumption that the sine qua non of oppressive imperial power was only European, and whatever Other political power resided in the colonized nation was its subaltern. That this novel is set in Nigeria is particularly to the point, for, unlike Kenya, where the increased expropriation of land led to the Kikuyu rebellion, Nigeria did not suffer white settlement and independence was achieved peacefully. Highlighted by this dual absence is the Emir, who, interestingly enough, as a Muslim ruler, is absent from much postcolonial theory but is a key player in *The Walled City*. This local ruler has a fair share in what Huxley identifies as oppressive practices, including a long, precolonial history of "slavery and extortion," mostly involving indigenous blacks (22). Of course, the Emir's presence could easily be interpreted as Huxley's rationalization of imperial indirect rule. On the other hand, it may be one of her more acute insights that there is agency in the very decision to be manipulated and thus to stabilize one's power.

As it works through Freddy's consciousness, the progressive disorder of imperial rationalization is expressed in the prologue, set in 1942, at the zenith of his powers and at a decisive moment in the global struggle against fascist racism. Freddy views his political policies in the light of how his arch rival, Robert Gresham, would have decided the fate of the colony on the brink of the Axis attack on Africa and internal rebellion. Cynical about both the colonizer and colonized, Gresham represents a critique that, as it attempts to articulate the damage caused by their enmeshed relationship, cancels any romantic idealism about either. In response to Begg's tax scheme, Gresham retorts:

> [The natives are] used to being conquered, . . . and they'll merely think (as they think already) that one lot of masters has replaced another, and that both are equally greedy. The greatest mistake we make is to imagine that because we know we're different from all the other conquerors who've come to Africa, the conquered know it too; or that because we want to change the inhabitants into good little democrats like ourselves, patient and kind to animals and fond of cricket, the inhabitants really want to make this transformation, or would be capable of it if they did. People don't reverse their natures overnight just by being conquered. (Huxley 1948b, 21)

Ridiculing the stream of conquerors recalls Olivia Manning's resistant Egyptians in her *Levant Trilogy*. But if the tone and content are the same, Huxley is creating a different forum here among different actors. Between the British administrators, Gresham and Begg, she smashes the notion of a univocal colonial ideology and presence. Begg's conservatism rationalizes colonial policies by seeing them as self-justifying ideals. On the other hand, Gresham's liberalism rationalizes the bitter consequences of pragmatic politics by seeing them as the corruption of colonial ideals. In the light of being threatened by another empire and its horrific ideals, Begg's pragmatism mocks the foundational ideals of all colonialism while Gresham's cynicism mocks their consequences. It is only in debate that the colonial mission and its practices are exposed as self-canceling.

Huxley's idea of a debate about British colonialism does not feature only its administrators. Working the interstices between the Emir, who wields a wily position of his own, the rebellious natives, and the local colonial office, another perspective connects them all by articulating the relationship between ideal intentions and dire consequences. Ibrahim, the Moslem court interpreter, translates the Empire's rhetoric of moral superiority into one of "many foolish tales" by showing it to be no better than the Emir's "extortions" (Huxley 1948b, 25). This critique of colonialism's sense of its universal ideals moves the narrative back to 1929, suspended between two world wars, the import of which must be denied by the colonial agents in order to perpetuate colonialism's belief in its own omnipresent beneficence. And while the Muslim Ibrahim derides the Africans' fearful "hearts of slaves," his prejudices are also spread evenhandedly among all those specious justifications for power, including the British "aim to help the common people" (25, 26).

It is, of course, easily argued that since the British held overweening power, figuring a multilayered colonial relationship only deflects attention away from the powerlessness of the colonized. But Ibrahim's two-way critique offers agency to the colonized by arguing and enacting the interdependence of colonial relations. If his status depends on the need of the British for his spying, it also indicates a radical separation. In dialogue with Gresham, who believes in the power of negotiation and the superiority of Western scientific thinking as solutions to differences and assimilation, Ibrahim asserts a cultural identity that represents an opposition. Asserting unassailable allegiance to its own historical evolution, Ibrahim's Islam will not be seduced by the timeless "Christian doctrine of universal brotherhood" into an assimilation that guarantees the erasure of his own faith and the Other's subordinate status as a dependent foster child (Huxley 1948b, 283). Supporting Ibrahim's oppositional independence, the narrator joins consciousness with Gresham to aver: "Between two faiths there could be no compromise—the world was flat or it was round, it could not be both at once; between the cypress and the date-palm no union could be fertile" (283). The rhetorical consequence of this trialogue positions Ibrahim's Islamic faith as a powerful contender to the confidence and historical mission of Western Christian and political culture. The assertion of religious culture adds a significant category of colonial analysis to Huxley's life work: the realization "that men are divided with greater potency by faith than by race or pigment" (26).

Squeezed between the battle of equally powerful if differently deployed systems of belief is a struggle that takes Huxley disturbingly close to her own identity politics. Defined by racial politics, this struggle represents a challenge to her arguments in this novel. At the moment of the novel's publication, when racism is being transformed into industrialized murder, Huxley is asking her readers to consider the primacy of religious or ideological differences over that of race. The politics of race are represented through the character of the black African, Benjamin Morris, who, as a child, is rescued by Catholic missionaries from the human sacrifice to which his own people had committed him. While it might seem that no rescue is possible for this imperialist plot, Benjamin is awakened soon enough to the double messages of Christianity and the colonial mission. It does, however, take a young English chemist, albeit one who has left "old-fashioned liberal[ism]" behind, to guide Benjamin in reading Western empiricism and "social consciousness" critically (Huxley 1948b, 141). The effect is to catapult Benjamin into a journey of recognizing racial oppression in its most disguised forms and then converting to political protest. Huxley's complex portrait of Morris grants him acute critical powers as well as inconsistent personal and political desires. By the end, however, this complexity may be compromised by her own contradictory agenda and the question of whether she considers her representation of race in the light of the racially marked moment of her writing.

Even as Gresham argues against essentializing "the native," the intelligence and integrity he grants to Benjamin Morris are presented as a racialized first impression (Huxley 1948b, 161). What elevates Morris to intellectual prowess is the integration of characteristics denied to blackness. Race becomes a mind-body problem. Blackness can only signify the physical or the body, lacking the other substance of complex thought. In the racial logic employed by Gresham, this weakness or lack integral to blackness is overcome by reading into Morris's physical appearance the presence of "fiercer blood" than blackness by itself has the capacity to produce (137). A combination of attributes—physical, intellectual, and temperamental—adds up to signs of an "Arab" presence in Morris's genealogy, all of which are taken by Gresham as an evolutionary improvement over the indolent state of blackness. Recalling the assurance of Ibrahim, Morris's hybrid persona resonates with a passionate intellectual propensity that legitimizes his oppositional stance to colonialism. But if blackness by itself constitutes inadequacy, the promise of Morris's mixed racial profile turns out, as Huxley's narrative strategies assess this mutation, to be an evolutionary dead end. Instead of embodying and animating either a viable alternative to the superiority of whiteness or a cultural critique of race, Morris represents "a queer unstable mixture"(138). As his story is plotted, this instability may even be the explanatory key to the trajectory of his increasingly violent political life. For Huxley, who throughout her writings pondered the vexed scientific and political meanings ascribed to race, the insertion in Morris's character of an "Arab" lineage confuses her earlier assertion of culture and belief as determinants of character. Not only is the idea of blackness as a separate racial category complicated by a genealogy of mixed blood, but its cross-reference with a people who define themselves linguistically as well as ethnically, and with various religious beliefs, undermines the signifying credibility of the physical. Gresham's role as racial reader, harkening back to nineteenth-century race science and anthropology, is therefore marked by unreliability and, by extension, calls his political acumen and moral stature into question.

If the narrative questions Gresham's association of race and the physical with character and fate and intertwines them as determinants, the reverse also holds sway in this novel. The critical challenge to Gresham reflects back on the narrator as well. Registering sympathy for Morris's condition, the narrator proffers the difficulty of theorizing the meaning of a people from the case of an individual: "For it was no easy task to realize in a single career the aspirations of a people" (Huxley 1948b, 139). And yet despite such disclaimers that we find in all of Huxley's ethnographic narratives, the narrator here moves from the direct discourse of Morris's and Gresham's conversation to present the social context from which Morris emerged. The language through which the narrator constructs the black African social environment is, as though confirming Gresham's reading, constitutive once again of an organically physical universe. Like Gresham's logic of blood, this universe obeys laws which cannot be altered, and so Morris's people are seen as being caught in an "immemorial pattern" (139). All of a piece, this pattern does not constitute a relationship among diverse and individuated entities. Instead, the individuals who populate this landscape are conflated by the narrative into a single, essential personhood, constructed out of a combination of material elements that collapse into each other: "His sisters and cousins planted and hoed among the crops under an exacting sun, and in the cool of the evening returned to their crude shelters, to the rounding up of goats, the fistfuls of porridge, the long droning talk that, like a cow in pasture, was hedged in by the petty events of the day" (139). This long sentence creates a people who are merged with, are indeed inseparable from, their environment. The parallel alignment of climate, people, livestock, and expression, all objects of a pattern of endless circularity, elides differentiation or hierarchy. The arrangement of language signifies a literalness that denies the people any symbolic relationship to the landscape, such as that vouched for by Chinua Achebe. Reclaiming the black Africans' "completely different story," Achebe insists that it is "founded on a mystical, immemorial relationship between them and the red earth of their homeland" (2001, 63). Achebe's reference to "immemorial" is especially interesting because of Gresham's invocation of the same word. Though it points to different interpretations, the word creates a slippage in its sense of creative forces beyond the black Africans' grasp. The difference lies in Achebe's insistence on a "relationship" constructed by the black Africans themselves, while, for Gresham and Huxley's narrator, the black Africans are planted too deeply in their "red earth" to emerge as separate subjects. Locked into the single meaning offered by the narrator's reading of an equal opportunity landscape, none of Huxley's black Africans can make a difference, either to themselves or to their environment. Instead of producing change over time, their labors have only recycled sameness. If they are dominated by the natural cycles of climate, they not only possess the same adaptive impulses but are of the same constitution, the same essential physicality as their livestock.

In its parallel and repetitive syntax, this passage resembles the rhythmic and heuristic structure of a fable or myth. And in the choreographed simplicity and totality of its logical balance, the passage asserts a truth claim that forecloses critical intervention by providing a story that is so complete in itself that it offers itself as both obvious and mystifying in its meaning. It is this meaning which exposes the dangers in Huxley's confusions and literalized renderings, for they add up to a story about the evolutionary stagnation of a people. And to lure the reader into submission and sympathy with the narrative form, the juvenile appeal of the passage also runs parallel to its infantilization of the objectified native.

Benjamin Morris's individualized difference is a result of his "unstable" hybridity. Out of his Arab assertiveness and English education is born the desire to alter the landscape which gave him life but would have sacrificed it in submission to the cosmic laws his people understand only as immutable. As he recreates himself through different laws—those of the colonial mission— Morris understands that his position is constructed by external agents and not part of a mystified indigenous primordial eternity.[27] This understanding, however, cannot counter other forces heaped against him. As his character is allowed to develop, it is further destabilized by having no place to nurture it. His critical intelligence and education are no match against the British. They may claim to respect his mind, but their arguments are won by restrained manners elusively encoded and designed to reject those not born to share them. Equally debilitating, the Africans with whom he would share his interests "could not discuss" them and the Arab community sees him only as a pawn in their designs against the British (Huxley 1948b, 261). Morris is thus a resident of a colonial no-man's-land, belonging nowhere, "and so, from lack of nourishment, the plant of his culture had shriveled and drooped. . . . Without family, without equals, with neighbors he despised, his solitary spirit had encased itself in a cocoon of dreams" (261).

Readers might easily expect this sympathetic understanding of his complex plight to pave a level narrative playing field, one that grants Morris a fate interweaving his constricted heritage, his struggle for individuation, and the political and social circumstances of the intercolonial power plays which constrain him once again. Such a strategy would also coincide with the narrative assumption that Gresham's struggle to find integrity within the colonial structure is serious, an assumption that is fulfilled with the novel's finale. The probity of Gresham's investigation is affirmed as he abandons the colonial project and begins a quest for knowledge about North Africa that is unsullied by colonial interests. The performance of this shifting quest, however, requires that once again the self-determining fate of the Englishman depends on the subordination of the colonized. With all the attention Huxley gives to the consciousness of Benjamin Morris, unlike Gresham, his desires and dreams are not supported or legitimized by being inscribed in a cultural tradition of quest literature. Instead, Morris's dreams of gaining political authority by editing the first black African newspaper are corrupted by his vengeful pride and exploited to fulfill his desire for the daughter of a Muslim. While his life begins as an object of colonizing pity, his development is derailed by having his desires turn to paranoia and hysteria. No longer shaped by sympathy, Morris's real tragedy lies in the narrative twist of fate that makes him the butt of a joke, unlike the Kikuyu of Huxley's other writing, who know how to resist British humor. When we last see Morris, he is running from the black prostitute substituted for his Muslim beloved by her father, a punishment for interfering with the latter's business with the British. Duped, humiliated, feminized in his hysteria, the promising black leader is exposed as an exploding body of irrational desire. In effect, Morris is denied the Arab "fierceness" and acuity that should have been part of the genetic promise of his mixed blood. Instead, the novel rejects not only Morris's promise, but the very idea of legitimizing his pathway to power through Britain's colonial agents.

When Gresham reflects that "fifty years ago there would have been no Benjamin," the novel is asserting a determining power that defies race as a genetically constitutive category. This same narrative power, however, also reifies Morris's mixed race as though it resists cultural intervention and historical conflict (Huxley 1948b, 279). Gresham's claim that Morris "was entirely a British creation" does not merely demonstrate the obvious intervening power of the colonizing mission (279). The definitive tone of the statement gestures toward British responsibility for Morris's character and fate, and this is part of an anticolonial critique that reaches a crisis in Gresham's conclusion: "If the empire fell . . . it would not be from abuses or oppression, but simply from lack of imagination" (280). Such a vexed disclaimer also represents a critical question for Huxley's own narrative strategies, one that obtains for other colonial writers as well: Is she representing the failed black leader as constructed and then destroyed by a failure of colonial imagination or does this rationalize colonial "abuses or oppression"? That the answer may very well point to the latter is evidenced in a passage from her 1954 west African travel chronicle, *Four Guineas,* where she reflects, "Impatience with British rule is . . . called a revolt against imperialism, but in truth I think it is, in part at least a revolt against *ennui,* and that when the British Empire finally crumbles we might write as its epitaph: 'We bored them to death' " (1955, 140). If the languid wit of these lines recalls Evelyn Waugh's bright young things, we are reminded as well of the horrifically comic irresolution that distinguishes the end of his novel, *A Handful of Dust,* where Tony Last is trapped into rereading Dickens to a crazed missionary in a South American jungle.

Trapped by words may just be Huxley's own fateful script, for, most problematically, her construction of Benjamin Morris questions whether he represents the failure or success of her own imagination. For Abdulrazak Gurnah, Huxley represents a "failure of the imagination to conceive the landscape [and its indigenous people] other than within its own discourse," and the rhetorical result is that the "essence" of the native is "always unstable and in danger of corruption" (2000, 285, 289). When Huxley's narrator in *The Walled City* applauds Gresham's abandonment of the colonial project, she begs the question of whether the narrative has abandoned Morris as well. But in his case, she is denying him the same appeal as Gresham is granted, to an open-ended "fortune" (Huxley 1948b, 318). The development of Morris's rage provides a clue to this conundrum. His brief tenure in the geopolitical world is no match for the triumphalist confidence of the British and the Muslims. What looks like meetings of intellectual equality is exposed by the novel as webs of political deceit. For example, the authority of Morris's barbs at Christian hypocrisy is overwhelmed by the pragmatic political logic which forms the foundation of British conquest and which, in the novel's World War II conception, may represent a hope that herein lies the power that will defeat the irrationally racist Nazis. In turn, Morris's passion for justice and equality is undercut by the theological zeal on which, according to the Muslim Ibrahim, the history of his own people's survival rests, no matter who the conqueror.

The combined feminization and impotence of a black African resistance is highlighted by the critical presence of two colonial women. Each in her own way rejects the roles prescribed by imperial domesticity and ascribed to them by postcolonial critics. Married to colonial officials, neither Priscilla Gresham nor Armorel Begg are good wives or happy settlers. Though Priscilla brings to the minds of Englishmen romantic memories "of English summers and country gardens," her own view of the British Empire is represented as follows: "a factory for sepulchers, her young men forced outward from their kindly center by some strange . . . force as unaccountable as the impulse that sent the ants hurrying over the surface of their own world, and perhaps as purposeless" (Huxley 1948b, 27). As it connects the carnage of war with that of colonial conquest, this statement may be seen as a crucial move for the novel's integrity, especially as it challenges any romantic perspective on the imperial project. Priscilla's weak heart, like the tropical diseases that afflict colonists in so much colonial fiction, is attributed to the self-destructiveness of the imperial project and not to an imagined inscrutable malignancy inherent in the tropical soil and body. The romantic is debunked further by linking Robert Gresham's belief in "imagination" to both his failure as a love partner and his trust in the possibility of colonial beneficence. Recognizing the source of her disorder, Priscilla rejects the possibility of being rescued by romantic love from her failed marriage and from imperial myths.

Assuming responsibility for her own weakness, Priscilla understands that settler women comply with the myth of colonial adventure by thinking it will free them from the social constraints of England. What they deny is that colonial social codes intensify those constraints while camouflaging them in a different landscape. If the colonial lens cannot focus on itself as a subject, Priscilla finds it refracted in the "imprisonment" of the Emir's palace, where his women consider themselves "among the fortunate: safe, well-fed, valued" (Huxley 1948b, 56). Both the "placid" faces of the Emir's women and Priscilla's weak heart show that despite the different ideologies which govern their lives, men can "occasionally . . . choose their lives; women hardly ever" (27). Though Englishwomen may learn the rhetoric of "freedom" by rote, the life lesson colonialism teaches them is that, like the Emir's women, they are "the ornaments—the glitter, not the solid stuff underneath" (182).

If this juxtaposition between the harem and the bungalow seems too balanced and therefore fails to hold the more powerful Empire culpable, Huxley
rejects the solace offered by "the bleak comfort of futility," that is, a retreat
from responsibility into a victim identity (1948b, 311). Instead, Armorel Begg,
the more assertive but defeated colonial woman, realizes "that it did matter
. . . which path you chose. Hers . . . had led her into a tunnel with walls of glass
. . . you could see through them . . . sweet gardens, but, try as you would, you
could not break out. . . . Better the craggy path over the rocks than this . . . for
it was the wind of freedom, and here in the tunnel was the calm not of death
but of sterility" (311). What shatters colonial "tunnel" vision and smashes its
"walls of glass" is the conjunction of native insurrection, the sterile debates of
the two women's husbands about what is good for the natives, and, last but not
least, world war. For Huxley herself, participating in this same debate many
years later during the Mau Mau uprisings, the Second World War shows a
complicated, deromanticized battle for and against freedom. Beginning the
novel, the war shows the British defending imperial interests which turn out
to be more sand than "sweet gardens," but they are also, in that very risky space
between, fighting for "the wind of freedom" against Hitler's drive for world
conquest and enslavement. In tandem, we can read all of Huxley's African
writing as raising discomforting questions for a writer interrogating her
own colonial history and identity. As the Second World War raised troubling
questions about the connection between imperialism and fascism, she
never stopped questioning it. The "cloud of red dust" that at the very end
"obscure[s]" the colonial "horizon" also becomes an apt metaphor for the
novel's unresolved vision (1948b, 319).

A THING TO LOVE AND A MAN FROM NOWHERE: THE VIOLENT AND INEVITABLE END OF EMPIRE

It may be that a new Africa, based on the European ideas and dreams for which
it is so avid, will be the issue: an Africa of the materialist, the bureaucrat, the
trade union, the lawyer and the technician; or it may be that the goat will leave
the boa-constrictor stronger, but oddly unchanged. "The white man brings his
canon to the bush" said a former king of Ashanti, "but the bush is stronger than
the cannon." Whether it will be stronger than the book is yet to be seen.

—Elspeth Huxley, *Four Guineas*

Traveling through west Africa in 1954, at the height of the Mau Mau
rebellions, Huxley shifts her ambivalence about British colonial rule to anxieties about African self-determination. Her travel chronicle through west
Africa, *Four Guineas,* is fraught with the tension of doubting—whether it is
her efforts to recognize the integral coherence of west African cultures and
traditions or the integrity of Britain's objective "not to rule, but to prepare the
way to cease from ruling" (1955, 187). If her own travel adventure cannot

resolve the tension, she will, in the same year, set her imagination to the task and write *A Thing to Love,* her much criticized novel of Mau Mau. Rather than start with a clean slate, however, Huxley infuses her new characters with those who failed her in *A Walled City,* as though testing her irresolution one more time. Combining qualities of Freddy Begg and Robert Gresham, Huxley creates Sam Gibson, a settler whose full complement of racist assumptions is matched only by his sexism and other forms of chauvinism. As the plot turns on the romantically charged rescue of his beloved from Mau Mau rebels, his character is treated redemptively, however, and as his machismo spends itself in battle, he mellows into "a new resolve," able to envision a multicultural Kenya: "We are in it together, he wanted to say, and we shall come out battered but safe in the end . . . the Home Guards, the chiefs and the laborers, the Christians and schoolboys and teachers and farmers who won't, in the long run, accept the tyranny of fear, the religion of hatred, the code of revenge and the degradation of cruelty—not if we stand fast, not if we can show them the way and the future, and travel side by side" (1954b, 255–256).

Gibson's lofty sentiments beg the question of whether Huxley recognizes the special pleading in her representation of his "new resolve," and this emerges from contradictions between the insistent symmetry of Gibson's vision and the fact that he cannot bring himself to utter it. In effect, this contradiction works metonymically, as though the entire narrative is trying to express but cannot overcome Huxley's own inability to speak, the lack of her "resolve" to characterize Gibson's change (1954b, 255). And while it is plausible that Gibson is tongue-tied by his beloved's resistance, even at the very end, when he proposes marriage, she is not treated to his vision. But we are. Invoking the reader as Gibson's audience has the effect of a final plea, just in case the evidence Huxley has planted doesn't convince us. But the vision itself is encumbered by the drama of Gibson's silence, which may very well express the ineffectuality of both him and his vision, raising the question of whether Huxley is so unsure of it and of his transformation that she cannot allow him to articulate it. This tension creates another uncertainty—about Huxley's search for the viability of white settlement. Instead of a détente granting the Kikuyu "a share of Western progress in exchange for the loss of their past," Huxley's uncertainty raises too many doubts about "Western progress" (Tucker 1967, 150). How can Gibson's vision of a future shared "side by side" be realized when what prevails is the Western belief in the "degradation of cruelty" that identifies and condemns the rebels as followers of "the religion of hatred" (Huxley 1954b, 256).

Embodying "the religion of hatred" and therefore lending narrative support for Gibson's vision is the Kikuyu insurrectionist, Gitau. Many critics have noted his resemblance to Jomo Kenyatta, who, for the period during and until independence, remained an icon of Huxley's resistance to Kenyan self-determination.[28]

Like Kenyatta, Gitau's London education has taught him to recognize the mockery and "hidden purpose" contained in the colonizers' polite social discourse and
lofty yet commonsensical rhetoric (Huxley 1954b, 102). His progress from critic
to radical is inspired by his African education, where, like Benjamin Morris in *The
Walled City,* he learns that "two thousand years of Christian civilization" has led
only to more killing and oppression of others (103). Unlike Gibson, however, but
like Morris, Gitau is not redemptive. Instead, he loses all vestiges of his critical fac-
ulties and becomes a murderous savage, erasing any possibility of viewing him
either as a complex individual or as a freedom fighter. Like Benjamin Morris,
Gitau has been betrayed by his European education and initiated into rebellion by
the empirical evidence of colonial exploitation. But Huxley is so terrorized by the
Mau Mau uprisings and so betrayed by their universal condemnation of the settlers that she executes an angry justice in retaliation. As her indictment, judgment,
and sentence are delivered to both Gitau and Morris, they fall victim to her narrative counterinsurgency.

If the plotting of *A Thing to Love* destroys both the integrity and the
agency of Mau Mau, it also lays waste to that of the colonial project. As Huxley shows in so much of her writing, when the settlers reconstitute the
African wilderness in the romantic image of their own green and pleasant
land, the English education they impose destroys the Kikuyu sacred bond
with their lands. As Ngugi wa Thiong'o portrays this bond in his novel *Weep
Not, Child,* Kikuyu land is a divine legacy from Murungu, the Creator, and
bears the responsibility "to rule and till in serenity sacrificing only to me,
your God" (1964, 28). The English missionary education that shapes both
Benjamin Morris and Gitau is also instrumental in planting the linguistic
seeds that grow into their powerful arguments, expressed not only to other
characters but to readers as well. As these political arguments fall on deaf
colonial ears, they transmute into rage at the politely silent condescension
toward their wish for self-determination; in turn, rage develops into political
rebellion. Though this rebellion leads to independence, its own sanctification
and violence overwhelms and, by implication, sacrifices the sacredness of the
land, both in its Mau Mau ceremonial oathing and in its unifying principles
and meaning.

The problem, of course, is that Huxley finds the methods of this rebellion
so heinous and its colonial objects so misunderstood that she always represents
it as self-destructive, if not self-parodying.[29] And yet despite Huxley's rejection
of African nationalism and anticolonial uprisings, the polemics of her fictional
insurrectionists, Morris and Gitau, highlight the promises and language of the
missionary project as a betrayal of its own principles. This is not the end of the
story, however, for the missionaries' Christian ethics remain imprinted on the
political consciousness of those students who refuse the object lesson of

becoming subservient mimic men.[30] If the violence depicted in *A Thing to Love* is indeed barbaric, it represents the self-fulfilling prophesy of imposing both Christian charity and "absolute standards" on those very people diagnosed as congenitally deformed by "fecklessness and impotence" (Huxley 1954b, 144). Huxley's frustration with this colonial failure leads her to question her own hope for reconciliation. In her 1948 East African travel book, *The Sorcerer's Apprentice,* she writes: "What are we doing in Africa today? Educating the people to despise their lot and to aspire to something better, and then tying them to a system which prevents them from satisfying their desires. There's only one answer to that: discontent, and one day revolution. We must give up clinging to the old ways for fear of disrupting tribal society. It's falling apart already. We must plunge boldly into the methods of the future; mechanization, scientific production, collective farming—with co-operation as the goal" (1948a, 141).

Huxley's struggle to reconcile indigenous claims with her own argument for the settlers' legitimacy implodes with Sam Gibson's silence at the end of *A Thing to Love.* But we can see her taking a more valiant offensive in the same novel with the character of Pat Foxley, the daughter of a settler, who rebels, ironically, by becoming a missionary. For Huxley, the identity that was nurtured by an abiding love for the African wilderness is tested by Pat's passion for improving the lives of the African people. For example, Pat's devotion to teaching Kikuyu children is driven not only by her delight in their intellectual gifts and growth, but by the narrator's mixed feelings about Colonel Foxley's twenty-year "battle with natural forces" to build a farm (Huxley 1954b, 22). Its daffodils and "herd of Ayrshires" may be show worthy, but the narrator also assesses these displays as a "painful" memorial to a "graveyard of unsuccessful experiments"(22). Having inherited a legacy of colonial failure, as did Huxley, Pat diagnoses its etiology: instead of following "the inclinations of nature," her father would "strain and twist them to his own purpose" (24). Like his twisted, arthritic body and that of a neighbor's crippled son, colonial settlement suffers from its own unnatural forces. Recalling Huxley's decision, Pat leaves home, disappointing the expectation that she would carry on her parents' work. What the novel asserts that Huxley's memoirs cannot is that this decision is driven by the recognition of an unhealthy imposition of an English farm onto the African landscape. Nonetheless, because Pat's Anglo-African identity is inseparable from the English settlement of Africa, her own consciousness and project can't completely escape it either. We can see how this ontology determines Pat's purpose and destiny when she transfers her love for the uncolonized African landscape to its young people, but imposes her goals on them. As she teaches Kikuyu children the English language and the skills legitimized by their

English sense of purpose, her work at the missionary school participates in the colonization of its African students. In effect, even as it represents a rebellion against her father's project, Pat's work threatens to replicate it.

Interestingly enough, in all the indictments of *A Thing to Love,* there is no mention of Pat Foxley. I wonder if this is because she is positioned, like Armorel Begg and Pam Gresham in *The Walled City,* as the critical voice that preempts that of the postcolonial critic. Resisting the idea that they love only the land and are blind to the natives' subjectivity, these female characters teach us how to read colonial relations as interweaving the settler, the landscape, the black African people, and the writer struggling to discover what Africa means to her and what she means to Africa. The guided tour led by these women characters shows us that in its transplanted state, the English garden has become a deadly mutant. Like the seemingly romantic bower that protects Sleeping Beauty, the English settler farm is also a prison. Most threateningly, the Foxley's farm breeds poisonous attitudes that seem to infect the entire novel, including Pat's mission to educate black children. For example, Mamie Foxley is ashamed of her daughter "drumming a lot of useless nonsense into those black woolly heads—turning out future prostitutes, and swollen-headed youths who thought themselves too grand for manual work" (Huxley 1954b, 26). Mamie typifies colonial racism and sexism, but Pat's character opposes her as well as the missionaries for whom she works. As Pat negotiates her emotional and political identities and attitudes, hers is the voice given to criticize not only her father's failed mission, but the missionaries' repressive rigidities and willful ignorance of the logic of Kikuyu beliefs. Nowhere is her critique more powerfully represented than in relation to Sam Gibson's silent thoughts, which seem predominant. In her rejection of Sam's desire, in her own unexpressed reflections, Pat revises the missionary and colonial project. Whereas Sam imagines a community of settlers, missionaries, and loyal Kikuyu, Pat distinguishes herself from his "reason" and theirs with a "compassion" that is "absolute" and that frees the self from the "desire" that marks the colonizing purpose (254, 255).

For many readers, this "compassion" will simply not suffice. All too suggestive of the condescension of imperialist supremacy, compassion looks like a feeble attempt to resurrect another kind of "divine" mission that predicates against the self-determination of black Africans (Huxley 1954b, 255). Further damning Huxley's case for Pat's compassion is its immediate object at the novel's finale. Matthew, a Christian Kikuyu working for the British District Office, and saved by Pat's ministrations from Gitau's brutal Mau Mau attack, is also her mediating partner in the question of whether "Europeans" are the "saviors of his people, as they claim, or its oppressors, as the Spokesman said" (123). Most critics have indicted this mediating representation as a sellout to colonial accommodation, to "the loyalist tradition" (Githae-Mugo 1978, 122).

In 1954, as the Mau Mau rebellion still raged, Huxley was searching for ways to accommodate the needs of black, Asian, Arab, and European Africans and create a "multi-racial state" led by a revised British colonial principle (Huxley 1954a, 9). Her pamphlet *Kenya Today*, written the same year as *A Thing to Love,* acknowledges that Mau Mau has exposed "a serious flaw in [a] society" ruled by European missionary and political policies and practices which, with "all the talk of 'partnership,'" did not allow the Kikuyu to "feel themselves to be partners in the enterprise" (Huxley 1954a, 31). This pamphlet is an important gloss on the mediating partnership she imagines at the end of *A Thing to Love.* The society she imagines that Pat and Matthew, a white European woman and a black African man, will share is predicated on the hope that the mutually exclusive claims on Africa of both Europeans and black Africans will yield to their equal and "natural" demands for "political rights," a situation that can only occur when Europeans no longer "fear . . . for their own position" (1954a, 9). This fear, she argues, drives part of the supremacist doctrine of such overzealous missionaries as the Macalisters in *A Thing to Love,* and in turn legitimizes the "social injustice" that cuts across economic, educational, and political lines (1954a, 10).

There is no doubt that Huxley's arguments rested on her belief in the benefits European knowledge could bring, such as health care, moral education, and agricultural training. Her trips to Africa after its independence involved her attempts to become an instrument of these benefits, offering her expertise on soil and forest conservation to government agencies and farmers across the continent. These messages, however, were accompanied in her writing by her efforts at the very same time to come to grips with the failure of European settlement. And despite the broad spectrum of these efforts, rather than unfolding as a process of understanding, they express a frantic, unappeasable confrontation with the tragic consequences of European settlement. How this failure would affect these Europeans forms a climactic scene in *A Thing to Love* in which the Europeans' fears materialize in the murder of Pat's parents by Mau Mau. So violent is this murder that it can't be put to rest by the mediating vision that ends the novel—its resonances overwhelm all other narrative effects.[31] We see how images of that murder almost overwhelm Huxley's critical imagination as they become the impetus for Huxley's last novel, *A Man from Nowhere,* where a white settler seeks revenge for the violent death of his family as black rebels take over. I read this last novel as Huxley's dirge for the brutal but necessary end of Empire in Africa. Read in tandem, the two novels, *A Thing to Love* and *A Man from Nowhere,* put the lie to the vision of a partnered "multi-racial state" as they plot a different kind of mutuality—mutual violence.

One of the most startling plot turns in *A Man from Nowhere* is that the revenge Dick Heron seeks for his family's murder and his wife's suicide is not aimed at the violently victorious blacks but at the cabinet minister in charge of the London colonial office, Peter Buckle. As the novel plots Heron's stalking and confrontation with Buckle, it seems enervated by its own confrontation with the end of Empire. With no settlement to call home, as Heron stalks the man he holds responsible for colonial failure, a narrative reparation and revenge are being sought in vain. And so the novel enacts a mourning process that can only end with profound melancholy. It cannot work through the profound sense of losing the place that formed a powerfully magnetic force drawing together the writer's identity, narrative sense of self, and purpose. Neither the listless sexual attraction and encounter with Buckle's daughter nor the drawn out and ineffectual debate between the two men can provide either closure or a new impetus on which the settler can build a life. Most significantly, this exhaustion extends to the fact that this novel is Huxley's last. That she cannot find the arguments to win the debate for Heron, that he kills himself at the end instead of Buckle, only testifies to the depressed self-destructiveness of colonial Africa. The cause of the depression may very well be as follows: "It was just that Mr. Heron didn't quite fit into any of the niches, he didn't belong and yet he must belong to something, somewhere—no man was by himself in the world, he must have a family, an origin, a position, however obscure. To be without a position was not to exist, to crumble or perish like a lone brick without a wall, a bee that had lost the hive" (Huxley 1965a, 14). Heron, the colonial settler who belongs nowhere, does not even occupy the position of Other in the land which has rejected him. Like the English spinster governess in *The African Poison Murders,* mirroring a sterile and self-dissolving colonial presence, he is not only nowhere, but no one. Twenty years after the Allies' victory over fascist racist oppression, two years after Kenya has won its independence, there is no triumph for the white settler. In this novel, with this beginning and with its suicide ending, we can see all of Huxley's previous pleading on behalf of the worthiness of European settlement confronting its own illusions and dead end. As she was to declare many years later, "They came in quest of adventure, stayed to make a colony and, in the process, destroyed what they had come to seek" (Huxley 1987, 132).

Nearly sixty years after her parents took her along on their great adventure of building the new garden nation, it is all over, trampled by those whose own gardens were expropriated and for whom the benefits of the imperial project were too meager to compensate for having never been granted more than alien status in their own land. As Huxley begins and ends *A Man from Nowhere,* black Africans are nowhere to be seen or heard, an ironic sign that they have totally demolished the imperial presence and perhaps its narrative as well. With poetic justice, this absence exposes the good intentions of the colonial project as a lack; despite their promises to lead Africans into educated self-determination, the colonizers never developed a lexicon to represent this new status. As Huxley's biographer observes, "Through the book runs a theme of the waste and uselessness of white endeavor in an African country" (Nicholls 2002, 345). In their struggle for independence, the Africans have removed themselves from the settler narrative and can only be felt in the self-canceling confrontation between the settler and the colonial administrator. With the suicide of the European settler, the novel represents the voided imagination that would only be restored when postcolonial critics needed it to serve as a tale of their own revenge.

CHAPTER 4

Island Strangers

PHYLLIS SHAND ALLFREY
AND PHYLLIS BOTTOME

Beauty and disease, beauty and sickness, beauty and horror: that was the island.—Phyllis Shand Allfrey, *The Orchid House*

SO MUCH OF what we respond to in the fictional representation of colonial and postcolonial relations of the Caribbean derives from the tiny island of Dominica. Its colonial native, Jean Rhys, who left to build a literary career in England, wrote what is now the iconic fiction of West Indian colonial studies, *Wide Sargasso Sea*. Written late in her career, over many years, the novel is Rhys's critical response to Charlotte Bronte's demonizing representation of the traumatized colonial woman, Bertha Mason. Less well known but certainly as important to modernist colonial literature are another Dominican, Phyllis Shand Allfrey (1908–1986), and a British writer, Phyllis Bottome (1882–1963). While Allfrey lived abroad for many years, unlike Rhys, she returned to Dominica, where she built a career of political activism on behalf of the island's workers and then as the first woman and first white to serve in the Cabinet of the West Indies Federation. Phyllis Bottome's interest in the West Indies focused on the island of Jamaica, where she and her husband, Ernan Forbes-Dennis, not only visited many times, but helped build a progressive school that would educate both black and white children. By the time they were writing their Caribbean novels, both writers had already established themselves as working for humanitarian causes. While living in London during World War II, Allfrey worked as a welfare officer on behalf of both war-torn Londoners and newly arrived Dominicans. After living in Germany and Austria during the 1920s and 1930s, Bottome returned to England to rally on behalf of Hitler's victims.

COLONIAL GOTHIC: PHYLLIS SHAND ALLFREY'S
THE ORCHID HOUSE

Allfrey's political activism could not have been predicted by her colonial background. But instead of blending in, she escaped her racially segregated country village and the household that, despite its aristocratic connections, was beset by financial decline and the shadowy presence of a shell-shocked father.[1] Her stays in New York and London began her political education in Fabian Socialism, expressed in local London Labor Party involvement and in her writing. Returning to Dominica after twenty-one years, in 1951, she "almost single-handedly educated the Dominican peasantry in the principles of democracy" (Paravisini-Gebert 1997, xvi). After sacrificing her literary career for her duties as Minister of Social and Labor Affairs of the West Indies Federation, the collapse of the Federation in 1962 was a devastating blow. She and her husband then left its seat in Trinidad to return to Dominica, where she addressed the island's racial tensions in editorials she wrote for the *Dominica Herald*. It was her public criticism of the Dominica Labor Party that led to her dismissal, an "expulsion widely believed to have been racially motivated" (Paravisini-Gebert 1997, xvii). Depressed but undaunted by this debacle, Allfrey and her husband organized the *Star,* a newspaper that stood in opposition to the government. After decades of political courage, financial struggle, and personal tragedy, Allfrey was a neglected and almost completely unknown figure at her death in 1986.

Allfrey's 1953 novel, *The Orchid House,* was published at the time Jean Rhys was writing her novel and, with its modern setting on the island of Dominica and experimental style, provides a necessary addition to the critical space Rhys occupies. Instead of concluding with the colonial exile and terror of a colonized colonial woman, Allfrey's novel brings that terror home to the colony, examining the fate of Dominica itself as it struggles to loosen the grip of imperial power. In contrast to Rhys's modern rendering of the Victorian exploitation of a colonial woman, Allfrey presents the persistence of the colonial past as its legacies of racial and gendered exploitation haunt all the male and female characters in the present.

Like Rhys, Allfrey finds inspiration in her own family's history and experience, including their economic and social devolution and the corrupting lure that a destabilized colonial infrastructure offers. Written from a post–World War II perspective and set in the interwar years, *The Orchid House* depicts a declining British gentry and other colonial forces hanging on for dear life as they struggle with the shock of the Empire lurching toward its end. The disorientation that marks this modern story is tightly plotted around a colonial family that, like Allfrey's own, traces its settlement in the West Indies to the seventeenth century. But whatever wealth and position the family once claimed, by the end of World War I, it has retreated from any socially important role or involvement in the life of the island. The family's self-enclosure, as its current state is haunted by its white colonial past, finds its metaphor in the orchid house, a highly artificial environment designed to nurture hybrid blooms. As a colonial edifice, however, this orchid house nurtures the opposite: suffocation. This is highlighted by the three daughters who have made their homes abroad and whose visits and attempts to reinvigorate those they left behind set the plot in motion. The first part of the novel, written in a languid narrative style, depicts their childhood life of colonial leisure. As each of the daughters returns, however, she disrupts the family's retreat into anachronistic fantasies and exposes the Empire's final, desperate grasps for power. Expressing this disruption, the novel assumes "a Janus-like" form which, as Paravisini-Gebert observes, "looked back with nostalgia at a world about to disappear, while depicting the process through which its death could be expedited" (1997, xix). We see this self-disruptive narrative as the sisters come and go. For example, even as Joan, the political-activist daughter, plans to stay in Dominica and foment a workers' movement, Allfrey shows us how the cultural identity of her family remains deeply enmeshed in the colonial history that allowed it to claim belonging to Dominica. In its confrontation with the end of Empire, however, Allfrey's novel also severs ties with that dissolving past and present and offers an alternative view of colonial responsibility, one that raises new questions about a postcolonial future.

Where writers like Phyllis Bottome and Olivia Manning drew connections between imperial and fascist racism, the warrants of World War II, and those to end Empire, Phyllis Shand Allfrey, like Elspeth Huxley, looks back to World War I as a watershed event that would shadow the interwar years. Allfrey finds the heart of imperial decline in the protracted disorder of the earlier world war, but as we shall see, she also connects this decline to the war on the horizon. Through the character of a shell-shocked colonial veteran her novel exposes the bankruptcy not only of the romantically charged myths that shaped the narrative of the Great War but of the colonial tradition that supported them. Just as the island's lush landscape is deromanticized by its pervasive poverty, so the returning soldier, like the Empire for which he fought, is damaged beyond repair. Taking the fate of Great Britain beyond its own island identity, Allfrey's novel extends the critique of its aristocratic traditions that Rebecca West also located in the war-torn consciousness of a veteran of the Great War. The psychic condition and the return of Allfrey's veteran bear strong resemblance to Chris Baldrick in West's 1918 novel, *Return of the Soldier*. Like Baldrick, Allfrey's Master, the father of the three sisters, has lost his way home. As in both novels, this is a place that, despite its physical beauty and resonance of power and position, is now devoid of meaning for both veterans. But where West's soldier clings to the nurturing memory of a romantic love and is surrounded by a competing trio of desirous women, Allfrey's Master is oblivious to the claims of all the women who love him.

Both writers, thirty years apart, show the persistent dangers of the Great War's haunting allure by having their veterans inextricably attached to it. In West's novel, Chris Baldrick returns to the battlefield when he is forced to confront his aristocratic responsibilities as an equally grim exercise. Allfrey's Master doesn't have to return to the war in body. As his broken spirit reveals, he never left it. His two years at a convalescent hospital in Scotland (clearly modeled on the famed William Rivers's Crocklehurst) have only restored him to an ongoing sense of loss. He now knows that the catastrophic experiences of the war only prepared him to face an insupportable and anomalous heritage. The war exposed the reality that the costs of his colonial heritage were as damaging for the colonizer as the war that was supposed to protect its power. That this damage will lead to another explosion is presaged at the novel's end.

As a site of decaying colonial power, the home to which the Master returns mocks the fervent patriotic spirit which lured so many men to the western front. British through inherited colonial identity, the Master has suffered through a war to save an Empire that exploits but disavows responsibility for his colonial home and its people. Though long freed of slavery, the island is now captive to the reconfiguration of white economic power as its various factions join forces. In actuality, as Allfrey's biographer notes, Dominica never developed the plantation wealth of other West Indian colonies, and by the early twentieth century, the white colonial class was already being eclipsed by the rise of a mulatto elite (Paravisini-Gebert 1997, ix). *The Orchid House* targets the recalcitrant and opportunistic remnants of the white landed gentry and the Catholic clergy. If the Great War freed Europe from the Kaiser's imperial expansionism and wrenched it into a new modernity, in Allfrey's novel, its victory does not extend to Britain's Caribbean Empire. The returning soldier only highlights the tight reins of Dominica's colonial dependence on both colonizer and colonized.

It is in this context that the mystery behind the Master's delayed return can be solved. His traumatized condition combines the wartime horrors he experienced and witnessed with the shock of recognizing that the real threat to his island colony home has not been vanquished, but will prevail. The mental fog of his shell shock is not, therefore, just a pitiable impairment that prevents the Master from coping with ordinary civilian life. Like the drug-laced cigarettes to which he becomes addicted, his war-torn condition also protects him from confronting his own role in his home front crisis. He is now immobilized from acting either on behalf of or against a society that the war has exposed as essentially corrupt. Like that society, however, his wounded and addictive state marks him as resistant to change. Signifying the self-enclosed and myopic culture to which he returns, his family's support of his addiction protects them as well from confronting change and the replay of global danger.

The idea that such reinforcing resistance to change is a totalizing condition of colonialism pervades the entire novel, both in its characterization and in its interpellation of a disruptive gothic narrative. Though the gothic's sense of indefinable horror has been deconstructed since Jane Austen's *Northanger Abbey*, it persists as a favorite genre through which to narrate the emotive power of deeply disturbing psychological states. Truly disturbing, however, for modern literary analysis is the discovery that the gothic has been implicated in Orientalist depictions of exotically dangerous places. With its shadowy figures and frights, the gothic is all too capable of connecting a sense of the unholy with the savagery of the native, as in depictions of the ceremonial rites of indigenous peoples, whether it is Mau Mau oathing in colonial Kenya or the practice of obeah/voodoo in the Caribbean islands. For Allfrey, however, the anachronistic sense of gothic horror works metaphorically to dramatize a decaying Empire that should have ended long ago. As it wrenches colonial politics out of the gothic attic, her novel shows how the horrific life supports of colonial politics have been concealed.

The Orchid House anticipates Jean Rhys's deconstruction of the colonial gothic and the fiendish occupant of its secret attic. Rather than providing the story behind and before Bronte's, however, Allfrey's novel can be seen as imagining the consequences of both versions as shaping the character and future of the colonial island. I will also show how the characters of Bertha Mason and Rochester resonate in both Allfrey's Master and his demonic drug dealer. For example, just as we now read the demonized Bertha Mason as an object of Rochester's colonizing desire,[2] so we can see Allfrey depicting the fulfillment of that desire at the end of Empire. In *The Orchid House,* colonial desire has produced a codependent relationship between the "monster" drug agent and the drug dependent Master (Allfrey 1997, 64). Like Bertha Mason, the Master retreats so far into the defensive shadows of his mind that he disappears from much of the narrative. Though, unlike Bertha, the choice is his, the Master also spends most of his time confined to a space that conceals him from the other characters. As we will see, however, this custody does not protect him from their plotting. In this resemblance to Bertha, in his wounded, passively dependent and constrained state, the Master is not only emasculated and feminized as an individual male character, but represents the collective loss of patriarchal colonial power.

Like the anxiety that lurks inside Rochester's Byronic machismo and that Rhys links to his exploitation of Bertha/Antoinette, the Master's weakness is exposed as chronically related not only to drugs, but to his dependency on the women who support him. In order for the orderly facade of their power base to be maintained, the weakness of both men, which is symptomatic of their illusory order, must be kept secret. Thus Bertha, whose intense sexuality and fiendish strength mock Rochester's virility, must be kept hidden. In Bronte's novel, Rochester's deficiencies are only exposed when Bertha's destruction of his house leaves him blind and lame and he calls for Jane, who must then nurse him. As part of her colonial critique, Allfrey narrates the family's efforts to keep the Master's weakness secret. For Allfrey as for Rhys, the chronic disease afflicting both men can be traced to the incipient decay that has eaten its way through the walls of the colonizing country house order. Moira Ferguson's assessment of Rochester in both his incarnations would thus also apply to the Master: "He lives back home as an insider and outsider, a historical anachronism" (1993, 115). In Allfrey's analysis, it is this endlessly recombining disordered order, as it resounds from Dominica's history, through Bronte's narrative, and glosses Rhys's analysis, that explains the resistance to change. As the novel's title suggests, this order can only be maintained in a hothouse, a carefully tended environment where its fragile, hybrid, orchid-like inhabitants are protected from external vicissitudes. The Master, his forbears, and heirs are members of that endangered species—the white Creole—that, as Gayatri Spivak designates this identity category, is "caught between the English imperialist and the black native" (1986, 269). As Rhys's Rochester concurs, this trap predicts the Creole's dead end: "Creole of pure English descent she may be, but they are not English or European either" (Rhys 1966, 67).

To further develop and complicate this analysis of a tense Caribbean colonial identity, Allfrey creates the drug dealer as a doppelganger who taunts the Master by reminding him that without colonial power his identity and subjectivity are in jeopardy. There is no Master without his ability to control and dominate. By contrast, the uncanny, inexhaustible supplies of the drug dealer, Mr. Lilipoulala, endow him with an immeasurable power that contrasts with the Master's declining, near-absent state. Recalling Bronte's racialization of Bertha Mason, Mr. Lilipoulala is portrayed as a dark island figure. But despite the dangerous powers they represent, both are denied any expressiveness that would allow them a character of their own. Instead, they are reduced to speechless embodiments of a poisonous allure—the Caribbean woman's excessive sexuality and Mr. Lilipoulala's drugs. Bertha's intermittent escapes and violent visitations are responses to Rochester's expropriation of her fortune and predict his comeuppance. Mr. Lilipoulala's recurring visits deplete the Master's fortune and character to the extent that there is nothing left with which to make restitution for colonial expropriation and exploitation. Just as Jean Rhys ascribes the demonizing of Bertha Mason to colonial power, Allfrey situates "that evil creature," Mr. Lilipoulala, as a critical question about the legitimacy not only of the colonial presence, but of its narrative (Allfrey 1997, 64). Rhys rescues Bertha's subjectivity by reclaiming her as Antoinette and offering her a history of her own. Allfrey shows that even though the Empire is coming to an end, the monstrousness of its lingering oppression can still be felt in its progeny—the demonized colonial subject who has neither name nor face nor voice.

Like so many silhouetted portraits of dangerous Others, Allfrey's can easily be written off as racist and reinscribing colonial oppression, especially

because we never hear Mr. Lilipoulala's side of the story. This absence can also
be seen as an erasure of the Other's language and therefore a reflection of a
history particular to the Caribbean. As Ashcroft, Griffiths, and Tiffin explain,
those who were imported as slaves suffered "the loss of their own 'voice'" and
found that psychic survival depended on their facility for a kind of *double
entendre*. They were forced to develop the skill of being able to say one thing
in front of "massa" and have it interpreted differently by their fellow slaves.
This skill involved a radical subversion of the meanings of the master's
tongue" (1989, 146). The doubling of the drug dealer and drug addict, however, tells a different story. One side of this reflexive portrait depicts Mr.
Lilipoulala as "such a man of darkness and mud that it would take more than
a rainstorm to keep him from sucking the blood of a corpse" (Allfrey 1997,
84). The vampire image here, with its insatiable desire for the life blood of the
other, is very mutual, however. Having arisen from the "darkness and mud" of
the Great War, the Master is left with no desire except that which drains the
remaining life of his colonial estate. In turn, as the drug dealer exists only in
relation to the Master, he has no self-determination; his evil is a function of a
history of parasitic colonial desire. Because it is a reflection of the colonial
order, the demonized colonial Other threatens the romantic, affirming version
of the pioneer adventure, so both Bertha Mason and Mr. Lilipoulala must be
destroyed. The gothic night of terror in which the drug dealer makes his only
appearance resounds with narrative memories of Bertha Mason bringing
down the house which has imprisoned her. Though Mr. Lilipoulala is killed
off as well, and the Master, like Rochester, is being cared for, instead of representing a new beginning, Allfrey's novel turns back on itself. Every hope for
regeneration and progress is situated to examine the forces that keep the colonial order in thrall to the past. And then, as though testing the grounds of her
own revisionary analysis, Allfrey moves her narrative from the gothic into the
modern.

The modern, in *The Orchid House*, consists of the reactionary politics that
institutionalize the resistance to change. Even the change from its French
imperial hold to British dominion has only reinforced the island's colonizing
forces. Allfrey's indictment of the remaining Catholic clergy shows the willingness of ideological enemies to become allies when the stakes are the economic and political power of Dominica's future. Her portrait of the priest,
Father Toussaint, in league with the dissolute but opportunistic British colonial Rufus depicts a political offensive of traditional colonial hierarchies
against the threat of workers' economic and human rights. Even at the end of
the novel, when the Master's socialist daughter Joan has enlisted the partnership of their black servant Baptiste to launch a workers' initiative, she realizes
that she can only succeed if she accedes to the combined and therefore
impenetrable power of the immutable Catholic Toussaint and her all too

resilient uncle Rufus. If the novel accepts this unholy alliance as necessary to effect any progressive change, it does so by viewing it as also integral to that change. In reaching their own détente, the centuries-old rivalries of French and British colonial interests and secular and religious politics are forced to sacrifice their separate hegemonic spheres. In so doing, they acknowledge the power that will succeed them—the black workers.

Father Toussaint and Rufus represent the reactionary forces that would keep the islanders ignorant and passive. The newspaper over which Rufus gains control presents itself as a voice of progress while insisting on the necessity of gradual change, a policy that, in effect, reinforces the status quo of a racist system of education and workers' inequities. Together, Toussaint and Rufus impose and enforce a politics that crushes the will of the people they supposedly serve. Rufus, who has produced several mulatto children by black women, seems, on the one hand, to have abandoned the racial strictures that govern white colonial society. On the other hand, he becomes enraged when Baptiste questions the editorial positions of his newspaper, not only because Rufus is being confronted with the hypocrisies of his own personal and professional life, but because the challenge is articulated by a "foolish Nigger" (Allfrey 1997, 120). That such racism is integral to Rufus's double life becomes clear when Lally, the Master's family housekeeper and nursemaid, reveals why he begins to publicly acknowledge the mulatto Cornélie as his daughter. White self-interest overcomes racial barriers when Cornélie inherits property from her enterprising black mother. Reinforcing Rufus's racist recognition of Cornélie, Toussaint retains the vise-like hold over her consciousness, a hold that began with her education in a Catholic convent. After Andrew, her lover and father of her child, is taken away from her, with no community of her own, she turns to religious retreat for comfort. Toussaint and the religious hopefulness that supports his power thus loom in the background as the arbiters of her desires. Cornélie may be another prototypical tragic mulatta, but instead of the melodrama that usually determines her fateful demise, Allfrey leads her into a more indeterminate, modern, and perhaps even more oppressive plot.

Just as this religious vestige of colonial rule is still powerful enough to infect the will of a free mulatta, so it is shown to be equally self-destructive. We see this as Allfrey projects the ravages of colonial settlement metaphorically onto the diseased and inert landscape still in its thrall. Instead of providing nourishment for its people, the lush beauty of the island is presented as alluring but poisonous, much like Mr. Lilipoulala, like the refuge offered by the Church, and like the duplicitous paternalism of Cornélie's father, Rufus. A particularly telling scene illustrates this when the eldest sister, Stella, takes Helmut, her young son, to Petit Cul-de-Sac, the home of Cornélie, Andrew, and their daughter, Roxelane, in the interior of the island. Stella's concern that the "great glory" of the island's "beautiful secrecy" is threatened by tourism is blind to the colonial damage that is its real secret (Allfrey 1997, 66). If Stella never gains this insight, it becomes visible to the reader when her child becomes ill from the delicious and bountiful food he is fed at Petit Cul-de-Sac and when she finds her beloved Andrew "chilled and blue" in the landscape she takes for "paradise" (Allfrey 1997, 67, 68). Rather than an invasion from abroad, the coughing and weakness afflicting Andrew have a local and critical etiology. A child of the island's Creole gentry, Andrew suffers from an inertia that is symptomatic of the lack of will and direction he inherits from a self-indulgent colonial past. As though portraying the consequences of this history, Andrew's indolent irresponsibility toward his child and her mother resembles that of Rufus toward his many black lovers and mulatto offspring. Instead of a healthy hybridity, these interracial relationships have created an unhealthy mutation, a colonizing inbreeding that weakens or distorts the self-determining instincts of parents and progeny. Thus the older, respectable Rufus should not be seen as having recovered from his dissolute youth, but as converting his sexual prerogatives into political domination of the very people who include his heirs.

Dramatizing the self-destructiveness of this exploitation, Andrew's consumption represents not the cause of his coughing, but a symptom of being "as beautiful as Narcissus," a self-consuming disease which mirrors the dissolution of the Empire itself (Allfrey 1997, 71). Like the Master, as though inheriting an incurable imperial disorder, Andrew recedes into himself from the battles over Empire. In a telling exchange, when Stella asks him if there is any hope of a cure, he ascribes his resistance to "the news of all the blood that is being spilt or is just going to be spilt over the world" (55). Traumatized by the lack of meaning in such warfare, he, too, like the Master, is addicted to withdrawing from action, only to perform the horrors of war on himself. But war is not presented as only a figment of their narcissism. Between the two men, the memory of the Great War and the Spanish Civil War circulates and intensifies to presage the coming of the next global outbreak. And just as the Master retreats from the ghosts of his war experience, so Andrew shrinks from assuming responsibility for his own haunting. Unable to face the global explosion, he implodes. Because he refuses medical help, his condition worsens, threatening to kill him. When Stella first sees him, he looks to her "like a young boy," not energetic or anarchically playful, but passively dependent, playing the feminine role of powerlessness like her father (67). The combination of abrogating responsibility and preferring dependency plays into the hands of the manipulative power of Toussaint and Rufus and therefore perpetuates a condition that threatens to rival that of "spilt blood." As part of the political desire that Allfrey's plot expresses, this neocolonial domination, is equally inward-

turning and self-absorbed. Refusing to adapt to the needs of a people struggling to be free, this dominion is doomed.

Stella's blindness about the island's "secrecy" masks her own romantic narcissism and colonial legacy. What has poisoned her son is not an overindul-
gence in native strawberries and the cooking by a "dirty old Obeah woman"
(Allfrey 1997, 76). Instead, the atmosphere has been poisoned by Stella's complicity with colonial domination. Her self-indulgent fantasy that the island's
beauty and bounty are meant for her recuperation takes none of the island's
needs into account. Paying no attention to Cornélie's desires and claims on
Andrew, Stella flirts with Andrew as a recapitulation of her own childhood, an
imaginary time when consequences have no reality. But several narrative
voices combine to mock her. The Edenic landscape that has been poisoned by
colonial history takes its vengeance not only on her child. The defiled island
also recalls the grueling farmwork and disillusionments that characterize her
marriage. And finally, even Andrew responds to her "bookish talk" by assessing
it as "grandly *impossible*" (70, italics in original). If, as Andrew reminds her, her
flirtation with fantasy is "not innocent," the novel implicates her in a plot that
tests the innocence of its own self-conscious critique of colonial forces (75).
While Stella's two sisters are given the work of reform and rescue, she enacts
the revenge of colonial decline against itself.

Stella's revenge tale, a legacy from her father's story, but one that disrupts
it, occupies an appropriately gothic space. During a stormy night, while her
father waits feverishly for Mr. Lilipoulala, Stella strikes back. Decked out with
cape and lantern, Stella is typecast as one of those hapless heroines of an earlier age, caught up in plots that veer between the ghost story and its objective
correlative, the tale of sexual terror. The doubly duplicitous nature of the
gothic serves Allfrey's novel throughout, for it enables her to expose the emotional excesses and exotic dark powers associated with Caribbean tales of
obeah and the sexually volatile Creole as disguising a modern realist drama:
the persistent terror underlying colonial power. Like those gothic narratives of
the eighteenth and nineteenth centuries, the primary danger in Stella's story is
not to her body but to her inherited position and privilege. Driven to despair
by her father's drug addiction and the secrecy and denial that ensure it and its
economic and social costs, Stella makes a melodramatic attempt to rescue him.
Confronting the grisly reality of Mr. Lilipoulala's cadaverous figure, Stella goes
to meet him and, enlisting the help of the stormy black night, makes sure he
falls off the rickety bridge carrying him to deliver his ungodly goods.

Instead of a cure, however, killing off the drug agent only exposes the
inherent insubstantiality of the Master and the late colonial order. Stella's
actions entrap her in a plot that cannot extricate itself from the colonial politics that have determined her family's fate. These politics, moreover, turn out

to be a great deal darker than either the gothic night or the specter of evil. Stella may have executed the agent of her family's dissolution, but, as in her relationship to Andrew, her flirtations with her own unbridled desire have created new dangers. Waiting in the wings of this modern melodrama is another figure associated with the gothic: the evil Catholic priest. Allfrey unabashedly exploits this icon, which she justifies through her reading of Dominica's history. As Paravisini-Gebert recounts, "Allfrey was never shy about attributing Dominica's ills to the tyranny of '300 years of Catholic morality,' and in *The Orchid House,* the church emerges as the most conservative and powerful force in Dominica" (1997, xxv). Aligned with Lilipoulala's demonic figure, who is also Catholic, Toussaint seizes the knowledge of his disappearance as political currency. The Father pieces together Stella's guilt and, with the threat of going public, not only drives her back to the United States, but compromises her sister Joan's political activity. In its combination of modern political acuity and gothic melodrama, Allfrey's novel provides a guide to reading the perplexity of abstract evil in colonial modernity. No longer mysterious or beyond comprehension or unrelated to material experience, the evil in her modernist gothic melodrama is sensational only in its revelation that danger emanates quite logically from the clash of interdependent power fostered by an archaic and oppressive colonial feudalism.

Even with the rescue mission engineered by the youngest sister, Natalie, the novel asserts the island's resistance to change. Armed with the millions she inherited from her elderly late husband and airborne to the island by her current paramour's seaplane, Natalie cuts a modernist swathe through the gothic hold on a colonial past. With mischievous wit and the narrator's support, she undercuts the ineffable power of Father Toussaint's religious authority: "'Nearly all the people in this island were born in sin, as you say,' remarked Miss Natalie, losing her formal air of reverence. 'What would you do for parishioners otherwise?'" (Allfrey 1997, 168–169). As though usurping the priest's celestial domain, when last seen, she is airborne. Having packed her father and Andrew aboard her lover's plane, she will take control of the retrogressive plot in which they have been complicit. But as we don't know if either the Master or Andrew is saved from their life-denying fate, despite her reality-testing pragmatism, Natalie's plot may be as romantically illusory as theirs or Stella's, in short, a flight of fancy. With its comic overtones, however, Natalie's mocking voice is also self-deprecating and therefore enacts one of the novel's several self-critical perspectives. Having characterized the three sisters as becoming outsiders to their inherited colonial position, Allfrey questions the definition of colonial and of colonizer. Like herself, her parents, and grandparents, the sisters were born in Dominica. They were not taken there like Elspeth Huxley and Rumer Godden, to be settlers in a land occupied by a more indigenous people. The sisters have no other cultural identity; nor are they raised to yearn for return to England. Being a Dominican is not a state of exile; leaving it is.

The sisters claim the identity into which they were born as not only self-defining but as entitling them to define Dominica's fate. As each one returns, she experiences Dominica as a magical place, endorsing the power she feels to effect progress and cure its ills. But as we have seen with each of their plots, Dominica asserts a resisting power of its own. And so even Joan, whose only self-indulgence is to assert herself on behalf of the workers, learns that her uncle Rufus and Father Toussaint are able to hold dominion over the island because they also serve the purposes and needs of many of the island's people, colonizer and colonized alike.

The most expressive voice of the island's resistance to change is one that remains critically controversial—that of the novel's narrator, Lally, the black servant and nursemaid whose name and relationship to the family are based on Allfrey's own nurse. As Paravisini-Gebert summarizes the criticism, "Lally's obdurate resistance to join the wave of political change [is] seen as emblematic of Allfrey's 'conservatism' " (1997, xxiii). Lally's resistance derives not only from the only stability she has known—her subordinate, subjugated place in the family—but from the need to protect herself against social and emotional isolation, both of which are features of her position and of the possibility of change. For despite her servitude and the social and racial hierarchies that define it, she professes for the family a love that is rewarded by the knowledge that they are as dependent on her as she is on them, albeit in different ways. Allfrey measures this difference very acutely; the family's need for Lally to keep their domestic lives in order extends to their emotional indulgences, which they can confide in her without the social censure they could expect from an equal. This intimacy, however, works only one way. While she knows the Master and his wife and their three daughters all too well, and therefore can narrate their story even when she lacks access to their behavior, they know little or nothing of her and are about as interested. She is there to serve them, and through her very invested narrative, the novel focuses on their lives and her reactions and assessment of them. This focus, moreover, raises the question of whether she is given an emotional life apart from her dependent love for them. We hear very little of her feelings about herself and her condition, most of which she dismisses in favor of ministering to the family. Does she even have a story beyond her servitude? Such questions extend to that which plagues postcolonial theory more generally: Who speaks for the subaltern, especially if the words she speaks for herself reflect the ways in which her subjectivity is totally bound up in those for whom she is a blank slate? On the other hand, as the white family's story rests in her words, is Lally being granted a shaping and interpretive power over their "machinations?" (Allfrey, 1997, 110).

Paravisini-Gebert argues convincingly that in order to track the process which Dominica must endure if it is to progress toward social justice, Lally must be made to represent internalized oppression. As the character of the socialist sister, Joan, shows, there is no reason for any of the island's white institutions to yield their power if those like Lally submerge their subjectivity in them. I am going to argue with Paravisini-Gebert's claim that Lally has "been oblivious" to "the corruption that rules the economy and political life of the island, the hypocrisy of the press, the repression of the estate workers, and the unyieldingness of the Catholic church" (1997, xxiii). Instead, I see Lally as expressing a critical understanding of this economic and moral corruption and as constituting the environment that created her. In one particular instance, she tells us how proud she is of her "skin, not Frenchy and Catholic" and without "a drop of white blood," the combination of which, for her, would constitute racial, cultural, and political vice (Allfrey 1997, 4). Such an assessment, especially as it follows Allfrey's own analysis of Catholic abuses, should make us wary about Lally's modesty, that she cannot "understand Miss Joan's special words, words which would never perfectly reach my ears" (112). In light of Lally's otherwise astute powers of observation and understanding, her modesty can be seen as also mocking those who might assume she cannot "understand . . . special words." That Lally's rhetorical strategy is also a negotiation with white colonial power is made clear in her ironic barb at Miss Joan's high-minded resolve: "'The people, the people. I don't understand the sacred way you say that word, Miss Joan. I don't understand it at all. You only know about a dozen of them, anyhow'" (110). If we understand Lally's point as deflating the all-knowing self-righteousness of political good intentions, it would also attest to Allfrey's self-critical powers. For not only is the political activist Miss Joan based on her own character, but, for Allfrey, Lally is the novel's "heroine," whose creation required Allfrey "to jump out of [her] own skin and into . . . Lally's" (quoted in Paravisini-Gebert 1996, 79).

Constructing the Caribbean subaltern with this critical voice, of course, anticipates the character of Christophine in Rhys's novel. Although Lally is nowhere as defiant as Christophine, they both occupy similar critical positions. Both women challenge the reactionary thinking that supports the island's self-deluded political culture, but Lally also mocks the progressivism that suffers from a lack of political reality testing. Such characterization forms a pattern among several women writers I consider in this study. The Egyptian porters in Olivia Manning's *The Levant Trilogy*, the Kikuyu workers in Elspeth Huxley's memoir and novels, and the Kashmiri servants in Rumer Godden's *Kingfishers Catch Fire* also express an ironic bewilderment at the self-deluded relationship the colonial settler or sojourner imagines with indigenous people. As though questioning the integrity of their own narratives, these writers create a heuristic that not only anticipates postcolonial questions but challenges them with their own self-consciousness. Of course, one can accuse these writers of letting themselves off the hook since self-deprecating humor can be as self-defensive as it might be honest. Moreover, how can the colonial writer take credit for granting subjectivity to the colonized when she controls what they say and do?

Lally's ongoing dependent relationship with the Master's family is the key to Allfrey's controversial narrative form. As the servant narrates it herself, she enacts recognition of her position in relation to the island's power structure. At first, we might not think so, for when each of the three sisters returns, Lally all too willingly takes on the work as their children's nursemaid. Though by this time she is elderly and suffers her own illness, this work provides her with the critical perspective through which she can both remain allied with the family and construct a narrative distance from their perfidies.[3] As her narrative negotiates this relationship, it also keeps her from facing the death of the self that would result from severing their mutual dependency. Having tied her identity and selfhood to them, there is no other family or community to which she could turn for substantiation and identity. As Paravisini-Gebert emphasizes, Lally is "a foreigner in Dominica" not only because she is from Montserrat, but because she is "a Methodist in a Catholic island, and educated black woman who speaks English in a country peopled by a patois-speaking illiterate peasantry, and 'the last of the slaves' in a novel about the empowerment of the black population" (1996, 83). While it is clear that the family intends to take care of her, the narrative thrust is that Lally nurtures herself.

The black servant asserts the power of her own substantial character by caring for her white colonial employers, by keeping them from fading into their insubstantiality and retreating into the hothouse of colonial fantasy and disappointments—the orchid house. In turn, the physical suffering Lally endures, and in silence, indicates the cruel price she pays for allegiance to a system that cannot grant her subjectivity but that feeds her knowledge that this is her constructed, not natural state of being. Her story does not, however, end there. Her silence is broken by her narrative. Her expressed understanding that Joan can create a political rhetoric that sacralizes "the people" includes a critical question: Where are these "people" as individuals in the white woman's construction of an aggregate black body? Just as her own critical comments are dismissed by Joan as naive and "unjust," so Lally is made to disappear into a mass that confirms Joan's mission (Allfrey 1997, 111).

It is the persistence of Lally's voice over the course of the novel, through its final pages, that affirms not only her intelligence but that of the novel itself. As Lally constantly asks questions of each of the sisters, their cumulative effect addresses the novel itself, as though Allfrey is creating Lally as a critical voice through which to construct her own assessment, not only of the island's colonial history and present, but of her own involvement in its future. Written just before Allfrey returned to Dominica to organize the Dominica Freedom Party, its dialogue between her fictional counterpart, Joan, and Lally antici- pates critical questions about such activism and its imaginative vision. Each of Lally's questions addresses the negotiation of power that would lead to the island's independence and the emotional needs that drive the returning sister's efforts. Between the idealism that Joan would translate into political action and a productive postcolonial future lies the open question of whether the political imagination of the colonial woman can understand the nature of the colonized people's self-determination. The novel's ending makes it clear that this knowledge lies in Lally's hands; she asserts that she, "too, had [her] wider reaches beyond the family" (Allfrey 1997, 185).

These "wider reaches" extend to the entire novel and its time line. Tar- geting World War I as the beginning of the end of Empire, the novel takes us into the crisis years of the Spanish Civil War, where Joan's husband has been wounded, and the first rumblings of World War II. Though the flight plan of the seaplane carrying the Master and Andrew includes the New World, Canada, and the possibility of their recuperation, and though the new war is never mentioned, its storm clouds are present. They are embedded in the anx- iety from which the Master may not recover and which accompanies Natalie's romantic optimism. The expression of this dread is given, as we should expect by now, to Lally: "It seemed certain to me that something final would happen, that the seaplane with its anxious load would run into the fiercest of hurri- canes and become a few splinters of metal and board—the youngest mermaid would be cast into the deep sea, while the spirit of the Master—who could say where that turbulent spirit would find rest?" (Allfrey 1997, 179). Having already been tested and subverted, we can ask, What is this melodramatic and mythic imagery doing in the novel's last words? If, however, we see this figu- ration in light of the novel's analysis of late colonial politics, we can see how Allfrey is connecting the disintegration of imperial power to the trajectory of war that will climax shortly.

The imagery in this passage is positioned against that of romantic travel writing, which subjugates the timeless place and its Others to the discovery or recuperation of the self. Writing in the immediate postwar period, as she is planning to return to Dominica, Allfrey implicates her own activist travel plans in the island's imperial past and present. She is unlike Elspeth Huxley, who fer- vently believed that bringing her expertise in agricultural environmentalism back to Africa could benefit the land and its people. Allfrey confronts the pos- sibility that the idea of modern progress is itself a mythic construct that car- ries the dangers of obliterating the colonial subject.[4] As her novel presents it, the history of Dominica's colonial subjectivity has created identities that are felt by the colonizer and colonized as theirs, as that which they claim for themselves as having inherited and experienced that history.[5] Together, this inheritance and these identities also reclaim and revise the idea of home as it relates to the mobility of the colonizer as she moves within the colonial sphere and exiles herself.[6] As Allfrey's three sisters come and go and experience their sojourns as "exile, mobility, difference, modernity," and as the hybrid identity they are creating, it is not their "knowledge of a Self, society, and nation" that is being generated, but ours (Grewal 1996, 4). For the island's people, settlers and colonized alike, there is no postcolonial future without the recognition and affirmation of their contesting colonial identities and identifications with their colonial home. In this way, *The Orchid House* engages the island's future as struggling not only against the persistence of its self-indulgent colonial past and claims, but with its identity and role as the very idea of imperialism is about to be blown up. Allfrey argues that the future into which Natalie's plane is flying will explode into that "fiercest of hurricanes," the Second World War, carrying with it and splintering all the romantic myths that colonial power can be restored. Where Bronte rescues the colonizer from his own perfidies, and Rhys traces their costs, Allfrey confronts both imperial devastation and the responsibilities that must accompany a postcolonial future and identity. Allfrey said of *The Orchid House,* "I wanted to write a book about an island. . . . The island is the real hero. It was probably nostalgia. It's a life that's gone now" (quoted in Paravisini-Gebert 1996, 81).[7]

PHYLLIS BOTTOME:
ANTIFASCIST ANTICOLONIAL ACTIVIST

Phyllis Bottome's politically activist career did not begin with the necessity to end the Empire. She had already proved her political mettle in her antifascist rallying and writings, but even as victory was declared over the Axis powers, she felt that the struggle against political oppression was not over. It was while living in Austria and Germany in the 1920s and 1930s that she first recognized the urgency that would lead her to assume this responsibility.[8] As the Nazis rose to power with a rhetoric of racial purity and supremacism and she connected the designs of all imperial conquest and expansion to all racialist ideologies, she began to write her polemical novels. Early in her career, her 1924 epic novel, *Old Wine,* dramatized the inbreeding of Central European antisemitism with the political and economic union of old and new guard. Their opportunism led not to political change but to new opportunities to scapegoat Others for their frustrated consolidations of power. This was a failure of political responsibility that would lead to oppression. Though predictive of fascist persecution, the novel also introduces a powerfully optimistic voice in the character of an American feminist who resists the romantic lure of Central Europe's old aristocracy. For the rest of her writing career, Bottome would continue to create women characters who challenge political infamy.

Bottome's 1937 novel, *The Mortal Storm,* was a political and dramatic plea for Britain to involve itself in the fate of the Jews who were now victims of the Nazis' racial policies and persecution. Though sanitized of its specifically Jewish and feminist content, the 1940 MGM film version also appealed to American involvement. With its star-studded cast, including James Stewart, Margaret Sullavan, and Robert Young, with its romantically tragic ending (also drastically different from the novel), the film was a blockbuster success, commercially, critically, and in its propaganda.[9] Despite the efforts of Bottome and so many other British women writers, as well as the reports that were reaching Britain from Europe by 1942, Jewish victims, along with Gypsies and Others, would be ignored by the Allies' war aims of World War II.[10] Bottome viewed this inaction as morally reprehensible and historically linked to the racial ideologies that underwrote the imperial history of her own nation. As she interpreted it, the emphasis on winning the war did not include concern about Hitler's targeted victims, but rather consigned them to a racial category that made them unsuitable subjects even for colonization. Their stateless condition endowed them with no homeland and, for all too many in the British home and foreign offices, marked them as unworthy of one. Bottome challenged not only her own people, but all the Allies to exercise their democratic ideals by saving Hitler's victims from his exterminationist racial policy. In her books of reportage, pamphlets, letters to editors, radio talks, and public lectures, in *The Mortal Storm* and two other novels of the 1940s, *Within the Cup* and *The Lifeline,* she developed a lifelong activism on behalf of oppressed Others. She expected Britain and its Allies to guarantee all peoples the right to their lives and, following that emergency, to their different identities and cultures.

Phyllis Bottome was subject to dismissal by audiences in her day; her rallies for the endangered Jews could not dent the armor of official war aims and a pervasive antisemitism. But despite her own political defeats, she would never consider herself anything but an active agent who is neither a victim of her government nor complicit with it. Tirelessly seeking and finding outlets for her campaign, she would therefore never claim the status of victim for herself. In her belief that speaking on behalf of the victims was a moral and political imperative, Phyllis Bottome has much to say about the vexed relationship between racialized discourse and the rhetoric and narratives of democratic actions and inaction. And in so doing, she reweaves the racialized relationship between colonized and colonizer, addressing the question so relevant in today's postcolonial theories: Who can speak for the colonized? As though responding to the postcolonial claim that colonial writers can only further oppress their colonized subjects by representing them, Bottome's writing constructs critical dialogues between colonial subject and object. The shape of these dialogues creates a tense intimacy and possibilities for a transforming politics within the radical alterity and irreconcilable differences of colonial subject and object. What she recognized was the interweave of two histories, that even as the Allied nations were fighting for the lives of their people, other peoples were fighting them for the legitimacy to define their own lives and nationhood. That this was the moment of truth in the name of an argument about democracy drives the narrative forms of her novels of the 1930s through her 1950 novel, *Under the Skin*. Each of these novels gives voice to the subjects and victims of World War II and of imperialism.

While anticolonial struggles simmered worldwide long before and after World War II, Bottome recognized that whatever victories could be claimed against empires had been indecisive and, worse, hadn't even won the legitimacy of being identified as war. Despite this willful political neglect, these struggles could claim a literary victory in writing by Bottome, Storm Jameson, who was president of British Pen during the war, and other British women writers. Their writing represents protracted efforts to bring the consciousness of racialized Others into the cultural mainstreams that still continued to reflect the whiteness of so many other modernist writers.

This complicated and possibly vexing political position embraces one of literary modernism from its origins in the 1920s through the 1940s, when theorists until recently believed the experiment had come to an end, and through the postwar periods in which the British Empire was dissolving. At the same time that Bottome was writing a political consciousness, she was working against that modernist mainstream which was representing the decentering consciousness of the psychologically and socially besieged modern subject. While Bottome was dramatizing the political silencing of her subjects, modernists were endowing their psychologically tormented characters with self-expressive language. At the same time that Bottome was self-consciously polemical and even propagandist, modernist writers were questioning the possibility of constructing a coherent political statement. In turn, fragmented characters are made to mirror the vexed modernist consciousness of the writer while calling attention to the questionable power their writing endowed. Bottome, Storm Jameson, and Rebecca West, by contrast, had staked their careers on different political and literary questions. Even as they witnessed and then fled Germany in 1934 to face Hitler's bombs falling on their own heads in the battle of Britain, they were asking, What literary forms can represent this treacherous reality? Even after victory was declared, they recognized that the battle against racial persecution wasn't completely over, but had to be fought as a global struggle against the remains of imperial domination. But instead of being "caught between the European values they renounce and the alienated colonial spaces [modernists] narrativize," these women wrote novels that question those values and spaces (Gikandi 1996, 48).

ANTICOLONIAL MELODRAMA: *UNDER THE SKIN*

It is the juncture of the Allies' victory and the struggle to end the Empire that takes Phyllis Bottome to a new frontier of political consciousness and modern literary history. After her own battle against fascism, Bottome mourned the world's losses and faced the horizon of a new world crisis. Her novel *Under the Skin* plots the racialized bridge from the end of World War II to the end of Empire. A politicized version of the familiar genre of female development, it locates its energy from the explosive effects of those forms of engagement Homi Bhabha calls mimicry and hybridity. *Under the Skin* links the world's indifference to the fate of Hitler's victims to the violation of human rights in imperial conquest by weaving a political argument into a melodrama of sexual intrigue. Questioning her own narrative form as well, Bottome portrays powerful connections between the realpolitik of colonial relations and the literary politics of narrative history and form. While so much British fiction of the 1950s revived traditions of sensibility and elegiac comedies of upper-class manners, Bottome dramatized historical linkages between the oppressive practices of domestic and imperial ideologies. Such linkages, she argues, define the social structures which seemed to sustain traditional fictional forms as well as the Empire, but actually foretold the self-indulgences of the former and the self-destructiveness of the latter. As she establishes these politicized fictional linkages, moreover, Bottome shows how the political themes of modernism could not and would never go far enough to engage the fates of those the world still considered Other.

Under the Skin constructs its bridge across these moral landscapes by sending a young Englishwoman, Lucy Armstrong, on an odyssey of emotional and political recovery after her own war service and after her parents, her husband, and then a new love are killed in the war. Left alone to face the bare cupboards of Britain's postwar austerity, she finds that even a Labor Party victory cannot defeat "a tradition of patriotic snobbery" (Bottome 1950, 54). Lucy understands that her nostalgic memories of a just war—"Dying together if we had to, but not to be beaten" (247)—have already become a political and social anachronism, and so she decides "to get away from a life that didn't seem real after the war" (203). Like Allfrey's anachronistic myths of a romantic colonial order, the patriotic slogans of wartime will be tested by the violations of imperialism. While Britain wrestles with its bankrupt coffers and diminishing world power, Bottome confronts the remains of its imperial mission by creating a novelistic form that can dramatize its damaging effects and articulate an interdependent future. Thus, with high hopes for a more bracing challenge than England's domestic recovery, Lucy takes a job in a Caribbean British colony as headmistress of a girls' boarding school. Though Bottome never names the island, we can assume from her own travel writing that it is Jamaica, a colony that didn't win its independence from Britain until 1963.

Bottome combines two genres in this novel to create her anticolonial melodrama: romance and political thriller. In the first instance, her heroine struggles with her romantic attraction to the school's doctor. Then, employing another implication of romance, there are those factions in the novel, both within the school and outside, who are threatened by Lucy's romantic political agenda; she wishes to build harmonious race relations within the school community. As the novel performs the intermarriage or hybridization of these genres, it also tests the romantic assumptions underwriting their conventions, including elements of the gothic, such as the inevitable raging storm that is so important to *The Orchid House* and a mysterious murder attempt. Instead of tragic renunciation, heroic rescue, or happily-ever-after writ large on the bodies of love, Bottome exploits the conventions of melodrama so that they come to reflect the extremist social, cultural, and racial assumptions which form the basis of colonial and postcolonial conflict. In turn, she juxtaposes these conventions with provocative references to the Holocaust as central to her anticolonial critique. In this way, the conventions of genre fiction perform the work of a stringent historical and ideological analysis.

Lucy's journey carries her across racial lines that, as we might expect, are fertile grounds for melodrama. But most tellingly for this postwar, pre-postcolonial novel, Lucy's emigration puts her at risk of conflict, not only with the colonial squirarchy who thoroughly disapprove of her progressive ideas, but with the racially mixed women students and administration who have their own vexed hierarchies to protect. At the eye of the storm—and what makes this novel both sensational and potentially sensationalist—is the fact that Lucy's new love, the school's doctor, is half black. Despite the transgressive politics of their racial constructions, despite the possibilities they might represent for a productively collaborative political and social future, these characters and their relationship cannot in any way be seen as a blossoming hybrid species. As we will see, their relationship defies such optimistic gleanings, especially in the theoretical terms of a negotiated peace or settlement, either among colonized subjects or between the resisting colonized and the reluctant colonizer. In Bottome's plotting, instead of grafting a progressive, anticolonial persona onto these vestiges of colonial history, her colonial and colonized subjects represent the unstable byproducts of racialized colonial relations. They embody the dark truths of the persistence of colonial racism in a presence that is kept invisible by two formidable curricula—that taught by the school and that taught by the colonial community. The school is designed to take in girls whose mixed race identities make them unacceptable to the town, from which it is conveniently set apart. Its lessons include teaching the girls to be not quite indigenous islanders as they dress them up in British accents and a 1950s set of Edwardian manners. The colonial community makes sure that they can never be quite British or, as Bhabha observes of mimicry, *"Almost the same but not white,"* a performance that highlights "the difference between being English and being Anglicized" (1998, 156, italics in original). The girls may pass their Anglophone exams with flying colors, but their racial lack of Englishness guarantees only rejection by the settler community, which arms its clubs and gated communities with a color bar.

As Bottome dramatizes the school, it represents the sexual rivalries and racial tensions that issue from a position of being not quite anywhere or anyone, and that instability in turn reflects the stalwart political and social fragility of the colony and the colonizing idea itself. While many postcolonial critics have noted how postwar black emigration destabilized English identity, Bottome takes Englishness to the colony to confront it with the emerging identity of those who are struggling to be free of its mythic and political power. To engage the characters of schoolgirls in this struggle highlights the sense of emergence as they are at a critical juncture in the development of their personal and social identities. Typical adolescents in one sense, the girls form cliques whose members switch allegiances as quickly and as often as their moods shift. But as Bottome shows, in a racialized society, isolated from their families and with no communities to call their own, these girls become part of a deadly politics. Having internalized their own marginalized position, they then project it onto Lucy, who has chosen to isolate herself among them. As she becomes the scapegoat of their frustrations, but continues to offer her guidance, the novel defines their relationship as the late colonial moment of rebellion. On the verge of maturity, the girls could be seen as the object of colonial condescension, just like all those natives who so many imperial powers assumed just weren't ready for self-determination. As Bottome plots the end of Empire, however, the colonial subject has been educated and understands the presence of the English headmistress all too well. No matter how sympathetic and supportive, instead of being a role model, Lucy is situated as another colonizing agent. As war breaks out among them, the very lessons brought by colonial missions are turned against them.

This novel challenges its own position in relation to the persisting presence of the reluctant colonial agent. Through the character of the English headmistress, Bottome asks: Can the white colonial writer represent an authentic or indigenous colonial experience if the language of her representation can only be figured in the European political history and cultural traditions that constitute it? Is it possible to imagine a narrative that analyzes oppressive colonial relations through the lens of a just war? And can the collective experience of racial subjection be addressed through the narrative of individual development, that is, of a white Englishwoman whose sense of self has been built on fulfillment and agency as the pathway to social and political responsibility? In my reading, Bottome makes it very clear that while she would never renounce her celebration of the Allied victory in World War II, she would neither represent nor rationalize her nation's imperial inequities so that they were rendered invisible by that victory. And just as she demonstrated in her earlier writing, she would insist on making the otherwise invisible colonized peoples visible to an audience that would more than likely prefer to look the other way. Bottome would also never yield to the kind of political complacency that would allow her to create subject peoples as victims of the modernity mission or as objectified by competing theories of imperial or postcolonial discourses. Her novel offers full recognition that the racial and political oppression of colonial rule in Jamaica was derived from the same sense of moral superiority that gave her nation its sense of indomitability during the Battle of Britain. And if the ultimate goals and effects of World War II were worthy, they would, in her moral imagination, have to expose the Empire as an iniquity. Her warrant in *Under the Skin* became the exposure of race wars that did not merely signify the end of the Empire but its beginnings and racist legacy. Her novel predicts that these race wars would not merely cut the Empire in two, but would make it resemble the shards of vainglorious empires of ancient infamy.

Like Allfrey, Bottome undercuts any romantic vision of an island paradise. Just as the three sisters in *The Orchid House* try to appropriate Dominica as the object of their desires, so Lucy envisions her island as just waiting to be conquered by hers; in this case the island is an escape from the constraints of her own tight little island. Bottome corrects this vision by constructing her novel as Lucy's process of political discovery, a journey that is also translated into a travel advisory for readers. At the start of her journey, Lucy is moved by a "strange, nostalgic childhood memory," a colonial vision of being sent exotic gifts from the island whose Edenic bounty is hers for the taking (Bottome 1950, 15). As the fantasy of a war-torn adult, the island's paradisial powers of nurture and delight are also recuperative. Unlike Allfrey's Master, for whom the island represents the reality of failed colonial fantasies, the English sojourner feels entitled to "invent whatever life she liked, out of the deep purple shadows" (15). Bottome's metaphor here may seem, at first glance, to represent just another case of the colonial tourist whose adrenaline rush is induced by the exotic and erotic "purple shadows," especially as these shadows conceal such irritants to the colonial fantasy as natives. But as the novel progresses, those "deep purple shadows" represent a reality check, a life created beyond the Englishwoman's imagination.

The deep "purple" flesh that camouflages the natives reconstitutes them in a colonial vision: they remain invisible as they mimic their mysterious environs, but in so doing, they represent the preternatural. In their shadowy presence, the human and the landscape are lost to each other. Because Lucy's sighting renders the natives conveniently invisible, without content or context, they are all the more available to the colonial fantasies she projects onto them. This same invisibility, however, also inspires the anxiety of what is unknown, and therefore probably threatening. But this apparition does not remain in the sphere of the uncanny, as the Freudian concept relates to individual, internalized trauma. Rather than being demonized and relegated to the shadows of the gothic, this unknown presence is humanized and historicized. One of Bottome's great achievements in this novel is to dramatize the political implications of colonial fantasy by having the fantasy materialize into a violent struggle against it by its colonized objects. As the fantasy of England as a green and pleasant island is threatened by the violent resistance of the fantasied island colony, English identity is threatened by its own ideological foundations. As the novel's title plays out, what is "under the skin" of both colonizer and colonized, white woman and "purple" man and woman, is certainly about race and racially based oppression. Rather than reinscribing an inherent racial difference that pits colonial subject against its objectified Other, however, the novel traces the history of a seething colonial relationship. In turn, that history can only lead to an explosion, not only in human relations, but in narrative form.

By raising the following questions, the narrator leads us to see this clash not as a surprise ambush, but as a process that can be assessed as both destructive and productive. The questions also suggest a new take on hybridity, that which recognizes it as both generative and degenerative, as the result of organic forces growing out of political and social history and then fusing with human agency and action: "Was this Island wavering towards bankruptcy, a civilization coming to birth, or a civilization crumbling into decay? Whose responsibility was it? Whose interests were guiding it?" (Bottome 1950, 25).

Bottome's interest in the political and narrative effects of assigning moral and political responsibility leads her to question the meaning of that word, "Island," by using the word "wavering," which in its verbal form denotes process. In other words, that "Island," "wavering" so tenuously in her sentence, designates an unnamed, destabilized, and therefore ambiguously claimed space that suggests two islands, not one. I believe she is asking the following: How do we understand what has to be considered the problematic relationship between "this Island"—Britain—and that Other Island—its colony? In conflating the two islands as one, "this Island," it is as though Bottome is looking at them through a telescopic lens that maneuvers their contours to show how, under the pressures of imperial self-interest, they can so easily appear as one unified but unstable whole. The result of this vision is an island that has lost both its topographical integrity and its name as it has become engulfed by the British Empire. At the same time as she makes this sighting, Bottome's lens dis-mantles the apparent unity as a decadent illusion about to implode. Like the "purple shadows" sighted by the narrator, this conflation of two Islands is constructed so as to conceal a fault line underneath, a friction that signals an erratic, explosive relationship which can never fulfill a myth of a primordial harmonious past. First of all, the reality of geological history is one of turbulent process, where island formation either bursts forth volcanically from the ocean's depths or is torn from other land masses. In the novel's political representation of this organic process, when the Islands get too close—geologically and politically—one crushes the other, or, in a degeneratively developmental sense, the "bankruptcy" of one erodes the stability of its Other. These Islands may be oceans apart in geological time, but in Imperial time, a connecting bridge has been built that is designed to bear only one-way traffic.[11]

Under the Skin dramatizes this explosive relationship as it originates in the already bankrupt Island of Britain when a white British woman assumes the legitimizing mantle of a British passport to leave it on that one-way bridge to colonial convalescence. Lucy Armstrong's subjectivity as a traditional English heroine has been impoverished and wounded, but not lost in her Island's history. She has suffered sacrifice in body and psyche but in a war that did save her native Island. In her need, as the novel tells us, to come "to birth," Lucy assumes that the Island is her compensation; the colony serves the purpose of reconstituting herself. But Lucy's character is constructed to ask what it means to be a white intruder on a colonial space struggling to be as free as those for whom her nation fought. In Bottome's construction, Lucy's colonial encounter with "this Island" complicates the categories of colonized and colonizer along racial lines that are not dressed up as black and white, but as mixtures reflecting the submerged but festering history of interracial sexual relations in the colony. Like the relationship between the imperial and colonial Islands, the various hues of the characters' skin color are more like a crushing fault line than a bridge to mutuality. As Lucy asks herself when she sees her schoolchildren for the first time: "How could she ever reach or understand these strange children, with their mask-like faces? Why were they so frightening—or was it because they themselves were afraid?" (Bottome 1950, 36).

We only get the answer as Bottome's romance turns to thriller and one of the older girls, caught between sexual and political jealousy, tries to engineer Lucy's death. Though depicted as psychologically unstable, the girl is not demonized, as is Bertha Mason; her motives and character are not lost in the spectral shadows of the gothic or in the repressed past of Freud's uncanny. Instead, they emerge within the political reality of her social position. As in so many of Bottome's novels, characters are drawn in light of Alfred Adler's theories of individual psychology, developed in opposition to Freud's insistence on the prevalence of infantile fantasy in the adult's unconsciously driven behavior. For Adler, instability and destructive behavior can be traced to social causes and are considered treatable through the assumption of social responsibility. It is in this sense that we can see the girl as representing the explosion of social rejection into avenging rage. As it builds in momentum, this rage becomes a collective emotion as it defines the character of the colonized island.[12] Presented as melodrama, a crushing tropical storm expresses the release of not so natural forces and brings those "purple shadows" into focus. What the children's faces "mask" is the fear of both colonizer and colonized being crushed by the other, a fear which is the only "birth" that issues from the relationship between sexual, racial, and political violence in the Empire.

The mask, of course, replicates the fear it conceals because if it is worn too long, it is suffocating in itself. We see this played out as a critique of the idea of a productive hybridity in two characters: Lucy's arch rival and enemy, Elvira Loring, and the man Lucy loves, Philip Calgary, both of whom are light-skinned blacks. Neither black nor white, neither quite visible or invisible, combining intellectual brilliance and physical beauty, each is nonetheless, as Elvira points out, "very slightly, but unmistakably to the Island, a colored person" (Bottome 1950, 22). Like so many mulatto characters, they are betwixt and between race and culture, and, therefore, even though they may become exotically attractive sexual objects, they fit no social category into which they can be integrated. Robert J. C. Young explains this position as representing the fear that interracial unions produce degeneration because Europeans and Africans are not only different races, but different species (1995, 16). We see this representation of degeneration in the way Elvira's character turns out to be a witch's brew of uncontained, irrational rage and terror, not quite human, an inspiration, in fact, for the character of the student with whom she is deeply enmeshed. The double trouble of these harridans allows us to see that, as in Bertha Mason's character, femaleness, read as dark and dangerous, remains a mysterious, shadowy blank slate. The convenience of this blank slate suits the society which projects the terror of the Other onto it in order to keep her out of the way.

In Bottome's version, however, this dark femaleness is not innate or essential, but rather a condition of social and cultural position. The explosion of the student's and Elvira's rage against Lucy represents personal reactions against the white Englishwoman who stands for the powers that marginalize these dark women. In another sense, Elvira embodies the collective frustration of the students who are being educated into a social void. Like them, Elvira has no viable emotional or professional outlets in her marginalized position. Instead, even her administrative position at the school represents an inward-turning self-defense against the prejudices of the white colonial society that has isolated the students and staff, interning them into yet another island colony within their own. Philip, by contrast, becomes a noble healer as a result of the opportunities afforded to his male hybrid identity. As a result of his education and experience outside the Island, he can both exploit Western scientific rationality and question it in his empathy for the students. The combined hybridity of Elvira and Philip embodies not only the agency to struggle against the insidious "shadows" of invisibility, but the agony of being birthmarked by the Island as signs of the "stigma" of "illicit miscegenation" (Bottome 1950, 202).

If we can also imagine this combination as a trope for a hybrid genre, what Bottome is doing here is grafting the genres of social historical analysis and polemic onto a romance thriller. In so doing, she challenges those who might ask if the conventional love story of overwhelming individual passion and enforced renunciation takes priority over the writing of social and political responsibility and agency. The result in this novel is that instead of a declaration of love and passion, Philip treats Lucy to the history of what he calls "our straitjackets": "It's been burned into my blood. . . . We dark people in countries owned and run by white ones drink in this agonizing sense of inferiority with our mother's milk. If we try to escape into the life of the mind we find you there before us! Our thoughts are colored by your thoughts—inhibited by your restrictions" (Bottome 1950, 204). Bottome's hybrid genre may represent a fertile and equal opportunity for narrative form, but its harmonious play in this novel exposes the political sterility produced by a racial mixture in a racist society. If this alloy suggests a lack of fixed identity, the people Philip refers to as "mixed races" are not free of racial boundaries or their cognate, intellectually rationalized imperialism. When, as he says, "Our thoughts are colored by your thoughts," a union is taking place that is not the cognitive pathway to racial harmony or a productive fluidity, but a paradoxical and preconscious form of mind rape or brainwashing. This is also what we can aptly call a whitewashing, in which the color white reflects its dominance by depriving the colored, half white person of any relationship to white identity. Moreover, in this conquest, the color white insists on its own purity. It suggests that what has been "burned into [the] blood" of what Philip calls "the dark people" (Bottome 1950, 204) is the cognition that they do not represent the blossoming of a new and healthy race but a freakish mutation, recalling Houston Chamberlain's racist construction of "hybridized . . . mongrel races" (Gilman 1991, 174). It is in this sense that the character of Elvira can be viewed with any sympathy and raised from the level of the stock figure of the dark vampire woman. In a politically determining construction of character, the destructive sense of self that can emerge from the imbibed lesson of white superiority and one's own genetic degradation dons a new mask of fear, what the narrator describes as a face of "icy blankness" (Bottome 1950, 202).

The meanings embedded in this "icy blankness" become more apparent as Lucy's involvement with Philip becomes both more intimate and more political, and, as a result, her romantic odyssey of regeneration becomes estranged from its origins in fictions of self-definition. In addition to figuring "icy blankness" as a mask of fear, the novel constructs it as an inhospitable space that keeps Lucy uncomfortable in her romantic ambitions. Despite its "blankness," it is not an empty space, for what emerges are figures that disturb traditional British fictions of a woman's search for selfhood. Bottome sets this emergence, or I should say, emergency, as an all too familiar colonial scene, indeed, as we shall see, so familiar that it parodies itself: it is "a hot noon hour" and Lucy has her students writing an essay on "Shelley, who was her favorite poet" (Bottome 1950, 80). Suddenly "a ripple of excitement spreads" among Lucy's hot-blooded adolescent girls because Philip, in an instance that parodies the concept of mimicry by relating it to its mythological antecedents, as the not-so-white knight, rides up on his "golden" horse: " 'That was a man,' the girls' eyes said, 'a real man.' . . . More than a thought, a quickening of their whole being invaded them. They turned their eyes on Lucy challengingly, as if they were demanding what this man's image meant to her—this man who was one of themselves! Did she, too, recognize his male significance or—because he was dark—was he merely a shadow from the underworld?" (80).

Bottome's figuration here sets up a complex and critical colonial relationship. The half-black, half-white doctor is a product of the biological and political colonial history of the Island, on the one hand, a regenerative force, and on the other, a sign of degeneration. As Bottome expounds her positive views of miscegenation in her essay "Pirate's Isle," we can hear her still arguing against a form of racialism that World War II has not defeated: "unless the observer is a victim to Goebbel's philosophy, he is bound to admit that" the progeny of Jamaica's white colonial planters and slave women "are amongst the most outstanding and successful human beings to be found on the Island" (1955, 194, 195). What makes the difference is not a hybrid romance, but education.[13] If "Goebbel's philosophy" represents a degenerate lesson in biological difference, Philip Calgary's identity as doctor of color signals an evolutionary change. In its unsettling parody and resistance, Philip's adaptive change does not merely mimic Anglicization or, as Homi Bhabha asserts, represent a "threat" to colonial power and authority (1997, 157). Philip's colored identity may mock England's foundational myths starring white knights, but his rhetorical and medical skills and his analysis of colonial oppression and the Nazi death machine derive from acquired, not innate, intuitive, or instinctive knowledge. By dint of his British education, he has accumulated layers of hybrid knowledge that celebrate the questioning authority of the English empirical tradition, a form of inquiry that recognizes and internalizes, in Bottome's texts as in other British writers' work, the self-reflexive, self-mocking, and self-critical impulses of mimicry.

These impulses fuse in the collective character of the black girls who watch Lucy gazing at Philip. Their adolescent, that is, their unsettled, unsettling, but very wise sexuality challenges the romantic fantasy that originally drew Lucy to the Island: that she could "invent whatever life she liked" out of the Island's "deep purple shadows." From the perspective of their own shadowy social and cultural position, coupled with their acquired knowledge of English mythologies and literary history, the girls are able to see something all too palpable hidden behind Lucy's English romantic shadows. It turns out that Lucy's fantasied blank space of self-fashioning has less to do with the murky topography of the Island than with her own cultural tradition, as the reference to Shelley testifies. For joining Shelley in this tradition is the presence once again of Charlotte Bronte. Instead of *Jane Eyre,* however, Bottome's novel invokes *Villette,* where another schoolteacher, also named Lucy, is beset by ghostly presences that obscure the culture shock she endures as an Englishwoman struggling between self-determination and the lure of a foreign sexual love.

As Bottome's schoolgirls use their politicized sexuality and Anglicized education to interrogate the literary tradition Lucy teaches, it becomes clear that the ghosts of English romanticism have been all too intimate with fantasies of cultural and moral superiority. For Bottome, these are fantasies that support racialized myths of a manifest imperial destiny and that in turn support the Englishwoman's dream of self-determination and regeneration. The noble knight of old England, in historical reality, a conqueror, is mocked by the half-black Philip, one of the conquered but also constructed as a model of a new kind of humane leadership. As the schoolgirls turn "their eyes on Lucy challengingly," they enact a resistance to imperialism. The girls force Lucy and us to see that the Island's exotic "deep purple shadows" are already filled with the dark man whose "male significance" defies another cultural myth, a Shelleyan construction, this time from Mrs. Shelley. Here I mean the myth of the monster who can best be understood as representing the sexuality of a racialized male Other. In a challenge not only to her heroine, but to her readers, Bottome represents the black man as resisting his image of a sexual icon. He embodies a complex of political realities that contest not only the threatening if romantic image of "a shadow from the underworld," but the political lesson that white racial supremacy has not been vanquished by the just war.

This figure of "a shadow from the underworld" also haunts the novel in ways that build connections between the fantasied absence of the Empire's dark people, World War II, and the end of the Empire. This is a connection, moreover, that Bottome suggests is both more intimate and more dangerous than the liaison between the black man and the Englishwoman. When Philip recounts the damaging history of the Island's race relations to Lucy, he invokes a persecution whose rationality is as "shadowy" as the reasons for oppressing his people: "People talk of a color bar, but what they mean, of course, is a psychological disgrace. Jews were less despised—in the countries where they are still despised—*before*—than *after*—six million of them were murdered for the sake of their inferiority. It was not, you see, so obvious that they *were* inferior until they were murdered" (Bottome 1950, 202, italics in original). For readers in 1950, what may very well have been as startling as the novel's advocacy of love between a black man and an Englishwoman was the exposure of a relationship between racist ideologies held by both the Third Reich and the British Empire. The jolt would have been especially sharp at a time when Britain was still trying to recover from the economic and human losses of World War II. In contrast to the speedier recovery of Europe, including the German economic miracle, Britons were still experiencing the deprivations of an austerity program, enforced shortages that deflated memories of their heroic war. But Bottome's novel is relentless in insisting that the ideological relationship between racism and imperialism persists in Britain so long as it claims any colonies and assumes no responsibility for the colonized of past and present. In fact, the narrative only allows the love between Lucy and Philip to be realized in the language of this ongoing colonial relationship.[14]

When Lucy expresses passion in response to Philip's, it is a confession not of personal ecstasy but of political accountability. Admitting that we English "are responsible for" keeping the Island blacks "uneducated and . . . backward," she goes further in her indictment: "We made, or helped to make, the whole muddle about Hitler, didn't we? Well, then, we made the muddle about the slaves here, too; we actually *brought* them here—to *be* our slaves! It was, if anything, worse than Hitler! We took away their rights as human beings—just as he took away the rights of the Jews. . . . [I]t isn't just enough to *free* slaves. You have to help them to make themselves free! (Bottome 1950, 247–248, italics in original). Bottome's "we" implicates the British woman writer and any fellow travelers who cannot see that "the whole muddle," like the land of "purple shadows" or the "underworld," is that imagined site where there is no political responsibility, just an expediently romanticized lack of definition, what Bottome inspires us to call a cognitive invisibility. This shadowy language derives its rhetorical power from the romantic imagination which constructs the underworld as an imagined place of eroticized fears, and, while this has been translated into the stuff of myth and gothic fun, its associations with hell materialize all too realistically as the slave market and death camp. Bottome underscores this association in "Pirate's Isle" by narrating the history of Jamaica as a succession of not so romantic piracy: "Nor was the British Empire at all behindhand in barbarity, for as soon as we had conquered Jamaica from the Spaniards, we proceeded to carry on the same [slave] trade, in a manner that, for sheer insensate cruelty, outrivaled Belsen under the Nazis" (1955, 189).

The underworld that emerges in Bottome's historical account may be as hot as the mythical hell but its source is neither mythic nor gothic. Instead, the source of its deadly heat is as real as the colonial sun of Jamaica and the ovens of Auschwitz. As though responding to postcolonial theories of colonial history and war, Bottome and Allfrey as well find no iconic moments or texts to represent the ongoing struggles and stories that negotiate the difficult relationships among reluctant and purposeful colonizers and resisting or enraged colonized. Asserting a different vision, the dystopic future sighted by these writers in their Caribbean colonial outpost becomes a continuous present in another, as Bottome finds the historic evidence that allows her to do more than just notice the shadows of persecuted Jews in the history of black slavery.

The statements about Hitler and slavery that Bottome scripts for Lucy and Philip create a two-way bridge between the histories of World War II and worldwide imperialism by constructing a postimperial interracial romance. As though responding to the question, Who can speak for the colonized? the twin statements mate Lucy and Philip by having each of them speak for themselves and for the absent racialized Other—the exterminated Jew. Taking each of them out of the immediacy of imperial hostility and into the history of another Other does not transform their romance into a hybrid relationship, but rather gives them equal parts in a duet in which their opposed political histories converge, not in harmony, but in harmonized dissonance. This dissonance, however, is not a negative force. In its recognition of the historically real Others of the Nazi death camps and of colonial oppression, it grants integrity to their distinct if related experiences and events by refusing to construct any of these as a universalized, iconic narrative. This distinction works as a critical check on those postcolonial analyses that universalize originary, foundational models of colonial purpose as applicable to selected colonial moments or to contemporary postcolonial conditions. In its transhistorical sweep, this strategy disallows historical change and the integrity of historically different fates. By contrast, in *Under the Skin* and in *The Orchid House,* Bottome and Allfrey create a new critical genre: the utopian thriller that models historical change. Even as their villains—the palpable presence of racist and antisemitic persecution—are represented as different but related historical forces and events, continuous and perhaps even irrevocable, their novels invoke change through human agency that assumes responsibility for it. And so the forces of evil in these novels are exposed and judged by the unlikely partnership, in Bottome's novel, of a white colonial teacher and a black colonized healer and, in Allfrey's, of a white colonial political activist and a black servant. Even if empathy is an impossible condition of their differences, it is in their trust of the humane tensions that bind them together that Bottome and Allfrey create and fight the last battle of the last just war as the end of Empire.

Conclusion

"There are two great and adversarial myths inside which we live: the dream of staying and the dream of leaving," [Rushdie] said. "The dream of staying has been incredibly privileged because it relates to the idea of belonging, of roots, of nations, of tribe, of clan. All kinds of very important cultural constructs require us to think that staying put is a very good idea. . . . [But] the itch to leave home—the dream of away—is actually as important as the countervailing dream of home, though it gets much less cultural airtime."
                                                          —Salman Rushdie

SALMAN RUSHDIE CHALLENGES the cherished idea of home from the position of having been elsewhere—incarcerated in exile and then adapting to the freedoms exile can represent. As an Indian Muslim sheltered by Britain from the fatwa on his life and now as a New Yorker, his postcolonial manifesto is cannily universal. I am taking the license to claim that his "we" and "us" would not exclude the British women writers who, for different reasons, didn't stay put and who discovered how the idea of empire was the "adversarial myth" that propelled their writing. Among these women, there are those who grew out of their settler childhoods to build personal lives and careers in England and one who tried to alter the "dream of staying." Elspeth Huxley chose to move on from her parents' romantic "dream of staying" and "idea of belonging," and then dramatized the impossibility of both for the rest of her writing life. Rumer Godden was uprooted from her Anglo-Indian home by the "countervailing dream" that India belonged to its own people, a trauma that she translated into satires and elegies of colonial and neocolonial self-deception. Phyllis Shand Allfrey escaped from the stultifying world of the Caribbean white Creole, but it was her activism in wartime England that propelled her return to Dominica to foment a revolutionary idea: that by helping to build a new postcolonial nation, she could belong. Her novel *The Orchid House* charts the marginalization of this dream. As these women move between the centers and margins of colonial privilege, their writing develops tensely poised relationships to the mythic "dream of staying and the dream of leaving." For these white British women of the Empire, writing its end means that instead of either leaving or staying, instead of belonging to a nation, tribe, or clan, they live inside a journey that never ends and that positions them as always betwixt and between the dreams of Empire and its nightmares.

In the end, one can't even describe their positions as "in between" because that suggests a space of its own, too definable and stable. Instead, their movements back and forth, crisscrossing the terrains of colonial memory and postcolonial history, defy claims that they fit any one category of identity. This transitory, self-doubting identity mocks the charge that they are colonial solipsists or translators and exploiters of the native's experience. As Elspeth Huxley traverses Africa as a map of her evolving political consciousness, as Rumer Godden deconstructs the romance of Anglo-India, and as Phyllis Shand Allfrey revises her dream of integrating her anticolonial activism into a postcolonial narrative, they do more than complicate that genre to which they are mostly consigned—colonial discourse. Instead, they create an intercolonial dialogue and an intersecting, oscillating position that jostles the relationship between colonial and postcolonial representation and between colonial representation and postcolonial criticism. If they are anywhere, it is, as Jane Marcus (1989) puts it, in the woman writer's "elsewhere."

Equally elsewhere, but moving in a different direction, are those writers whose outsider positions lie betwixt and between their identities as Englishwomen and their exile from it as political wanderers. Phyllis Bottome, who chose to return to England to protest the fascism and Nazism whose rise she had witnessed, is at home in no empire. At the same time, however, she exploits her position as British subject and citizen to fill the silence that imperial oppression creates. She constructs a new language of resistance—the native interracial, multicultural voice that speaks not only for the colonized self, but for Others, totally silenced and extinguished victims. Olivia Manning was driven into exile by the Nazi siege and made running away her home base. It is from this unsituated perspective, with its last-minute escapes to unknown destinations and sudden entrapments, that she bears witness to the exile of Others from their own "idea of belonging." Ethel Mannin's travels among and on behalf of the world's dispossessed moved her to take up the cause of a people in the throes of exile from their homeland. But the nightmare of leaving that she narrates for them expropriates the narrative of another people's exile, and as a result, she ousts these Others from their own ancient roots and foundational memories. Unlike Manning's "exodus," Mannin's is not a pathway to knowledge but the construction of an "adversarial myth." In turn, we can find a response to Mannin's dangerous distortions and elisions in the fiction of Muriel Spark. Instead of a search for "roots" or "belonging," the religious pilgrimage of Spark's character, Barbara Vaughan, charts the moral vulnerability of constructing a unified, coherent foundational myth at the expense of historical knowledge or any people's sense of belonging.

For so many of their fictional characters, exile from Britain and its colonial lands becomes a test of whether it is possible to identify or empathize with or even to understand the exiled conditions of colonized and resisting subjects. Phyllis Bottome, political voyager, and Elspeth Huxley and Phyllis Shand Allfrey, colonial truants, eschew the very possibility of colonial identification, and even empathy, as they distance their British characters from the emotional, cultural, and political experiences of the colonized. In these cases, melodrama is the distancing method that involves the British character in the fate of the colonized. But rather than achieving any objective or empirical knowledge through this distancing, their melodramas underscore the idea of mystery. Not mystery as manifest in the idea of the mysterious Other, but as a way of stonewalling any assumption that the Other is available as a dispenser of knowledge to satisfy either the curiosity of the British sojourner or the desire for the thrill of the exotic or strange. Most importantly, their idea of mystery does not obscure or deny the history of British colonial encroachment, conquest, and settlement. In fact, the only substantial revelation to emerge from their mystery melodramas is that colonial history is always present as a motivating force in crimes that are staged in colonial sites but perform charades of personal, psychological conflicts.

Other writers engage comedy to achieve distance, not from the colonized, but from a colonizing consciousness and identity. To dream of knowledge or identification may be solipsistic for Sophie in *Kingfishers Catch Fire,* but its comic drama shows us how Godden works through a radical separation from a childhood identity she could no longer claim. Creating a tension between genres, Godden pairs an elegy of personal loss with a satire of misbegotten political gains. Ernst Van Alphen's (1997) concept of "moral friction" is manifold here and raises questions for my revisionary postcolonial critique. Does the history of colonial oppression and the subjectivity of the colonial Other disappear into the literary experiment of the British woman writer? For Godden, Huxley, Manning, and Spark, satire, the genre which allows British culture to accept its own injustices as genial eccentricity, is the critical means through which they confront their own participation in British colonial consciousness and imaginatively effect its grand finale.

This "moral friction" is particularly resonant in the novels of Olivia Manning and Muriel Spark, where their satires of British colonialism and neocolonialism are set against the grim history of the Holocaust. Without political or moral compromise, but with withering irony, these writers argue that the continuing myopia of Britain's geopolitical self-interest only broadens the scope of colonial racism. Their own broad canvases include the multicultural dimensions of resisting colonial subjects whose dreams of belonging to themselves are frustrated by the nationalist tensions exacerbated by a colonial history. It is the setting and memory of World War II that exposes the wandering British subject to those Others who are stuck, with no exit from the nightmare scenario of belonging to someone else.

"STRANGERS" IN "STRANGE LANDS": ZADIE SMITH'S *WHITE TEETH*

Our children will be born of our actions. Our accidents will become their destinies. Oh, the actions will remain. It is a simple matter of what you will do when the chips are down, my friend. When the fat lady is singing. When the walls are falling in, and the sky is dark, and the ground is rumbling. In that moment our actions will define us. And it makes no difference whether you are being watched by Allah, Jesus, Buddha, or whether you are not. On cold days a man can see his breath, on a hot day he can't. On both occasions, the man breathes.

—Zadie Smith, *White Teeth*

If World War II and the knowledge of oppression it represents are absent from all too many postcolonial studies, fifty-five years after its ending, the event and its lingering effects have found a critical position in the remarkable novel *White Teeth,* by Zadie Smith, Britain's most celebrated postcolonial prodigy. In *White Teeth,* the last days of that war mark the beginning of an escape from the nightmare of belonging to someone else and chart a journey to somewhere else. *White Teeth* proclaims a declaration of independence not only from the haunting and constraining memory of the war's catastrophes and racist oppression, but from the very idea of belonging. After centuries of colonial oppression and decades of postcolonial depression and anger, *White Teeth* imagines the grand finale of Empire as the construction of a multicultural, multiclass British bazaar. Acknowledging its colonial history and debt to postcolonial studies, the novel creates a set of unanticipated mutating connections among historical and imagined events and identities interwoven among first-, second-, and third-generation postcolonial citizens of Britain. The end of World War II meets the creation of a new Britain when a younger generation seizes the monocultural ground of Englishness on which their racialized conditions originated. As this younger generation remaps the future of their interrelated history, the narrative and political effects of their takeover represent a response not only to postcolonial critics, but to British women writing the end of Empire.

Born in 1975, of a Jamaican mother and English father, in the epicenter of "British racism of the 1970s and 1980s," Zadie Smith writes *White Teeth* as a rebellion against her confinement in the role of marginalized victim in an ongoing history of oppression (Sharpe 1993, 142). Neither she nor her characters will accept their places as objects of an interminable and global racist plot.

Instead, she insists that "her own education at a comprehensive school and then at Cambridge shows that "life changes, my family is a picture of change" (Hattenstone 2000, 3). The novel's hyperkinetic romp across interracial, multiethnic London veers from the marriage of working-class Englishman Archie Jones to biracial Jamaican Clara, from his friendship with his Bengali Muslim army mate, Samad Iqbal, to their children's entanglements with the Jewish Chalfen family. As their children hip-hop unimpeded through London's jumble of social and cultural identities, *White Teeth* understands, toys with, and then refuses inclusion in the "official racism of Britain in the 1970s" (Sharpe 1993, 142). These characters and the whole of *White Teeth* will not play into the hands of Enoch Powell's racist rhetoric—"the triumph of barbarism over civilization" (Sharpe 1993, 143). Powell's rallying cry against the postwar waves of postcolonial immigration reverses that slogan used by colonial conquerors and also by the Allies in their war against Nazi conquest—the triumph of civilization over barbarism. But Powell's slogan also exposes what all the antagonists of World War II had to deny: though their ideas, goals, and practices of "civilization" differed radically, the word "civilization" claims superiority and so also justifies the "barbarism" of its right to dominate Others. As so many British women writers realized, neither their testimony nor the Allies' victory could eradicate the many brands of racism in their own civilization.

In its construction of a multivocal civilization, *White Teeth* represents a counterplot to "official" British racism, which, paradoxically, like the pessimistic postcolonial critic, determines the fate of "Afro-Asian citizens" as indeed very dark (Sharpe 1993, 142). In Smith's novel, even as they persist, both racist and antiracist positions are echoes of the past her zigzagging narrative will not accept as determining. Instead, *White Teeth* embraces the power of the past as a haunting or binding presence but also subjects it to a restless striving that ventures even beyond antiracist resistance. Smith's novel lays the oppressive past and its critique to rest. *White Teeth* articulates the demands of postcolonial questions on historical memory and then integrates those demands in the characters of a younger, decidedly non-Anglo British generation that insists on speaking for itself. The dissonant harmonies of their voices do not, moreover, represent a unified body that can be labeled Other, but rather an agitated, squirming dismissal of conceptual, social, or political confinement.

I do not think that Zadie Smith's carnivalesque plotting denies the oppressively racist history and conditions of either colonialism or postcolonial Britain. In fact, these historical conditions can be seen in the light-skinned Jamaican faces of her characters Hortense, Clara, and Irie. These women were born of their great grandmother's seduction a hundred years earlier by a well-intentioned Englishman who managed, by "accident," to avoid the responsibilities of his actions (Smith 2000, 299). Recalling Phyllis Bottome's and Phyllis Shand Allfrey's portrayals of biracial characters, Smith makes sure we know that "just as the English loved India and Africa and Ireland; it is the love that is the problem, people treat their lovers badly" (299). But like her younger characters, Smith has moved on from this formative history and from Bottome's and Allfrey's tentative endings. *White Teeth* forges newly unsettling fates out of the past, in particular, out of the racist tragedies of colonial history. These include her own references to the Sepoy Mutiny of 1857 and on to World War II and the oppressive residue that led up to and formed a racist continuum between these events. Her characters not only chafe against the dominant mythology of the war's heroic morality and Britain's monoculturally racist character, but struggle with their own desires to insinuate their racial, class, and cultural differences into British modernity.

It is in the flux of their settling in and remaining dislocated that a new generation with new voices is born to challenge the relationship between the legacies of World War II and British cultural identity and difference. With a nervous energy that drives them to choose exile from their parents' conflicted histories, dreams, and desires, as well as from dominant narratives of racially determined doom and gloom, Smith's younger generation chooses to be travelers "betwixt and between." They will not be pinned to the structures that define postcolonial status and identities. And so near the end of the novel we learn that Irie, part black, Jamaican, and white English, has had sex with both Iqbal twins, and her child's identity will be only partially knowable. The child is a hybrid of the twins' sameness and of their different characters and actions. His biological determination is merged with indeterminacy, and so his very nature rebels against being bound by one's origins in history: "If it was not somebody's child, could it be that it was nobody's child? . . . A perfectly plotted thing with no real coordinates. A map to an imaginary fatherland. But then, after . . . rolling it over and over in her mind, she thought: *whatever*, you know? What*ever*. It was always going to turn out like this, not precisely like this, but *involved* like this. (Smith 2000, 427, italics in original).

As though in league with these younger generations, the end of the novel will not settle down either. Embracing "the confusing transcripts" of its characters' fates and actions, the ending marks a narrative that keeps defying the expectations and closure of an oppressively plotted past or future (Smith 2000, 448). Situated in a Britain bounded by the historically verified racist origins and remains of colonialism, Zadie Smith dramatizes a kind of fundamentalist agency that allows her young characters to free themselves from those postcolonial lessons that reify victimhood. As a genetically altered "FutureMouse" escapes the trap of its programming, the only finality is Smith's theme of defiance: "Choosing chance I dare defy darkness," spoken by Ava Kadishson Schieber, a Holocaust survivor and artist (spoken presentation, 2003).

The chances, defiances, and fates of *White Teeth*'s characters are also drawn between and around lines that extend beyond the London roamings of its younger generation. They lead us to a far distant past. Invoking that iconic instance of colonial resistance and postcolonial studies, the Sepoy Mutiny, Smith casts Mangal Pande, the Bengali soldier who fired the first shot, as Samad's great grandfather, a "hero" whose legacy includes the dictum, "You must live life with the full knowledge that your actions will *remain*. We are creatures of consequence" (Smith 2000, 86). For his descendent, however, "consequence" is more elusive. The idea of consequence is set up at the beginning of the novel with an ambiguous last shot fired in the waning days of World War II, the facts of which neither we nor Samad discover until the end of the novel. This suspended ambiguity thus raises questions about the relationship between knowledge, actions, and consequence. It is in that ambiguous and sprawling space between the beginning and end of the novel, between individual and historical actions and accidents, and in a historical relationship between these events and World War II that Smith maps a double meaning of "consequence." For the Sepoy Mutiny only realizes its goal ninety years after its occurrence when, facing the costs of its victory over Nazi barbarism, Britain is forced to give up India. By the same token, that latter-day World War II victory is only fully realized fifty-five years later when, in a decisive action of its own, *White Teeth* liberates its characters from Britain's own racist barbarism. In addition to her plotting of the concordance of fate, accident, and choice, Smith means her characters to matter, to make a difference as they redraw the face and boundaries of a postmodern, crazy-quilt, metropolitan, and peripheral Britain.

We can imagine how they matter if we position Smith's post-Indians, post-Jamaicans, post-black and white, and all-Jewish characters in relation to Bottome's Jamaicans. Smith's dramatis personae establish intimacies and chafe at each other in a Britain that, against its will, encourages and harbors them. Among Bottome's Jamaicans, there can only be mutually destructive intimacy. The masks of fear, the "icy blankness" they wear, express the source of this psychological friction as their enforced alienation from their own island nation. As for the Jews of Bottome's novel, they are entirely deprived of shelter or masks. They can only be present in the voices that grieve for them and keep their memory alive in antiracist and anticolonial passions. In Smith's postwar, postcolonial Britain, the masks of alienation represent Samad's mourning for an authentic, unthreatened, indigenous identity, safe from war and colonial domination.

In a desperate move to rescue at least one of his twin sons from the experience of alienation, Samad sends Magid back to Bangladesh, but both sons defy his plotting: "The one I send home comes out a pukka Englishman, white-suited, silly wig lawyer. The one I keep here is fully paid-up green-bow-tie-wearing fundamentalist terrorist. . . . These days, it feels to me like you make a devil's pact when you walk into this country. . . . [I]t drags you in and suddenly you are unsuitable to return, your children are unrecognizable, you belong nowhere" (Smith 2000, 336). Samad's mockery of his own delusion that origins can be authenticated and recoverable in the new empire, the United Kingdom of exile, paradoxically attests to the mutability of identity as well as of place itself. Just as Elspeth Huxley destabilized the identity of the colonial subject by leaving Kenya and writing the story of why, so Samad is forced to recognize that by coming to England he has spawned his own changeling children. In turn, the England occupied by the postcolonial subject doesn't remain still long enough to be identifiable except as a remote memory of a mythic past or, as with Magid's Bangladeshi Englishness, the subject of parody. If Magid's identity suggests hybridity, its instability undermines it. If we view this parody in relation to Rumer Godden's *Kingfishers Catch Fire,* we have an even more graphic picture of how the England that Toby offers Sophie is an impossible anachronism worthy of only wistful but portentous satire. Like Samad, Sophie would be making "a devil's pact" if she accepted England on its own terms as a mythic construction. The ambiguous ending of Godden's novel invites us to consider the identity of the colonial exile as crossing a meandering path with that of the postcolonial exile. They both represent identities that no longer have a category or place in the end of Empire. Both Godden and Smith also suggest that the postcolonial concept of hybridity may already be an anachronism.

For the young in Smith's novel, belonging "nowhere" is neither comic nor wistful, but means instead that they can create their own "elsewhere." Instead of enforced alienation, her young post-Jamaicans, post-Bangladeshi, and Jews construct a London of their own, as a dressing room where they try on the masks and costumes for their parts as the devil's advocate, "a scientist Jew and an unbelieving Muslim"—"strangers" in their own "strange lands" (Smith 2000, 383, 351). They perform in a masquerade that Smith designs as part of her carnival of identities in the making or, as she portrays her young, on the make. Perhaps inspired by her own Jamaican heritage, Smith invokes the ebullient spirit of the Caribbean carnival, which celebrates the mestizo performance of African and local traditions while incorporating the spasmodic chic of popular culture. Extending Bakhtin's idea of heteroglossia, Smith's carnival projects voices that in their intergenerational quarrels don't seem to hear each other, but the cacophony they produce effects a cultural transformation. What emerges is a cultural riot against the English value of knowing one's place. As Smith's adolescents thumb their noses at English propriety, overturn their parents' expectations, and even subvert their own, they also mock "the idea of belonging, of roots, of nations, of tribes, of clans" by celebrating alienation; but Smith's carnival is not just a free ride on a carnival float, emblematic of a "Happy Multicultural Land" (384). The identity game of "musical chairs" doesn't stop on command; instead, they come up against "their past, that place where they have *just been*. Because this is the other thing about immigrants (fugees, emigres, travelers): they cannot escape their history any more than you yourself can lose your shadow" (351, 385, italics in original).

Like Bottome's anticolonial and Spark's postcolonial invocations of the Holocaust, Zadie Smith's narrative engraves the origins of a revolutionary postcolonial Britain on a map of history. It is during the waning days of World War II that Smith's history of Britain's multicultural identities begins and we witness the end of Empire as a cross-cultural friendship is formed between two subalterns in the British army. As their actions and accidents of fate entwine them more intimately than any romantic love, Samad Iqbal and Archie Jones emerge from behind their guns and masks of depression to forecast the consequences for Britain of the complex array of anticolonial scenarios played out among British women writers. Even their Churchill tank is "a bridge-builder . . . not tied to English county allegiances" (Smith 2000, 74). As the tank lumbers across the back roads of the Balkans on April 1, 1945, it connects the history of World War II to postcolonial theories. As these men are then marooned in a Bulgarian town, as "freaks and fools," members of "the Buggered Battalion," they carve their nation's future in a tragic comedy of errors marked as April Fool's Day (74, 77). In the month that follows, Archie and Samad, ignorant of the war's European finale, suffer nonetheless from its residual horrors, including the murder of their tank mates by a Frenchman who may have helped the Nazis' sterilization and euthanasia programs. Only when they are joined by Soviet soldiers out "to catch themselves a Nazi" on their way to liberating "the work camps," are we made to understand that the justice and injustices of this war will not be laid to rest (89). Omnipresent in the unfolding fates of Archie and Samad, their families, and the Jewish Chalfens is the ghostly presence of this global war with its planned mass exterminations. But reappearing as well is a spontaneous, accidental heroism that quells the violence threatening the novel's ending. For at that very final moment at the end of the novel, when the idea of a multicultural Britain is about to implode on New Year's Eve, 1992, we are taken back to World War II. This scene is where Salman Rushdie's "dream of away," that is, the freedom of getting away as opposed to the horror of being sent away, begins to achieve reality.

As Smith returns to the World War II scene left hanging at the beginning of her novel, its history and consequences remind us that the carnival floats of "Happy Multicultural Land" are shadowed by the death transports that only stopped when World War II ended. We learn that the French doctor who Archie was supposed to kill lives only because chance conspired with the Englishman's hesitation. Forty-seven years later, at the public demonstration of FutureMouse, portending a linkage of action, accident, and consequence, Archie sees Millat Iqbal about to shoot the Frenchman. But interrupting any poetic or moral justice in the young "fundamentalist terrorist" killing off the old one, Archie throws himself into the fray, saves the doctor, and is wounded in his efforts once again. Most tellingly, the crash of his body against a glass container sets FutureMouse free. This comic celebration of ambiguous cause and effect, of the instability of moral action, also suggests that literary endgames may just collide with those of history (Smith 2000, 447), for sitting at the table with the French doctor who may be a Nazi eugenicist is the Jewish geneticist Marcus Chalfen. To have them join forces is no carnival of ambiguity. It represents neither a healthy hybridization of villain and victim nor a satiric juxtaposition. The scientific project of this odd couple, to double the life span of a creature who will die at a scheduled date while losing its skin pigmentation, creates a moral friction that defiance, comedy, and celebration may not resolve. Smith clearly intends comic irony in the press release for this experiment; the release concludes with "the tantalizing promise of a new phase in human history, where we are not victims of the random but instead directors and arbitrators of our own fate" (357). The problem is that this scientific experiment reflects a historical narrative that cannot be parodied in a literary experiment. What Smith is playing with is all too suggestive of the nonrandom selection of the Jews as subject and object of the lethal science of racial difference that constructed them as "black" and unable to lose the skin pigmentation assigned to them. It was this construction that arbitrarily and unambiguously scheduled the reduction of their life spans.

As these scenes interlace, the linkage of past and present becomes increasingly intense, as though Smith is weaving an urgent postmodern historical fiction that will override if not reconcile the moral friction she has created. In one movement, the cataclysmic Sepoy Mutiny invades this final scene as we are told that "Millat is reaching like Pande" (Smith 2000, 442). Hurtling over the intervening centuries, Smith's designated "endgames" begin with a list of liberatory events, "the independence of India or Jamaica, the signing of peace treaties or the docking of passenger boats" (447–448). The claim at the very end of the novel that this sequence of events signifies "the beginning of an even longer story" draws our attention to a gap that cannot be leapt over or woven together (448). The absence at this end point of any reference to World War II as the beginning of the final chapter in the story of the end of Empire or as part of her own narrative may just dampen her own celebratory rhetoric, for without this reference both the end of Empire and the postcolonial condition are truly fictions. "FutureMouse" may "leap" and "disappear" into freedom, and seven years later Irie and Joshua Chalfen may be lovers, but, as Smith confesses, "surely to tell these tall tales and others like them would be to speed the myth, the wicked lie, that the past is always tense and the future, perfect" (448). As past and present converge with the future in this novel, the indeterminate conclusion is destabilized by a very "tense" past. We can celebrate the takeover and makeover of the postimperial metropolitan center by the heirs of those historical Others who are the new selves, but this brilliant comedy of postcolonial fluidity is also haunted. Within the moral friction between a postcolonial imaginary and a fictionalized World War II, haunting the freedom of the albino FutureMouse and the Caribbean vacation of the lovers, is the nightmare tragedy of the Holocaust, of having no place to go, no "elsewhere."

If this nightmare tragedy represents an all-too-determinate ending, putting the lie to the fruitful possibilities of fluid identities and hybrid relationships, and so incommensurate with the genres of tall tales and myths, Smith's ending reminds us that World War II brought an end to another real tragedy. In the very scene that solves the mystery she left open at the beginning, we also learn that Archie's inability to kill the doctor is not a response to any or all of the latter's full complement of philosophical hypotheses. Instead of being persuaded by rationalist rhetoric, Archie responds to the impulse that saves the doctor once again fifty-two years later: an inability to reduce another human being to an argument for killing him. Because we never discover whether the doctor is really a Nazi eugenicist, because his identity can't be fixed in the way Nazi eugenics decreed, Archie's hesitation bears even greater moral consequence. It is an action that celebrates the clumsy but decisive ending of a necessary war, and the destiny it leads to is the friendship—of a brown Bangladeshi Muslim and an Englishman—that puts "the wicked lie" to racist eugenics.

If we position Zadie Smith's *White Teeth* as a response to British women writing the end of Empire, the narrative and historical boundaries between them would give way under the pressure of the past meeting our own present. Like other novels discussed in this book, *White Teeth* belongs as much to the tense past as it does to an open, uncertain future and so engages in a dialogue with them. These other British women challenge us to disrupt our distinctions and resolve the tensions between colonial and postcolonial narratives through an act of memory. Imaginatively and historically returning us to that tense past, they enable us to assimilate the knowledge offered by the voices silenced by our cataclysmic modern history. How else can we understand fully the urgent need to end the British Empire and the obliteration of racial theories by Zadie Smith's postcolonial British characters unless we confront the racial exterminations perpetrated by that other empire? Smith's conclusion suggests a debt not only to colonial resistance and liberation, but to the end of that cataclysmic modern imperial history. The agitated insertion of the ending of World War II into her conclusion also suggests an ongoing and painful payment for this combined debt. There is no way of paying it except by narrating it as a presence that haunts the open-ended choices of her young characters. If we see this agitation as a productive moral friction between imaginative literature and historical narrative, then the celebratory ending of *White Teeth* is no timeless tall tale or myth but is deeply implicated in the literary history of the end of Empire that my book constructs.

In this way, the ending of *White Teeth* can also be read as an invitation to include those other white British women writers in Smith's celebration of the end of Empire. They would be included among those whose lives were shaped by the experience of colonialism and recognized as writing back to their own colonial power base, to the colonized, to the postcolonial subject, and to the postcolonial critic. This inclusion then constructs new definitions of self and Other and margin and center. Instead of replicating the divisions of colonialism, they could be seen as repairing them. Like Samad and Archie, these writers matter because they enable us to see that as the margins and center of Empire clash and shift as a result of World War II, and the very idea of empire is being destroyed, so the identities and positions of colonial and postcolonial self and Other can no longer remain fixed as adversarial myths. As they take the risk of representing and speaking for the colonial Other, as they remind us of those who had no one to listen to them, they activate a new postcolonial integration. Like Samad Iqbal, they know, "When the walls are falling in, and the sky is dark, and the ground is rumbling, our actions will define us" (Smith 2000, 87). Now it is our turn to act by listening to them.

Notes

Introduction

1. Benita Parry (1997) contests the term postcolonial, while Barker, Hulme, and Iversen distinguish between "post-colonial" as temporal and "postcolonial" as an "analytical concept" (1994, 4). Michael Gorra views "postcolonial" as both temporal and oppositional: concerned "with what comes after empire as with the anticolonial struggle itself"(1997, 6). The multidisciplinary approach of Frederick Cooper and Ann Laura Stoler addresses questions central to my own, including whether a "stress on contingency, contested categories, and engagement within colonial states and societies should not lead to a reexamination of recent scholarship on 'postcolonial' situations" (1998, 4).
2. Catherine Hall claims, "It is clear that neo-colonialism, informal economic domination by, for example, the United States, continues to flourish" (2000, 3). Sara Suleri holds the United States' "economic and ideological support" of Afghanistan's military regime responsible for oppressive Islamic laws against women (1998, 124).
3. Antoinette Burton agrees with so many critics who assume that the nostalgia that seems to perpetuate the Raj revival represents "a disavowal of the end of empire" (2001, 230). The women writers I consider in this book should not only answer but challenge Burton's query "about what aesthetic forms postcolonial memory takes when empire is apparently gone, but continues to 'vanish' again and again before our very eyes" (2001, 230).
4. This power is all too evident in the iconic status of the 1857 Sepoy Rebellion in India and its related rumors of rape. Together, these narratives are persistently replayed as evidence for finding the Empire and its patriarchal structure everlastingly if not omnipotently violent and controlling. Jenny Sharpe asserts that the colonizer's anxiety appears as the "threat of the dark rapist," a sign of "a crisis in British authority . . . managed through the circulation of the violated bodies of English-women" (1993, 3, 4). Despite their struggles and victories for self-determination, women are seen as suffering "colonization by Englishmen" well into the twentieth century (Janaki Nair 2000, 239). Proliferating postcolonial debate shows that no monolithic view prevails, but claims persist that imperial history is "a means of justifying British imperialism," leading to hostile "doubts about the possibility of constructing non-Eurocentric historiography" (Claire Midgley 1998, 4, 5). Many postcolonial critics focus mainly on events of violent oppression and rebellion as representing the temper of colonial relations while the less dramatic chronicles of administrative and commercial relations are rarely recounted or used as reference points. See for example, Anne McClintock (1995).
5. Typical of this elision of World War II is Anne McClintock's survey of anticolonial struggles in India and South Africa from the end of the nineteenth century through the 1990s and their relation to nationalism. Her brief note about Afrikaner nationalism adopting Nazi "politics of fetish symbol and cultural persuasion" ignores huge

distinctions in definitions, policies, and practices of fascist, democratic, and nationalist forces that led to two world wars and wartime literary productions that analyzed those distinctions (1995, 373). Sangeeta Ray's study ranges from the Sepoy Rebellion of 1857 through India's 1947 partition, but ignores any impact of World War II (2000, 7), as does Elleke Boehmer's survey (1995). Vron Ware dismisses the war's significance by having it "overshadow . . . the immediate memory of Empire [of] many white women in Britain" (1992, 227). Perhaps most significantly, Aimé Césaire, who many consider the founder of postcolonial studies, rages against Nazism and its application of European "colonialist procedures," but because he sees no difference between the Third Reich and the continuation of many different types of racism into the postwar period, he is able to ignore the impact of World War II (2000, 36).

6. At the same time, however, I could not, in the interest of open inquiry, omit those other writers who turned out to be more ambivalent or even compromised in their colonial and postcolonial representations. My concern was not balance or evenhandedness, which, as I discovered from the experience of the British in Mandatory Palestine, can be predicated on self-delusion. I must thank Carol Troen for her wisdom about this.

7. Sander Gilman's *The Jew's Body* (1991) expands definitions of race to intersect with antisemitism and so should be required reading for postcolonial critics.

8. Though Hitler's concentration and death camps were lethal to all inmates, his extermination plans were intended mainly for Jews. According to Guenter Lewy (2000), accurate statistics about the murder of Gypsies are difficult to ascertain, but up to 60 percent of European Roma may have been killed. See also Donald Kenrick (1999). In all his rants against Hitler, with full knowledge of the Holocaust when he writes *Discourse on Colonialism*, Aimé Césaire (2000) never mentions either the Jews or the Gypsies.

9. Ruth Roach Pierson sees the European bourgeois "cult of domesticity" as interdependent with colonialism (Pierson and Chaudhuri 1998, 5). For other analyses of gender and colonialism, see Joanna Trollope, Margaret Strobel, Vron Ware, Rosemary M. George, and Helen Calloway.

10. Lynne Hanley finds that the "consciousness" of Lessing's black Moses in *The Grass Is Singing* "remains . . . maddeningly inaccessible to the reader" (1991/1992, 499). Louise Yelin grants that white women writers are "looking beyond the old order" for ways of imagining "new kinds of relationships" with "postcolonial, postimperial nations," but criticizes Lessing and Gordimer for their attachment to European cultural identities (1998, 174). Gayatri Spivak (1986) decries Western narrative's reliance on individual character development and suppression of the subaltern's voice. Leela Gandhi argues that even if colonial white women were feminists and memsahibs sympathized with native women, "the postcolonial critic is prevented from . . . unreserved celebration by the recognition that these women's constitutions" were "inextricable from the hierarchies which inform the imperial project" (1998, 93). Debates persist about the true and false consciousness of those fictions critical of the imperial project, with Forster's *A Passage to India* as the ubiquitous test case. See Jenny Sharpe (1993), Benita Parry (1998a), and Zakia Pathak, Saswati Sengupta, and Sharmila Purkayastha (1991).

11. Linda Alcoff defines privilege as being "in a more favorable, mobile, and dominant position vis-à-vis the structures of power/knowledge in a society. . . . Certain races, nationalities, genders, sexualities, and classes confer privilege, but a single individual . . . may enjoy privilege" related to "parts of their identity and a lack of privilege with others" (1991/1992, n. 4, 30). Alcoff sees "the problem of speaking for others," as "epistemological and metaphysical," but its "political consequences . . . can increase or reinforce the oppression of the group spoken for" (1991, 8, 7). Penelope

Ingram asks if "retrieving an authentic voice for the native" might just "reproduce the epistemic violence of imperialism by erecting an ideal voice and full subjectivity in the place of an always already silenced one" (1999, 80). Like Ingram and so many postcolonial critics, Alcoff is inspired by Gayatri Spivak's essay, "Can the Subaltern Speak?" (1988) and prefers the idea of " 'listening to' " (1991/1992, 22). But as writers like Phyllis Bottome and Olivia Manning recognized, some events prevent persecuted people from being heard or speaking, and if someone else didn't speak for them, all would be lost, including lives.

12. Margaret Strobel studies "those European women who tried to make a positive contribution in the colonies" and tried "to move beyond the ethnocentrism and sexism of their culture and period" (1991, xi). Most cogently, Benita Parry alerts us to the dangers of "attack[s]" on "political binaries" that ignore "the obstinate material, social and cultural conditions of colonialism's histories"(1998a, 7).

13. Jenny Sharpe's revised history of the image of English colonial women in India grants them greater authority and agency to commit their own oppressions (1993).

14. These phrases are from Indira Karamcheti's castigation of Nancy Paxton for claiming that the voices of British women and "the subaltern classes" are heteroglossic and dialogic, in Bakhtin's sense of disrupting and yet hearing each other to create newly complex conversations (1999, 127). I am only too happy to share Paxton's guilty claim.

15. There is considerable infighting among those critics who claim, in different ways, to deconstruct such categories and create more fluid and historically applicable methods of analysis. See, for example, Sara Suleri's attack on bell hooks and Trinh Minh-ha for their brands of "postcolonial feminist criticism" (1998, 124).

16. Louise Yelin (1998) discusses these issues in Christina Stead, Doris Lessing, and Nadine Gordimer.

17. These writers do not fulfill a "pattern of projecting upon, rather than drawing from, Asian cultures," which Philip Darby sees "has been characteristic of nearly all American fiction set in the Asian region" (1998, 46).

18. Jane Haggis notes the "net of interaction" between white women and those "of other social groups" in order "to restore conflict, ambiguity and tragedy to the center of historical process" (1990, 114, 115). Cooper and Stoler show that "the notion of the civilizing mission gave way after World War II to the notion of development, embodying in a subtler way the hierarchy that civilizing entailed" (1998, 35).

19. Without studying any of these writers, Ian Baucom can claim that "the modern English literature of nostalgia is vast," turning "a resentful back on the present and a teary eye toward the image of a dying England" (1999, 175).

20. Susan S. Friedman's chapter "Beyond Difference" (1998) analyzes evolving strands of hybridity.

21. Without regard to their various views, John Hutnyk (1996) speaks for the colonized in his critique of Bhabha's linguistic pyrotechnics which ignore the radical political dissent he favors. Hutnyk's reading of the unified desires of the colonized and fixed position of the colonizer is addressed by questions posed by Ananda Abeysekara about postcolonial theories which insist that culture is either "reified, solid, fixed, and essential" or "unbounded, nonunitary, fluid, [and] changing. . . . For *whom* is 'culture' unbounded? For the anthropologist [and like-minded scholars] or the native. That is, for (Western) theory, or for the (local) discourse which theory is endeavoring to engage, inquire upon?' " (Abeysekara 1999, 1–2).

22. Ballhatchett notes that once Indians with Western education could "compete successfully . . . the British could no longer assert their right to power on grounds of superior knowledge or intellect: instead they turned to arguments of racial superiority" (1980, 7).

23. See Paul Scott's novel, *Staying On* (1997). Gikandi notes that "the value" that is "nullified" with "the collapse of the empire" is the racism inherent in the imperial

history that constitutes English identity (1996, 70). While there is a growth industry about Empire coming home and writing back, little attention is paid to colonials who didn't necessarily choose to become postcolonial, and especially those in the unsettling space of being anti-imperial and calling a colony home.

24. Where Bhabha identifies "figures of farce" and a self-reflexive "comic turn" in subjecting colonial power to "mimicry," Godden and Manning show colonizer and colonized mimicking each other in a "farce" of respective self-deception and misappropriation (Bhabha 1998, 153). Rosemary M. George complicates the dynamic of mimicry in her assertion that colonizer and colonized collaborate in their shared history of colonialism (1996, 4). She questions contested uses of "colonial subject": "Can one be subject to someone else and tied to one's own identity at the same time?" (1996, 25).

25. Benita Parry argues that Forster's "perplexity . . . reconfigures the distant, alien complex of cultures" and "signals an anxiety about the impasse of representation" (1998b, 176). Her contrast of Forster's indirect "aversion to empire" with even less critical modern "novels of "manners" ignores those like Godden's, which, though mild mannered in its parody, depicts insurrection not as a transcendent gesture but as violently real (1998b, 178).

CHAPTER I   STRANGERS AT THE GATES

1. Of course, the shock of this neglect is that the founder of postcolonial studies, Edward Said, has shown no interest in any of these writers and has inspired none in his followers. Interest in Lawrence Durrell's late colonial writing is sustained by the International Durrell Society, but it would be a pity if the baroque *Alexandria Quartet* were taken as typical of British literary representations of its Middle East presence.

2. I deal with Agatha Christie's Middle East detective novels in "The Mysterious New Empire: Agatha Christie's Colonial Murders" (2004).

3. There is still too little critical work on Manning, who felt she never received the serious attention and wider audience her work deserved. I analyze her complex representation of the Jew in *The Balkan Trilogy* in my *British Women Writers of World War II,* and a complete bibliography of her writing has been compiled by Gyde Christine Martin (1989). Morris (1987) shows much appreciation of the trilogies, but no political or historical analysis.

4. When Italy entered the war in 1940, extending it to North Africa, and "Rommel threatened to occupy Egypt and advance on Palestine and Syria, an agreement was made between the Hagana and the British Middle East headquarters" to arm and train the Hagana as "an underground resistance force" (Bentwich and Bentwich 1965, 165). Despite concerns about ongoing Arab-Jewish tensions in Palestine and political pressures from each side, the British felt it necessary to exploit "indigenous resources," and three Jewish and three Arab independent companies were raised from their communities (Cohen 1978, 99, 103).

5. Iraq fought against the British in World War II and, as a result, according to Cohen, except for "the loyal Ibn Saud and Emir Abdullah . . . Unlike after the First World War, the Arabs would have no claims on the victorious Allies" (Cohen 1978, 62–63).

6. Elizabeth Monroe, who worked for the Ministry of Information during the war, questioned the meaning of Britain's hold on the Middle East: "What constitute interests? Are they purely material—supplies, markets, airlines, pipelines—or are they also psychological, entailing prestige and moral ties such as alliances?" (quoted in Wilson 1998, 64). Despite victory over the formidable Rommel at El Alamein at the end of 1942, Britain was now increasingly dependent on the United States. Britain thought its "unrivalled experience and oversight of Middle Eastern affairs"

could "influence the very expression of Arab nationalism," but this was undercut by pressures from the Arabs and Jews of Palestine for independent statehood (Cohen and Kolinsky 1998, xiii). Louis argues that the British felt that "the Empire was not in a state of dissolution but rather of transformation. Formal rule would be replaced with more modest informal influence, but Britain would remain the dominant power" (1985, 396). But, by the end of the war, "the challenge that [the British] faced was too complex—and the struggle availed them very little"(Shepherd 2000, 247).

7. Louis reports that at the end of the war Britain's "economic troubles were accentuated by the necessity of a $3.75 billion loan from the United States" (1985, viii).

8. The following quote illustrates the source of British anxieties about their hegemony in the Middle East:"In Palestine our difficulties are much greater than in other subject states, as the thinking classes definitely accuse us of promoting an unjust policy, of taking sides . . . It is a fallacy to think the Oriental content with high wages and no power. If the Indian in whose country we have made untold improvements, would throw off European control were it possible, how much sooner would the Arab of Palestine do so. . . . Whatever the aims of Zionism, it is clear that old methods of government are no longer adequate. Nationalism is a very real thing, which cannot be neglected nor abolished. . . . We have either to hand over much power or rule by force" (Lt.-Col. F. G. Peake, Resident in Amman, Sept. 21, 1929, writing to Sir John Chancellor, the third High Commissioner in Palestine, after the 1929 riots, quoted in Shepherd 2000, 179). This recognition marks a shift in British colonial policy, a shift which is illustrated, ironically, by the case of Kenya, where early settlement possibilities included the idea of declaring 3 million acres of highland as a Zionist "refuge" from east European pogroms (Best 1979, 49–50). Zionists saw this offer "as an official admission that Palestine was never to become theirs" (Best 1979, 50).

9. Mark Williams's discussion of different modernist responses to the disasters of modernity in New Zealand writing suggests the space in which Manning writes (2000, 250).

10. Stevie Smith sees Miss Bohun as "a mean maniac" whose power is thwarted only by Felix's adolescent agility (1951, 4). Niamh Baker, by contrast, finds that Miss Bohun's inhumanity "becomes more complex" because of "the very tenacity with which [she] clings to life" (1989, 71). Baker doesn't consider Miss Bohun's relation to the novel's Jewish refugees. Manning's concern about the plight of European Jews under fascism is explored with greater breadth in *The Balkan Trilogy* with the complicated and sometimes problematic portrait of the Drucker family, who are forced to leave Germany for Rumania.

11. While bombing raids killed people in Haifa and Tel Aviv in 1940, Jerusalem was considered "a privileged enclave, safer than elsewhere in the Middle East" and the British community continued with its "ordinary life" (Sherman 1997, 153).

12. By 1943, the British were trapped in their own vacillating politics in Palestine. Though they had crushed the 1936–1938 Arab riots against Jewish immigration, because their 1939 White Paper acceded to Arab demands to limit the number of Jewish immigrants, they faced the continued frustration of Jewish nationalists. And so they found themselves "neither able to delegate power, nor to continue to rule by force" (Shepherd 2000, 180). Louis explains Britain's dependence on the United States for "a viable solution" to the partition of Palestine and the creation of a Jewish state, but "co-operation was impeded because of the American anti-colonial tradition" (1985, 394).

13. Shepherd notes that although "British forces repeatedly offered safe conduct out of the field of fire to Jews and Arabs," the Arabs accused the British of conspiring with the Jews against them and the Jews were convinced "that the British were aligned

with the Arabs" (2000, 235). Britain's "pro-Transjordan policy" during the Palestine War of 1947–1949 "placed it in direct opposition to the Arab League objective of establishing a Palestinian Arab state of the whole of Mandatory Palestine. The creation of Israel and the Arab defeat was to undermine Britain's influence in the Middle East" (Thornhill 1998, 42).

14. Though Manning's invocation of the Holocaust postdates full knowledge of its horrors, and Jewish refugees were present in England from the late 1940s, it was the Eichmann trial in 1961 that introduced the survivors' voices into public discourse.

15. Manning's account of the *Struma* is confirmed by recent historical investigation of Douglas Frantz and Catherine Collins (2003). By summer 1942, the Allies had learned of the Germans' extermination of Europe's Jews. In December 1942, the *Times* published the story "Deliberate Plan for Extermination," and on December 17, Anthony Eden responded to the news in Parliament (Zweig 1986, 135). For British obstruction of Jews' attempts to escape Nazi-occupied Europe, including internment and deportation for those who managed to reach Palestine, see Wasserstein (1999) and London (2000). Churchill expressed sympathy for the Jews in many ways. In 1942, he charged that refugees from the ship *Darien* be allowed to remain in Palestine when others were preventing this rescue and that of other ships headed for Palestine (Gilbert 1981, 24–25; Zweig 1986, 116). In addition to urging President Roosevelt to help "remove refugees to safety," he supported the formation of a Jewish Brigade (Gilbert 1981, 141). Despite large numbers of unused legal immigration certificates and the willingness of the Palestine Jewish community to cut their own rations to save the refugees, the Colonial Office led "the belief that the refugee traffic was a proven . . . security risk" and that Britain needed to defend itself "against the spectre of a 'flood of gatecrashers'" (Zweig 1986, 116, 125). Sherman argues that the "British Government . . . in England and Palestine, 'could not see the connection between the tragedy overwhelming the Jews in Europe and the intensification, indeed the transformation of Zionism'" (1997, 159).

16. Recalling a visit to a Middle East Harem, Manning "was painfully conscious of the women's boredom and narrowness . . . but [she] noted that British officers tend to treat the Mohammedan institution with a half-envious respect. Men find it convenient to exclude women even if they do not actually shut them away." She connects this memory to E. M. Forster's response to admitting "a few exceptional young women . . . to [the Apostles]. . . . The presence of young women would . . . distract the men from the elevated mental striving that was their aim" (Manning 1974, 734).

17. Baruma's essay about the dangers of identity politics shows how "absolutist" identities and "blood-and-soil nationalism" erase how "we are all made up of a mixture of loyalties and identifications, regional, linguistic, religious, ethnic, national, social, or professional" (2002, 12, 13).

18. Most historians today agree that by the end of the war Britain was too embroiled in its own political debates and a contradictory evenhandedness to be held responsible for the 1948 Arab-Israeli war. Between the politics of oil and other resources were the different views of Churchill and the Labor government which followed his tenure. Labor believed that a "revolution in Imperial attitude" was necessary for "the prosperity and defense of the Empire and Commonwealth," and this involved "dealing with the peoples of the Middle East and Asia, and eventually those of Africa, on an equal footing" (Louis 1985, 8). Churchill's 1946 comments indicate a self-critical if paternalistic sense of responsibility where he rejects the idea of fighting "it out to the death" in Palestine. "For what reason? Not, all the world will say, for the faithful discharge of our long mission but because we have need, having been driven out of Egypt, to secure a satisfactory strategic base from which to pursue our Imperial aims" (quoted in Louis 1985, 433).

19. The British occupied Egypt in 1882 and left in 1954. According to Derek Hop-

wood, "Britain had invaded the country under the pretext of reestablishing law and order and restoring financial stability. Egyptian finances were admittedly in a mess and needed sorting out" (1989, 17). Britain never made Egypt part of the Empire, but declared it a protectorate, choosing its rulers. In 1922 the British signed a treaty granting Egypt some independence until Mussolini invaded Ethiopia. They only left when Gamal Abdal Nasser overthrew King Farouk and took over the government in 1952.

20. Rod Edmond discusses the fears of being contaminated by native cultures, fears that form the imperialist discourses of degeneration in turn-of-the-century British fiction (2000, 45). These maladies reappear metaphorically in twentieth-century novels. Having developed immunity to fears of native contamination, imperial contenders are now infected by the colonized soil they themselves contaminate with the wars they bring to it.

21. "Tanks designed for muddy European fields were . . . torn by the rocky ground, their air-filters choked with sand," (Cooper 1995, 44–45). The Allied troops were 220,000 strong and their losses amounted to about 1,000 a day (Cooper 1995, 216).

22. William Louis analyzes Egypt's value to British interests as "compelling"; its geography made it "an essential link in British world security" (1985, 226). This dependence was complicated by British diplomats' assumption that the Egyptians needed "a strong but essentially a fair and helpful hand to guide them," an approach reinforced by their view of Egyptian political differences and King Farouk's pro-Axis sentiments (Louis 1985, 227).

23. The pro-Axis revolt in Iraq in 1941 is a backdrop for this statement and for Manning's novel *School for Love*. The Mufti of Jerusalem, Haj Amin el Husseini, who was perhaps the leading figure among Arab Nationalists in Palestine, sought refuge with the Germans and helped organize a European Muslim brigade which fought with the German Army. When members of the Egyptian ruling family began negotiations with Italian fascists, the British surrounded the royal palace. The comments of Manning's Egyptian porter about the British going and Germans coming would reflect a sentiment commonly detected among certain Arab circles in the Middle East at that time. See Louis (1985, 413).

24. Artemis Cooper notes that while the British saw their own Middle East mission in World War II as part of "a war for freedom and democracy," their Allies felt "mistrust of British imperialism" (1995, 225, 226). Soldiers from South Africa and New Zealand "said that it was the Dominions who had borne the brunt of the fighting" (Cooper 1995, 226).

25. Cairo was deeply segregated at this time, between British-, French-, and English-speaking Egyptian upper classes and "ordinary, Arabic-speaking people" (Cooper 1995, 35).

26. Whittaker relates this issue "to the paradox [Spark] seeks to convey—the absurdity of human behavior in the context of a divine purpose" (1982, 27). Edgecombe (1990) views Spark's determinism as an issue of authorial control. From early Catholic history, there has been a central debate regarding divine foreknowledge and predestination.

27. Whittaker finds the novel impeded by an "untidy and crowded" canvas of characters (1982, 78), and Massu finds the characters "unsatisfactory . . . round but come out flat (1979, 61).

28. See Cheyette (2002, 52), and see Whittaker, who has read Spark's letter to her agent describing those events (1982, 32). John Glavin argues that after this, "she set about converting all her energies into writing the absolutely opposite sort of book" (2000, 298).

29. Richmond interprets the novel's evocation of history as mythic and transhistorical: "The dramatic events" of the pilgrimages "are set against a larger story of history,

itself only temporary and dimly suggesting the possibilities of a celestial Jerusalem" (1984, 105). Hynes also takes Spark's religiosity as an invitation to a spiritualized interpretation, focusing on "the role of the inexplicable in realism's sweaty doings" (1988, 53).

30. Many different perspectives on the history of the 1967 war can be found in *The Six-Day War: A Retrospective*, ed. Richard B. Parker (1996).

31. Kemp sees Barbara Vaughan's identities as cohering and representative of the novel's "aesthetic, metaphysical, and ethical harmonies" (1974, 104, 110).

32. Shepherd describes how, until the very end of the British Mandate, the policy of the last high commissioner, Sir Alan Cunningham, was "'holding the ring': trying to ensure what in British eyes could be a fair fight between Arabs and Jews, but at the same time keeping the sides apart until the British withdrawal" (2000, 232). This failed when Jews and Arabs attacked each other and "resented any British interference with their plans" (Shepherd 2000, 232).

33. Spark was born Muriel Sarah Camberg, of a Jewish father and Protestant mother. Recently, her Jewishness has come back to haunt her as a family scandal. Her son Robin made public his discovery of a certificate proving his grandparents had a synagogue wedding, a claim she denies. Whittaker sees this novel as "an attempt to reaccommodate the Jewishness which for several years had been subordinated to the Catholicism" (1982, 32).

34. Cheyette notes that Spark "does not describe herself as a 'Christian Jew' or 'Jewish Christian' which would have reinforced a traditional Catholic view of the transcendent power of the founders of the Church" (2000, 17). He finds her use of the term "Gentile" "deliberately open," suggesting "both a non-Jewish pagan and a rather prim and comic Edinburgh gentility," but he doesn't mention that for Jews, "Gentile" means non-Jewish (2000, 17).

35. Jacqueline Rose interprets the guide's questions as having "interrogated [Barbara] with hostility" (1996, 69) and finding her "presence acceptable only if she is willing to shed the non-Jewish part of her identity" (1996, 13). Rose's own hostility is consistent with the professed "identity politics" through which she interprets the novel (1996, 14). While she acknowledges that "Israel came into being to bring the migrancy of one people to an end" and "give the Jew her place as fully modern citizen," she can't bring herself to accept Israel's legitimacy, as when she suggests that its foundation occurred "as if it had symptomatically to engender within its own boundaries the founding condition from which it had fled," and as in her construction of "Israel/Palestine" which denies each people a separate state, which is, after all, what they want (1996, 13).

36. Interestingly, the Holocaust plays no role in Rose's interpretations of the Eichmann trial in Spark's novel or of Hannah Arendt's book, *Eichmann in Jerusalem*. Evading confrontation with the specific magnitude of the twelve-year-long event, she chooses the term "horrors of modernity," which allows her to ignore the Holocaust either in its own right or as part of the impetus for the creation of the State of Israel. Her only use of the word in a book that deals with antisemitism from Shakespeare to South Africa refers to Clive Sinclair's reference (1996, 75) and to "the issue of the victim/aggressor" as related to the writing of Bessie Head about South Africa (1996, 111).

37. Cheyette importantly observes that Spark's 1979 novel, *Territorial Rights*, with its scathing portrait of an anti-Semite, confronts the failure of conversion to "expunge the infectious and impure presence of her unconverted self from either her life or her art" (2002, 110).

38. What has been particularly controversial about Arendt's analysis is her proclamation, in her "Postscript": "When I speak of the banality of evil, I do so only on the strictly factual level, pointing to a phenomenon which stared one in the face at the trial.

Eichmann was not Iago and not Macbeth.... Except for an extraordinary diligence in looking out for his personal advancement, he had no motives at all.... He *merely*, to put the matter colloquially, *never realized what he was doing*" (1994 287). Felman argues that "the banality of evil is not psychological, but rather legal and political" (2001, 204).

39. Fotini Apostolou studies Spark with a postmodern "emphasis on the intertextual games" which offer new readings of her work (2001, xv). That this study excludes *The Mandelbaum Gate* highlights the way this novel's "promise of dominance" is not "embroiled in [a] playful atmosphere" (2001, xv).

40. Cheyette proposes that in addition to the novel's "unrestrained form," it continued to be disturbing to Spark because of its "Jewish subject matter" (2002, 65).

41. I discuss this revisionary movement in *British Women Writers of World War II*. For a longer-range view of women writers' concerns with political and social issues, see Maslen, who discusses Mannin; and, for women's postwar fiction, see Baker and Phillips and Haywood.

42. The need for Arab support also shaped Britain's Arab policy in 1943, which was based on the White Paper policy of May 17, 1939, promising "a Palestinian state based on its majority Arab population within ten years. Earlier promises to the Jews were ignored" and Jewish immigration was "curtailed" (Thornhill 1998, 43). The winter of 1942–43 was a turning point: the victories against Germany "led to a spate of rumor and lobbying by both Arabs and Zionists on the political future of the Middle East" (Cohen 1978, 144). The lobbying was a result both of "long-term proposals that had been held up owing to the military situation" and of "American sympathy for the Zionist cause" which had "increased in the autumn of 1942" with the reports of Nazi mass exterminations (Cohen 1978, 161).

43. Mannin's foreword (1963) quotes Harry Truman, whose memoirs recount how "disturbed and annoyed" he was at such "pressure," but she omits his simultaneous belief in the need for a Jewish state. She also never mentions Churchill's support for a protective homeland for the besieged Jews. Without any Jewish "pressure," Churchill foresaw its necessity in 1939 when he protested the White Paper as "a disastrous policy and a breach of an undertaking for which I was prominently responsible" (Gilbert 1981, 171). Churchill asked the House of Commons, "What sort of National Home is offered to the Jews of the world, when we are asked to declare that in five years' time the door of that home is to be shut and barred in their faces'" (quoted in Bentwich and Bentwich 1965, 164). Of course, as a Tory, Churchill would not be found credible by the socialist Mannin. She would not have been alone in questioning the sincerity of Churchill's support for the Jews, viewing it as more political than heartfelt, and would probably have approved the policies of the Labor Party, which appointed Ernest Bevin as foreign secretary. Rather than a Jewish state in partitioned Palestine, Bevin advocated "an Advisory council with Arab and Jewish members," granting "minority rights" to a Jewish population that would be limited to "33⅓ or 40 per cent in the whole country" because "what justification is there for putting 360,000 Arabs under the Jews?" (Beeley 1990, 123, 125). Harold Beeley, an official serving the Palestine desk in the British Foreign Office from 1945 to 1948, defends Bevin's policy not only on the grounds of recognizing the demands of an Arab majority, but because of "two fears": Britain's dependence on the United States and on Arab support against Soviet expansion in the Middle East (1990, 129). Beeley defends Bevin against charges of antisemitism but cites his statement to the 1946 Labor Party Conference in response to American support for a Jewish state in Palestine: "The demand for the 100,000 immigrants [to Palestine] was proposed with the purest of motives. They didn't want too many Jews in New York" (Beeley 1990, 121). Beeley notes that this "particular indiscretion ... drew a fierce protest from the two Senators for the State of New York" (1990, 121).

44. Mannin's novel of wartime Germany, *The Dark Forest*, presents all occupations as evil but humanizes Germans in large measure by avoiding mention of their death camps.

CHAPTER 2   STRANGERS IN A WALLED GARDEN

1. The term Anglo-Indian has changed meanings over time. Today it designates a combined Indian and European racial identity, but since it referred to British settlers before independence, I follow Godden's usage. Teresa Hubel notes that Godden's novels *The Lady and the Unicorn* and *Black Narcissus* should not be considered nostalgic (1996, 219).
2. Margaret Macmillan notes that though most British in India were middle class, in the big cities, their social hierarchy was rigidly ordered: "Merchants and their families were acceptable, but those in the retail trade, no matter how rich, were not" (1988, 48). According to Ian Stephens, a journalist stationed in India between 1937 and 1951, the British had their own caste system: "the pukka Brahmins," "member[s] of the topmost British Government service," were "the so-called heaven-born," and in descending order were "the military caste, the box-wallahs or businessmen (no matter how wealthy, and subdivided hierarchically between commerce and trade), and finally, the Eurasians, people of mixed blood analogous to the despised Hindu lower castes" (quoted in Allen 1995, 96–97). Cooper and Stoler offer comparative evidence that commercial colonial agents participated in "the multiple circuits of person, ideas, and institutions" that formed a "global experience and produced alternative routes to class mobility" (1998, 28).
3. From its founding in Bengal, the East India Company became the British image of India. As Embree argues, the British constructed out of Bengal society an Indian "national character" that justified imperial rule: "the poverty of India was rooted in [its] social and cultural fabric," and its culture was "confused, complex and incapable of comprehension under any reasonable categorization" (1989, 105, 107). It was clear to the British that Bengal was "the richest and most fertile" region of India (James 1998, 30).
4. Lynne Rosenthal sees Godden's fiction affirming a "sense of continuity and time-lessness despite change" (1996, ix). There is actually a narrative tradition and logic to India's aura of timelessness and even mystery, insofar as Herodotus (ca. 480–425 B.C.) depicted it with untold wealth and unimaginable flora and fauna, and as the outer limits of civilization. See Embree (1989) for an extensive discussion of India's images in ancient Greek thought.
5. Godden's statement should be read in ironic contrast to Lord Curzon's statement, at Calcutta University, "that truth was a virtue unknown in India" (quoted in Embree 1989, 103).
6. Michael Powell and Emeric Pressburger, best known for their wartime films, *49th Parallel* and *The Life and Death of Colonel Blimp*, produced, wrote, and directed *Black Narcissus* in 1947 at the J. Arthur Rank studio. It starred Deborah Kerr as Sister Clodagh, David Farrar as Mr. Dean, Sabu as the young General, and introduced Jean Simmons as Kanchi. Hassell Simpson reports that despite Rank's preface that the nuns were Protestant, American Catholics protested because the film's nuns were "'worldly, neurotic, and frustrated' and therefore an abnormal case; and the National Legion of Decency condemned it as 'an affront to religion and religious life'" (1973, 141). Pressburger, a Jewish refugee from Hungary and Berlin, often wrote dialogue that, speaking in "the voice . . . of every refugee from Nazism," was "admiring, deferential, skeptical [of Britain]" (Snowman 2002, 164).
7. Tony Williams interprets the nuns' mission as representing the "psychologically crippling aspects of British colonial and cultural imperialism" (2000, 131).

8. Ella Shohat and Robert Stam provide an overview of cinematic colonial films. But in seeing the "textual norms" of *Black Narcissus* "embodied by the British man," they don't acknowledge how Mr. Dean's drinking and cynicism undercut those norms; their view of the nuns as "privileged . . . centers of consciousness in relation to the 'natives'" ignores Godden's own powerful narrative, including the women of the harem (1994, 166).

9. In addition to its economic costs, "by the end of the war, there was a loss of purpose at the very center of the imperial system," due also to the fact that the "countryside had slipped beyond control" (Cain and Hopkins 1993, 195). Darby's incisive analyses of late colonial novels of India show them also preparing for the end of Empire, especially as they plot failed relations between Indians and the British (1998). He does not consider any modern British women writers after Flora Annie Steel and Maud Diver.

10. Priya Jaikumar's discussion intertwines the melodrama of "place" in the film with the nuns' failed expectations, concluding that Sister Clodagh remains "admirable" (2001, 71). She does not see how the film's expressionistic technique critiques this relationship and conclusion. Godden's short story "Rahmin" is also concerned with the exploitative colonial relationship to Indian artisans. Here the narrator becomes entwined with but fires an embroiderer in bad economic times: "I never saw him again except in my mind, where he remains as a small and shameful scar," embroidered on her consciousness (1989b, 31).

11. As a reminder of the achievements of feminist scholarship, we need only to review Hassell Simpson's guidelines for Louise: "Although, in general, the wife should submit to her husband, a mutual respect and forbearance should characterize the marriage relationship. . . . When the male is weak, of course, the female partner in a marriage may be encouraged to take the initiative" (1973, 47).

12. Ironically, the Bengal famine, in which millions of peasants paid exorbitant rents to landowners and were exploited by the British colonial administration, occurred a year after this novel was published. See Paul R. Greenough's study of this event (1982).

13. Lawrence James discusses how Hitler opposed an alliance with Indian nationalism and not only disdained Indians in *Mein Kampf* and was "amazed by the lengths to which the Raj" would accommodate the Indian National Congress, but told Lord Halifax "that Britain ought to shoot Gandhi and as many Congressmen as were needed to 'make it clear that you mean business'" (1998, 553–554).

14. After conquering Singapore on February 15, 1942, the Japanese captured Burma, a severe blow to British belief in its own rightful power, especially because Japan claimed to be liberating Asia from European rule. Adding insult to injury, India's defense now depended on the U.S. Navy.

15. By the end of the war 13 million Indians were employed in war work. On September 3, 1939, the British Viceroy, the Marquess of Linlithgow, declared war on Germany and "committed over 300 million Indians to a conflict without consulting a single one," showing "that Britain was ultimately still master of India" (James 1998, 539). The Muslim League decided to support Britain "as much out of hope for future favors as conviction," while the Indian National Congress opposed Nazism "on principle" (James 1998, 539). The Indian army in 1941, totaling 418,000 men, was composed of "37 per cent Muslims and 55 per cent Hindus, mainly Rajputs, Jats and Dogras, whose warrior traditions remained strong" (James 1998, 542). In 1940 an Emergency Powers Act was passed to curtail political activism that would harm the war effort.

16. Thomas Dukes claims that Godden creates a female "*Bildungsroman*" in her writing, but the character of Louise shows how emotional or social development may be thwarted by an imperial psychology (1991, 17).

17. I am grateful to Elizabeth Maslen (2001) for her comprehensive distinction between a "confrontation with modernity" and what have become all too slippery uses of the term "modernism." Modernity cuts across the timelines of different cultures.

18. Much feminist scholarship, especially that combined with postcolonial studies, argues that gender itself is an unstable category, but when allied with nationality, class, and ethnicity is unsettled even more. See Sangeeta Ray, Rebecca Saunders, and Inderpal Grewal.

19. Margaret Strobel shows how British modernizing practices were made doubly problematic by the response of Indian nationalists who claimed a "spiritually superior" culture that associated Indian women with "the inner," spiritual realm and thereby "made their adoption of Western practices and education" difficult (1993, 21). Sangari and Vaid discuss how the colonial administration codified "high caste Hindu norms . . . to the disadvantage of *all* Hindu women whether rural or urban" (1990, 7). Godden's character Narayan fits their description of the Indian middle-class professional who "develop[s] ideologies of 'Hindu' and 'Indian' womanhood" different from "actual patriarchal norms" practiced by "other classes" and Western marriages (Sangari and Vaid 1990, 9).

20. Feminist research puts the lie to British respect for indigenous tradition. Joanna Liddle and Rama Joshi show the oppressive results for all castes of Hindu women of the British translation of Brahmanic customs into law at the end of the eighteenth century: except for wedding gifts, property ownership was prohibited and divorce outlawed (1986, 26). Strobel discusses how the British Civil Procedure Code in 1859 gave husbands the right to force unhappy wives to stay with them instead of returning to their families (1993, 15).

21. The rabid dog is based on two incidents in the Goddens' childhood: when their father secretly shot their dog when he found its cries unbearable after its broken leg was set, and when Rumer developed rabies after being bitten by their three spaniels and underwent the painful stomach injections.

22. George Mosse's discussion of the modern construction of masculinity is particularly relevant here, contrasting the image of the civilized European male as self-controlled and controlling against that of the uncivilized, hysterical, passive, and homosexual or feminine male of less-esteemed cultures (1996, 55–76).

23. Ronald Inden's critique of Orientalist or Western representations of India revises "caste" "as a form of subject-citizenry" that includes the "agency" for oppression, not only by rulers but by the peasant classes (1990, 217). Overall, Inden criticizes Western writers for depicting Indians as distorting "normal and natural thoughts and institutions" (1990, 39). He doesn't consider how Western, indeed, colonial writers of imaginative narratives could also criticize the conventions that embed these problematic cultural assumptions.

24. Suleri refers to a "strikingly symbolic homoeroticism" to replace the metaphor of colonialism as rape (1992, 17). Paxton (1992) sees the discourse of rape fading in English fiction at the end of the eighteenth century but reemerging between 1830 and 1947, when it is used to test social progress. Her view of British fiction as mirroring colonial oppression would be tested by considering such fictions as Godden's. Hubel (1996) shows how British imperialism could manifest both a "liberal reformative ethic and conservative Orientalism" and was always shifting in its ethos. Her study is exemplary in its melding of literary and historical analysis.

25. In her historical survey of the zenana, Janaki Nair shows how some Western feminists find the Indian woman "fully empowered by her (natural primal) position in the family" and able to "make the transition to the wider 'civic' world quite easily since the family was only a cellular form of society. . . . Through her very domesticity, . . . the Indian woman was a repository of resistance" (2000, 237). Phillip Darby notes that the "feminization of Asian peoples" reflected threats to "the structure of

imperial power" because it "subverted, compromised, spoke with a different voice; what it would not do was to stand up and fight" (1998, 73). Shila's resistance is to the structure of colonial relations.

26. Like many historians today, Embree resolves debates about India being a nation or a continent of nations merged by imperial conquest. He sees India as many strands of civilizations, linking an "ideological, Brahmanical tradition and the historical experience resulting from the impact of two alien civilizations, the Islamic and the Western" (1989, 9).

27. The incident, in 1944, led to "charges of defamation" that made her feel "she could never go back to Kashmir" (Chisholm 1998, 177). Chisholm shows that Godden's two versions of the story, in *Kingfishers* and in her 1987 autobiography, combine emotional with literal truth," leaving a disturbing sense of authorial vulnerability that may explain why Godden later came to dislike the novel (1998, 177). In her 1989 memoir, Godden admits that if only she had "kept to" the "almost peasant simplicity" she began with, instead of the "British Raj customs" brought by the friend who came to share the house, "trouble" might have been avoided (Godden 1989a, 21).

28. Gikandi connects women's comedy and colonial fictions: "because of their liminality in the culture of empire . . . women writers came to read colonialism as . . . a threat because it was a patriarchal affair in which women were excluded in the name of a stifling domestic ideology; it was an opportunity because it destabilized the very categories in which this ideology was formulated"(1996, 121).

29. Godden moved into Dove House, Dhilkusha's model, in 1942, she said, "when we were desperate, ill and so poor that Srinagar's Mission Hospital had taken us in" (1989a, 21). She "paid five rupees, the equivalent then of seven shillings and six-pence, or a dollar and a half, for the house and nine acres of land 'under the trees'— the landlord kept the fruit" (1989, 21).

30. Lynne Rosenthal analyzes how "Sophie chooses the aesthetic, her vision of the ideal, over the reality of the Kashmirian world and her own children" (1996, 43).

31. Vron Ware argues that despite the popularity and "high" female "profile" of such 1980s films as *Jewel in the Crown* and *Out of Africa,* there "has been little feminist cultural criticism," perhaps because it is assumed that British-made depictions of colonial society make them "racist"(1992, 230). It may also be because their female characters challenge postcolonial assumptions that they are either solely victims or complicit with imperialist ideologies.

32. George analyzes how "homesickness," the "search for the location in which the self is at home[,] is one of the primary projects of twentieth-century fiction in English" (1996, 3).

33. Until it became a French mandate after the end of the Ottoman Empire at the end of World War I, Lebanon was part of the Ottoman's province of greater Syria; as a national entity, its borders were established in 1923 by European powers at a conference in San Remo.

34. See *The Greengage Summer* (1958), *The Peacock Spring* (1975) and her children's stories.

35. Sophie's romantic scripting of the colonized supports Suleri's contention that "an anxious impulse" rendered "colonized peoples . . . interpretable within the language of the colonizer," but this cannot be claimed for all colonial women writers, as Godden's satire shows (Suleri 1992, 7).

36. In *A Time to Dance,* volume 1 of her autobiography, Godden asserts that she "will never countenance a word against missionaries, knowing at first hand the depth of their selflessness, courage, endurance and kindness," but because she refers to medical and not teaching missionaries, she raises questions about her novel's critique (1987, 182). Ballhatchet notes, "Like Eurasians, missionaries also occupied an

ambiguous position on the margins of the social distance between the ruling race and the peoples of India" (1980, 111). For extensive study of the role of women teachers and medical missionaries and reformers, see Kumari Jayawardena, who shows how "they saw their task as 'saving' their Asian sisters from devilish beliefs, moral degradation and from sexual and social oppression" (1995, 4). Colonialism was the tool of reform.

37. See Anne McClintock (1995, 140).

38. Although the Sepoy Mutiny is so often made the model for all others, Lawrence James sees differences that highlight the problems with a universalizing history (1998, 564–569).

39. Mrinalini Sinha notes how "imperialist thinking" divides "the so-called 'manly' peoples of the Punjab and the North-West Frontier Provinces [from] the 'effeminate' peoples of Bengal and the more 'settled' regions of British India, or between virile Muslims and effeminate Hindus" (1999, 447).

40. Sophie fits most of Ware's description of "the Foolhardy" feminist British character in India, "finding India fascinating, and bringing "disastrous consequences both for herself" and others (1992, 232). But Sophie also defies the idea that India's "exotic mysteries . . . repel her" with her honest if self-deluded desire to understand and work with the Kashmiris (Ware 1992, 232). Sophie's actions, at the end of the Empire, can be translated into comedy; what is ominous is the lack of imaginative space, neocolonial, postcolonial, or English, that can accommodate her "unwillingness to conform" (Ware 1992, 232). Chisholm argues that, unlike Godden's own experience, "Sophie is able to put things right" and the novel "could be seen as an extended tribute to Kashmir . . . , a country and a people whose beauty and natural nobility are shown in striking contrast to the drab, conventional nature of England and the English" (1998, 180).

CHAPTER 3   RED STRANGERS

1. The African writer Ngugi wa Thiong'o argues that when "confronted by the white man," the "will to act" of Huxley's "African characters . . . melts away even without the kind of inner conflict which we would normally expect in any human being confronted by alien forces he can hardly comprehend. Her good characters . . . live in stupid, perpetual puzzlement about the ways of the white man. The others are thugs and crooks" (quoted in Heywood 1971, 6–7).

2. Most historians agree about colonial policies that supported settlers like the Grants. Bruce Berman explains how "easy terms" on "hundreds of acres" were given to small farmers to help them "fulfill their imperial role in export production rather than simply live off the land" (1990, 56). While this alienated land from the Kikuyu, who were then pressed into becoming laboring squatters on white estates, it also afforded them revenue from tending their own crops and livestock. Hut and poll taxes exposed "patronage" as another form of oppression (Berman 1990, 62). Tabitha Kanogo (1987) analyzes the relationship between squatters and settlers.

3. Maughan-Brown typifies this claim: "The myths and stereotypes" which shape "colonial settler ideology" are shared "by the white authors writing about 'Mau Mau'"; we can predict "what the white settler writer will have to say on almost any issue" (1985, 73). Hariclea Zengos (1989) agrees. Gillilan Whitlock argues that Kenyan settler "polemics" doesn't "deny the presence of African people but [rather their] integrity, authority and agency" (2000, 125).

4. Huxley recalls studying with the anthropologist Malinowski along with Jomo Kenyatta, Kenyan liberation leader and first prime minister after independence (using the name Johnston), and being concerned that Malinowski might treat the

"effrontery" of her work with "contempt," not the least because he was writing his own anthropological study, *Facing Mount Kenya* (Huxley 1987, 197, 196).

5. Willis condemns Huxley's "vision of change" as being consistent with Lord Delamere's. He also notes that she was mentored about the Kikuyu by Louis Leakey, whose "prolonged and vicious" rivalry with Kenyatta's interpretations coincided with the "considerable unease" the latter caused settlers and officials (2002, 5).

6. Reinhard Sander condemns *Red Strangers* as typical of the work of "a person who belongs to a self-proclaimed dominant race" and who "is unable to see the injustice and oppression directed against a different race and people" (1976, 28). This view overrides any critical perspective in the novel by insisting that it is a "defense of British colonialism in East Africa" (Sander 1976, 28).

7. Like Achebe, Willis finds Huxley consistent about "colonialism's promise of progress [being] dashed by metropolitan interferences and African political aspirations" (2002, 5).

8. Huxley explained how, if not why, she began to write mystery novels: "In the 1930s my husband's job took us both on many [sea] journeys . . . and I took to writing crime stories to . . . avoid playing bridge" (quoted in Bargainnier 1984, 35).

9. Bargainnier claims that however they may reflect an empire in decline or "the exoticism of Africa," Huxley's mysteries "are suffused with that profound knowledge and an unsentimental love of Africa" (1984, 35–36).

10. Abdulrazak Gurnah sees Huxley and Karen Blixen representing the European experience in Kenya as "a crisis of contradictions," alienated from the exotic land and people and insecure representing it "within Western discourse" (2000, 286). Though characterized as "'liberal,'" this settler writing is "always unstable and in danger of corruption" (2000, 289). I argue that this is the dilemma Huxley's writing emplots.

11. Bargainnier sees *The Merry Hippo* satirizing the "failure" of colonial administration, through "corrupt, malicious, uncooperative or simply fatuous" officials (1984, 40).

12. In *Nellie: Letters from Africa*, Huxley notes that while her mother helped her write this memoir "by recalling various incidents . . . , she disapproved of the whole idea" (1973, 226). Until 1920, Kenya was officially the East Africa Protectorate, and then became a Crown colony. By 1939, it had a European population of 21,000. Its indigenous peoples "outnumbered the white settlers by approximately 175 to one" (Kennedy 1997, 1). Its Indian population, which outnumbered Britons, was scorned by both the British and black Africans.

13. Despite 999-year leases, hard work, love of the land, and experiments with scientific techniques, many European farms required constant subsidy; neither crops nor cattle could earn the revenue to support them (Best 1979, 163). Karen Blixen's coffee farm is typical in succumbing to frost, drought, and locusts, and then the Wall Street crash "wip[ed] out the mainstay of Kenya's economy at one cruel stroke" (Best 1979, 119).

14. Justin Willis criticizes those like C. S. Nicholls, her biographer, who find Huxley's "particular experience of Kenya . . . gave her unusual 'understanding' of whites and Africans," and while he avers that "Huxley herself was cautious of this sort of rhetoric of authenticity," he also claims that her writing exhibits "little" change in its attitudes toward colonialism (2002, 4). Nicholls provides vast and varied sources to demonstrate such change. Criticisms of Nicholls's work continue the stereotyping and dismissal of those British women who spent formative years in the colonies and wrote about them.

15. Tidrick (1990) discusses Huxley's debates with Perham. Interestingly, Huxley's defense against Margery Perham's indictment of settler domination is based on economics, seeing the settlers as betrayed by the colonial office's limited support. Berman shows that by World War I, "a clash of interests" between colonial administrators and settlers was fomented by "constant rows between secretaries of state in

London and Kenya's governors and in the emergence of clear limits to metropolitan control over the colonial state" (1990, 67).

16. Whitlock notes that the child's innocent voice enables Huxley to convey colonial settlement "with a clear sense of its absurdity and imposture" (2000, 126). Mary Louise Pratt sees the European bourgeoisie maintaining their innocence while claiming superiority and dominance (1992, 78). In *Nellie: Letters from Africa*, Huxley notes that *The Flame Trees of Thika* is "*a semi-fictional account of my childhood . . . not always sticking exactly to factual details*" (1973, 226, italics in original).

17. Maughan-Brown disdains such close reading as "traditional," favoring, instead, ideological "interpellation," which, in my view, overwhelms any complex relationship "between character, narrator and author" (1985, 11 4).

18. Wendy Webster discusses a "shift in Huxley's work between 1935 and 1964 from a confident assertion of imperial identity to "anxieties" about "homophobia, 'miscegenation,'" and the displacement of working-class masculinity (1999, 530). While *Flame Trees* is written in this period, its depiction of an earlier time reflects cultural concerns that accrue to these later ones. Dane Kennedy notes that "settler culture . . . isolate[d] and institutionalize[d] white settlement within a rigid set of physical, linguistic, social, economic, and political boundaries" (1997, 189).

19. Huxley's father had exhausted various money-making schemes before a farm in Kenya became his last chance at professional success. Nellie Grant was the granddaughter of the Marchioness of Westminster and the daughter of Lord Grosvenor, but her tiny income hardly matched the prestige of her status.

20. Githae-Mugo notes that Huxley's attitudes, "inherited" from her family, were more "liberal than the average settler['s]," but her "benevolent" treatment of the natives is attributed to their treating her "as a memsahib" (1978, 19).

21. Webster sees Tilly's rugged individualism "outdo[ing] men in . . . adventurousness, resilience and persistence," but this also includes domesticating black men (1999, 531). I find Huxley more critical of Tilly's relations with both black and white men, as well as with those "students of colonial discourses and postcolonial theory [who] do not," according to Simon Gikandi, "know what to do with the women of empire" (1996, 121).

22. Kennedy notes that despite their remoteness from indigenous Africans, their homes were "literally over run with African employees," challenging "the maintenance of social standards and racial differences" (1982, 1, 2). Because safeguards against threats of interracial sexual relations assumed only settler men were tempted, employing African women as domestic workers was prohibited. Because African men were assumed to be sexually voracious, they were feminized, infantilized, and dressed in "special caps, smocks, and other garb . . . intended to define and delimit their role" (1982, 5).

23. Kennedy shows how language signified "the barrier constructed by the European community between itself and the African population" (1997, 155). Instead of easing communication and despite the Africans' eagerness to become proficient "in the language of the ruling race," the English opposed its instruction (1997, 156). To cope, Africans developed "mongrel dialects" that communicated inefficiently and reinforced the belief in black stupidity (Kennedy 1997, 156).

24. Githae-Mugo objects to Huxley calling the medicine man "a magical practitioner," but Huxley shows his method as empirical (1978, 42). Elizabeth Fenn (2001) and Jonathan Tucker (2001) show that smallpox inoculation was devised in Africa or Asia in the early eighteenth century and cut the death risk from 30 to only 1 percent. The method is exactly as Huxley describes.

25. David Boxwell's insights into the role of imperial science in British popular fiction show "a terrifying vision of the entire British Empire brought to a halt by a quasi-tropical disease" (2002, 10). The absurdity of that terror is exhibited by the Happy

Valley crowd, who "argued in their own defense that it was the rarified air" of the highlands "that made them unusually randy and more than a little potty" (Best 1979, 106). While Huxley is criticized for this novel's bleak picture of Africa, she argues that the historically verified "ecological crisis of the 1890s," including "cattle plagues and drought," that "wiped out up to a quarter" of Kenya's people "and produced squabbling over the means of subsistence" was also a result of the white man's plague—smallpox (Berman 1990, 53).

26. The economic and human losses of the Anglo-Boer War of 1899–1902 drew many white settlers to Kenya, including Afrikaners who trekked to German East Africa only to find their numbers restricted by the German government. Some crossed into Kenya only to be governed by the British, whom they had fought. Afrikaner collaborators with the British were politically if not socially welcomed (Kennedy 1997, 26).

27. Simon Gikandi corrects assumptions about Africans' reliance on any mystical notion of their relationship to their land or polity. He argues that they fought colonial rule not "to return to a pre-colonial past but because they wanted access to the privileges of colonial culture to be spread more equitably" (1996, xix).

28. Huxley's critics take her to be very disdainful of Kenyatta, but with their first meeting at the London School of Economics in 1936, she recalls him as "fluent, alert, cogent and authoritative—one of the stars" (Huxley 1964, 171). Later she distinguishes between him as leader of Mau Mau and his "grace and candor" as the first prime minister of independent Kenya, especially as he eased tensions with white settlers and among his own divided people in a powerful message of "forgive and forget"(Huxley, 1964, 174; 1987, 202–203). She saw Mau Mau as a terrorist movement, "rooted in a deep, emotional hatred, not merely of Europeans but of all they represented, of the whole Western world, the whole twentieth century" (Huxley 1960, 236). As an expert agronomist, she also disagreed with Kenyatta's attitude toward the soil erosion she feared.

29. See for example, Maughan-Brown (1985), who finds no differences between this and any other colonial novel about the Mau Mau rebellions. Sharon Russell is almost alone in assessing Huxley as having a "fair evaluation" not only "of the Mau Maus," but of "the complex structure of [colonial] society" (1991, 24). Martin Tucker also sees *A Thing to Love* holding Gibson "as responsible for the tragedy as any extremist" (1967, 136).

30. The role of British missionaries has been explored and deplored, but Huxley shows that even when they supported colonialism, women missionaries could also challenge its policies. Margaret Strobel discusses several, including Mary Slessor, who, in 1901 Nigeria, "opposed such practices as slavery; human sacrifice upon the burying of an important person; poison ordeals; and the putting to death of twins, whose births [as depicted in Achebe's *Things Fall Apart*] were thought to be ritually dangerous" (1991, 54).

31. From its inception, the Mau Mau rebellion was considered by Europeans to be a "mass psychosis" (Berman 1990, 353), an "irrational, and atavistic response to problems of rapid social change," a reversion to African primitivism, and a rejection of modern Western progress (Rosberg and Nottingham 1966, 330). Denying the movement any political intelligence, Europeans accused Mau Mau of being "a secret, tribal cult, led by unscrupulous agitators, mere confidence tricksters" (Rosbert and Nottingham 1966, 330). The social and political structures of Mau Mau were much more complex, however. Its leaders were divided by unequal access to "education, land, and wealth," but their "secret mass oath" produced political commitment as well as "the discipline and will for sustained resistance in the face of great hardships"; oathing also isolated the Kikuyu from other Kenyan Africans (Rosberg and Nottingham 1966, 242, 243, 261). Huxley, who depicts oath taking in

A Thing to Love as involving animal sacrifice and symbolic sexual acts and in 1985 still argues that oaths "were enforced with much obscenity to kill, maim and destroy white people and their livestock and property," based her judgment in part on a journalist's report (Huxley 1987, 103; 1973, 200). But almost no historical study of Mau Mau describes oath ceremonies. Nicholas Best recounts a description by a prominent Kenyan leader, which includes placing his penis into a hole of the thorax of a skinned goat (1979, 164). It doesn't stretch the imagination to understand how such ceremonies would strike Europeans of the time as "depraved" (Githae-Mugo 1973, 119). Perhaps the ghost of such judgment haunts the absence of descriptions even today, especially in light of concerns about depicting indigenous peoples as guilty of bestial sexuality and therefore dangerous and warranting colonial domination. Compounding the perceived savagery of oathing ceremonies was the majority belief that "Mau Mau committed 'unspeakable atrocities'" against settlers, though this has been disputed by medical studies (Berman 1990, 356). Nellie Grant and Nicholas Best report murders of settlers by panga-wielding Mau Mau (Huxley 1973, 192; Best 1979, 176)). Huxley's mother calls the uprising "a civil war" (quoted in Huxley 1973, 195), a view that reflects conflicted attitudes in England, where "if evidence appeared that colonial control depended too heavily on . . . too rough a justice, then the humanitarian instincts on which the champions of empire had played so artfully for so long . . . might be roused successfully against the continuation of empire" (Darwin 1988, 20).

CHAPTER 4   ISLAND STRANGERS

1. My information about Allfrey is based on the extensive research of Lizabeth Paravisini-Gebert (1996).
2. Gayatri Spivak views Rhys's Bertha Mason as a silent subaltern in Bronte's exploitation of her for the sake of Jane's success (1986); Benita Parry accuses Spivak of ignoring the defiant voice of the black Jamaican, Christophine (1987). Penelope Ingram argues for "the distinction between the undeniably more privileged position of the white Creole and that of the so-called doubly oppressed silent subaltern" (1999, 91). I see Allfrey dramatizing the power relations among them as she reconfigures their presence among her own characters.
3. Kathleen Renk (1999) sees Allfrey's representation of Lally's relationship to her employers as romantically harmonious while she remains subordinate to white domination.
4. Renk classifies *The Orchid House* as a "nationalist" anticolonial novel indebted to nineteenth-century realism in its concern with feminist individualism, but its experimentation with the characters and perspectives of the three sisters as well as gothic conventions seems awfully modern (1999, 4–6).
5. Benita Parry argues "that there is a move to restore affect to the fiction of identity, and rather than the toleration extended to its expedient use in political mobilization, we see it embraced as a pleasure, and one that is all the greater because identity is now perceived as multi-located and polysemic—a situation that characterizes postcoloniality and is at its most evident in the diasporic condition" (1994, 175).
6. Inderpal Grewal's discussion of "'Home'" is applicable to the return of Allfrey's three sisters to the home they fantasize they can regenerate and where they can effect a "consolidation of the Self," but instead of this being "enabled by the encounter with the 'Other,'" their sense of self becomes the object of criticism in the anticolonial engagement of Allfrey's experience and imagination (1996, 6).
7. Allfrey's unpublished sequel to this novel, *In the Cabinet*, adds to the family's tragedies with the murder of Joan's little boy, Ned, "in retaliation for Stella's murder of Mr. Lilipoulala" (Paravisini-Gebert 1996, 89).

8. For biographical information on Bottome, see Marilyn Hoder-Salmon (1998).

9. Despite the substitution of Hollywood romance and glamour for Bottome's feminist analysis, as well as the erasure of the word Jew, Bottome felt that the film version was extremely important because its 1940 release represented a plea for the United States to enter the war. See my analysis of this in *British Women Writers of World War II.*

10. See the new introduction to the recent reprint of *The Mortal Storm.* The BBC canceled her radio talks that pleaded with German women to resist their sons' Nazi indoctrination. This and many other examples of her political rallying are now available to scholars at the British Library, which has recently acquired her papers.

11. Susan S. Friedman theorizes spatial narrative movement as boundaries and borderlands, emphasizing intercultural encounters among those of variously hybridized identities in order to complicate notions of "sameness and difference that [are] embedded in the double meaning of the term *identity*" (1998, 143). While she and others give complex recognition to the ambiguities and ambivalences in this movement, what is missing is the recognition that part of human agency is to choose difference and a fixed identity, and that intercultural contact may have negative, even destructive results.

12. "The Pirate's Isle" charts Jamaica's history of "eneffaceable cruelty and shame" back through the Spanish conquest, its extermination of the Arawaks and introduction of African slaves (1955, 188–189).

13. In "The Pirate's Isle," Bottome distinguishes between Spanish policies, which kept most Jamaicans illiterate, and the success of various British Christian groups which, despite their dogmatic condescension, worked "hand in hand, with teachers, doctors, nurses, welfare and research workers" to relieve much "misery and ignorance" (1955, 193).

14. Vron Ware notes the frequency with which "interracial sex . . . leads to death in colonial fiction," and how this calls for the study of "plots and characterizations . . . in such dangerous territory" (1992, 233).

References

Abeysekara, Ananda. 1999. Contested Religious Identities: Debating Monkhood and Buddhism in Sri Lanka. Ph.D. diss., Northwestern University, Evanston.

Achebe, Chinua. 1992. *Things Fall Apart*. New York: Knopf.

———. 2001. *Home and Exile*. New York: Anchor Books.

Alcoff, Linda. 1991/1992. The Problem of Speaking for Others." *Cultural Critique* 20 (winter): 5–32.

Alexander, Joan. 1983. *Voices and Echoes: Tales from Colonial Women*. London: Quartet Books.

Allen, Charles. 1995. *Plain Tales from the Raj: Images of British India in the Twentieth Century*. London: Abacus.

Allfrey, Phyllis Shand. 1997. *The Orchid House*. 1953. Reprint, New Brunswick: Rutgers University Press.

———. n.d. In the Cabinet. Two unpublished manuscripts.

Apostolou. Fotini. E. 2001. *Seduction and Death in Muriel Spark's Fiction*. Westport, Conn.: Greenwood Press.

Arendt, Hannah. 1994. *Eichmann in Jerusalem: A Report on the Banality of Evil*. New York: Viking Press.

Ashcroft, Bill, Gareth Griffiths, and Helen Tiffin. 1989. *The Empire Writes Back*. London: Routledge.

Bailey, Susan. 1987. *Women and the British Empire: An Annotated Guide to Sources*. New York: Garland.

Baker, Niamh. 1989. *Happily Ever After? Women's Fiction in Postwar Britain, 1945–60*. New York: St. Martins.

Bakhtin, Mikhail. 1981. *The Dialogic Imagination*. Ed. Michael Holquist. Austin: University of Texas Press.

Balibar, Etienne, and Immanuel Wallerstein. 1991. *Race Nation Class: Ambiguous Identities*. London: Verso.

Ballhatchet, Kenneth. 1980. *Race, Sex, and Class under the Raj: Imperial Attitudes and Politics and Their Critics, 1793–1905*. London: Weidenfeld and Nicolson.

Bargainnier, Earl F. 1980. *The Gentle Art of Murder*. Bowling Green, Ohio: Popular Press.

———. 1984. The African Mysteries of Elspeth Huxley. *Clues* 5, no. 2 (fall/winter): 35–47.

Barker, Francis, Peter Hulme, and Margaret Iversen. 1994. *Colonial Discourse/Postcolonial Theory*. Manchester: Manchester University Press.

Baruma, Ian. 2002. The Blood Lust of Identity. *New York Review of Books* 11 (April): 12–14.

Baucom, Ian. 1999. *Out of Place: Englishness, Empire, and the Locations of Identity*. Princeton: Princeton University Press.

Beeley, Harold. 1990. Ernest Bevin and Palestine. In *Studies in Arab History: The Antonius Lectures, 1978–87,* ed. Derek Hopwood, 117–130. Basingstoke, Hampshire, U.K.: Macmillan.

Bentwich, Norman, and Helen Bentwich. 1965. *Mandate Memories, 1918–1948.* London: Hogarth Press.

Berman, Bruce. 1990. *Control and Crisis in Colonial Kenya.* London: James Currey.

Berman, Bruce, and John Lonsdale. 1992. *Unhappy Valley: Conflict in Kenya and Africa.* London: James Currey.

Best, Nicholas. 1979. *Happy Valley: The Story of the English in Kenya.* London: Secker & Warburg.

Bhabha, Homi. 1986. The Other Question: Difference, Discrimination, and the Discourse of Colonialism. In *Literature, Politics, and Theory,* ed. Francis Barker et al. London: Methuen, 148–172.

———. 1994. *The Location of Culture.* London: Routledge.

———. 1998. Of Mimicry and Man: The Ambivalence of Colonial Discourse. In *Tensions of Empire: Colonial Cultures in a Bourgeois World,* Frederick Cooper and Ann Laura Stoler, 152–160. Berkeley: University of California Press.

Boehmer, Elleke. 1995. *Colonial and Postcolonial Literature.* Oxford: Oxford University Press.

Booth, Howard J., and Nigel Rigby, eds. 2000. *Modernism and Empire.* Manchester: Manchester University Press.

Bottome, Phyllis. 1932. *What Are Dictators?* London: Trustees for Freedom Publications.

———. 1940. *The Mortal Storm.* Directed by Frank Borzage. A Metro-Goldwyn-Mayer Film.

———. 1942. *Within the Cup.* London: Faber.

———. 1943a. *The Lifeline.* London: Faber.

———. 1943b. Our New Order—Or Hitler's? In *Our New Order—Or Hitler's? A Selection of Speeches,* ed. Phyllis Bottome. Harmondsworth: Penguin, 78–116.

———. 1950. *Under the Skin.* London: Faber & Faber.

———. 1952a. *The Challenge.* London: Faber.

———. 1952b. Note, July 11. Phyllis Bottome Papers, British Library.

———. 1955. The Pirate's Isle. In *Not in Our Stars,* by Phyllis Bottome. London: Faber & Faber, 187–196.

———. 1957. *Alfred Adler: Portrait from Life.* 3rd ed. New York: Vanguard Press.

———. 1962. *The Goal.* New York: Vanguard Press.

———. 1998a. *The Mortal Storm.* 1937. Reprint, Evanston: Northwestern University Press.

———. 1998b. *Old Wine.* 1924. Reprint, Evanston: Northwestern University Press.

Boxwell, David. 1999. On the Edge of the Precipice: The Cultural Work of the Archers' *Black Narcissus.* Paper delivered at the Modernist Studies Association.

———. 2002. The Germs of Empires: Tropes/Tropics/Diseases in Joseph Conrad's *The Shadow Line* and Edgar Wallace's 'The Black Grippe.'" Paper delivered at the Modern Language Association.

Broe, Mary Lynne, and Angela Ingram, eds. 1989. *Women's Writing in Exile.* Chapel Hill: University of North Carolina Press.

Burton, Antoinette. 1992. The White Woman's Burden: British Feminists and "The Indian Woman," 1865–1915. In *Western Women and Imperialism,* ed. Nupur Chaudhuri and Margaret Strobel, 137–157. Bloomington: Indiana University Press.

———. 2000. Who Needs the Nation? Interrogating "British" History. In *Cultures of*

Empire: Colonizers in Britain and the Empire in the Nineteenth and Twentieth Centuries, Catherine Hall, 137–153. New York: Routledge.

———. 2001. India, Inc.? Nostalgia, Memory, and the Empire of Things. In *British Culture and the End of Empire*, ed. Stuart Ward, 217–232. Manchester: Manchester University Press.

———, ed. 1999. *Gender, Sexuality, and Colonial Modernities.* New York: Routledge.

Cain, P. J., and A. G. Hopkins. 1993. *British Imperialism: Crisis and Deconstruction, 1914–1990.* London: Longman.

Callan, Hilary, and Shirley Ardener, eds. 1984. *The Incorporated Wife.* London: Croom Helm.

Calloway, Helen. 1987. *Gender, Culture, and Empire: European Women in Colonial Nigeria.* London: Macmillan.

Calloway, Helen, and Dorothy O. Helly. 1992. Crusader for Empire: Flora Shaw/Lady Lugard. In *Western Women and Imperialism*, ed. Nupur Chaudhuri and Margaret Strobel, 79–97. Bloomington: Indiana University Press.

Césaire, Aimée. 2000. *Discourse on Colonialism.* Translated by Joan Pinkham. New York: Monthly Review Press.

Chatterjee, Partha. 1993. *The Nation and Its Fragments.* Princeton: Princeton University Press.

Chaudhuri, Nupur, and Margaret Strobel, eds. 1992. *Western Women and Imperialism.* Bloomington: Indiana University Press.

Cheyette, Bryan. 2000. *Muriel Spark.* Tavistock, U.K.: Northcote Publishers.

———. 2002. Writing against Conversion: Muriel Spark, the Gentile Jewess. In *Theorizing Muriel Spark,* ed. Martin McQuillan, 95–112. Basingstoke, U.K.: Palgrave.

Chisholm, Anne. 1998. *Rumer Godden: A Storyteller's Life.* Basingstoke, U.K.: Macmillan.

Cohen, Michael J. 1978. *Palestine: Retreat from the Mandate: The Making of British Policy, 1936–45.* New York: Holmes & Meier.

Cohen, Michael J., and Martin Kolinsky, eds. 1998. *Demise of the British Empire in the Middle East.* London: Frank Cass.

Cooper, Artemis. 1995. *Cairo in the War, 1939–1945.* Harmondsworth: Penguin.

Cooper, Frederick, and Ann Laura Stoler. 1998. *Tensions of Empire: Colonial Cultures in a Bourgeois World.* Berkeley: University of California Press.

Darby, Phillip. 1998. *The Fiction of Imperialism.* London: Cassell.

Darwin, John. 1988. *Britain and Decolonization: The Retreat from Empire in the Post-War World.* London: Macmillan.

Dick, Kay. 1974. *Friends and Friendship: Conversations and Reflections.* London: Sidgwick & Jackson.

Donaldson, Laura E. 1992. *Decolonizing Feminisms.* Chapel Hill: University of North Carolina Press.

Doyle, Michael W. 1986. *Empires.* Ithaca, N.Y.: Cornell University Press.

Dukes, Thomas. 1991. "Evoking the Significance": The Autobiographies of Rumer Godden. *Women's Studies* 20: 15–35.

Edgecombe, Rodney S. 1990. *Vocation and Identity in the Fiction of Muriel Spark.* Columbia: University of Missouri Press.

Edmond, Rod. 2000. Home and Away: Degeneration in Imperialist and Modernist Discourse. In *Modernism and Empire*, ed. Howard J. Booth and Nigel Rigby, 39–63. Manchester: Manchester University Press.

Embree, Ainslie T. 1989. *Imagining India.* Delhi: Oxford University Press.

Felman, Shoshana. 2001. Theaters of Justice: Arendt in Jerusalem, the Eichmann Trial, and the Redefinition of Legal Meaning in the Wake of the Holocaust. *Critical Inquiry* 27 (winter): 201–238.

Fenn, Elizabeth A. 2001. *Pox Americana: The Great Smallpox Epidemic of 1775–82*. New York: Hill and Wang.

Ferguson, Moira. 1993. *Colonialism and Gender Relations from Mary Wolstonecraft to Jamaica Kincaid*. New York: Columbia University Press.

Finney, Gail. 1994. Introduction: Unity in Difference? In *Look Who's Laughing: Gender and Comedy*, ed. Gail Finney, 1-16. Langhorne, Penn.: Gordon and Breach.

Four Feathers. 2002. Directed by Shekhar Kapur. Performed by Heath Ledger, Wes Bentley, Kate Hudson, and Djimon Hounsou. Miramax.

Frantz, Douglas, and Catherine Collins. 2003. *Death on the Black Sea*. New York: Ecco.

Friedman, Susan Stanford. 1998. *Mappings: Feminism and the Cultural Geographies of Encounter*. Princeton: Princeton University Press.

Gandhi, Leela. 1998. *Postcolonial Theory*. New York: Columbia University Press.

Gardiner, Judith Kegan. 1989. The Exhilaration of Exile: Rhys, Stead, and Lessing. In *Women's Writing in Exile,* ed. Mary Lynne Broe and Angela Ingram, 133–150. Chapel Hill: University of North Carolina Press.

Gasiorek, Andrzek. 1995. *Postwar British Fiction*. New York: St. Martins.

Gates, Henry Louis. 1991. Critical "Fanonism." *Critical Inquiry* 17: 457–470.

Gender and History. 1993. Vol. 5, no. 2 (summer). Special issue on gender, nationalisms, and national identity.

George, Rosemary Marangoly. 1996. *The Politics of Home*. Cambridge: Cambridge University Press.

Gikandi, Simon. 1992. *Writing in Limbo: Modernism and Caribbean Literature*. Ithaca, N.Y.: Cornell University Press.

————. 1996. *Maps of Englishness: Writing Identity in the Culture of Colonialism*. New York: Columbia University Press.

Gilbert, Martin. 1981. *Auschwitz and the Allies*. London: Michael Joseph.

Gilman, Sander. 1991. *The Jew's Body*. New York: Routledge.

Githae-Mugo. 1978. *Visions of Africa: The Fiction of Chinua Achebe, Margaret Laurence, Elspeth Huxley, Ngugi wa Thiongo*. Nairobi: Kenya Literature Bureau.

Glavin, John. 2000. Muriel Spark: Beginning Again. In *British Women Writing Fiction,* ed. Abby Werlock, 293–313. Tuscaloosa: University of Alabama Press.

Godden, Rumer. 1942. *Black Narcissus*. 1939. Reprint, London: The Reprint Society.

————. 1946a. *The River*. Boston: Little Brown.

————. 1946b. *Rungli-Rungliot or Thus Far and No Further*. Boston: Little, Brown.

————. 1951. *The River*. Film Adaptation. Written by Rumer Godden and Jean Renoir. Directed by Jean Renoir. Produced by Kenneth McEldowney.

————. 1957. *Mooltiki: Stories and Poems from India*. New York: Viking Press.

————. 1958. *The Greengage Summer*. New York: Viking Press.

————. 1975. *The Peacock Spring*. London: Macmillan.

————. 1985. *Breakfast with the Nikolides*. 1942. Reprint, London: Futura.

————. 1986. A Cool Eye in a Parched Landscape. *New York Times Book Review* (May 25): 1, 20.

————. 1987. *A Time to Dance, No Time to Weep*. New York: William Morrow.

————. 1989a. *A House with Four Rooms* . New York: William Morrow.

————. 1989b. Rahmin. In *Two under the Indian Sun,* by Jon Godden and Rumer Godden, 25–32. London: Macmillan.

————. 1991. *Coromandel Sea Change*. New York: William Morrow.

————. 1994. *Kingfishers Catch Fire*. 1953. Reprint, Minneapolis: Milkweed Editions.

————. 2000. *Black Narcissus*. Film Adaptation. 1948. Written, produced, and directed by Michael Powell and Emeric Pressburger. MGM Home Entertainment Video.

Godden, Jon, and Rumer Godden. 1966. *Two under the Indian Sun*. London: Macmillan.

————. 1972. *Shiva's Pigeons: An Experience of India*. Photographs by Stella Snead. New York: Alfred A. Knopf and Viking Press.

————. 1989. *Mercy, Pity, Peace, and Love: Stories*. New York: William Morrow.

Gorra, Michael. 1997. *After Empire*. Chicago: University of Chicago Press.

Greenberger, Allen. 1969. *The British Image of India: A Study in the Literature of Imperialism, 1880–1960*. New York: Oxford University Press.

Greenough, Paul R. 1982. *Prosperity and Misery in Modern Bengal: The Famine of 1943–1944*. New York: Oxford University Press.

Grewal, Inderpal. 1996. *Home and Harem: Nation, Gender, Empire, and the Cultures of Travel*. Durham: Duke University Press.

Gupta, Brijen Kishore. 1973. *India in English Fiction, 1800–1970*. Metuchen: Scarecrow.

Gurnah, Abdulrazak. 2000. Settler Writing in Kenya. In *Modernism and Empire*, ed. Howard J. Booth and Nigel Rigby, 275–291. Manchester: Manchester University Press.

Haggis, Jane. 1990. Gendering Colonialism or Colonising Gender. *Women's Studies International Forum* 13, no. 1–2: 105–115.

Hall, Catherine. 2000. *Cultures of Empire: Colonizers in Britain and the Empire in the Nineteenth and Twentieth Centuries*. New York: Routledge.

Hall, Stuart. 1995. Negotiating Caribbean Identities. *New Left Review* 209 (Jan.–Feb.): 3–14.

————. 1996. Cultural Identity and Diaspora. In *Contemporary Postcolonial Theory: A Reader*, ed. Padmini Mongia, 110–121. London: Arnold.

Hanley, Lynne. 1991/1992. Writing across the Color Bar: Apartheid and Desire. *Massachusetts Review* (winter): 495–506.

Hartley, Jenny. 1997. *Millions like Us: British Women's Fiction of the Second World War*. London: Virago.

Hattenstone, Simon. 2000. White Knuckle Ride. *The Guardian* (Dec. 11): wysiwyg: //26/http://books.guardian.co.uk/whitbread2000/story/0,6194,417437,00.html.

Hausner, Gideon. 1966. *Justice in Jerusalem*. New York: Holocaust Library.

Heywood, C., ed. 1971. *Perspectives on African Literature*. London: Heinemann.

Hoder-Salmon, Marilyn. 1998. Phyllis Bottome. In *British Novelists, 1919–1939*, ed. George M. Johnson. Columbia, S.C.: Bruccoli Clark.

Hogan, Patrick Colm. 2000. *Colonialism and Cultural Identity*. Albany: State University of New York Press.

Hopwood, Derek. 1989. *Tales of Empire: The British in the Middle East, 1880–1952*. London: I. B. Taurus.

————, ed. 1990. *Studies in Arab History: The Antonius Lectures, 1978–87*. Basingstoke, Hampshire, U.K.: Macmillan.

Hospital, Janette Turner. 1988. Review. *A Time to Dance, No Time to Weep*. *New York Times Book Review* (Jan. 3): 13.

Hubel, Teresa. 1996. *Whose India? The Independence Struggle in British and Indian Fiction*. Durham: Duke University Press.

Hutchins, Francis G. 1967. *The Illusion of Permanence: British Imperialism in India*. Princeton: Princeton University Press.

Hutnyk, John. 1996. *The Rumour of Calcutta: Tourism, Charity, and the Poverty of Representation*. London: Zed Books.

Huxley, Elspeth. 1939. *Red Strangers*. London: Chatto and Windus.

———. 1948a. *The Sorcerer's Apprentice: Journey through East Africa*. London: Chatto and Windus.

———. 1948b. *The Walled City*. London: Chatto and Windus.

———. 1954a. *Kenya Today*. London: Lutterworth Press.

———. 1954b. *A Thing to Love*. London: Chatto and Windus.

———. 1955. *Four Guineas: A Journey through West Africa*. 1954. Reprint, London: Reprint Society.

———. 1959. *The Flame Trees of Thika*. London: Chatto and Windus.

———. 1960. *A New Earth: An Experiment in Colonialism*. London: Chatto and Windus.

———. 1964. *With Forks and Hope: An African Notebook*. New York: William Morrow.

———. 1965a. *A Man from Nowhere*. 1964. Reprint, New York: William Morrow.

———. 1965b. *The Merry Hippo*. 1963. Harmondsworth: Penguin.

———. 1967. *White Man's Country: Lord Delamere and the Making of Kenya*. Vol. 1: *1870–1914*. Vol. 2: *1914–1931*. 1935. Reprint, New York: Praeger.

———. 1968. *Love among the Daughters*. London: Chatto and Windus.

———. 1969. *The Red Rock Wilderness*. 1957. Reprint, London: Hodder Paperbacks.

———. 1973. *Nellie: Letters from Africa*. London: Weidenfeld and Nicholson.

———. 1981a. *The Flame Trees of Thika*. Videotapes. Vols. 1–4. Directed by Roy Ward Baker. London: Euston Films Ltd.

———. 1981b. *The Mottled Lizard*. 1962. Reprint, London: Penguin.

———. 1987. *Out in the Midday Sun: My Kenya*. New York: Viking.

———. 1988. *The African Poison Murders*. 1939. Reprint, New York: Viking Penguin.

———. 1989a. *Murder at Government House*. 1937. Reprint, New York: Viking Penguin.

———. 1989b. *Murder on Safari*. 1938. Reprint, New York: Viking Penguin,

———. 1992. *Nine Faces of Kenya*. 1990. Reprint, New York: Penguin.

Huxley, Elspeth, and Margery Perham. 1954. *Race and Politics in Kenya*. London: Faber and Faber.

Hyam, Ronald. 1976. *Imperial Century, 1815–1914: A Study of Empire and Expansion*. London: Batsford.

Hynes, Joseph. 1988. *The Art of the Real: Muriel Spark's Novels*. Cranbury, N.J.: Associated University Press.

Inden, Ronald. 1990. *Imagining India*. Oxford: Basil Blackwell.

Inglis, Ruth. 1969. Who Is Olivia Manning? *The London Observer* (6 April): 24–27.

Ingram, Penelope. 1999. Can the Settler Speak? Appropriating Subaltern Silence in Janet Frame's *The Carpathians*. *Cultural Critique* 41 (winter): 79–107.

Jaikumar, Priya. 2001. "Place" and the Modernist Redemption of Empire in *Black Narcissus* (1947). *Cinema Journal* 40 (winter): 57–77.

James, Lawrence. 1998. *Raj: The Making and Unmaking of British India*. New York: St. Martin's.

JanMohamed, Abdul R. 1983. *Manichean Aesthetics: The Politics of Literature in Colonial Africa*. Amherst: University of Massachusetts Press.

Jayawardena, Kumari. 1995. *The White Woman's Other Burden*. New York: Routledge.

Kanogo, Tabitha. 1987. *Squatters and the Roots of Mau Mau, 1905–63*. London: James Currey.

Karamcheti, Indira. 1999. Writing Rape and the Difference It Makes. *Novel* (fall): 125–128.

Karkar, Sudhir, and John Munder Ross. 1986. *Tales of Love, Sex, and Danger*. New York: Unwin.

Karr, Mary. 2002. The Domestic Verses of Salman Rushdie. *Chronicle of Higher Education* (13 Sept.): B7–B10.

Kemp, Peter. 1974. *Muriel Spark: Novelists and Their World*. London: Paul Elek.

Kennedy, Dane. 1982. Master and Servant in the White Settler Household: Kenya and Rhodesia, 1900–1939. Staff Seminar Paper 11 (1981–82). Nairobi: University of Nairobi Dept. of History.

———. 1996. Imperial History and Post-Colonial Theory. *Journal of Imperial and Commonwealth History* 24, no. 3 (Sept.): 345–363.

———. 1997. *Islands of White: Settler Society and Culture in Kenya and Southern Rhodesia. 1890–1939*. Durham: Duke University Press.

Kenrick, Donald, ed. 1999. *The Gypsies during the Second World War: In the Shadow of the Swastika*. Hatfield: University of Hertfordshire Press.

King, Anthony. 1976. *Colonial Urban Development: Culture, Social Power, and Environment*: London: Routledge and Paul.

Lagaan. 2001. Directed by Ashutosh Gowarikar. Produced by Amir Khan. General Movie.

Lanchester, John. 2001. The Land of Accidents. Review of Zadie Smith's *White Teeth*. *New York Review of Books*. (8 Feb.): 29–31.

Langer, Lawrence. 2002. Recent Studies on Memory and Representation. *Holocaust and Genocide Studies* 16, no. 1 (spring): 77–93.

Lassner, Phyllis. 1998. *British Women Writers of World War II*. New York: St. Martin's Press.

———. 2004. The Mysterious New Empire: Agatha Christie's Colonial Murders. In *Inroads and Outposts: British Women Write the 1930s*, ed. Gay Wachmann and Robin Hackett. Gainsville: University Press of Florida.

Lewy, Guenter. 2000. *The Nazi Persecution of the Gypsies*. New York: Oxford University Press.

Liddle, Joanna, and Rama Joshi. 1986. *Daughters of Independence: Gender, Caste, and Class in India*. London: Zed.

Little, Judy. 1983. *Comedy and the Woman Writer: Woolf, Spark, and Feminism*. Lincoln: University of Nebraska Press.

———. 1991. Humoring the Sentence: Women's Dialogic Comedy. In *Women's Comic Visions*, ed. June Sochen, 19–32. Detroit: Wayne State University Press.

London, Louise. 2000. *Whitehall and the Jews, 1933–1948: British Immigration Policy and the Holocaust*. Cambridge: Cambridge University Press.

Louis, William Roger. 1985. *The British Empire in the Middle East, 1945–51: Arab Nationalism, the United States, and Post-War Imperialism*. Oxford: Oxford University Press.

Mackenzie, John M. 1986. *Imperialism and Popular Culture*. Manchester: Manchester University Press.

Macmillan, Margaret. 1988. *Women of the Raj*. New York: Thames and Hudson.

Mannin, Ethel. 1936. *South to Samarkand*. London: Jarrolds.

———. 1946. *The Dark Forest*. London: Jarrolds.

———. 1963. *The Road to Beersheba*. London. Hutchinson.

Manning, Olivia. 1944. Middle East Letter. In *Modern Reading*, ed. Reginald Moore. London: Phoenix, 74–79.

————. 1967. Cairo: Back from the Blue. *Sunday Times Magazine* (Sept. 17): 46–55.

————. 1970. The Tragedy of the Struma. *The Observer* (March 1): 8–17.

————. 1974. Olivia Manning on the Perils of the Female Writer. *The Spectator* (Dec. 7): 734–735.

————. 1975. *Artist among the Missing*. 1949. Reprint, London: Heinemann.

————. 1981. *The Balkan Trilogy*. 1960–1965. Reprint, Harmondsworth: Penguin.

————. 1982a. *The Levant Trilogy*. 1977–1980. Reprint, Harmondsworth: Penguin.

————. 1982b. *School for Love*. London: Heinemann, 1951. Reprint, Harmondsworth: Penguin.

Marcus, Jane. 1989. Alibis and Legends: The Ethics of Elsewhereness, Gender, and Estrangement. In *Women's Writing in Exile*, ed. Mary Lynne Broe and Angela Ingram, 269–294. Chapel Hill: University of North Carolina Press.

Markandaya, Kamala. 1958. *Some Inner Fury*. New York: Signet.

Martin, Biddy. 1998. Lesbian Identity and Autobiographical Difference(s). In *Women, Autobiography, Theory,* ed. Sidonie Smith and Julia Watson, 380–390. Madison, University of Wisconsin Press.

Martin, Gyde Christine. 1989. Olivia Manning: A Bibliography. *Bulletin of Bibliography* 46, no. 3 (Sept.): 160–170.

Maslen, Elizabeth. 2001. *Political and Social Issues in British Women's Fiction, 1928–1968*. Basingstoke: Palgrave.

Massu, Allan. 1979. *Muriel Spark*. Edinburgh: Ramsay Head Press.

Maughan-Brown, David. 1985. *Land, Freedom, and Fiction: History and Ideology in Kenya*. London: Zed Books.

McClintock, Anne. 1995. *Imperial Leather: Race, Gender, and Sexuality in the Colonial Context*. New York: Routledge.

McQuillan, Martin. 2002. *Theorizing Muriel Spark*. Basingstoke: Palgrave.

McWhirter, David. 1994. Feminism/Gender/Comedy: Meredith, Woolf, and the Reconfiguration of Comic Distance. In *Look Who's Laughing: Gender and Comedy*, ed. Gail Finney, 189–204. Langhorne, Penn.: Gordon and Breach.

Metcalf, Thomas R. 1995. *Ideologies of the Raj*. Cambridge: Cambridge University Press.

Midgley, Claire, ed. 1998. *Gender and Imperialism*. New York: St. Martin's.

Miller, Rory. 2000. *Divided against Zion: Anti-Zionist Opposition in Britain to a Jewish State in Palestine, 1945–1948*. London: Frank Cass.

Mills, Sara. 1991. *Discourses of Difference: An Analysis of Women's Travel Writing and Colonialism*. London: Routledge.

Miriuki, Godfrey. 1974. *A History of the Kikuyu, 1500–1900*. Nairobi: Oxford University Press.

Mohanty, Chandra T., Ann Russo, and Lourdes Torres, eds. 1991. *Third World Women and the Politics of Feminism*. Bloomington: Indiana University Press.

Mooney, Harry J., Jr. 1982. Olivia Manning: Witness to History. In *Twentieth-Century Women Novelists*, ed. Thomas F. Stoley, 39-60. London: Macmillan.

Moore-Gilbert, Bart. 1996. *Writing India: 1757–1990*. Manchester: Manchester University Press.

Morris, Robert K. 1987. Olivia Manning's *Fortunes of War*: Breakdown in the Balkans, Love and Death in the Levant. In *British Novelists since 1900*, ed. Jack I. Biles, 233-252. New York: AMS Press.

Mosse, George. 1996. *The Image of Man: The Creation of Modern Masculinity*. New York: Oxford University Press.

Mukerjee, Meenakshi. 1985. *Realism and Reality: The Novel and Society in India*. Delhi: Oxford University Press.

Munt, Sally R. 1994. *Murder by the Book? Feminism and the Crime Novel*. London: Routledge.

Naik, M. K., S. K. Desai, and S. T. Kallapur. 1971. *The Image of India in Western Creative Writing*. Madras: Macmillan.

Nair, Janaki. 2000. Uncovering the *Zenana*: Visions of Indian Womanhood in English-women's Writings, 1813–1940. In *Cultures of Empire: Colonizers in Britain and the Empire in the Nineteenth and Twentieth Centuries,* Catherine Hall, 224–245. New York: Routledge.

Ngugi (James) wa Thiong'o. 1964. *Weep Not, Child*. London: Heinemann Education Books.

Nicholls, C. S. 2002. *Elspeth Huxley: A Biography*. London: Harper Collins.

Nichols, Victoria, and Susan Thompson. 1998. *Silk Stalkings: More Women Write of Murder*. Lanham, Md.: Scarecrow Press.

Ondaatje, Christopher. 2002. Cruel Cuts for Excising PM. Review of C. S. Nicholls' *Elspeth Huxley: A Biography*. *Times Higher Education* (12 July): 27.

Orwell, George. 1953a. Marrakech. In *A Collection of Essays*, by George Orwell. New York: Harcourt Brace Jovanovich.

———. 1953b. "Shooting an Elephant." In *A Collection of Essays*, by George Orwell. New York: Harcourt Brace Jovanovich.

Paravisini-Gebert, Lizabeth. 1996. *Phyllis Shand Allfrey: A Caribbean Life*. New Brunswick: Rutgers University Press.

———. 1997. Introduction to *The Orchid House*, by Phyllis Shand Allfrey, vii–xxvi. New Brunswick: Rutgers University Press.

Paravisini, Lizabeth, and Carlos Yorio. 1987. Is It or Isn't It? The Duality of Parodic Detective Fiction. In *Comic Crime*, ed. Earl F. Bargainnier, 181–193. Bowling Green, Ohio: Popular Press.

Parker, Richard B., ed. 1996. *The Six-Day War: A Retrospective*. Gainesville: University of Florida Press.

Parry, Benita. 1987. Problems in Current Theories of Colonial Discourse. *Oxford Literary Review* 9, no. 1–2: 27–58.

———. 1994. Resistance Theory/Theorizing Resistance or Two Cheers for Nativism. In *Colonial Discourse/Postcolonial Theory*, ed. Francis Barker, Peter Hulme, and Margaret Iversen, 172–196. Manchester: Manchester University Press.

———. 1997. The Postcolonial: Conceptual Category or Chimera? In *Yearbook of English Studies: The Politics of Postcolonial Criticism*, vol 27. London: Modern Humanities Research Assoc.

———. 1998a. *Delusions and Discoveries: Studies on India in the British Imagination, 1880–1930*. London: Verso.

———. 1998b. Materiality and Mystification in *A Passage to India*. *Novel* 31, no. 2 (spring): 174–194.

Pathak, Zakia, Saswati Sengupta, and Sharmila Purkayastha. 1991. The Prisonhouse of Orientalism. *Textual Practice* 5, no. 2 (summer): 195–218.

Paxton, Nancy L. 1992. Complicity and Resistance in the Writings of Flora Annie Steel and Annie Besant. In *Western Women and Imperialism,* ed. Nupur Chaudhuri and Margaret Strobel, 158–176. Bloomington: Indiana University Press.

Perham, Margery. 1961. *The Colonial Reckoning*. London: Collins.

———. 1974. *African Apprenticeship: An Autobiographical Journey in Southern Africa, 1929*. New York: Africana Pub. Co.

————. 1983. *West African Passage: A Journey through Nigeria, Chad, and the Cameroons, 1931–1932*. London: Peter Owen.

Perrault, Jeanne. 1998. Autography/Transformation/Asymmetry. In *Women, Autobiography, Theory*, ed. Sidonie Smith and Julia Watson, 190–196. Madison: University of Wisconsin Press.

Philips, Deborah, and Ian Haywood. 1998. *Brave New Causes: Women in British Postwar Fictions*. London: Leicester University Press.

Pierson, Ruth Roach, and Nupur Chaudhuri. 1998. *Nation, Empire, Colony*. Bloomington: Indiana University Press.

Plain, Gil. 1996. *Women's Fiction of the Second World War*. Edinburgh: Edinburgh University Press.

————. 2001. *Twentieth-Century Crime Fiction: Gender, Sexuality, and the Body*. Edinburgh: Edinburgh University Press.

Prakash, Gyan. 2000. Subaltern Studies as Postcolonial Critique. In *Cultures of Empire: Colonizers in Britain and the Empire in the Nineteenth and Twentieth Centuries*, Catherine Hall, 120–153. New York: Routledge.

Pratt, Mary Louise. 1992. *Imperial Eyes: Travel Writing and Transculturation*. London: Routledge.

Raiskin, Judith L. 1996. *Snow on the Cane Fields: Women's Writing and Creole Subjectivity*. Minneapolis: University of Minnesota Press.

Ramusack, Barbara N. 1992. Cultural Missionaries, Maternal Imperialists, Feminist Allies: British Women Activists in India, 1865–1945. In *Western Women and Imperialism*, ed. Nupur Chaudhuri and Margaret Strobel, 119–136. Bloomington: Indiana University Press.

Ray, Sangeeta. 2000. *En-Gendering India*. Durham: Duke University Press.

Regard, Frédéric. 2003. Life-Writing as Mediating Criticism. In *Mapping the Self: Space, Identity, Discourse in British Auto/Biography*, ed. Frédéric Regard, 323–338. Saint-Etienne, France: Publications de l'Universite de Saint-Etienne.

Renk, Kathleen J. 1999. *Caribbean Shadows and Victorian Ghosts*. Charlottesville: University Press of Virginia.

Rhys, Jean. 1966. *Wide Sargasso Sea*. New York: W. W. Norton.

Richmond, Velma Bourgeois. 1984. *Muriel Spark*. New York: Frederick Ungar.

Rigby, Nigel. 2000. "Not a Good Place for Deacons": The South Seas, Sexuality, and Modernism in Sylvia Townsend Warner's *Mr. Fortune's Maggot*. In *Modernism and Empire*, ed. Howard J. Booth and Nigel Rigby, 224–248. Manchester: Manchester University Press.

Rimmer, Douglas, and Anthony Kirk-Greene, eds. 2000. *The British Intellectual Engagement with Africa in the Twentieth Century*. New York: St. Martin's.

Rosberg, Carl G., Jr., and John Nottingham. 1966. *The Myth of "Mau Mau": Nationalism in Kenya*. New York: Praeger.

Rose, Jacqueline. 1996. *States of Fantasy*. Oxford: Clarendon Press.

Rosenthal, Lynne M. 1996. *Rumer Godden Revisited*. New York: Twayne Publishers.

Roy, Parama. 1998. *Indian Traffic: Identities in Question in Colonial and Postcolonial India*. Berkeley: University of California Press.

Rubin, David. 1986. *After the Raj*. Lebanon, N.H.: New England University Press.

Rushdie, Salman. 1991. In Good Faith. In *Imaginary Homelands: Essays and Criticism, 1981–1991*, by Salman Rushdie, 393–414. London: Granta.

Russell, Sharon A. 1991. Elspeth Huxley's Africa. In *Mysteries of Africa*, ed. Eugene Schleh, 21–34. Bowling Green: Bowling Green University Popular Press.

Sage, Lorna. 1974. A Nasty Piece of Work. *London Observer* (31 March): 38.

Said, Edward. 1978. *Orientalism*. London: Routledge.

———. 1993. *Culture and Imperialism*. London: Chatto.

Sander, Reinhard W. 1976. Two Views of the Conflict of Cultures in Pre-emergency Kenya: James Ngugi's *The River Between* and Elspeth Huxley's *Red Strangers*. *Ikoro: Bulletin of the Institute of African Studies University of Nigeria, Nsukka* 3, no. 1: 28–42.

Sanders, Dennis, and Len Lovallo. 1985. *The Agatha Christie Companion*. London: W. H. Allen.

Sangari, Kumkum, and Sudesh Vaid. 1990. *Recasting Women: Essays in Indian Colonial History*. New Brunswick, N.J.: Rutgers University Press.

Saunders, Rebecca. 1989. Gender, Colonialism, and Exile. In *Women's Writing in Exile*, ed. Mary Lynne Broe and Angela Ingram, 303–324. Chapel Hill: University of North Carolina Press.

Scott, David. 1994. *Formations of Ritual*. Minneapolis: University of Minnesota Press.

Scott, Paul. 1977. *Staying On*. London: Heinemann.

Segev, Tom. 2000. *One Palestine, Complete: Jews and Arabs under the British Mandate*. New York: Henry Holt.

Sharpe, Jenny. 1993. *Allegories of Empire*. Minneapolis: University of Minnesota Press.

Shaw, Carolyn Martin. 1995. *Colonial Inscriptions: Race, Sex, and Class in Kenya*. Minneapolis: University of Minnesota Press.

Shepherd, Naomi. 2000. *Ploughing Sand: British Rule in Palestine, 1917–1948*. New Brunswick: Rutgers University Press.

Sherman, Joshua. 1997. *Mandate Days*. London: Thames and Hudson.

Shirwadkar, Meena. 1979. *Images of Woman in the Indo-Anglian Novel*. New Delhi: Sterling Publishers.

Shohat, Ella, and Robert Stam. 1994. *Unthinking Eurocentrism: Multiculturalism and the Media*. New York: Routledge.

Shrapnel, Norman. 1974. Fashions of Guilt and Virtue. *Manchester Guardian Weekly* (4 May): 21.

Simpson, Hassell. 1973. *Rumer Godden*. New York: Twayne.

Singh, Jyotsna. 1996. *Colonial Narratives, Cultural Dialogues: "Discoveries" of India in the Language of Colonialism*. London: Routledge.

Sinha, Mrinalini. 1999. Giving Masculinity a History. *Gender and History* 11, no. 3 (Nov.): 445–460.

Smith, Sidonie, and Julia Watson, eds. 1998. *Women, Autobiography, Theory*. Madison: University of Wisconsin Press.

Smith, Stevie. 1951. New Novels. Review of *School for Love*. *World Review* (Oct.): 78–80.

Smith, Zadie. 2000. *White Teeth*. New York: Random House.

Snowman, Daniel. 2002. *The Hitler Emigres: The Cultural Impact on Britain of Refugees from Nazism*. London: Chatto & Windus.

Spark, Muriel. 1961. My Conversion. *The Twentieth Century* (autumn): 58–63.

———. 1965. *The Mandelbaum Gate*. New York: Knopf.

———. 1970. What Images Return. In *Memoirs of a Modern Scotland*, ed. Karl Miller. London: Faber & Faber, 151–155.

———. 1971. The Desegregation of Art. *Proceedings of the American Academy of Arts and Letters* 22: 21–27.

———. 1977. Interview: Frank Kermode. The House of Fiction. 1963. In *The Novel Today: Contemporary Writers on Modern Fiction*, ed. Malcolm Bradbury. London: Fontana, 132–135.

———. 1985. The Gentile Jewesses. In *The Stories of Muriel Spark*. New York: Dutton, 270–276.

———. 1992. *Curriculum Vitae: Autobiography*. London: Constable.

Spivak, Gayatri Chakravorty. 1986. Three Women's Texts and a Critique of Imperialism. In *Race, Writing, and Difference*, ed. Henry Louis Gates Jr., 262–280. Chicago: University of Chicago Press.

———. 1988. Can the Subaltern Speak? In *Marxism and the Interpretation of Culture*, ed. Cary Nelson and Lawrence Grossberg. 271–313. Urbana: University of Illinois Press.

Spurr, David. 1993. *The Rhetoric of Empire*. Durham: Duke University Press.

Steedman, Carolyn Kay. 1998. Stories. In *Women, Autobiography, Theory*, ed. Sidonie Smith and Julia Watson, 243–254. Madison, University of Wisconsin Press.

Stetz, Margaret D. 2001. *British Women's Comic Fiction, 1890–1990*. Aldershot, U.K.: Ashgate.

Stoler, Ann L. 1989. Making Empire Respectable: The Politics of Race and Sexual Morality in Twentieth-Century Colonial Cultures. *American Ethnologist* 16, no. 4: 634–660.

———. 1992. Sexual Affronts and Racial Frontiers: European Identities and the Cultural Politics of Exclusion in Colonial Southeast Asia. *Comparative Studies in Society and History* 34, no. 3 (July): 514–551.

Strobel, Margaret. 1991. *European Women and the Second British Empire*. Bloomington: Indiana University Press.

———. 1993. *Gender, Sex, and Empire*. Washington, D.C.: American Historical Assoc.

Suleri, Sara. 1992. *The Rhetoric of India*. Chicago: University of Chicago Press.

———. 1998. Woman Skin Deep: Feminism and the Postcolonial Condition. In *Women, Autobiography, Theory*, ed. Sidonie Smith and Julia Watson, 116–125. Madison: University of Wisconsin Press.

Thomas, Nicholas. 1994. *Colonialism's Culture: Anthropology, Travel, and Government*. Princeton: Princeton University Press.

Thornhill, Michael. 1998. Britain and the Politics of the Arab League, 1943–50. In *Demise of the British Empire in the Middle East*, ed. Michael J. Cohen and Martin Kolinsky, 41–63. London: Frank Cass.

Tidrick, Kathryn T. 1990. *Empire and the English Character*. London: Taurus.

Trivedi, Harish. 1994. *Colonial Transactions: English Literature and India*. Manchester: Manchester University Press.

Trollope, Joanna. 1983. *Britannia's Daughters: Women of the British Empire*. London: Hutchinson.

Trotter, David. 1990. Colonial Subjects. *Critical Quarterly* 32, no. 3: 3–20.

———. 1991. Theory and Detective Fiction. *Critical Quarterly* 33. no. 2 (summer): 66–77.

Tucker, Jonathan B. 2001. *Scourge: The Once and Future Threat of Smallpox*. New York: Atlantic Monthly Press.

Tucker, Martin. 1967. *Africa in Modern Literature*. New York: Frederick Ungar.

Van Alphen, Ernst. 1997. *Caught by History: Holocaust Effects in Contemporary Art, Literature, and Theory*. Stanford: Stanford University Press.

Viswanathan, Gauri. 1989. *Masks of Conquest: Literary Study and British Rule in India*. New York: Columbia University Press.

———. 1998. *Outside the Fold: Conversion, Modernity, and Belief*. Princeton, N.J.: Princeton University Press.

Ward, Stuart, ed. 2001. *British Culture and the End of Empire*. Manchester: Manchester University Press.

Ware, Vron. 1992. *Beyond the Pale: White Women, Racism, and History*. New York: Verso.

Wasserstein, Bernard. 1999. *Britain and the Jews of Europe, 1939–1945*. Rev. ed. Oxford: Oxford University Press.

Waugh, Patricia. 1989. *Feminine Fictions: Revisiting the Postmodern*. New York: Routledge.

Webster, Wendy. 1999. Elspeth Huxley: Gender, Empire, and Narratives of Nation, 1935–64. *Women's History Review* 8, no. 3: 527–545.

West, Rebecca. 1987. *The Return of the Soldier*. 1918. Reprint, Harmondsworth: Penguin.

Whitlock, Gillian. 2000. *The Intimate Empire: Reading Women's Autobiography*. London: Cassell.

Whittaker, Ruth. 1982. *The Faith and Fiction of Muriel Spark*. London: Macmillan.

Williams, Mark. 2000. Mansfield in Maoriland: Biculturalism, Agency, and Misreading. In *Modernism and Empire*, ed. Howard J. Booth and Nigel Rigby, 249–274. Manchester: Manchester University Press.

Williams, Tony. 2000. *Structures of Desire: British Cinema, 1939–1955*. Albany: State University of New York Press.

Willis, Justin. 2002. Of Mice and Mints. Review of C. S. Nicholls' *Elspeth Huxley*. *Times Literary Supplement* (16 August): 4–5.

Wilson, Rodney. 1998. Economic Aspects of Arab Nationalism. In *Demise of the British Empire in the Middle East*, ed. Michael J. Cohen and Martin Kolinsky, 64–78. London: Frank Cass.

Yapp, M. E. 1999. Suez Was Not the Turning Point. *Times Literary Supplement* (16 July): 10–11.

Yelin, Louise. 1998. *From the Margins of Empire: Christina Stead, Doris Lessing, Nadine Gordimer*. Ithaca, N.Y.: Cornell University Press.

Young, Robert J. C. 1995. *Colonial Desire: Hybridity in Theory, Culture, and Race*. New York: Routledge.

Zengos, Hariclea. 1989. *"A World without Walls": Race, Politics, and Gender in the African Works of Elspeth Huxley, Isak Dinesen, and Beryl Markham*. Ann Arbor: University of Michigan Press.

Zweig, Ronald W. 1986. *Britain and Palestine during the Second World War*. London: Boydell Press for The Royal Historical Society.

Index

Achebe, Chinua, 118–119, 126, 148, 217n7; *Things Fall Apart*, 183–184, 219n30

Adler, Alfred, 183–184. *See also* Phyllis Bottome

Afrikaner nationalism, 203–204n5

Allfrey, Phyllis Shand, 3, 8, 10, 15, 21, 124–125, 178, 194–195; life, 160–161, 174, 190–191; *The Orchid House*, 12–13, 34, 38, 137, 160–175, 179, 181, 188, 220n4; *In the Cabinet*, 220n7

Anglo-Boer War, 219n26

antisemitism, 5, 20–23, 44, 54, 175–176, 189, 204n7, 211n43. *See also* fascism; Holocaust; Jews; race and racism; Nazis and Nazism

Arabs: as colonial subject, 27, 33, 149–150, 211n42; as literary characters and stereotypes, 29–30, 47–49, 52; nationalism, 3, 62, 207n6, 209n23; and Palestine, 24–25, 31, 45, 61–69, 211n42; and race, 157. *See also* Ethel Mannin; Olivia Manning; and Muriel Spark

Arab-Israeli 1948 war, 24, 61, 208nn13, 18. *See also* Israel; Palestine; and Ethel Mannin

Arab-Jewish relations, 46, 58–59, 65, 206n4, 210n32. *See also* Israel; Palestine; Ethel Mannin; Olivia Manning; and Muriel Spark

Arawaks, 221n12

Arendt, Hannah, 56, 210–211n38

Austin, Jane, *Northanger Abbey*, 164

Axis powers, 3, 87, 144, 175; Iraqi pro-Axis revolt, 209n23. *See also* Nazism; the Third Reich; Benito Mussolini; and Japanese Empire

Bakhtin, Mikhail, 109, 125–126, 197, 205n14

Bevan, Ernest, 211n43

Bhabha, Homi, 5, 12–13, 70, 178, 180, 186, 205n21, 206n24

bildungsroman, 20, 124, 213n16

black and blackness. *See* race and racism

Bollywood: *Lagaan*, 2

Blixen, Karin: *Out of Africa* (film version), 215n31; 217n13

Bottome, Phyllis, 2, 5, 7, 11, 15, 21, 39, 66, 127, 160, 162, 181, 194–195; life, 175, 191; *The Lifeline*, 176; *The Mortal Storm*, 221n10; "The Pirate's Isle," 186, 188, 221n13; *Old Wine*, 175, 176; *Under the Skin*, 6, 7, 11, 175–189; *Within the Cup*, 176

Bronte, Charlotte: *Jane Eyre*, 13, 160, 164–165, 175, 187; *Villette*, 187. *See also* Phyllis Shand Allfrey, *The Orchid House*; and Jean Rhys

Caribbean. *See* Domenica; Phyllis Shand Allfrey; and Phyllis Bottome

Catholicism. *See* Muriel Spark and Phyllis Shand Allfrey

Cesaire, Aime, 204n5

Chamberlain, Houston Stewart, 5, 185. *See also* Hitler; race; and racism

ABOUT THE AUTHOR

Phyllis Lassner is the author of two books on the Anglo-Irish writer Elizabeth Bowen as well as *British Women Writers of World War II: Battlegrounds of Their Own*. She has written extensively on British women writers of the interwar era and has worked on several reprint projects, including two novels by Phyllis Bottome. She is currently writing about British women writers haunted by the Holocaust.